## Praise for *Bad Influence*

'Uncomfortable but essential reading. Your definitive guide to separating medical facts from online fiction.'

Adam Kay, author of *This is Going to Hurt*

'This superb book is an essential guide to the wild world of internet health – a series of cautionary tales, brilliantly told, about the perils of health influencers and the messages they peddle.'

Chris van Tulleken, author of *Ultra-Processed People*

'Exhaustively researched – documents the tensions between amazing modern medicine and twenty-first-century quackery that circulates on our screens. An important reminder of how technology's tentacles are reaching into every corner of our lives, and the challenge to work out what's real.'

Laura Kuenssberg

'Combining first-class medical journalism with her instinct for the digital zeitgeist, Deb Cohen serves up a health warning for those of us looking to social media for a quick-quack health fix. In a world where dodgy online medical opinions come thick and fast, this is the perfect antidote.'

Prof. Kevin Fong

'Razor-sharp, prodigiously researched and written with a balance that is the hallmark of true intellect, *Bad Influence* is essential reading for anyone needing to navigate the increasingly murky interface between medicine and the online world which – let's face it – is all of us.'

Dr Gabriel Weston, author of *Direct Red*

'This book tackles one of the most important health issues of our time. It is brilliant, thorough and vital. Empowering for anyone who has ever come across health information, stories, or advice online – which is pretty much all of us.'
Prof. Daniel M. Davis, author of *The Beautiful Cure*

'This book is a much-needed prescription for the unregulated world of online health misinformation by an expert, who knows and understands what she is talking about. The influence we are all under now to buy products, tests and gadgets that often have no proven value for our health is terrifying for society and actually bad for our health. I'll be telling my patients to read this!'
Dr Ellie Cannon

'With a reporter's eye and a scientist's precision, Deborah dissects the interventionist claims of the wellness industry and exposes the shaky evidence underpinning it. Her diagnosis is uncomfortable but urgent: that those selling us control over our health may, in fact, be the ones making us sick... a must-read.'
Natasha Loder, Health Editor, *Economist*

'Eye-opening and concerning. This book will hopefully influence how you access healthcare information and maybe think twice before you make (often complex) decisions about your body based solely on your social media feed.'
Prof. John Tregoning, author of *Live Forever?*

'A timely and eye-opening investigation into how social media is reshaping the way we think about health... Essential reading for anyone with a social media account – or anyone who cares about the future of evidence-based medicine in an age of influence.'
Rebecca Coombes, Head of Journalism, *British Medical Journal*

# BAD INFLUENCE

## HOW THE INTERNET HIJACKED OUR HEALTH

**DEBORAH COHEN**

A Oneworld Book

First published in Great Britain, the Republic of Ireland and
Australia by Oneworld Publications Ltd, 2026

Copyright © Deborah Cohen, 2026

The moral right of Deborah Cohen to be identified as the Author of this work has been
asserted by her in accordance with the Copyright, Designs, and Patents Act 1988

All rights reserved
Copyright under Berne Convention
A CIP record for this title is available from the British Library

ISBN 978-0-86154-988-7
eISBN 978-0-86154-989-4

Typeset by Geethik Technologies
Printed and bound in Great Britain by Clays Ltd, Elcograf S.p.A.

No part of this publication may be reproduced, stored in a retrieval system, or
transmitted, in any form or by any means, electronic, mechanical, photocopying,
recording or otherwise, or used in any manner for the purpose of training artificial
intelligence technologies or systems, without the prior permission of the publishers.

The authorised representative in the EEA is eucomply OU,
Pärnu mnt 139b–14, 11317 Tallinn, Estonia
(email: hello@eucompliancepartner.com / phone: +33757690241)

Oneworld Publications Ltd
10 Bloomsbury Street
London WC1B 3SR
England

Stay up to date with the latest books,
special offers, and exclusive content from
Oneworld with our newsletter

Sign up on our website
**oneworld-publications.com**

**To Effie**

This book would not have been possible without the unwavering friendship and support of Effie Webb. From the very beginning, her ability to dive deep into the far reaches of social media has offered insights that I alone would not have found. Her sharp thinking and camaraderie have helped shape the ideas in this book. Modest and kind yet determined, she's a star in the making.

# CONTENTS

| | | |
|---|---|---|
| 1 | A Confluence of Change | 1 |
| 2 | Are Stories Making Us Sick? | 30 |
| 3 | The Weight-Loss Race, or the New Drug Market | 57 |
| 4 | A Diagnostic Odyssey | 94 |
| 5 | Sick Until Proven Healthy | 120 |
| 6 | Expanding the Symptom Pool | 144 |
| 7 | The Optimisation Trap | 175 |
| 8 | Who's Really Empowered? | 206 |
| 9 | A Hormonal Quick Fix | 242 |
| 10 | The New Preventive Medicine | 274 |
| | Epilogue: The Commodified Self | 306 |
| | *Acknowledgements* | 316 |
| | *Notes* | 321 |

# 1

# A CONFLUENCE OF CHANGE

It was a rainy summer's day in Liverpool at my aunt's birthday party. Like any determined group of Scousers, we resolved to defy the weather and, huddled under a gazebo, pretended we were in the tropics drinking chilled champagne instead of lukewarm prosecco. My cousin's friend, Anna, turned to me and announced, 'I've just bought an AMH test to see if I can have a baby.'

'Do you think it's going to tell you that?' I asked. She looked at me suspiciously. 'That's what the clinic I saw on Insta said,' she replied with a scornful expression.

Anna was sharp as you like. A successful lawyer, she'd been trying to get pregnant for some time and it simply hadn't happened. With the health service failing to give her answers, she'd turned to social media for help.

AMH stands for anti-Müllerian hormone. It's a hormone produced by the cells in the ovarian follicles. In women, AMH is related to egg count and, as such, declines with age. Higher AMH levels in principle mean more eggs and a higher ovarian reserve. But that's just one factor affecting pregnancy.

While these tests help guide fertility treatment medications, they can't predict your chances of getting pregnant, how long it will take, or your reproductive timeline. Research suggests that after accounting for age, women with low AMH levels have similar pregnancy rates to those with average levels.[1] Despite insufficient evidence that AMH testing reliably predicts reproductive potential in the general population, it continues to be marketed as such.

I asked her if she knew if the test was accurate. Many direct-to-consumer tests aren't. But they're ubiquitous on social media platforms, often targeting their advertising to particular demographics.[2]

'What will you do if the results are abnormal?' I asked.

'Go see my GP...' she answered.

'And what if they're normal?'

Anna paused. 'Go see my GP,' she said slowly. 'If I can get an appointment, that is.'

'You've just wasted £160,' I replied. 'The test isn't going to tell you what you think it is. And whatever the results, you'll see your GP who probably won't be able to use them.'

Anna was just one of several friends I saw that summer who, for one reason or another, were taking their health into their own hands. Admittedly a select bunch: largely university educated, employed and in their thirties, forties and fifties. They came from across the political spectrum, but most had faith in scientific progress and medical institutions. A few experimented with supplements, while the Covid-19 pandemic left others sceptical of the pharmaceutical industry and mistrustful of public health.

But they all had one thing in common: the National Health Service (NHS) no longer worked for them. Social media had become their go-to resource to learn more about their health and, they hoped, take control of it. Some were looking for private hormone replacement therapy doctors; others for full-body MOTs; attention deficit hyperactivity disorder (ADHD) information for their children; advice about weight-loss drugs; and some of the men had started to take their lead from a growing pool of doctors and scientists with a high-profile online presence advocating a range of individualised preventive health measures.

They weren't people likely to fall for some of the more outlandish claims of the wellness industry. But they were interested in what looked like serious medical products, seemingly backed by reams of evidence and endorsed by apparently credible healthcare professionals. This wasn't just about some of the well-documented slurry of 'misinformation' churned out by so-called conspiracy theorists and wellness gurus, but health content creators, companies, clinics and a whole host of other players profiting from people's desire to take charge of their health by offering supposedly tried-and-tested solutions.

I noticed my friends were grappling with the same issues that I faced in my day job as a journalist investigating healthcare stories. What is the evidence for this claim? What are the benefits and harms of this treatment? Does this disease even exist? How well is this product regulated? What conflicts of interest are involved here? And who is making the money? Awash in an ocean of contradictory information, skimming myriad articles filled with terms they don't fully understand, wrestling different demands on their time and purses, how do they – or you and I – make a decision about who to trust?

In some ways this is nothing new. The mainstream media has rightly been criticised for hyperbolic headlines about the benefits of new treatments, distorting evidence and overstating harms – or even ignoring them entirely. One minute, coffee causes cancer,[3] the next, it decreases the risk of type 2 diabetes.[4] At its worst, the mainstream media, alongside the *Lancet*, stirred up a scandal about the MMR (measles, mumps and rubella) vaccine, whipping up fear it was linked to autism, with some authorities suggesting it played a role in causing vaccination rates to drop.[5] Twelve years later, the *Lancet* was forced to retract the paper, and it was exposed as an elaborate, intentional fraud in a series of articles in the *British Medical Journal* (*BMJ*).[6]

But increasingly, eyes are turning away from mainstream media to the internet. How does this affect our choices? How does it make us view our symptoms? And how is it shaping our expectations about health? As our culture changes, so too does our perception of health. Medicine doesn't exist in its own silo of objective scientific facts. It is influenced by the world around us. This book reveals what can happen when entertainment, commerce and health collide.

Since the 1990s, Professor John Powell – with a background in social sciences, medicine, and public health – has watched how digital technology is reshaping healthcare, from the way people manage their health to how they engage with services. Based at Oxford University's Department of Primary Care Health Sciences, he helps UK healthcare organisations like NICE (National Institute for Health and Care Excellence) and the MHRA (Medicines and Healthcare products Regulatory Agency) figure out how to use digital tools in healthcare. He tells me:

> I remember when I first started studying digital health in the late 1990s, I was fascinated by how the internet was supposedly changing things. But I ended up being fairly sceptical at the time. It didn't seem like the internet was fundamentally changing much – big players were still big players, and patients remained largely disempowered and uninformed. Despite the promise of this fantastic new technology that would supposedly democratise access to information, I just didn't see it happening. It felt more like an evolutionary change than a revolutionary one.

## THE PROSUMER EFFECT

But all that has changed. He argues that the ubiquity of mobile phones and data, affordable home broadband, and a young generation for whom entertainment, education and socialising are all online and in the palms of their hands have shaped how people view doctors and healthcare settings. 'For them it's how everything is done, so why wouldn't healthcare work that way too?' he posits, adding: 'It could also be the "prosumer" effect, where people are both producers and consumers of information through social media, reviews, and rating sites. Whether it's about health or food, people are contributing to the knowledge ecosystem.'

Covid-19 also had an impact. As strict lockdowns confined many to their homes, hospital visits and doctor's appointments were discouraged, as posing a safety risk. Healthcare, which had long resisted telemedicine and remote care, was forced to adapt quickly. Institutions that had been concerned about what might be lost in the transition to digital suddenly had to make it work.[7] 'This shift also affected patients, who became more self-reliant and more open to remote care – even care provided from another country,' Powell says.

Social networks and media became primary sources for health information – surpassing traditional reliance on doctors – and redefining who is perceived as a reliable source of knowledge.[8] You no longer just type in 'I have frequent migraines' and your search engine directs you to the NHS website or a similar source. On social media platforms, you can see people just like you who also say they have frequent migraines, here's how they manage them, what triggers doctors might not mention and which products seem to help. On Instagram, TikTok and Facebook, patients don't just consume health information – they shape it, share it and build communities around it. Content creators have group chats with each other and get ideas for videos from other creators. They may analyse which content resonates with audiences and adjust their strategy accordingly.

These platforms also amplify health conversations far beyond traditional limits. A patient's story that might once have reached a dozen people in a support group can now influence millions. They also enable users to share deeply personal medical experiences through videos and threads, sparking conversations with strangers worldwide. Healthcare professionals harness these platforms to generate research ideas, draft academic papers and arrange media appearances through connections they've made. As we'll see, the impact goes beyond individual health decisions. As social media platforms reshape how we discuss and manage disease, they're beginning to influence many aspects of health from clinical practice to medical research.

## WHEN THE SAFETY NET FRAYS

These changes have come at a critical juncture. In the UK, for example, the NHS is facing unprecedented challenges. Since its founding on 5 July 1948, the NHS has guaranteed free healthcare at the point of use for all UK residents and has typically been a source of immense national pride.[9] But now barely a day goes by without a negative headline about NHS crises and whether people can access the services they need. It is experiencing a crisis of faith. Data from the 2024 British Social Attitudes survey show that only 21% of British adults reported being 'very' or 'quite' satisfied with the NHS – a record low since the survey began in 1983, marking a sharp 39-point drop since 2019. Just 2% expressed being 'very' satisfied, down from 4% in 2023.[10]

Satisfaction with A&E services has plunged to 19%, while dissatisfaction has surged to 52%, making it the least satisfactory NHS service for the first time. NHS dentistry has hit a record low, with satisfaction dropping to 20% (down from 60% in 2019) and dissatisfaction reaching 55%, the highest for any specific NHS service. GP services have continued their downward trend, with satisfaction falling to 31% from 34% in 2023.

Across the board, dissatisfaction with waiting times and appointment availability is widespread, with only 11% believing there are enough NHS staff. Furthermore, 69% of respondents think the government spends too little on the NHS, highlighting concerns about resource allocation and staffing. Noticeably – and relevant in the social media era – there is a divide between generations, with satisfaction lower overall and falling in younger age groups.

The numbers behind this perhaps explain why. The NHS waiting list in England swelled to 6.29 million people waiting for treatments at the end of February 2024, roughly 10% of England's population. Median waiting times have nearly doubled from 7.6 weeks before Covid-19 to 14.2 weeks in 2024. Behind these figures lie countless delayed surgeries, postponed treatments, and lives put on hold. Diagnostic test waiting lists have reached 1.57 million, with many patients waiting longer than the six-week target. Even as the number of monthly tests returns to normal levels, it cannot keep pace with growing demand. The system appears caught in a vicious cycle:

longer waits can lead to delayed diagnoses, which in turn create more complex and urgent cases.

The pandemic, while not the source of these problems, acted as an accelerant. When Covid-19 hit, non-urgent services were suspended and vulnerable patients stayed home. As services resumed, the system faced a backlog of delayed care. Staff shortages and strict infection controls only complicated recovery efforts. The waiting list, already growing before the pandemic, surged as patients who had delayed care finally sought treatment.

In the UK, public commitment to the NHS's founding principles seems unshaken. An overwhelming 91% believe healthcare should remain free at the point of use, while 82% support both universal access and tax-based funding. This creates a peculiar tension: Britons simultaneously hold record-low satisfaction with the NHS's performance and record-high belief in its core mission.[11]

Surveys and studies in other countries have shown a decline in the public's trust in healthcare professionals and the healthcare systems too. Factors contributing to this decline include the Covid-19 pandemic, increased reliance on telemedicine and exposure to conflicting health information from various sources, including social media.[12]

The problems facing healthcare are not going to be short term, particularly in developed, westernised societies with ageing populations and fewer people of working age.[13] 'This challenge is going to persist for a long time, leaving health systems under strain, with increasing waiting lists and limited resources,' Powell tells me. 'This pressure is one of the drivers behind people seeking help elsewhere, even in parallel to the NHS. Whether it's through private health insurance, other private providers, or even turning to platforms like TikTok for health advice, people are increasingly looking beyond the NHS for solutions.'

As technology advances at a rapid pace, public expectations grow. It can be frustrating to learn that a seemingly ground-breaking treatment available elsewhere is not accessible on the health service in your own country – even when the scientific evidence for its effectiveness is uncertain. But there are plenty of providers willing to step into the gap. Health is big business. The global pharmaceutical industry chalks up a revenue of roughly US $1.3 trillion.[14] In the UK, even with the NHS, private healthcare is worth £12.4 billion.[15] And that's before we even look at the booming industries of healthcare-related products, apps, wearables, homeopathy, specialist pillows… Companies endlessly market treatments and technologies, turning measurable aspects of human health into a marketable product. Wellness becomes a commodity turning healthy consumers into potential patients. After all, as we hear some content creators say, how can you put a price on your own life?

## THE WELLNESS INDUSTRIAL COMPLEX

In the UK government's 2025 *Fit for the Future: 10 Year Health Plan for England*,[16] technology takes centre stage. The ambition is to move the NHS away from being a twentieth-century technological laggard to a twenty-first-century leader using innovation to tackle today's pressures and secure the system's long-term sustainability and effectiveness.

Many of these are positive developments. But at the same time daily life becomes subjected to medical interpretation and diagnosis, with normal variations reframed as conditions requiring intervention. There's a cure for every ill and a litany of ways to optimise, enhance and transform your health, all available for purchase. Fitness trackers quantify our steps while meditation apps monetise our peace of mind. Online health companies offer subscription-based care, while AI-powered apps promise personalised health insights. Companies now sell everything from genetic testing to personalised nutrition plans, each promising a better, healthier you. This nexus of pharma, tech, testing and supplement companies is perhaps best described as the wellness industrial complex.

'Just as the pandemic magnified issues already present in society, technology amplifies patterns that were already underway, such as the commodification of medicine and the rise of influencer-driven commerce,' Chris Stokel-Walker, a technology journalist, tells me. Now influencers on a grand scale monetise themselves: their health conditions, their stories, their lives. The internet has created low barriers to entry into the healthcare marketplace. Setting up a website, let alone a business, is now so easy that anyone can create an online front door to their 'clinic' in a matter of hours. Accessibility is one of the drivers, Powell says. A professional-looking website coupled with strategic advertising is relatively cheap, but the potential returns are substantial.

A 2025 report by Ofcom found that 76% of UK internet users seek health and wellbeing information online, with 35% of adults using websites and apps to research health symptoms. Media technology is playing an ever-increasing role in health, fitness and wellbeing. But this growing dependence on digital health resources comes with a drawback – only 51% of search engine users in the report could identify sponsored content.[17]

And now there are large language models (LLMs) such as ChatGPT, Claude, Gemini, and Copilot added to the mix. In Australia, for example, one nationally representative survey suggested adults are turning to them for health advice, including information about their symptoms, medical conditions and terminology, and treatment options.[18] LLMs work by predicting what words should come next in a sequence, allowing them to generate human-like text responses to prompts. They're being used to answer questions, create content and even simulate conversation.

However, AI models can 'hallucinate' – that is, produce incorrect, misleading, or nonsensical information, often seeming plausible to a non-expert but lacking any factual basis. Studies also show AI safeguards are inconsistent and easily bypassed. A 2024 *BMJ* analysis found that GPT-4 could be 'jailbroken' to generate inaccurate health information more easily than other models. Without stronger protections, those working in bad faith could mass-produce deceptive health content – from articles to deepfake videos of doctors – that appears legitimate to most people, researchers warned.[19] A study analysing ChatGPT's responses to patient inquiries found they were rated similarly in quality – and even more empathetic – than human doctors' answers online. However, while experts identified unsafe advice, patients struggled to distinguish between helpful and potentially harmful responses.[20]

There is some scepticism – although this may change. A 2024 US survey found that 25% of Americans under thirty and 17% of those over thirty reported using chatbots for health advice at least monthly, but most of those surveyed weren't confident that health information provided by AI chatbots is accurate.[21] Ofcom also found that 52% of adults aware of AI said they would be more likely to trust a human-written article than one written by AI.[22]

## THE RISE OF DR TIKTOK

However, when it comes to social media, 90% of UK internet users engage, with usage nearly universal among younger adults. While Facebook is the most popular platform overall, Instagram, TikTok and Snapchat dominate among younger users.[23] Across the UK, US, Europe and Asia, TikTok has evolved from an entertainment platform to a search engine competitor, often outperforming Google in certain sectors and becoming a primary health information source.[24] Health-related content on TikTok has surged 600% since 2021, attracting 3.8 million healthcare providers.[25] One 2024 survey published in *JMIR Infodemiology* suggests that among American women aged 18–29 across different demographics, 65.5% actively seek health information on the platform, while 92% encounter it passively while scrolling.[26] 'TikTok has become a dominant force, transforming not just social media but how we talk about almost everything. Its influence, from cultural shifts to geopolitical implications, has been enormous,' says Stokel-Walker. At this point, it's virtually inescapable. Users are receiving, whether they want it or not, their health information from influencers who, in general, have little obligation to be accurate.

As social platforms continue their expansion – projected to reach 5.84 billion users by 2027 – the implications for healthcare are immense. To be clear, this is not all bad. Social media and digital platforms have had a bad press and at times, rightly so. But for some, the platforms are critical parts of their health journey, allowing them to access support they can't find in real life and encouraging them to pursue interventions that improve their wellbeing and quality of life.

Researchers are trying to understand how exposure to online health information translates to real life. Information can shift attitudes and intentions, but proving it changes the choices people might make is much more difficult. Behavioural influence is hard to quantify. The problem is the kind of data collected tends to be observational, so while we can see correlations (how two variables move together), establishing causation is much harder. To prove cause-and-effect relationships, researchers need randomised controlled trials, which require significant time and financial resources.

Dr Amrit Purba Kaur is assistant professor at the Medical Research Council Cognition and Brain Sciences Unit at Cambridge University, where she investigates the health impacts of social media use. 'Health behaviours are influenced by a wide array of factors – such as socioeconomic circumstance, family dynamics, cultural context and other personal and environmental elements,' she tells me.

The problem is teasing apart all these different influencing factors. Without tracking them, we can't determine social media's unique impact on health choices and behaviours. And, while researchers can track how health behaviours spread through social networks, proving direct causation between social media content and real-world health choices is remarkably complex. The challenges are both technical and ethical. How do you track someone from watching a TikTok video to making a doctor's appointment? When does correlation become causation?

Ideally, we'd have longitudinal studies (a type of research design used to gather data on the same people repeatedly over a period of time), including detailed data showing exactly what health content people view, how frequently and for how long, data on these influencing factors and specific health behaviours or choices. 'It is challenging to obtain this rich, objective data from social media platforms due to opaque data-sharing policies,' Kaur says.

For example, measuring time spent on social media doesn't reflect how users engage with health content. Simply tracking hours on platforms like Instagram or TikTok overlooks the nature of the interactions. One person might spend three hours passively scrolling through their feeds with only occasional exposure to health-related posts. Another might spend just half an hour actively seeking out and engaging with specific health influencers and bookmarking or commenting on posts. Despite less screen time, the second user engages more meaningfully than the first and this might have a different impact on their health choices and behaviours.

Privacy concerns and data limitations make it difficult to connect online engagement with offline actions. If we don't have data on different age groups, sex, ethnicities and socioeconomic circumstances, we can't examine how social media affects different groups of people – teens might be more influenced by social media health trends than older adults; people with health conditions might understand health information differently than others. Making things more complicated is the reinforcement loop of the social media algorithm. The health content you see depends on what you have liked before, keeping users in 'echo chambers'. Meanwhile, social media's functionality changes, influenced by political dynamics, regulatory changes, legal battles and the evolving ties between tech companies and governments. Likewise, LLMs continuously evolve, with each new version refining and expanding on previous developments.

Academic researchers often struggle to keep pace with rapidly evolving trends. In a conversation I had with Sir Michael Marmot, professor of epidemiology and public health at University College London, he bemoaned the contrast between academic and corporate research capabilities. While companies can quickly deploy market research to gauge consumer perspectives, academics face numerous hurdles – securing funding, navigating ethics committee approvals and completing the peer review publication process – all of which delay their ability to study similar phenomena in a timely manner. By the time researchers publish their analyses of TikTok or Instagram content, the digital landscape may have transformed completely – the viral trends, popular creators and platform features they studied already relegated to internet history. Distinguishing between passing fads and genuine influences is crucial for understanding how social media ultimately affects our health decisions.

Perhaps a snapshot of what big PR companies are promoting to prospective clients will give a sense of the impact they believe accessing health information is having: a 2024 Ogilvy survey of US adults reveals 70% of US adults engage with health content on social media. Among these users, 93% report taking action based on such content, with 54% scheduling medical appointments, such as a check-up or a screening test.[27] Nearly all engaged users (92%) cite positive impacts – 47% find it easier to learn about health conditions, while 42% feel more confident in health decision making. Market research company eMarketer found that 57% of doctors have changed their perspective about treatments based on information from social media platforms.[28] Content is perhaps not just having an impact on the public but on healthcare professionals too.

You might be thinking this is a rather rosy picture – where's the catch? But we need to be cautious of leaning too heavily on statistics from Ogilvy, a big international PR firm, as their own bottom line depends on people believing their social media medical marketing department will help boost a client's income streams. Moreover, it may well be a success for a marketing campaign for people to book an appointment or a screening test. But that says nothing about whether it's a good decision for their health. More on that later.

## A DIGITAL LIFELINE

Nevertheless it is clear people turn to social media for help and support – even if the extent to which they act on the information they receive is hard to quantify.[29] Traditional healthcare systems can leave needs unmet. Take Sneha Dave. She was diagnosed with severe ulcerative colitis, an inflammatory bowel disease, at six, and social media was a lifeline. Because her illness caused bathroom accidents, it was hard for her to talk about it, especially as she moved into her teen years – an embarrassing situation for anyone. She says: 'I was isolated from society for nearly five years during a crucial stage in my development.' After multiple surgeries, including the removal of her large intestine when she was fourteen, she founded Generation Patient, a global network helping young adults with chronic conditions to connect and support one another. It relies on social media networks to connect those who might be facing prolonged hospital stays or physical isolation – for example those shielding during the pandemic. 'These connections often span across the country or even the world, enabling them to find meaningful relationships despite physical distance,' she says. Some of these relationships have become meaningful offline friendships too.

But it's not just friendship. Studies show that people with cancer use platforms like X to discuss treatments and ongoing clinical trials and offer support during their ordeals, including the side effects of the treatments and the anxiety of scans.[30] Writing in the *Telegraph*, consultant breast surgeon Dr Liz O'Riordan described the 'community of care' she developed after turning to Twitter to share her own diagnosis, making online friends, most of whom she had never met offline. They gave her tips about how to cope with a change in how food tasted following her chemotherapy and ways to manage other side effects. They sent her blankets and quilts to snuggle up in on bad days and offered non-judgemental words of wisdom.[31]

'Social media can be a really powerful tool for exploring potential diagnoses,' Sneha reflects. 'Being able to access patient stories and information online can be incredibly helpful for evaluating one's own health and exploring potential solutions or options.' Sneha learned about mast cell activation syndrome – a rare condition involving episodes of severe systemic symptoms that appear like anaphylaxis – through social media. 'Understanding what it is and finding treatments and solutions for it was only possible because of the resources I found on social media,' she says. This allowed her to connect symptoms she might never have linked otherwise. For Sneha, this was empowering. But for others, the accessibility of medical information online can lead them down frustrating and expensive cul-de-sacs.

The democratisation of medical knowledge comes with challenges. For instance, information on the NHS website must be signed off by at least one clinician.[32] On social media, there are no such editorial checks, and you can reach millions of people instantly. Historically, doctors were the ultimate authority; they alone delivered diagnoses, referred a patient for further investigation and interpreted scans and test results. They spoke, patients listened. Now patients come equipped with their own view about their health and bodies and expect to be listened to. Paternalism is rightly a thing of the past. Indeed, there's been conscious advocacy for people taking responsibility for their health decisions by health professionals too.

Dr Jenny Wu, who specialises in obstetrics and gynaecology at Duke University in North Carolina, studies how health information is communicated on social media. For many of her patients, doctors are no longer the custodians of health information, although they still largely control treatment – but even this is changing, as we'll explore later. 'Our expectations of healthcare are undergoing rapid change,' she tells me. Her patients might endure fourteen-month waits for appointments while spending hours daily on social media researching their conditions. When they finally see a doctor, they get just twenty minutes. Their preconceptions about their health have had plenty of time to solidify. 'Healthcare professionals need to develop more effective approaches for addressing information patients find online,' she says – simply dismissing what they found isn't going to cut it.

## THE ILLUSION OF INTIMACY

Everyone knows the value of a good endorsement. In the 1990s and early 2000s, advertising on the internet was crude in many respects. It involved spam emails for penis enlargement pills, badly designed banners and pop-up ads. It was crass and annoying but overt. But the market has changed beyond recognition since then. Uniqlo went so far as to pay Roger Federer US $300 million to wear their products on the tennis court.[33] A single, respected voice telling you that a product works can be as effective as hundreds of billboards or TV adverts. Influencers or content creators use the same principle but rely on their perceived autonomy and accessibility. They curate their content to cultivate strong engagement, creating a community and loyal following around their 'brand'. While celebrities embody aspirational fantasies, influencers derive their persuasive power from portraying themselves as people just like you and me, with similar choices to make. When we see people like ourselves, messy kitchens, toddlers in the background, sharing information about their health with us, we feel more connected to their message. There's a reason we ask our friends and family for recommendations when it comes to needing a plumber or choosing a school for our child: we have faith in their judgement.

Content creators come from all backgrounds, ranging from celebrities and TV personalities to micro-influencers sharing well-meaning advice, alongside qualified scientists and medics. It's a crowded, competitive space, with each vying for attention. Professor Pete Etchells, a specialist in psychology and science communication at Bath Spa University, notes how 'previously, expertise was associated with someone who spent twenty years researching a specific topic. That was a marker of reliability – someone whose word you could trust. But now, trustability is often equated with being engaging, relatable, and likeable. People pay more attention to someone who can communicate well and seem friendly than to someone with decades of experience.'

This can lead to so-called one-sided parasocial relationships, which are deepened by the direct, personal nature of social media content. When it came to old-school celebrities, you could at most send them some fan mail and perhaps receive an autograph in return, if you were lucky. If you're a follower of a content creator, you can like their posts, comment under them, talk to other followers, even message them. Influencers might respond to questions in new posts, fostering an illusion of reciprocity and an equal relationship. 'There has to be a continuous flow of engaging information to build these parasocial relationships,' explains Dr Sophie Boerman, associate professor in persuasive communication at Wageningen University in the Netherlands. 'There also needs to be a level of interaction. It's not a one-way medium. People can respond, like posts, comment and even receive responses from influencers. This two-way communication, combined with consistent and interesting content, is key.'

Whereas healthcare professionals might have to be more dispassionate about how they communicate to potential patients online and uphold confidentiality, other content creators can be deeply personal. They may share intimate struggles over anything from mental health to chronic illness, creating a sense of closeness and a window into their life. Each personal revelation, each seemingly candid moment – from morning routines to health struggles – strengthens the follower's sense that they're developing a real friendship. This one-sided simulation of intimacy can create a powerful marketing dynamic. Consumers treat a recommendation from a practical stranger as if it came from a friend.

But a follower only sees what the influencer chooses to let them see. Many influencers fail to disclose when they have been paid for a post so what we see is a far cry from the full picture.[34] Yet a 2020 study in the *Journal of Marketing Management* found that when followers feel connected to or 'know' an influencer, they're more likely to trust their recommendations and buy their endorsed products.[35]

Why do people place so much faith in the words of these influencers and not the carefully vetted information you can find from healthcare authorities? It comes down to the stories influencers tell. Storytelling is how our brains are wired to process information – it's one of the most effective ways we learn and engage. We live our lives by narratives: where cause, effect and consequence seem to be clearly delineated. To hear a story, from our earliest childhood, is, in some sense, to learn how we ought to act.

One survey by a UK PR and digital communications agency in 2024 found that in health personal connection can matter more than credentials, charting changes in how consumers assess information.[36] About 35% of the people they surveyed say they won't trust information unless it comes from someone with first-hand experience. Another 17% need the source to be relatable. That same survey in 2020 found 70% of respondents said they would lose trust in a source of health information if it did not come from a healthcare professional. By 2024, this figure dropped to 45%. Additionally, more people are relying on their own health beliefs and experiences, with 29% of respondents in 2024 saying they wouldn't trust information that conflicts with their views, up from 17% the previous year. 'Consumers are increasingly ignoring health information that they can't relate to, even if it comes from trusted sources,' the report concluded.

## WHERE UNCERTAINTY DIES AND CERTAINTY SELLS

But individual stories may disappoint. What works for one person might not work for you, regardless of the seeming similarities in your symptoms. Our bodies are different and changes in our health often aren't always reducible to one cause and one effect.

Consider a gluten-free success story: 'I cut out bread and my fatigue vanished!' These testimonials flood social media, offering hope in neat narrative packages. A person might well have found boundless energy after going gluten-free. But in going gluten-free, they may have started eating more vegetables in the place of bread or pasta, or they drank less alcohol once beer was off the table. Put simply, the problem might not have been a gluten intolerance, but old habits they changed at the same time. This is known as the *post hoc ergo propter hoc* fallacy – 'after this, therefore because of this'.

Social media is about certainty. 'Social media has abolished doubt, it's like "God forbid you seem uncertain!" And yet real science – at least medical science – is always uncertain,' Dr Perry Wilson, associate professor of medicine and public health at Yale University, tells me. This is compounded by the fact we're desperate for 'one quick fix'. We crave medical certainty in an uncertain world. 'We have an understandable desire for miracle cures,' Wilson says, 'even though research is frequently about modest improvements, shavings of risk and close judgement calls.'

Medicine, at its core, is a science of probabilities rather than certainties. A doctor cannot predict with certainty whether a drug they prescribe will benefit you or if you'll experience a side effect. Likewise, the exact outcome of a disease can be uncertain. Instead, medical decisions are guided by statistical probabilities derived from scientific research.

Anecdotes are the lowest rung of evidence; no one would suggest extrapolating guidance for the whole population based on one story. This isn't to dismiss personal stories entirely. Anecdotal evidence can be a valuable signal, highlighting an area worth investigating further and prompting hypotheses. Much medical knowledge and research began with a health professional noting an unusual pattern in patient experiences and studying it further.

Well-designed research chisels away at uncertainty by comparing outcomes: does this treatment outperform that one, or no treatment at all? The results rarely offer guarantees, only probabilities. A drug might help seven out of ten patients while harming one – statistics that resist the comfort of black-and-white thinking.

However, while medicine speaks in probabilities, Instagram deals in absolutes. 'Social media allows anecdotes and testimonials to dominate. Testimonials are one of the most common ways to promote unproven therapies. A powerful, often celebrity-backed testimonial will outweigh hard evidence on safety and efficacy, which is why social media has become a "testimonial factory", Professor Timothy Caulfield, a Canadian health law and policy expert, tells me.

In this factory, a single, compelling personal story can outperform scientific evidence, manufacturing credibility through virality rather than verification. This alters our perception of what is normal or likely. For instance, a rare side effect when taking a medication might appear common simply because those experiencing it eagerly comment on relevant posts, while those who have no ill effects rarely feel compelled to share their uneventful experiences.

## TRACKED, TRACED AND TARGETED

Social media amplifies this effect, driven by algorithms that shape our feeds. These algorithms identify our preferences to maximise the time we spend fixed to our screen. In doing so, they create an illusion of understanding you personally, serving content that attracts engagement and keeps you scrolling for longer. There's a phrase I've heard repeatedly when talking to those who turn to social media for health information: 'The algorithm knows me better than I know myself.'

How do they seemingly learn about us? It's all about how we communicate online. We send emojis instead of smiling, tap 'like' instead of nodding and share posts to show we agree with them. These digital gestures have become our new body language. But these simple clicks and reactions reveal more than we think. When you double-tap a photo or share a post, you're leaving digital footprints. Companies track these tiny actions, building a detailed map of who you are. Your pattern of likes might reveal your political views. The posts you share could signal your interests, weaknesses and sensibilities. Even the emojis you choose can say something about your emotions and relationships. Tech companies use these digital breadcrumbs to predict what you'll do next and shape what you see. Each thumbs-up and heart emoji feeds the algorithms that decide what appears in your feed. It's a powerful system hidden behind simple taps as we move through the online world.

TikTok's algorithm works in a different way. Stokel-Walker describes the platform's departure from traditional models: 'Previous generations of social media, like Facebook, were based on the social graph. For example, Facebook would show you content that your friends posted or were interested in, reflecting their activity.' TikTok's system prioritises individual engagement patterns over social connections. 'Instead of focusing on what your friends are engaging with, TikTok's recommendation system is content-based. This means the algorithm prioritises your personal interactions with videos.'

'If you linger on a video, rewatch it multiple times, share it, comment on it, or like it, these actions send signals to the algorithm indicating your interest. The system ranks these behaviours in order of importance – watch time and re-watching are more significant than liking or commenting – and uses them to recommend more similar content,' Stokel-Walker explains. This feeds into what scientists call the 'illusion of truth bias' or the 'illusory truth effect': the more we see something, the more we believe it, regardless of whether it's accurate.[37] Our brains mistake familiarity for truth.

The algorithm amplifies this effect by showing us what's popular, not necessarily what's factual. When thousands share questionable health advice or conspiracy theories, this content feels credible. This 'social proof' exploits our tendency to trust crowds, even when they're wrong. Like a post about crash dieting, and suddenly your feed fills with similar content. Click on dubious health information, and you'll see dozens more claims, creating an echo chamber of dodgy information that feels truer and truer.

This can have insidious effects on vulnerable populations. A 2022 study by the Center for Countering Digital Hate found that when researchers created test accounts for thirteen-year-olds on

TikTok, the app's 'For You' feed quickly served harmful content.[38] Within three minutes, users saw videos about suicide. Within eight minutes, eating disorder content appeared. Mental health and body image videos played every thirty-nine seconds. Eating disorder content alone had gathered 13.2 billion views. TikTok has since clamped down on this content.[39] But it can't effectively police roughly 1 million content creators on its platform, and this is before we look at the content on other platforms.[40]

For health marketers, social media is perfect. A captive, somewhat fear-driven audience seeking wellness advice meets an algorithm designed to sell – creating an ideal environment to promote products and services. As my cousin's friend Anna who bought her AMH test online found out, this can be financially costly at the very least. Fortunately, though, her costs stopped there. After researching her low reading more thoroughly, she chose to disregard it and later conceived naturally, without needing IVF.

Social media influencers have become big business, transforming from a niche marketing trend into a $32 billion industry in 2025 – triple what it was in 2020.[41] Agencies are wise to the opportunity this presents for health and wellness and their social media spend is booming. 'With platforms such as Instagram, TikTok, and YouTube at the forefront of marketing strategies, and influencers trusted as valuable sources of information, the industry is set to continue expanding,' one marketing report said.[42]

## THE INFLUENCE LADDER

In the world of digital influence, reach and engagement have their own mathematics. At the summit sit the mega-influencers – the Kardashians and the Biebers – commanding audiences that surpass the population of many nations. Their posts can command fees in the hundred thousands, making them accessible only to the most deep-pocketed brands. One rung down, macro-influencers (100,000 to 1 million followers) hit a sweet spot of both visibility and authenticity. Think of fitness coaches whose workout videos reach hundreds of thousands, or chefs whose recipe reels spark kitchen trends across continents. Micro-influencers (10,000 to 100,000 followers) excel in engagement, fostering dedicated audiences despite their smaller reach. Nano-influencers, with under 10,000 followers, thrive on deep connections. A local fitness instructor with 3,000 highly engaged followers might drive more actual gym sign-ups than a celebrity athlete with millions of passive viewers.

In among these influencers are the podcasters. These podcast influencers use long conversations to build trust with their followers. They shape opinions and cultural trends through in-depth conversational content that can last for hours. They build strong connections with their listeners by putting out new episodes on a regular basis and talking to them by following up on their queries. People get the impression that they really know these hosts, almost like they're friends, and that's what gives them power. When these hosts endorse a product or brand, it often carries more weight than a traditional advertisement, because the recommendation feels like it's coming from a trusted friend rather than a paid spokesperson. Many also expand their reach by sharing podcast clips on platforms like Instagram and YouTube.[43]

And there's a new category of influencer that's emerging – those that are AI-generated. These computer-created characters simulate human behaviour and engage with audiences and promote products on social media much like their human equivalents.[44] They may be a caricature or even an avatar of the person themselves, only a computer is simulating their words and actions. They're already being used in some countries to talk about medical issues. The use of AI influencers, however, raises ethical concerns about transparency, potential audience deception and the implications of AI-driven persuasion techniques. Going forward it raises questions about which people and what platforms audiences will come to trust.

When it comes to health-related decisions, this influencer economy might not be in everyone's best interests. There's a reason that drug advertising is banned in nearly every country aside from the US and New Zealand; it's because the prevailing view is that decisions about medicines should be based on medical expertise and patient needs, not on commercial advertising. And even this legislation is being challenged by social media, as we'll explore later in the book.

## SELLING BY STEALTH

On social media, the line between someone sharing a personal experience of a product and someone advertising it becomes hard to draw – especially when influencers and companies alike are reluctant to disclose what content is paid for. Alice Bull has worked in digital marketing for over twenty years for major brands and PR companies. She has been dubbed a 'TikTok vigilante' for exposing how some of the biggest content creators are apparently skirting regulations designed to tell viewers when they are watching an ad.[45] Suffice to say, it doesn't always go down well. 'I don't think my husband could take it if I got any more legal threats on social media,' she says wryly. Bull says she's undeterred. Advertising in the UK is overseen by the Advertising Standards Authority (ASA). It responds to complaints, monitors ads and takes action to ban misleading, harmful, offensive or irresponsible advertisements. Bull tells me:

> There are so many rules and regulations about what you can and can't say. We see influencers breaking these rules all the time. Many are out there promoting supplements like their lives depend on it – which, in a way, they do because they're paid a fortune. But they make all sorts of unproven claims about the efficacy of the products, which is infuriating. For example, showing before-and-after photos and saying, 'This supplement grew my hair this much in six months.' Where's the evidence? Where are the studies? Unless you have data to back it up, it's just misleading.

In 2024, she pulled out of the Global Influence Marketing Awards – 'a significant industry event' – because, she says, that 'about 50%

of the entries hadn't disclosed their posts as advertising'. 'These were influencer posts up for awards, yet they weren't marked as marketing content. To me, that makes fair judgement impossible because algorithms always prioritise non-disclosed content over ads, and audiences are more likely to scroll past anything they recognise as an ad,' she says.

The distinction between an advert and a post is critical in how we assess information on social media. Posts which disclose that they are paid-for content can help children recognise when a YouTuber is trying to sell something, which research has shown dampens their enthusiasm for a product.[46] However, if a child has a parasocial relationship with an influencer, they will process paid-for content much in the way they would process 'genuine' enthusiasm from someone they like.

Professor Raffael Heiss, a digital media researcher at the Center for Social & Health Innovation in Innsbruck, has investigated this phenomenon. In one study, his team collaborated with over twenty schools where students analysed approximately 2,000 health-related influencer posts. The students examined whether posts contained advertisements and discovered that over 40% of all analysed content included promotional material. 'I'd argue they might have missed some, as influencers sometimes use subtle techniques like discount links,' he tells me. When students were asked to rate the content, there was no difference between sponsored and non-sponsored posts. They processed and responded to both types of content in similar ways. 'From all 2,000 posts, they classified only 4.7% as harmful, 30% as neutral and more than 60% as beneficial – which doesn't reflect reality,' he says.

The online world is much more challenging to regulate than traditional advertising media like TV, magazines and billboards. Social media enables private communication, allowing influencers to engage with their followers through direct messages. Not only do the algorithms prioritise direct messaging in terms of gauging your interest, but the seemingly personal relationship is also something that brands are keen to exploit, Alice Bull tells me. But regulating private exchanges between individuals is near enough impossible. How to apply advertising standards in the 'Wild West' of the internet vexes Jonathan Hardy, a professor of communications.

The varied range of health influencers adds to this challenge. At one end of the spectrum are amateur creators sharing their personal health experiences in good faith, though often without scientific backing. At the opposite end are professional influencers whose entire livelihoods depend on paid partnerships with health and wellness companies. Hardy references the case of British media personality Katie Price, who posted an Instagram Reel for The Skinny Food Co., showcasing her daily diet of only 755 calories – less than half of the NHS recommendation for an adult woman. In the video, Price was seen preparing meals and discussing her weight-loss efforts. The UK's ASA deemed the ad 'irresponsible' and banned it.[47] 'That's someone in a much more professionalised space who should know better,' he says. Between these poles lies a grey area where it's hard to distinguish between those who should be held to legal standards of advertisers and those who, regardless of what we think of what they say, are expressing themselves as private individuals.

Moreover, there's the issue of being able to say different things on different platforms. Consider the case of Davina McCall, one of Britain's most recognisable TV presenters. On television, her content faces strict oversight. But on social media, she can promote products in ways that would never clear TV regulations. This platform-hopping exploits what Hardy calls 'borrowed legitimacy' – using credibility earned in regulated spaces to sell products in unregulated ones. This is how influence flows across platforms outpacing regulatory frameworks.

'We're still in the early stages of figuring out how to enforce these rules effectively,' Hardy says. Transparency around financial interests has to go beyond disclosing sponsorships or marking a particular post as paid for. A wellness influencer might recommend supplements because they received free samples, hold stock in the company or have family ties to the brand, he says.

## CONFLICTS OF INTEREST

These conflicts of interest aren't, of course, limited to influencers. The medical profession has long grappled with the tension between providing impartial advice and commercial incentives. Drug company efforts to woo prescribing doctors have been debated for years and flagrant incentives are discouraged. The UK's General Medical Council, which regulates doctors, explicitly prohibits doctors from accepting any hospitality, fees or gifts that can be seen to affect how they prescribe or treat patients.[48] A doctor is required to state all reasonable alternatives when recommending a product or a service that they have a financial interest in. In principle, these safeguards exist to prevent doctors from exploiting their positions of authority for personal gain – though serious questions remain about how effectively these measures actually work. Companies still collaborate with health professionals – known as key opinion leaders (KOLs) – to whom they give platforms, training and resources to promote products through talks, publications and peer education. While KOLs may present valid scientific data, they play a role in shaping prescribing habits and perceptions,[49] and their content often aligns with commercial interests, blending medical expertise with marketing goals.

Most infamously, OxyContin, the drug that sparked the devastating opioid crisis in the US, gained widespread use through a sophisticated marketing strategy that featured prominent physician endorsements and strategic advertising in medical journals.[50] Other industries recognised the trust people place in medical professionals and leveraged this credibility to their advantage. In the 1940s, tobacco adverts appeared in the *Journal of the American Medical Association*, declaring 'More doctors smoke Camels', allegedly based on the results of a nationwide survey.[51]

In some ways, influencers have become the KOLs in consumer health. Using their own playbooks, they shape our perceptions and influence what we choose to purchase. It's a hard space to regulate but codes of practice are springing up. We'll explore their methods further throughout the book.

The holes in the claims made by celebrities and wellness gurus might be easy to spot, but it's much harder to argue with someone armed with a PhD, citing numerous scientific studies and claiming that a product really works. But just because someone is medically qualified doesn't mean that they have your best interests at heart. Nor does it mean that they apply the evidential standards required by clinical best practice to every product they endorse or recommend. 'Medical professionals on social platforms can command incredibly high fees when working with brands,' Bull says, citing one doctor who has worked with skincare brands like CeraVe and La Roche-Posay. They can charge premium rates because they have an 'unmatched authority' and it's a trend that is only going to grow, she adds. Furthermore, in the US, marketing agencies are encouraging health brands, including drug companies, to develop relationships with medical professionals.[52] In effect, we're continuously bombarded with health solutions, many of them driven by commercial interests rather than a genuine concern for patients' wellbeing. What does this all mean for us?

Even though measuring social media's impact is complex and robust data might be hard to come by, there are reasons to hypothesise that the platforms are reshaping the medical landscape in different ways, as we'll see throughout the book. The implications of this don't just affect individual health decisions but also public health policy, research and clinical practice. Healthcare providers must learn to navigate a world where patients confront them with tests and treatments they've used based on information gleaned from social media and on symptoms they've been told to expect. Public health officials face the challenge of communicating effectively on platforms that reward and amplify everything that sound medical guidance is meant to avoid.

But most of all, all of us need to learn how to assess information anew. Platitudes like 'Don't trust everything you read online' do not cut it on platforms abounding with seemingly credible, scientific guidance. We are in the middle of a global experiment in public health. It will take many years to understand the results. There are clearly benefits from its use. But there's a risk that, with unfettered advertising online coupled with the increasing commodification and commercialisation of health, we may be doing more harm than good. This book is about what can happen when entertainment, commerce and health collide.

# 2

# ARE STORIES MAKING US SICK?

In the winter of 2020, as the world wrestled with one kind of contagion, paediatric doctors found themselves tracking what seemed like another. While their colleagues donned N95 masks and studied viral loads, these specialists watched, with mounting curiosity, as a different wave of patients entered their clinic. They didn't have the dry cough, loss of taste, breathing difficulties and spiking fevers that accompanied Covid-19. Instead, they arrived with tics – sudden, involuntary movements typically associated with Tourette syndrome.

One doctor facing this influx of patients was Dr Tammy Hedderly, a consultant paediatric neurologist at Evelina London Children's Hospital who specialises in childhood-onset movement disorders, including tics and Tourette syndrome. 'We were seeing teenage girls with very florid movements,' she tells me. 'They were presenting with large physical tics; chest thumping; and hitting people, hitting their mum or dad. And they were making a lot of explosive movements such as jumping, hopping.' Prior to the pandemic, Hedderly's clinic would get four to six referrals per year for severe and sudden tics in teenage girls. Yet towards the end of 2020, this was up to three to four referrals per week.

The thing was the symptoms didn't look like traditional tics. In a typical case of Tourette's – which primarily affects boys from an early age – Hedderly would expect simple, fluctuating tics like blinking, coughing or clearing the throat. But these new patients were different. The surge of referrals consisted of adolescent girls with sudden onset of motor and phonic tics, leading to A&E visits. They followed a specific pattern and came with emotionally charged insults or strange phrases. 'Tics don't normally present like that,' Hedderly asserts.

Concerned about what she was seeing, Hedderly contacted a colleague at another London hospital, who was receiving similar referrals. Nor was this outbreak confined to the UK. From Toronto to Berlin to Sydney, a wave of tics seemed to sweep through young girls. On online forums, perplexed neurologists swapped notes. 'My practice has seen an unprecedented increase in young adolescent women with what appears to be acute explosive motor and vocal tics,' wrote a doctor from Kansas City, Missouri.[1] Neurologists at the Rush University Medical Centre in Chicago went as far as calling it a 'pandemic within a pandemic'.[2]

The patterns were similar. As well as the motor symptoms, in English-speaking countries the young people were repeating words like 'beans' and 'beetroot'. In Germany, along with specific movements, doctors reported patients shouting phrases, such as '*Pommes*' (chips), '*Bombe*' (bomb), '*Du bist häßlich*' (you are ugly), '*Heil Hitler*' and '*Fliegende Haie*' (flying sharks).[3]

What were the underlying reasons for a sudden surge in tics? How could clinicians help the young people coming into their clinics? Doctors in the US thought they may have found some of their answers on TikTok.

For some in the Tourette's community, TikTok has allowed those with the condition to challenge stigma and promote understanding. Social media has played an important role in destigmatising many conditions. Content creators share glimpses of their daily lives, showcasing how they navigate routine activities while managing their tics.[4] 'I wanted to show other people living with Tourette's that they are not alone, we are in this together,' one creator told *The Express*. 'I also hope to educate people who don't have Tourette's by answering their questions and showing them that we are human too.'[5]

But in this instance, the platform's algorithm had turned what was perhaps a neurological condition into a viral one. Researchers estimated that within a three-week period in March 2021 views of videos with the keywords #tourette and #tic increased by 7% to arrive at 5.8 billion views in total.[6]

The tics displayed by TikTok influencers were different to typical Tourette symptoms. There were far more tics per minute than normal. Symptoms typically considered rare in clinical settings were common online. These included coprolalia (involuntary swearing) and copropraxia (obscene gestures). Even more concerning was the prevalence of self-injurious behaviours like headbanging and self-punching – actions rarely seen in typical cases but featured prominently in the majority of TikTok videos.

'When a teenage girl walks into my clinic shouting "beans!", my first question is: "Have you been watching this influencer? Because I know all the names of the influencers,"' Hedderly says. Her patients would often deny this at first, she adds. The idea that they were imitating what they saw on TikTok seemed like an accusation of 'faking it' rather than an attempt at understanding their very real and distressing symptoms. But over time it became clear that they had spent hours watching influencers displaying particular tics, and then found themselves grappling with the same symptoms they had seen played out on their screens.

## WHEN SYMPTOMS SPREAD

Initially, the medical community attributed this to sociogenic illness, where members of a social group develop symptoms simultaneously without a physical cause.[7] Though these symptoms are real and can have serious consequences, what causes them is poorly understood, with extreme stress thought to play a role.

Sociogenic illness has been documented throughout history. For example, in Strasbourg in 1518, as many as 400 people found themselves dancing to the point of exhaustion and injury, as if by compulsion. This followed a series of famines and disease outbreaks in the city. This 'dancing plague' seemed to spread through the city like a contagious infection – although it's unlikely any pathogen was involved.[8] Medical historians have postulated that extreme stress was affecting the Strasbourg residents.

For the US neurologists, the pandemic-era surge in tics stirred memories of a series of recent events. In October 2011, Le Roy, a small town in New York state, experienced an unusual outbreak that began when a high school cheerleader suddenly developed inexplicable spasms during school. Within weeks, her best friend began showing similar symptoms, including a distinctive head-snapping movement. The condition then spread through the school in a pattern that tracked social connections, eventually affecting twenty people: eighteen teenage girls, one boy and one adult woman.[9]

The case quickly attracted national media attention, with affected students appearing on major news networks. As cameras rolled and speculation mounted, experts searched for culprits – environmental toxins or viral infections that could explain the sudden onset of symptoms. A wide range of blood tests and brain scans from those with symptoms came back largely normal.[10]

But one doctor, neurologist Dr Jennifer McVige, had a different hypothesis. Treating fourteen of those affected, she realised that all were under tremendous psychological stress. They'd been dealing with serious family illness and absent fathers, as well as the more standard pressures of adolescence. Understandably, some families were less receptive to this explanation.[11]

As far as stress goes for those pandemic tics, Covid-19 created a perfect storm. Teenagers spent their days at home, cut off from school and friends. Some worried for their loved ones and witnessed them become seriously ill or die from the disease. And social media, with its simulation of meaningful connection and potent algorithm, filled the void. It allowed teenagers to identify socially with strangers wherever they were, as they would do with their peers at school. Social media, it seemed, could spread symptoms across continents.

This does not mean that what these young people were experiencing was caused solely by social media. When patients came to Hedderly's clinic, each person needed careful investigation to understand what was really happening in their lives. 'They present in the same way, but every young person is different,' she says. The patients fell into several distinct groups. Some teens were unconsciously adopting these behaviours to connect with their peer group, developing tics as a way to express belonging – a physical indicator of group identity in an age of isolation. Then there were those whose medical histories pointed to something else. They'd had childhood tics that had come and gone, or siblings with similar conditions, suggesting an underlying genetic susceptibility. The pandemic had added its own layer of complexity, as isolation, anxiety and grief created new forms of psychological strain.

All these factors contributed to what the medical community calls functional tics. This is a neurological disorder where doctors can find no physical damage to the brain, no injury or disease to point to on a scan. The tics develop because people process their environment and bodily sensations in a different way leading to real physical symptoms. 'Some young people have a clear predisposition to neurodevelopmental difficulties. Research is at an early stage and there is so much more we need to try and understand about why particular people were affected, such as predisposing neurogenetic factors or precipitating events,' Hedderly explains.

Another group of affected young people seemed particularly influenced by their environment. 'We think that some people's brains are highly suggestible. So if you expose a brain to lots of images on social media, for example, there is a subgroup of the population that are much more likely to then exhibit those things,' she adds.

This posed a challenge for doctors. They would need to distinguish between transient tics that would resolve spontaneously and those requiring long-term psychiatric intervention. In doing so, they found themselves navigating a complex interplay of digital influence, psychological vulnerability and neurological symptoms. In medical journals, doctors advised one another to ask their young patients what they'd been watching on social media. 'A modern clinician thus needs to remain abreast of social media sources as they have now become essential in managing patients in the current environment,' the Chicago doctors wrote.[12]

## MONETISING DISTRESS

Hedderly's team tried to tackle the issue at source. They contacted the TikTok influencers whose videos depicted these symptoms, asking them to put some support on their websites or feeds. They received mixed responses.

'Likes and interactions are highly rewarding,' Hedderly explains. 'They activate that old part of the brain that responds to rewards, which can drive and perpetuate the behaviour. Human psychology is such that we are all driven by this desire.' Social media's reward system shapes what viewers see of these conditions. A video in which someone shows only minor tics is not as likely to get as much attentions as one in which someone is visibly distressed and jerking. This affects the content that influencers post – their curation of what they share.

But influencers aren't simply vying for attention. There's the promise of financial gain. The Chicago neurologists found that of the twenty-eight TikTok creators with over 100,000 followers they analysed, over 64% sold merchandise on their pages. 'It pays to become popular on social media platforms and thus following trends, such as tics and Tourette syndrome, can help these creators achieve this status,' they wrote.[13] Social media's promise of lucrative influence had turned medical symptoms into marketable content. Young people's pain, distress and need for belonging had been commercialised and commodified.

Given the stigma of the condition and the impact on quality of life, people with Tourette's began pushing back against the wave of social media cases. 'Some people with Tourette's became quite angry towards people experiencing functional tics, and saying, "you haven't got real Tourette's", and some people said "you're faking it,"' Hedderly says. Their resentment of social media cases is unsurprising. It's embittering to see a condition which shapes your everyday life being packaged as marketable content to millions. Unfortunately, it's not so straightforward as simply drawing a line between 'real' and 'fake'. Our consumption of social media, it seems, can induce conditions that are for all functional purposes devastatingly real.

## I WILL HARM

We're just beginning to understand how this content may influence our experience of health. Constantly seeing illness-related content online doesn't just raise awareness of particular conditions, or combat stigma, or help patients to connect with each other. Seeing and believing can translate into *feeling*.

We know this from the potency of the placebo effect when it comes to medication. If you believe you are being given pain relief, your brain will produce chemicals that make you feel better.[14] Our brains are not separate from our bodies – they are involved in every sensation we have. What we think and believe can have surprising effects on our physical health. You'll have some experience of this: your stomach churning before a job interview or feeling light-headed before an important presentation. These days we may view our forebears' fears of voodoo, witchcraft and curses as backward superstition. However, those who sickened after a supposed curse centuries ago are perhaps not too different from people experiencing symptoms like headaches and fatigue when exposed to Wi-Fi or wind turbines, despite no causal physical link being proven.[15] Convinced of our rational superiority to those who preceded us, we simply fail to realise how much we can still make ourselves sick.

We generally don't spend much time dwelling on the flipside of the placebo effect. It's called nocebo – literally 'I will harm'. Believing and expecting that you will fall ill can trigger real illness. These symptoms aren't imaginary or put on for show. When it comes to pains, involuntary movements or nausea to the point of throwing up, your mind can make all of that happen.

David Robson, a British science journalist, has direct experience of the nocebo effect. He first became interested in how our beliefs impact our health when he found himself struggling with depression and anxiety. He turned to his doctor for help who prescribed antidepressants. The pills stabilised his mood but brought on intense headaches, leading Robson to worry that something might be seriously wrong with him. Fortuitously, perhaps, he was working on an article about the placebo effect at the time.

Robson began to wonder if his headaches were caused not by the medication itself, but by his anticipation of side effects. The thought was a game-changer. 'The terrible pain I had been feeling while taking medication was perfectly real – but the product of my mind's expectation rather than the actual, chemical effects of the drugs,' he tells me. Once he grasped the power of the nocebo effect – that is the negative placebo, essentially – his headaches vanished. 'Expectations can shape our biology, within certain boundaries. Physiological changes can occur, and suffering from a nocebo effect doesn't mean someone isn't experiencing real physical symptoms,' Robson says.

Even before we seek treatment, our thoughts, emotions, experiences, exposure to media messaging and other expectations shape clinical outcomes and how satisfied we are. Researchers have long grappled with how to manage this problem. Many people stop taking cholesterol-lowering statin drugs because of uncomfortable side effects. To understand whether these side effects are genuinely caused by the medication or stem from patients' expectations, researchers at Imperial College, London conducted an experiment with sixty people who had previously quit statins due to adverse reactions.[16]

Participants cycled through three different treatment periods over twelve months: taking actual statin pills, taking placebo pills and taking no pills at all. Using a smartphone app, they rated their symptom intensity daily on a visual scale from 1 to 100. The researchers gave this a score. The results showed the negative effect of expecting to feel unwell. When participants took no pills, their symptom score was low, around 8 out of 100. However, when taking both real statin pills and fake pills, their symptom scores increased to 16, with almost no difference between the two. Similar numbers of people dropped out of the study after getting unwanted effects from either the statin or the placebo, and both groups felt equal symptom relief after stopping taking the tablets. 'Side effects from taking statin tablets are verifiable but are driven by the act of taking tablets rather than whether the tablets contain a statin,' the authors wrote.[17] This of course wasn't to say that statins have no side-effects – they do. But it shows how our expectations and prior experiences shape our symptoms.

MIND OVER BODY
Our past experiences can shape how we feel. But scientists have also been studying how we 'catch' negative health expectations from others. To demonstrate the power of suggestion, Dr Kate Faasse, who studies health psychology at the University of New South Wales, performs a simple experiment at the start of her talks about the nocebo effect. She asks her audience to imagine tiny bugs crawling on their skin. 'The entire room starts to squirm,' she says, as the audience begins to feel phantom itches. Their brains are activating the same neural pathways that would fire if actual insects were crawling across their skin.[18] 'People aren't making these things up. They're not malingering. They're not faking it,' she explains. The experiment shows how our minds process suggestion. The mere thought of an uncomfortable sensation can create that same discomfort in our bodies.

While stories about insects can make us squirm, our brains respond even more powerfully to visual cues. Consider the difference between reading about symptoms and watching them happen. A written description of a rash might make us slightly uncomfortable, but watching someone scratch at angry red welts can make our own skin tingle.

In a 2022 study, Faasse investigated how watching others experience symptoms may create those same symptoms in viewers, through social learning.[19] Researchers recruited ninety-seven college students for what they claimed was a trial of a 'fast-acting beta-blocker' medication for anxiety. The students heard about possible side effects – headaches, tiredness, dizziness, weakness, upset stomach – but weren't told they were receiving a placebo.

They were then split into three groups. One had no treatment, one had a sham treatment and one took a sham treatment and saw a video of actors reporting they had side effects after taking the pill. They then were then told to breathe through a narrow drinking straw for two minutes, following a fifty beats per minute rhythm set by a metronome. It's a way to induce mild anxiety. While almost everyone who took the sham medication reported some side effects, women who watched the videos of others experiencing sham symptoms reported significantly more symptoms compared to those who didn't watch the video.

In other words, social learning – our ability to pick up behaviours and physical responses just by observing others – has a role in the nocebo effect. When we observe or hear about someone else's negative health experience, we can start to feel similar symptoms ourselves even if there's no obvious physical reason for it.

A 2024 systematic review and meta-analysis looked at how this effect plays out in different cohorts. The researchers looked at common symptoms, like pain, itching, nausea and headaches, and found that what we see in others can show up in our own bodies.[20] And some people are especially susceptible: those who score high on particular measures of empathy report stronger nocebo outcomes. If you're someone who easily feels what others are feeling, you're more likely to experience similar symptoms after hearing about someone else's negative experience.

Simply being around other patients, whether in person or through online support groups, might influence how we experience our own illnesses. Our symptoms are shaped by the symptoms we've seen in others, as these are what our brains are conditioned to expect.

When someone describes their health experience in person, it has a more powerful effect on our own expectations and potential symptoms than videos. Researchers believe it's about the subtle, non-verbal communication we miss in videos – things like eye contact, body language and the nuanced way someone tells their story.

The internet has transformed how we share health experiences. Platforms like TikTok have shown how quickly health-related behaviours and perceptions can spread through video. A single viral video about medication side effects can reach millions, potentially influencing how entire communities think about a particular treatment.

This research highlights an issue that has become increasingly important in how we consume information. While a face-to-face conversation with a friend might be more immediately convincing, it's likely infrequent. Unlike the sheer volume of online health stories that are a click away on the sofa, on the train or after school drop-off. Someone might be more impacted by watching dozens of online videos about a medication's side effects than by a brief in-person conversation.

How we learn about health experiences matters, and the medium of communication can shape our expectations and potential symptoms. Early research by Faasse's team suggests content consumed on social media conditions our expectations. She and her team compared two ways of sharing the same health information. One came from leaflets that come with medications and the other from social media posts.

In her experiment, one group read formal medical language, the kind you'd find in any prescription package, listing potential benefits and side effects. Others saw the same information on social media. Both groups were presented with identical facts (like that 37% of people might experience certain side effects), only in different formats. Participants read around ten to fifteen social media posts describing a few different symptoms. The messages were fairly benign, like, 'I'm feeling very drowsy. I have to submit an assignment tomorrow. I hope this passes,' Fasse explains. 'They weren't particularly emotive or dramatic,' she says. Arguably they were more neutral than how they might be described on social media, as we'll see in later chapters.

The researchers then measured participants' expectations of side effects, asking them questions such as 'If you took this drug, how likely do you think it is that you'd experience these side effects?' 'If you did experience them, how severe do you think they'd be?' and 'How worried would you be about getting these side effects?'

'In every case, the ratings were significantly higher for participants who read the information via social media compared to those who read the formal information leaflet,' Faasse says. She does, however, urge caution as the study has yet to be published. It was also a controlled experimental setting and the way this plays out in the real world might be different.

## INFLUENCE AND ILLNESS

In Le Roy high school, you will remember, the first girl to come down with spasms was a popular cheerleader and the second person was her best friend. Although research is in its infancy, there are studies that suggest the level with which you identify with a person exhibiting symptoms – whether you trust them, how close you feel to them – is connected to the strength of the nocebo effect.[21]

On social media, we tend to follow and consume the content made by people we see as the most 'relatable'. This simulates the effect of knowing and liking someone, perhaps fortifying their authority and the weight we give to their experiences. There are compelling reasons to hypothesise that social media may contribute to the spread of nocebo effects.

'We typically follow people we trust, which is why their content appears in our feeds and resonates with us. This trust means we're more likely to heed their words and less likely to question the origins of their symptoms,' Robson suggests. 'That repetition on social media could play a significant role in amplifying your susceptibility, making you more likely to develop similar symptoms or concerns,' he adds. This means that the nocebo effect is no longer limited to cohesive communities in real life, such as schools and workplaces. In effect, an influencer in Sydney could make someone sick in London.

This might seem like a minor problem in the grand scheme of things. Does it matter if someone develops a headache after watching videos about migraines? But the psychogenic effects of social media have already had major public health consequences. In August 2012, the Colombian government introduced a school-based human papillomavirus (HPV) immunisation programme, initially starting with nine-year old girls and scaling it up. By the following year, the country had one of the highest HPV immunisation rates in the Americas, with coverage of over 90%.[22]

But on 29 May 2014, this started to unravel. A group of fifteen girls from one school in El Carmen de Bolivar, an agricultural town in the Montes de María mountain range, started to experience symptoms. These included a racing heart, shortness of breath and a numbness in their limbs. They were severe enough for the girls to be admitted to hospital.

Speculation started about what might have caused this cluster of symptoms. Was it water, lead or pesticide poisoning? Could it have been food they'd consumed? But parents were convinced that the second dose of HPV vaccine, administered two months earlier, was causing them. Soon more and more girls started to experience similar symptoms across Colombia. They were also fainting, twitching and arriving at the emergency department unconscious.

Puzzled, the authorities started to investigate. But after a thorough examination of over 500 girls, they found no biological cause for the symptoms. Reassured that the HPV vaccination was safe, the ministry of health stood firmly behind their programme.

The events in Colombia caught the eye of the Irish neurologist, Dr Suzanne O'Sullivan, who specialises in psychosomatic illnesses and epilepsy. She decided to fly to Colombia and investigate, documenting her observations in *The Sleeping Beauties*, alongside other case studies of psychosomatic illness.[23] It turns out the symptoms had little to do with the vaccine itself:

> There was no pathological mechanism through which a vaccine could have caused a mass outbreak of seizures, on a single day, a month after the vaccine was given. There is no association between the HPV vaccine and epilepsy, and, even if there was, the seizures I had seen were dissociative and certainly not caused by a brain disease.

Videos of girls who had received the HPV vaccine, showing them fainting, twitching and arriving unconscious at emergency rooms, began to surface in national news media and on social media platforms like YouTube at the time the first clusters of symptoms were seen.[24] The peak of emergency room admissions also coincided with intense media coverage and visits of ministry of health officials and politicians:

> Young women had been filmed in various stages of collapse: some lying still and pale, others with backs arched; some writhing, some shaking, and several being restrained by male relatives or boys from their class. These were clear dissociative seizures. There was no question.[25]

On 31 August, after over 200 girls had been hospitalised, the president of Colombia, Juan Manuel Santos, made a statement stating that there was no evidence that the HPV vaccine had caused the outbreak of symptoms in El Carmen de Bolivar. He described the girls as suffering from 'collective suggestion', or put more bluntly, hysteria.[26]

By the time ministry of health officials arrived in El Carmen de Bolivar to discuss the safety of the vaccine, there was already public outrage. Parents felt that their daughters' very real distress was being dismissed. No one is comforted by being told 'it's all in your head' when they are in pain. Even if someone's symptoms are being triggered by a social process, they have to be taken seriously. Even though Santos was correct, by bullishly insisting that the vaccine was safe and seeming to ignore those asking questions, he ended up further losing the trust of affected families. The Colombian public health response was botched.

Research shows that the effectiveness of health policies hinges on people's willingness to trust and follow guidance. When trust breaks down at any level people become less likely to comply with recommended health measures. Simply creating a policy isn't enough; establishing genuine credibility and understanding is crucial for ensuring that public health recommendations are actually followed.[27] By 2016, HPV vaccine uptake among eligible girls had plummeted in Colombia. Only 14% had the first dose and 5% the complete course.[28]

This HPV vaccine scare demonstrated the challenge public health authorities are up against when it comes to health panic spread online. How can a president speaking on national news – that many teenagers won't watch – compete with videos spreading like wildfire in the palms of our hands of girls collapsing with seizures? Those girls seem much closer to us than facts recited by a remote authority.

The risks of social media in effect creating illness through visibility doesn't stop at vaccines. Our awareness of everything that could go wrong with our bodies, born out of hours of consuming health-related content, could encourage us to pursue interventions and treatments that not only fail to solve our concerns but also have harmful effects on our bodies.

Some specialties are already witnessing the effects of online patient communities intensifying people's anxieties about their treatments. While neurological symptoms like tics don't require invasive treatments per se, the question of what to do becomes much more fraught when the proposed solutions can cause harm in their own right.

In her Tunbridge Wells consulting room, Ms Nora Nugent sees a whole range of concerns from some people about their breast implants. A consultant plastic surgeon based in Tunbridge Wells, she specialises in aesthetic and reconstructive breast surgery, now working exclusively in private practice. Some of the patients who come to see her describe a now-familiar pattern of symptoms. They have crushing fatigue, skin and hair conditions, brain fog and joint pain, which many attribute to their silicone breast implants.

'Some women associate these symptoms with the time shortly after receiving implants, while in others, they may have been symptom-free for years before the issues developed. It's not necessarily linked precisely to when implants were placed,' Nugent tells me.

It's a scenario playing out in clinics across the world. Since their introduction in the 1960s, breast implants have largely been used in post-mastectomy reconstruction and for cosmetic breast enlargement procedures. They're either made of silicone or saline, with silicone being the most common choice in the UK.[29]

When an implant is put into the body, a layer of scar tissue forms around it called a capsule. Varying in thickness, it acts like a natural bra, providing support and holding the implant in place. There are a number of recognised complications with breast implants, as there are with any major surgery, including scar contracture, rupture of the implants, bleeding, infection and fluid build-up.

However, over recent years, a growing number of women around the world have reported that they're struggling with symptoms, which has been dubbed 'breast implant illness' on social media platforms. It isn't an officially recognised medical condition and lacks specific diagnostic tests. Rather, it's a term that emerged to describe the collection of symptoms that some women with implants report experiencing.

There are over a hundred associated symptoms, including joint and muscle pain or weakness, memory and concentration problems, chronic pain, depression, fatigue, chronic flu-like symptoms, migraines and rashes and skin problems.[30] Many of the symptoms of breast implant illness are the same as those of autoimmune and connective tissue disorders, such as lupus and rheumatoid arthritis. However, only some people who have breast implant illness get diagnosed with a specific autoimmune or connective tissue disorder.[31]

## THE UNSETTLED SCIENCE OF IMPLANTS

The problem is there is no certainty around what causes it, and the mechanisms behind the illness are strongly contested. Some scientists think silicone implants might act as a constant trigger that can overstimulate the immune system, because your body wants to get rid of the foreign material, especially in people who are genetically prone to immune reactions. There are two main ways this might happen. Silicone directly affects the immune cells or it acts like a vaccine adjuvant – an ingredient added to some vaccines to boost the immune response – persistently activating the immune system.[32] They argue that we need better ways to identify which patients might be at risk for these immune reactions.

Others say bacteria can form thin layers called biofilms on implant surfaces and these persistent, low-grade infections may contribute to body-wide symptoms.[33] Then some medical experts suggest that psychological factors, including anxiety and stress, or even social media influences surrounding breast implants, could contribute to the development or intensification of breast implant illness symptoms. This might be exacerbated by an online echo chamber.[34] Some controversially suggest it might be a large-scale nocebo effect at work.[35] But others contend this theory struggles to explain cases with clear physical symptoms, such as hair loss,[36] with suggestions that breast implant illness could result from a mixture of several of the factors mentioned so far.[37]

Regulators on both sides of the Atlantic say that people wanting breast implants should be told about breast implant illness as a potential side effect.[38,39] Whatever the cause, Nugent stresses, the symptoms are real. 'The cause of the symptoms is what's unknown, not the symptoms,' she says.

From their earliest days in operating rooms, breast implants have been mired in controversy. When surgeons first began inserting them in the 1960s, they did so without meaningful safety research.[40] It was a flawed decision that would lead to decades of medical disputes and regulatory battles. Since then, silicone gel implants have faced ongoing scrutiny from both US and UK health regulators.

In the 1980s, reports linking silicone gel implants to developing arthritis, lupus and cancer were flagged in medical journals and by the Food and Drug Administration's (FDA's) own monitoring system.[41] The agency responded in 1992 by curtailing their use, limiting silicone implants to reconstruction after mastectomy, correction of congenital defects or replacement of existing devices. Europe continued to approve their use. Then, in 1999, the US Institute of Medicine released a hefty 400-page report prepared by an independent committee of scientists that seemed to exonerate silicone.[42]

The review of the existing literature found no evidence connecting the implants to systemic diseases like autoimmune disorders or breast cancer. It concluded that the main issues with implants were local complications – such as ruptures, hardening of the surrounding tissue, infections and pain – which, while problematic, weren't life-threatening.[43]

In 2006, after years of tracking women who received silicone implants during breast reconstruction, the FDA lifted the ban on silicone gel-filled implants. The agency's change of mind came after reviewing studies from two manufacturers that followed patients for just three to four years. Though the data revealed frequent complications, regulators determined that women could weigh these risks for themselves. Silicone implants could now be used for reconstruction at any age and for cosmetic enhancement in women twenty-two and older.[44]

The saga took another turn in 2010, when European authorities uncovered a scandal at Poly Implant Prothèse, or PIP. The French manufacturer had been secretly filling its implants with unauthorised industrial silicone, creating devices that ruptured at alarming rates. By the time regulators pulled PIP implants from the market, an estimated 47,000 British women had received them.[45] Many suffered anxiety and distress. They were left with the burden of making medical decisions about removal surgeries and what it all meant for their long-term health

Before the dust could settle on the PIP debacle, another revelation shook the industry. In 2011, health authorities in Europe and America raised concerns that certain breast implants were associated with a form of lymphoma, a cancer of the immune system. They called it breast implant-associated anaplastic large cell lymphoma (BIA-ALCL).[46]

The implants most associated with lymphoma risk have textured surfaces – a design typically preferred by surgeons over smooth implants. Yet even among textured implants, the risks aren't uniform; some texturing patterns appear to carry higher risks than others.[47] Although BIA-ALCL is treatable when caught early by removing the implant and the scar tissue in one piece (en bloc capsulectomy), the picture becomes more complicated when the disease has spread.[48]

The controversies continued to surface. In 2018, textured implants by a popular brand were withdrawn from sale in Europe on the instructions of the French health authorities.[49] The company in question, Allergan, wrote to clinics to say that, with immediate effect, it was 'suspending sales of textured breast implants and tissue expanders and withdrawing any remaining supply in European markets'.[50]

Given the history of changing policies and safety concerns around breast implants, it's not hard to see why women might feel anxious about what information manufacturers could be withholding and what potential harms regulators are failing to uncover. Women have been reporting strange, chronic symptoms after breast implants for decades. In 2020, the MHRA finally released guidance on 'Symptoms sometimes referred to as Breast Implant Illness', many years after online communities had emerged devoted to discussing the illness. But the authorities still say the link between implants and systemic illness is unclear.[51]

## HEARD AT LAST

Ultimately, many of the women affected by these symptoms feel that they are waging a lonely battle, unheard by the medical professionals who are meant to provide care. Those who received implants for cosmetic reasons describe an added layer of stigma and that their concerns sometimes met with judgement. With all the controversy and lack of clarity about breast implant risks, it's perhaps not surprising that women suspecting their implants of being the source of their illness have found solidarity on social media. It's a place where their experiences, finally, are heard and believed.

US health policy analyst Diana Zuckerman credits social media groups and patient activists with pushing the FDA and plastic surgeons to re-examine the safety of implants and with assisting many individual women who felt they had nowhere else to turn. 'I have no doubt that a lot of women who got their implants out and are feeling better now would never have done that if it weren't for the Facebook groups and websites,' she says. 'It's so unfair that women had to get the information from strangers online instead of their doctors, but it's also been so helpful to so many women.' She is frustrated by the lack of well-designed, long-term studies that include large numbers of women with breast implants.

On Facebook, one group has become a digital town square for nearly 200,000 women. The group 'Healing Breast Implant Illness and Healing by Nicole' offers the understanding and validation that its members say their doctors couldn't. The testimonies share a common thread of medical disillusionment. 'Doctors don't care to know whether these implants are harmful. They don't care to look at the studies,' one woman writes, her words echoed by a chorus of similar accusations. Another member's post is filled with scorn: 'My surgeon never told me about these horrible things that could happen after getting implants. Doctors just want to fill their pockets.'

For some women, finding these groups provides consolation. 'I started doing research, and I had all the same symptoms as all these people, and they all had the exact same implants as me,' one woman recalls. 'I was like "Oh, my god" that's what's been causing it.' Another member is more cynical: 'Misery loves company, I guess. Knowing that other women are going through the same exact thing that I have gone through validates my suspicion.'

Instagram and TikTok have become galleries of medical anxiety and devastating symptoms. Women document their symptoms with graphic imagery portending toxicity and death. One post shows a woman marked with a skull and crossbones across her chest, who is waiting to have the 'toxic shitbags' removed. She says her breast implants led to eye floaters, painful periods, gluten intolerance, hand tremors and neuropathy.

Their decisions on implants sometimes start in moments of vulnerability. 'I got breast implants before becoming pregnant with my third daughter. My older two daughters were still toddlers, and I was lost in the cycle of navigating motherhood and finding myself,' one mother confesses. She suddenly finds clarity when she stumbles across an article about breast implant illness: 'I nearly stood up out of my chair. "Omg, this is what's happening!"'

Some women describe their body rapidly ageing. 'I was 85 years old on the inside,' one writes, convinced her 'days were numbered'. Many recount years of inconclusive medical tests – enlarged livers, swollen lymph nodes, mysterious polyps – before diagnosing themselves. 'My gut was telling me it was because of having those toxic bags for 12 years,' one writes.

On the face of it, this seems like a story about the power of social media to help women. Its ability to support those who have been ignored in mainstream healthcare to reclaim control over their own lives and bodies. But professionals were concerned social media was creating anxiety and spreading confusion, perhaps overlooking the chaotic set of circumstances health authorities had created.

One study, with the title 'Breast implant illness: are social media and the internet worrying patients sick?', analysed popular tweets under the hashtag #breastimplantillness between February 2018 and February 2019. It found social media discussions often confuse breast implant illness with other conditions, like breast cancer, BIA-ALCL, and/or lymphoma, especially following FDA announcements. Most of this information is spread through non-medical sources and influencers, potentially creating misconceptions.[52]

Social media feeds can fuel a constant loop of symptom testimonials, with algorithms continuously promoting stories about severe illness. Faasse's research shows how this echo chamber can amplify health anxieties. When people enter a functional magnetic resonance imaging scanner (fMRI) – a machine that measures brain activity by detecting changes in blood flow – and are asked to focus on particular symptoms, the corresponding regions of their brains light up. This is not because of any physical stimulus but purely through the power of attention. 'It's real. It's happening in the brain. People aren't making it up or faking it. Imaging shows these activities genuinely occur,' she explains.

A 2022 study interviewed women with breast implant illness and revealed that, for some, exposure to social media group posts increased their anxiety about their symptoms.[53] As one woman said:

> I think they're very good for information but I think that they are also scary... I think that our mind is a powerful thing and so I think reading these stories and things over and over and over can also create problems too, that might not be there... You can start reading the stuff and almost stress yourself out more and worry that you have things maybe that you don't have.[54]

Science suggests she might be right. Our brains, Faasse notes, can amplify or dampen sensations based on what captures our attention.

Some experts worry that the digital amplification of fear and anxiety is pushing an increasing number of women to seek implant removal – what doctors call 'explant surgery' – without clear medical justification. The outcomes of these surgeries are mixed. Some women report improvements in their health after removal, while others find their symptoms persist. In a 2024 systematic review of the medical literature around 83% of women report improvement of symptoms, but there are weaknesses in the studies included in the review.[55] Even now, doctors cannot reliably predict which patients will find relief after surgery.

From her practice on the outskirts of Liverpool, Miss Leena Chagla takes the long view. With more than two decades spent in breast cancer care, she's seen the full spectrum of implant cases, including many seeking help after cosmetic procedures gone wrong, often performed abroad. 'I work purely in reconstruction after mastectomy,' she tells me.

What strikes her most is the difference between groups of patients. While some women specifically seek her out for implant removal, citing breast implant illness, her cancer reconstruction patients rarely report such symptoms. 'In twenty-six, twenty-seven years as a breast surgeon, I've never had to remove a reconstruction implant for this reason. That's really quite significant,' she muses.

It's a finding that surgeons in other countries have observed and studied too.[56] Chagla offered several possible explanations for this.

People with cancer might attribute symptoms like joint pain to their cancer medications rather than their implants. They might also be reluctant to consider implant removal after finally regaining their breast shape through reconstruction. This isn't just seen in those with cancer. Studies of transgender women with implants show they rarely report breast implant illness symptoms. Researchers suggest the psychological benefits of gender-affirming surgery might outweigh potential physical discomfort.[57]

The NHS, Chagla says, does remove breast implants in specific circumstances, such as if they're ruptured, leaking or causing severe capsular contracture. 'In those cases, we have clear surgical proof of a problem, and removal is warranted,' she says. But this doesn't extend to breast implant illness, and most NHS consultants will refer people back to their private surgeon. The NHS doesn't offer implant removal as a routine option because it's a major operation with risks involved, and there's no guarantee it will resolve symptoms. 'It's time-consuming, resource-intensive, and without solid evidence, we can't ethically or practically justify it,' she says. That isn't to say the NHS should ignore the symptoms women are experiencing. 'We'd want their condition thoroughly investigated rather than presuming the implants are the cause,' she adds. Doctors recommend exploring other potential causes for these symptoms, such as autoimmune conditions, thyroid problems or medication side effects – issues that some surgeons argue social media discussions might mistakenly attribute to breast implants.[58]

However, the surgery to remove breast implants has become its own source of controversy, especially when it comes to the capsule. If the capsule contracts, it has to be taken out along with the implant. This is called a total capsulectomy. It can be done with the implant removed first, or with the implant left inside. Social media groups have latched onto the most aggressive removal technique called an en bloc capsulectomy. This procedure, which removes the implant and its surrounding tissue capsule as one sealed unit, was initially developed for cancer treatment. It comes with more risks than standard removal methods, including increased bleeding, longer scars and, in rare instances, collapsed lungs.

The appeal of total removal is understandable. Remove everything to get rid of toxins in a similar way to how cancer surgeons aim to remove all traces of disease. But discussions tend to overstate the benefits of doing this while minimising the harm that can come with such invasive procedures. On TikTok and Facebook, the message has become absolute with some insisting that only an en bloc capsulectomy is curative. Any other approach is dismissed as inadequate. 'Make sure you go to a doctor who doesn't do implants at all but specialises in explants,' advises Star, a TikTok creator, to her followers. 'If those capsules are left inside, you can stay sick.' Monica, another TikToker who documents her explant journey, takes a similar view. 'I did not want those capsules left in my body.'

These social media testimonials have created a kind of parallel medical authority with its own certification process. One popular Facebook group not only insists on en bloc removal but directs women to YouTube videos of approved surgeons, warning members to demand photographic proof of a surgeon's expertise. The advice is that any doctor who suggests a less aggressive approach is to be distrusted. 'Some plastic surgeons may attempt to talk you out of explant or tell you a Total Capsulectomy is not necessary,' the Facebook group warns. 'Do not believe this.'

Yet the medical evidence is far from being that certain. Whether surgeons perform the aggressive en bloc procedures championed in Facebook testimonials or choose gentler approaches, the relief from symptoms has little connection to surgical technique.[59] But some surgeons are promoting en bloc capsulectomies as a cure-all solution, despite lacking scientific evidence for their claims. 'It's really disingenuous,' says Nugent. 'I've got to be honest – I think it's taking advantage of worried patients. There are reasons to do an en bloc procedure, but breast implant illness is not one of them.'

## SUPPLY-INDUCED DEMAND

The business of breast implant removal has found a home on social media, where surgeons post graphic videos of their handiwork on TikTok and Instagram. This marketing has drawn criticism from within the medical community, with other professionals condemning such practices in medical journals and filing formal complaints about misleading websites. When doctors market their services on social media, where does impartial medical advice end and exploitation begin?

Across the UK, private clinics now advertise these procedures on their websites, noting the increasing patient demand. Some surgeons themselves have helped create this through their participation on social media. Anxiety feeds demand, demand creates profit and profit drives more marketing, perhaps leading women toward riskier procedures than they might need.

Dr Caroline Glicksman, a surgeon in New Jersey has conducted multiple studies on breast implants and does not believe silicone to be the cause of the problems. She has been paid by implant companies to educate surgeons. This relationship between surgeons and implant companies is something that concerns Zuckerman and other patient advocates. Glicksman posed as a patient, contacting self-proclaimed, US-based 'breast explant experts' she found through Instagram and breast implant illness forums. She asked them about curing breast implant illness and about their surgical techniques. Costs were quoted at between $18,000 and $30,000, which is generally higher than other explant techniques, she says. The surgeons claimed to perform between 350 and 400 explant procedures each year when she asked them how many they did.

Many of these practitioners, Glicksman alleges, advertise their explant tallies like badges of honour on social media while making unsubstantiated claims about the treatment of breast implant illness to attract more patients. Social media has become a surgical marketplace. 'Do the math. These physicians are making between $11 and

$17 million a year, and many are receiving referrals from these sites,' Glicksman tells me.

Women who opt for the most aggressive surgery are not simply financially worse off. For some, their symptoms stay the same. Not only do they have to handle post-surgical recovery, they may be left with scarring and uneven breasts.[60] These stories don't always surface. In some breast implant illness forums, such testimonies vanish. They're deleted by moderators. Or the women quietly walk away from these communities, having paid an irreversible price for listening to influencers.

It's a challenge for medicine. How do you treat patients whose symptoms are exacerbated by their social media feeds – their bodies conforming to the expectations they are given through endless videos of people sharing symptoms? How do you help a patient whose presentation matches a viral TikTok video without dismissing their physical distress?

Healthcare has an uphill struggle in adapting to a world in which we are constantly pushed to pay attention to our bodies by an algorithm, and our bodies may in turn respond to the attention we pay them. We need to find ways of breaking out of algorithm-driven anxiety spirals and avoid a situation in which vulnerable people, lacking evidence-based guidance, pursue costly, unnecessary and harmful treatments. That's no easy task.

# 3

# THE WEIGHT-LOSS RACE, OR THE NEW DRUG MARKET

A diabetes medication does not typically ascend to the rarefied environment of the Academy Awards. Insulin or metformin have yet to reach such lofty heights. But in a moment that pharmaceutical marketing executives might have conjured in their most ambitious dreams, Jimmy Kimmel, surveying Hollywood's impossibly svelte stars, delivered a line that spoke to the elephant in the room: 'Everybody looks so great. When I look around this room, I can't help but wonder, "Is Ozempic right for me?"'[1]

Ozempic, a drug licensed for the management of type 2 diabetes, had been transformed into Hollywood's newest coveted accessory. It wasn't initially approved by regulators for weight loss, but it was being touted as a treatment for obesity.

It allegedly enabled Kim Kardashian to fit into the iconic skin-toned gown that Marilyn Monroe wore to serenade President John F. Kennedy on his forty-fifth birthday. In the run-up to the 2022 Met Gala, Kardashian apparently lost sixteen pounds in three weeks – impossible unless, her critics claimed, she had a little outside help. Kardashian, however, claimed it was due to nothing more than exercise, healthy eating and 'wearing a sauna suit twice a day'.[2]

Elon Musk showed none of the discretion associated with celebrity drug habits. When his followers praised his newly 'awesome, ripped and healthy' physique, he responded with characteristic bluntness, announcing to his 200 million Twitter (now X) followers the formula behind his transformation: 'Fasting + Ozempic/ Wegovy + no tasty food near me.'[3]

Ozempic has done the media rounds in the UK too. In 2023, a thin-looking Sharon Osborne took to the couch on *Good Morning Britain*, saying that she'd taken Ozempic because she was 'fed up of going back and forth' with her weight.[4] 'The world we live in today, everybody wants to be skinny,' she explained. 'I just thought, I've tried everything… And so I thought, well, might as well try it. And I did.' Where celebrities go, social media soon follows. As of August 2024, #Ozempic had 1.3 billion views on TikTok.

The drug has been credited for more than weight loss. Some claim it has helped them get pregnant – the so-called 'Ozempic babies' on social media – others assert taking Ozempic helped them 'switch off' anxiety. The testimonials aren't all success stories, however, with users sharing cautionary tales of aesthetic collateral damage. They're reminders of the unintended consequences that can accompany the pursuit of pharmaceutical perfection.

'Ozempic face' – characterised by hollow cheeks, prematurely sagging skin, and sunken eyes that results from rapid weight loss – and 'Ozempic butt' – wrinkly, loose, sagging skin – became trending search terms. Content creators share pictures of celebrities who they speculate exhibit the unwanted effects.

Away from the world of the rich and famous with slim celebrities questing for an even slimmer look, obesity is a genuine global health concern, affecting one in every eight people worldwide. Rates have quadrupled among children and teens and more than doubled among adults since 1990.[5] Obesity also increases the risk of a range of chronic illnesses. Global costs associated with the condition are predicted to reach US $3 trillion per year by 2030. Some estimate that obesity-related expenses could consume up to 18% of national health budgets in countries where 30% of the population is obese.[6]

In the UK, it's not the rich who are most affected, although they are the ones who can most afford the drugs. Obesity is strongly associated with social inequalities. The 2019 NHS Health Survey for England shows this difference is particularly pronounced for women: 39% of women in the most deprived areas are obese, compared with 22% in the least deprived areas.[7]

Governments around the world want to reduce the impact of obesity on their populations. Weight-loss drugs have the potential to change how we address it, but pills alone won't solve everything.[8] But for those with obesity the treatments offer hope.

Mr Ahmed Ahmed is an upper gastrointestinal and bariatric surgeon at West London's Imperial College NHS Trust, who runs publicly funded clinical trials into weight-loss surgery. He also sees private patients at his Harley Street clinic, a storied boulevard in central London where Georgian-styled buildings with their distinctive rectangular sash windows have housed private medical practices for generations. Even though the drugs are recommended for use on the NHS, it's very hard to get them, he tells me. In 2025, the government announced plans to expand access to weight-loss treatments on the NHS in England. However, many of those who could clinically benefit are still unlikely to receive them. If every eligible patient were to access these drugs through the NHS, it would consume a large proportion of the overall medicines budget.[9]

Plugging this gap is a private market for weight-loss drugs that's being played out across social media, with users having to negotiate bold claims about effects with marketing disguised as personal testimony. People are making clinical decisions based on abstracts (brief summaries of research articles), sponsored content or advice on Facebook groups, rather than evidence-based guidance. Meanwhile, pharmaceutical companies and online pharmacies exploit regulatory gaps, using patient influencers, unbranded campaigns and affiliate codes to create demand while bypassing traditional advertising restrictions. In 2025, it was estimated that around 1.5 million people in the UK every month already access these weight-loss drugs through private online pharmacies.[10]

It was against this backdrop that Charlotte (not her real name) made the decision to try to lose weight. Charlotte tells me she joined TikTok at the tail end of the Covid pandemic, after being encouraged to by her eighteen-year-old stepdaughter. She initially had no idea what her stepdaughter was talking about but went along with the suggestion regardless. It was a decision that would end up not only transforming how she managed her weight but also her day-to-day life.

'At that point, it was basically just funny dances and a good distraction from the awfulness of life,' she tells me. It didn't take long for TikTok to captivate her. She spent hours scrolling during the long pandemic lockdowns. At first, she just watched others' creations but soon felt compelled to join in.

Charlotte had been diagnosed with polycystic ovary syndrome (PCOS), a common condition that affects how a woman's ovaries work. Symptoms include irregular periods, difficulty getting pregnant, excessive hair growth and weight gain. As with many other women, her condition hadn't been picked up until she was trying for a baby, even though she'd experienced symptoms since her teens. 'I just kept going, struggling with my weight and other symptoms,' Charlotte says.

Initially she used TikTok to describe these specific concerns. But the more she posted about PCOS, the platform's algorithms, tuned into her interactions, started to populate her feed with videos about Ozempic. It was as if it was offering her the solution to her struggles, directing her to what she needed to do. Excited by what she saw, Charlotte approached her husband with newfound optimism. She told him she'd found a medication that would finally help her to shed some weight.

'He was so against it. He said to me: "Charlotte, what are you doing? Do not do this!"' she tells me, adding that he warned her that one of his friends had become 'very, very sick' after taking the drug.

A desperate Charlotte was undeterred. 'I'd done practically no research. I thought, "I'm just going to order it,"' she says. Soon enough, she was googling the best prices and pharmacies where she could buy it. 'Although this medication is expensive now, in the early days it was really expensive,' Charlotte adds.

She started out on Ozempic with a discount, paying £150 a month (£50 off the normal price of £200 monthly), through a three-month promotion from an online company. 'I didn't even speak to my GP, I just got it privately after a pharmacist consultation,' she told her followers on TikTok.

## NOW FOR THE SCIENCE

Ozempic is the brand name marketed by Danish drug company Novo Nordisk, while semaglutide is its generic name. This dual naming system is common in pharmaceuticals. The brand name is created by the company for marketing purposes, and the generic name identifies the active ingredient responsible for the medication's therapeutic effects.

The drug is what's called a glucagon-like peptide-1 (GLP-1) agonist. In pharmacology, an 'agonist' refers to a compound that attaches to specific cell receptors, triggering a biological response. GLP-1 drugs specifically bind to GLP-1 receptors, effectively mimicking the actions of the body's natural GLP-1 hormone. GLP-1 is mainly produced in the small intestine and has several important metabolic functions.[11]

The hormone has two important ways it regulates blood sugar. It stimulates the pancreas to release insulin, helping cells absorb glucose from the bloodstream, and simultaneously it blocks glucagon, a hormone that increases blood glucose. The combination of these blood sugar-regulating properties made GLP-1 medications candidates for treating type 2 diabetes, a common condition that causes the level of glucose in the blood to become too high.[12]

But GLP-1 agonists have other effects too. They slow stomach emptying, lengthening the digestion process and prolonging the sensation of fullness. They also influence key brain regions responsible for regulating hunger and satiety. This neurological effect increases feelings of fullness after meals, suppressing appetite, reducing hunger pangs and ultimately decreasing food intake. These combined effects are what's thought to lead to weight loss.

Throughout the 2000s, several GLP-1 drugs came onto the market and patients noticed that these drugs didn't just treat their diabetes; they also helped them lose weight.[13] When Ozempic received regulatory approval in 2017 as a type 2 diabetes treatment, doctors soon began prescribing it 'off-label' for weight loss. (The term 'off-label' refers to prescribing medications for conditions or purposes not officially approved in their licensing. It has implications for how companies can legally market their products, as we will see later.)

This 'side effect' had enormous potential. Novo Nordisk reformulated semaglutide into Wegovy, a distinct branded medication explicitly for weight loss. Following its 2021 US debut and subsequent 2023 arrival in the UK, the *Financial Times* reported that Novo Nordisk became Europe's most valuable public company for the first time.[14]

With financial success like Novo's, it's little surprise that other drug companies joined the fray. In 2022, Eli Lilly's Mounjaro – active ingredient tirzepatide – was approved in the US, and slightly later across Europe, as a diabetes treatment. Since then, it's been licensed for use in weight loss too. Its market entry signalled the downfall of Novo Nordisk's CEO. In May 2025, the company removed Lars Fruergaard Jorgensen amid fears it was losing its edge in the fiercely competitive obesity drug market.[15] Running a pharmaceutical empire is a volatile and unforgiving pursuit.

Charlotte initially started with Ozempic, using it for seven months before switching to Wegovy, and then to Mounjaro when it became available in the UK. When I spoke to Charlotte, she had just increased her Mounjaro dosage. Her decision to change medications stemmed from the dreaded plateau with Wegovy. 'I hadn't lost any weight in ages,' she explained. 'I was paying a significant amount of money every month, and it felt like the medication had stopped working for me.'

Taking to TikTok, Charlotte discussed why she had switched from Wegovy. She advised her followers to consider Mounjaro if they had the opportunity, drawing from her personal experience with the medications. 'The people who have made the switch from semaglutide to tirzepatide have noticed much better weight loss generally speaking,' she said. 'If you've made the switch, I would love to hear how much better it works for you, or vice versa, so maybe it didn't work as good for you as Ozempic.'

In December 2024, even Elon Musk announced his switch by posting a picture of his newly slimmed-down self, squeezed into a red-and-white, fur-lined suit, with the caption 'Ozempic Santa'.[16] 'Technically, Mounjaro, but that doesn't have the same ring to it,' he clarified, apparently concerned about pharmaceutical branding accuracy in his holiday humour. The 'high doses' of Ozempic had made him 'fart and burp like Barney from *The Simpsons*', leading him to seek another brand. 'Mounjaro seems to have fewer side effects and be more effective,' he said.

## THE EVIDENCE PYRAMID

But how much weight should you put on other people's opinions and experiences? Personal health stories are powerful. But they can be misleading. A person's experience might be influenced by countless factors – genetic predisposition, lifestyle changes, random chance or even the placebo effect. What works for one person may not work the same way for another. Changes someone attributes to an intervention could be coincidental or caused by something different.

Individual anecdotes are considered the lowest level of evidence. Medical researchers have developed a structured framework, a hierarchy of evidence, to rank the reliability of different types of studies. It's usually visualised as a pyramid, with the most scientifically rigorous research at the top and less reliable sources of information towards the bottom.

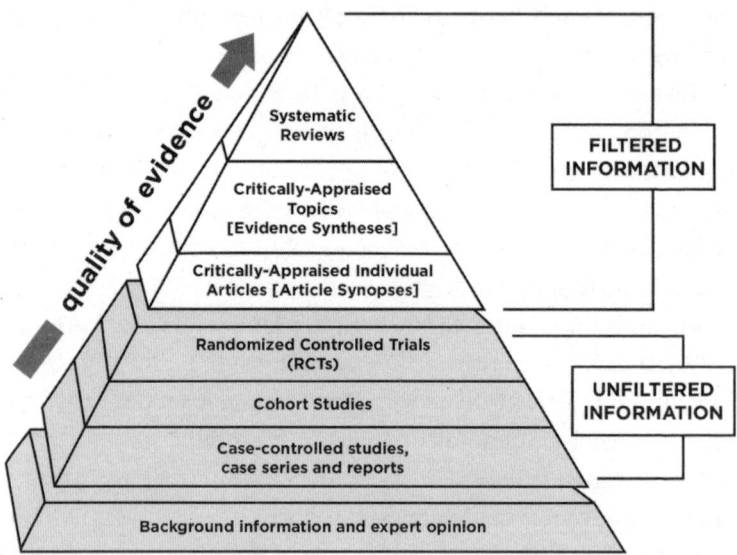

Dr Francis Perry Wilson is associate professor of medicine at Yale University. As well as being a trained neurologist running a clinic at Yale New Haven Hospital in Connecticut, he has also built a following on social media, unpacking medical research and explaining why 'Your Facebook Friend Is Wrong'. Anecdotes should never form the basis of a medical decision, Wilson says: 'We look for hope in anecdotes – googling the name of our condition and finding the occasional social media post encouragingly titled "How I Beat _____".'

Medicine requires results that are testable and repeatable. However, the complexity of scientific research doesn't easily translate into viral stories. Not only do we need to know if a treatment is effective; we need to know what harm it can cause as a side effect. The potential benefit of a treatment needs to be weighed up against the risks of potential harm. We may be unlikely to accept a 1% chance of certain cancers in exchange for losing a few pounds, but that calculus might change if the treatment was your only hope of avoiding imminent death. Balancing such benefits and harms is the cornerstone of clinical decision making.

This subtlety doesn't necessarily pay off on digital platforms that thrive on sensationalism rather than balance. A 2023 study published in the *Journal of Medicine, Surgery, and Public Health* examined the top 100 TikTok videos tagged with #Ozempic on a single day in June that year. It's only a snapshot in time, but collectively they had garnered around 70 million views.[17]

Around 60% mentioned Ozempic being used for weight loss and 35% presented it as a coveted drug, encouraging others to try it. Notably, only 29% of the videos mentioned potential side effects. The research also found that content highlighting positive aspects of the drug were more likely to be viewed, liked and shared compared to more balanced information.

But how do drugs like Ozempic make it to the market? Before they're granted a licence by a drug regulator, companies need to meet certain safety and quality standards. It all starts in the lab with preclinical research, where scientists test compounds to see how substances interact with cells and tissues. They then do animal studies to understand basic safety profiles and biological effects. This groundwork helps researchers identify promising candidates before any human is exposed to the treatment. Next come the clinical stages.

In phase 1, there are only a small number of participants. The focus is on determining the safest dose of a new treatment, identifying side effects and understanding how the drug is processed by the body.

In phase 2, the treatment is given to a larger group of people (several hundred) who have the condition the drug is meant to treat. The aim is to assess the treatment's effectiveness and further evaluate its safety.

And in phase 3, there are hundreds or thousands of participants. The clinical trial might compare the new treatment to the current standard treatment or a placebo to determine which is more effective. Side effects are monitored and more information is gathered to work out how to use the drug safely. It's the trials in this phase that tend to make news headlines about how well a drug works.

Throughout this process, researchers use randomised controlled trials or RCTs, which are the fairest way to investigate whether the effects from a treatment are caused by the treatment under investigation. To create a level playing field, participants are randomly assigned either to receive the new treatment or a comparison (control) treatment. This randomisation process helps to ensure any differences in outcomes can be attributed to the treatment itself rather than to other factors or biases.

If possible, in gold standard clinical trials, researchers 'blind' participants to their treatment group to stop them knowing whether they're receiving the medication under investigation or a placebo. This helps to eliminate the placebo effect and ensures similar behaviour across groups throughout the study. People may drop out if they discover they're not getting the real thing or change how they behave.

In an ideal world, the researchers stay 'blind' to who is getting what treatment until the study ends (this is known as a double-blind trial). They're susceptible to bias too and blinding stops them from skewing results based on their expectations. These safeguards help to ensure that any observed changes result from the medicine and not from people's beliefs. This system developed over many centuries of progress in medicine. But sometimes the way it works in the real world is imperfect and shaped by forces other than scientific rigour.

Trial results appear in medical journals written for specialists that are often locked behind paywalls that restrict full access to subscribers. Before research is published it usually undergoes peer review to ensure quality. These journals are part of the dissemination of scientific information and have a role in educating scientists and health professionals. But some take a more critical view.

My old boss at the *BMJ*, Dr Richard Smith, has written scathingly about the financial symbiosis between drug companies and medical journals. It's a lucrative business bridging science communication, pharmaceutical marketing and clinical practice. He argues that a favourable trial published in a medical journal 'is worth thousands of pages of advertising'. As he wrote in *PLoS Medicine*:

> A large trial published in a major journal has the journal's stamp of approval (unlike the advertising), will be distributed around the world, and may well receive global media coverage, particularly if promoted simultaneously by press releases from both the journal and the expensive public-relations firm hired by the pharmaceutical company that sponsored the trial.[18]

Journals in turn profit from selling bulk reprints of influential articles at high margins, primarily to drug companies for use in marketing and promotion. Inevitably, the copies they want to buy are those favourable to their commercial interests. This revenue stream risks creating conflicts of interest for journals, as it may incentivise the publication of studies that bring in money.[19, 20] For the companies themselves, media coverage of clinical trials can create premature excitement about new medications, sometimes before regulatory approval. Bold headlines may shape public perception, influencing policymakers and pressuring healthcare organisations to speed up approval and funding decisions.

Charlotte tries to inform her over 20,000 followers about these studies but says it's tricky: 'At the very least, I read the abstract for the study that I'm going to talk about. I feel like that's all that I can kind of do. I'm not a medical professional.' For many of those discussing studies on TikTok, or even patients in general, an abstract might be the only thing they see at all.

## WHEN HEADLINES HIDE THE WHOLE STORY

Sharing journal abstracts or press releases with followers might seem like straightforward information sharing, but these summaries only show part of the picture. Abstracts, for example, highlight key findings in a few paragraphs, typically emphasising positive outcomes without pointing out the limitations. The expectation is that interested readers in the field will then take the opportunity to read the article to examine the relevant findings about side effects, variations in results across patient demographics and any significant clinical observations.

When complex medical research gets reduced to simplified highlights, it can create unrealistic expectations about benefits while understating potential harms. Let's take a couple of Wegovy – or semaglutide used for weight loss – trials as examples. One major phase 3 trial, funded by Novo Nordisk, appeared in the *New England Journal of Medicine* in June 2021.[21] Many of the researchers involved had also received various forms of funding from Novo Nordisk and other GLP-1 manufacturers. This is standard for major trials of new drugs.

The double-blind trial enrolled 1,961 adults with either a body mass index (BMI) of 30 (classified as obesity) or 27 (overweight) if they had at least one weight-related health condition such as high blood pressure, sleep apnoea or cardiovascular disease. Participants were randomly divided into two groups: weekly 2.4-milligram semaglutide or placebo injections. Both groups also received lifestyle counselling that included diet and exercise guidance. The drugs, in other words, were given alongside other weight-loss and health measures.

The trial measured several outcomes, one of which was the percentage change in body weight from the beginning of the study to week sixty-eight. By week sixty-eight, participants who received semaglutide had lost an average of 14.9% of their initial body weight, compared to roughly 2.5% in the placebo group – a difference of 12.4%.

To understand how reliable this finding is, researchers calculated something called a 95% confidence interval. For this trial, that interval was 11.5% to 13.4%, meaning they're 95% confident that semaglutide's true effect (beyond lifestyle changes alone) falls somewhere between 11.5 and 13.4 percentage points of additional weight loss compared to the placebo. The narrow range suggests the results are quite precise. They also calculated the statistical significance or p-value. In the trial this was $p < 0.001$, which indicates that this difference is highly unlikely to have occurred by chance. Taken together, the statistics suggest that semaglutide causes greater weight loss than lifestyle changes alone.

For Dr Perry Wilson these numbers are a big deal. 'The degree of efficacy in terms of weight loss really are really impressive,' he says. There are all sorts of other health benefits being associated with the drugs too, he says, adding that they're among the most exciting drugs he's seen. But the picture behind these numbers is a little more complicated. Additional details tell us who was in the trial and who the headline figures apply to.

The abstract didn't include the mean body weight of the participants, which was 105.3 kg (16 stone 8 lb), nor the mean BMI of 37.9. It only noted 'nausea and diarrhoea' as 'the most common adverse events with semaglutide', which might seem like a reasonable trade-off for weight loss. A more granular look at the full paper showed that nausea affected 44.2% of participants taking semaglutide compared to 17.4% in the placebo group. Diarrhoea occurred in 31.5% of the semaglutide group versus 15.9% with placebo. Vomiting was experienced by 24.8% of those on semaglutide but only 6.6% on placebo.

The abstract also omitted less common but potentially serious complications. Gallstones developed in 1.8% of semaglutide users compared to 0.6% of those on placebo. Acute pancreatitis occurred in 0.2% of the semaglutide group with no cases in the placebo group. These might sound like small numbers, but Dr Igho Onakpoya, senior associate tutor at the Department for Continuing Education at Oxford University, who has studied weight-loss trials, offers a perspective: 'If there is just 1 serious adverse event in 500 in a trial [the equivalent of 0.2%], that might have a big impact on a population level when hundreds of thousands of people take it.'

Beyond safety concerns, other issues complicate the evidence. Not everyone responds identically to medication, and drug trials often restrict their initial test populations. The extensive exclusion criteria – defining those who weren't permitted to participate – were absent from the abstract and only available in linked online appendices. This particular semaglutide trial excluded people with a history of both type 1 and 2 diabetes; major depression in the last two years and others with serious mental health disorders; cancer within the last five years; and alcohol and drug use to name a few.

When designing clinical trials, drug companies tend to recruit the ideal participants. These might be the 'healthiest' sick people, such as those who have the target condition but fewer complicating factors that might interfere with treatment effectiveness or introduce safety concerns – or even those who are most likely to see the greatest benefit, such as those who are perhaps more obese, Onakpoya explains.

The trial population can look very different from real-world patients who end up getting the drug once it reaches the market. 'In real life, people who take the drug might have different clinical and medical histories and may or may not take other medications which might have an impact on a given drug,' he adds. The gap between ideal trial participants and the diversity of real-world patients means medications may perform better in studies than in everyday practice, where patients have more complex conditions and may take medicines less consistently.

Nor can all side effects be picked up at trial stage. We simply don't know the long-term effects of a drug until we've been using them for – well, a long time. We can't know if a particular treatment raises your lifetime risk of cancer or other illnesses that take time to develop until years, if not decades, later. Some side effects are the result of a drug's interactions with other medications; we won't see these until a wider population receives the drug.

After a drug is approved for use, the initial clinical trial participants may be monitored for longer and companies may have to do phase 4 studies to see what happens in the real world. This surveillance helps regulators evaluate the continued safety of the drug and also its long-term efficacy.

In the UK, the MHRA manages the Yellow Card reporting scheme that enables healthcare professionals and members of the public to report drug side effects. This helps identify trends in adverse events, and reports can lead to changes in the patient information sheet. For instance, reports by patients using the hormonal contraceptive Yasmin saying they'd had hair loss after taking it led to its information being updated to include this as a potential side effect.[22] We're also learning more about weight-loss drugs too. In June 2025, the MHRA advised women taking GLP-1 drugs to use effective contraception during treatment and, in some cases, for up to two months after stopping. These drugs shouldn't be used during pregnancy or breastfeeding due to limited safety data.[23]

And the tales online about women getting pregnant while taking Mounjaro might not be far off the mark. The agency said this drug may reduce the effectiveness of oral contraceptives in those who are overweight. They advised the use of a non-oral form of contraception.

Onakpoya points out that weight-loss drugs have a chequered history. Multiple 'miracle' weight-loss drugs have been withdrawn from sale because follow-up studies revealed serious adverse effects. In 2020, Belviq (lorcaserin) was withdrawn from the US market.[24] Lorcaserin had been approved in 2012 after clinical trials suggested nearly half of trial participants were able to lose 5% of their body weight in a year while taking the pill.

However, the FDA required manufacturer Eisai Inc. to conduct a safety study, tracking 12,000 patients over five years. It found that 7.7% treated with lorcaserin had a range of different cancers diagnosed, compared with 7.1% patients in the placebo group. Though this difference might appear small statistically, the FDA decided this risk of harm outweighed any benefit of weight loss, and the drug was withdrawn.

Follow-up studies have also flagged problems with other weight-loss drugs, such as sibutramine (Meridia).[25] This was suspended from the market in Europe and US in 2010 after a large-scale trial found an increased risk of heart attacks and strokes. This trajectory hasn't been unusual for weight-loss drugs. Onakpoya and a team of researchers at Oxford University found that between 1964 and 2009 at least twenty-five anti-obesity drugs were withdrawn from the market for reasons including psychiatric disturbances, cardiac toxicity and dependence.[26] Of course, this isn't to say the GLP-1 drugs will follow the same path. The drugs are very well-studied, but some doctors caution that we still do not know the longer-term effects in different groups of people.

How much weight someone loses and whether they have any side effects is only a part of clinical thinking. What health professionals also want to know is whether drugs like semaglutide reduce the risk of other illnesses that are associated with obesity, such as heart disease, high blood pressure, fatty liver disease and various cancers. Like side effects, this can take years to work out too. Already researchers are finding extra benefits. In a serious chronic liver condition that affects over 30% of adults worldwide, a trial found that 63% of people taking semaglutide showed reduced liver inflammation without worsening scarring, compared to 34% of those on a placebo.[27]

Evidence suggests there may be other benefits there too. In a large Novo Nordisk-funded double-blind trial of 17,604 high-risk adults with pre-existing heart disease and a BMI of at least 27, serious cardiovascular events – resulting in a stroke, heart attack or death – occurred in 6.5% of people taking semaglutide versus 8.0% on placebo over a period of three years and four months.[28] But it wasn't this 1.5 percentage point drop in risk of cardiovascular events, which was what the difference was in absolute terms, that made global headlines.

In Novo Nordisk's press release that hit the news, it was framed in much more dramatic terms as a 20% cut in heart attack and stroke risk.[29] Even before the trial had been fully published the *Wall Street Journal* announced to readers that 'Weight-loss drug Wegovy cuts stroke, heart-attack risk by 20% in new study'.[30]

This particular statistic is called the relative risk reduction and helps compare how much more or less likely an outcome is in one group versus another. It's not wrong but it tends to sound more impressive and lends itself to bold, breathless headlines about a treatment. The absolute change is more meaningful in practice.

Side effects were also different across the groups: 16.6% of semaglutide users quit due to adverse effects compared to 8.2% on placebo. These numbers weren't in the press release and didn't seem to make it onto the news pages either. This isn't to say that these figures mean that the drugs are not worth taking. It just shows the complexity of weighing up all the different factors in social media clips.

## RETHINKING WHO GETS THE DRUGS

After a busy day in his clinic, Ahmed explains to me how he uses the GLP-1s as part of weight-loss treatment. He tells me he's cautious about only offering it to people who are eligible to take it, calculating people's BMI to make sure it matches that of the people for whom the drug regulators have approved it – namely the population in the trial.

But in the US things have taken a twist. On the quiet, the FDA has removed the specific BMI requirements reflecting those studied in the trials from the drug labels of the GLP-1 drugs approved for weight loss. It now says that the medications are for patients 'with obesity' or those who are 'overweight in the presence of at least one weight-related comorbid condition'. It potentially broadens the pool of eligible people.

Writing in *The Atlantic* in May 2025, former FDA commissioner Dr David Kessler argued that this change is a recognition of the growing awareness that BMI is limited as a health metric. Effectively, BMI is a calculation involving height and weight.[31] '[BMI] doesn't distinguish between muscle and fat. It doesn't account for how fat tends to be distributed differently on male and female bodies,' he wrote. Nor does it account for people from different ethnic backgrounds who carry a higher risk of other illnesses from being overweight.

Critically, it doesn't distinguish between the fat that accumulates around the waist called visceral fat from that on your arms and thighs. Visceral fat is more harmful for health because of its impact on inflammation and metabolism. It is this fat in particular that is linked to the other diseases associated with obesity.

The debate around BMI aside, are the drugs working? Ahmed hasn't necessarily seen the maximum weight loss observed in the trials in his clinic. 'What we see in trials and what happens in the pragmatic world is slightly different,' he says. There are many reasons why there might be different patterns of weight loss. GLP-1 drugs curb appetite, so people eat less. They tend to be most effective for people who consume a high number of calories and need help in reducing their food intake. But for those who don't eat as much, the impact might not be as big, he explains. Studies of people taking these drugs in the real world rather than in trials have found this too.[32]

Compliance is also an issue. In trial settings, compliance may be better, as participants know they're being studied or are being encouraged to continue. The drugs only work while you take them, Ahmed emphasises: 'They're pretty good for three months, six months, and then sometimes compliance drops and people stop using the drugs and then they get the weight rebound effect,' he says. But lots of people seem to like them.

In the phase 3 trial funded by Novo Nordisk mentioned earlier, within twelve months of treatment ending, participants regained two-thirds of their prior weight loss on average.[33] This weight gain was accompanied by a worsening of some markers of cardiometabolic health, including diabetes and heart attacks. The authors concluded that 'ongoing treatment is required to maintain improvements in weight and health'.

Kessler contends that, given these are intended to be lifelong treatments, there's still much we don't know: 'Scientists do not have good data on whether and how to get off the drugs without regaining weight, whether they can be used safely and effectively on an intermittent basis, or how to adjust doses downward over the long term.'[34]

Ahmed is cautious about how he initiates the treatment: 'We start at the lowest dose for the different drugs and then we escalate month by month. I see them every three months to see how they're getting on with their weight-loss journey checking their objective weight-loss measurements and their side-effects profile.' Some patients are happy on lower doses because they want to maintain a certain level; others want to go to the max; and some can't tolerate the drug at all, he says. Ahmed sees managing patients' expectations about what the drugs can achieve, and in what timeframe, as part of his job

This contrasts with the self-treatment stories on social media. Users aren't just informing people about Ozempic or Mounjaro; they may be influencing how they use these medications. In Facebook groups dedicated to weight-loss drugs, people turn to their peers to find out how to use these medications, often resorting to unorthodox drug combinations and dosages that deviate from clinical guidelines.

'So I have a 5mg of chicken [a code name for Wegovy] but I'm unsure how many doses are in that (first time trying it) how do I figure out the math?' one user asks. Other forum members wade in with their recommendations. '4 doses and 12 lbs at 2.5, and I am supposed to move up this week... Should I stay another month at 2.5, or just follow the recommendations?' asks another. 'Can I take both [Ozempic and Mounjaro] for example take the non therapeutic dose of turkey [Mounjaro's code name] whilst still taking chicken [Wegovy]?' yet another asks.

These online groups tell stories of dramatic weight loss achieved by rapidly escalating or combining multiple weight-loss drugs together. What you won't always see is the full picture, such as a person's starting BMI, their diet and lifestyle or even if they are in fact taking the drug combinations they're recommending to others.

Another trend is 'microdosing' – a term associated with psychedelic culture. Users on Reddit, Facebook and TikTok exchange tips on taking lower GLP-1 doses than clinical guidelines suggest, citing fewer side effects and a more gradual weight loss.[35] Dedicated Reddit threads discuss benefits beyond weight loss, including reduced inflammation and improved concentration.

This may or may not be inherently a bad thing (although doctors warn about contamination drawing from open single-dose vials) but there's a lack of evidence about using the drugs this way.[36] Some suggest only 'super-responders' get an effect while others suggest it could be placebo.[37] It's fair to say, however, where there's consumer interest, there's a market. I've spoken to people who get their microdoses from private providers in the UK.

Influencers like Dr Tyna Moore have monetised it too. Her 'Ozempic Done Right University' charges $2,300 to teach GLP-1 'optimisation'.[38] Sporting a stethoscope slung around her neck – she's not a medical doctor – she promotes microdosing for everything, from high blood pressure to autoimmune diseases and brain fog. She's also made these claims on UK influencer Steven Bartlett's *Diary of a CEO* podcast and across his social media feeds. They've been watched and listened to millions of times. But these are claims drug companies would be prohibited from making.

Charlotte tells me about the excitement around Mounjaro (tirzepatide) for weight loss on TikTok when it became available in the UK. It's both a GLP-1 agonist and it imitates the hormone gastric inhibitory peptide (GIP), which is thought to improve how the body breaks down sugar and fat. 'Ozempic is like your "old, dependable pickup truck" that's definitely going to get you there, but you're going to be slow and steady. Mounjaro is a sports car, it's like the Ferrari of medication – that's how everyone was comparing it,' she tells me.

Content creators took to comparing the trials of the drugs online. In the phase 3 tirzepatide double-blind trial for weight loss, people with a BMI over 30 or 27 with another obesity-related illness were given different doses of the drug.[39]

Those who had 15 mg once-weekly injections had, on average, a 20.9% reduction in weight over seventy-two weeks compared to 3.9% for placebo. Participants in both groups had regular lifestyle counselling sessions that included healthy diet recommendations to reduce calorie consumption by 500 per day and to do at least 150 minutes of physical activity per week.

If you remember, for those taking a once-weekly 2.4 mg injection of semaglutide, the mean body-weight reduction was 14.9% over sixty-eight weeks. But it's tricky to compare different trials directly. While the participants in both the trials were broadly comparable in terms of weight and previous medical history, other factors could affect the results.

The semaglutide trial recruited participants from sixteen countries, while those in tirzepatide came from nine. These participants may have been recruited in different ways. The demographic make-up of trial participants may have an impact on the trial results that mightn't be immediately obvious or measured in the trial. Wealthier participants, for instance, may well have better resources to invest in dietary and lifestyle changes alongside taking the medicine. In the UK, people who participate in clinical trials tend to be White, British and affluent.[40]

The fairest way to compare treatments is in a head-to-head or comparative trial, in which each study group has similar characteristics and the measurements and follow-ups are consistent. But these kinds of trials don't happen that often in practice, particularly for drugs on patent. Wilson puts it bluntly: for drug companies it's all about risk management. A head-to-head trial which showed your drug was less effective than the competition would be a blow for your market share.

But Eli Lilly clearly had bullish confidence in Mounjaro and launched a head-to-head trial with Wegovy in 2023. 'Ozempic is the market leader and I suspect Lilly thought they had the better drug,' Wilson explains. The results were published in the *New England Journal of Medicine* in May 2025. The trial involved 750 obese people, with an average weight of 113 kg (nearly 18 stone). They were asked to take the highest dose they could tolerate of one of the two drugs.

The results showed that those taking tirzepatide (Mounjaro) had an average 20.2% weight reduction over seventy-two weeks, compared to 13.7% with semaglutide (Wegovy) – a 6.5 percentage points absolute difference. Waist circumference also decreased by 18.4 cm with tirzepatide and 13.0 cm with semaglutide, and those on the former had better blood pressure, blood sugar and cholesterol levels.[41] The findings enabled Eli Lilly to declare to investors that their drug produced 'superior weight loss over Wegovy'.[42]

## WHEN ADS SHAPE HEALTHCARE

This wasn't the only place where there was a head-to-head marketing battle occurring. Since 2019, US television viewers have probably had the catchy jingle 'Oh, oh, oh, Ozempic', an adaptation of the hook of 'Magic' by the 1970s' band Pilot, ringing in their ears.[43] As one US journalist put it, the ad 'has permanently imprinted the name of the medication' in her brain. The adverts featured a man cheerfully explaining that taking Ozempic for type 2 diabetes lowers blood sugar while also leading to weight loss. A mandatory disclaimer appeared on-screen clarifying that Ozempic is not officially a weight-loss medication to reflect US regulations that prohibit advertising prescription drugs for off-label uses. The ubiquity of these Ozempic adverts was partly why the drug took centre stage rather than Wegovy. Drug companies argue that this kind of advertising has benefits for patients. They say it helps people get medical care more easily, leads to faster diagnosis of health problems, reduces shame around certain diseases and encourages patients to take a more active role in managing their own health.[44]

In the UK, and most other countries, pharmaceutical companies can't advertise prescription medications to the general public. In the UK, medical advertising is governed by Part 14 of the Human Medicines Regulations Act (2012).[45] There are several reasons for this. A team of international researchers argued in the journal *BMJ Evidence Based Medicine* that direct-to-consumer advertising directly influences the doctor–patient relationship, encouraging consumers to request specific medicines.[46]

If someone goes to their doctor because they saw a drug advertised and they're wondering whether they should take it, it falls to the healthcare professional to decide what to prescribe (a doctor who's possibly also being marketed to). The researchers argue that this affects clinical appointments in several ways, including time spent discussing the advertised condition (which may not actually need medical treatment) and the promoted medication (which may not be the best treatment option).

Some studies suggest the ways drug ads affect how doctors prescribe, but they differ in their quality, and hence our ability to draw strong conclusions is limited. While drug ads might help people get treatments they want and need, they are associated with unnecessary, poorer quality, inappropriate and sometimes harmful prescriptions.

One review of the medical literature also said that direct-to-consumer advertising (DTCA) 'may result in inappropriate prescribing, create undue economic strain on an already overburdened healthcare system, and undermine the patient–physician relationship'.[47] 'Advertising begets demand, an axiom that is borne out time and again in studies of the impact of DTCA on prescribing practice,' the review authors added. It's something that's worth bearing in mind when we consider how much health advertising, in various forms, there is on digital media platforms.

Studies have suggested that patients exposed to more drug advertising were more likely to request advertised medications, and doctors approved most of these requests. Those who asked for advertised drugs were more likely to get a prescription, even if the doctor was ambivalent about the treatment.[48] Others suggest that both asking for a specific drug and a general request about drugs – even for conditions that don't require it – is more likely to result in a prescription.[49]

Some of the most robust evidence comes from California. An experiment using actors posing as patients found that when people specifically asked doctors for antidepressants, they were much more likely to get them – regardless of whether they actually needed the medication. The actors presented doctors with two different conditions: major depression (which can be treated with antidepressants) and adjustment disorder (a milder condition where antidepressants aren't usually recommended). Some actors asked for specific brand-name drugs they'd seen advertised, others made general requests for antidepressants and some made no requests at all.

When actors didn't ask for medication, doctors prescribed antidepressants in less than one-third of visits, even for major depression. But when patients requested them, prescription rates shot up, including for the milder condition where the drugs weren't appropriate.

In a nutshell, the study found that advertising may help people with serious depression get treatment they need. On the other hand, it may lead to overprescribing for people who don't need medication. This highlights how much influence patients have over their doctors' prescribing decisions, sometimes encouraging doctors to prescribe drugs in situations where they wouldn't normally consider them necessary.[50]

One explanation is that doctors who are pressed for time often find it easier to just prescribe the requested medication rather than have a difficult, time-consuming conversation about why it might not be necessary.[51] Another is that patients often leave consultations happier when they get a prescription. There's an argument that, in today's world of online doctor and clinic ratings, patient satisfaction could play a role in shaping prescribing practices.[52]

But consumer approval doesn't always tally with sound medical practice. Consider this through the lens of America's opioid epidemic, where the overprescription of painkillers has led to widespread addiction, deaths from overdoses and long-term public health crises. US research suggests that doctors who prescribed opioids for chronic non-cancer pain (where evidence suggests they have limited long-term benefit and carry risks of harm)[53] received higher patient satisfaction ratings.[54] Likewise, amid the growing global concerns about antibiotic resistance, patients tend to be more satisfied with telehealth sessions when they come away with an antibiotic prescription for upper respiratory tract infections (which are typically viral and unresponsive to antibiotics).[55]

In England, research suggests that remote consultations are associated with more prescriptions of antibiotics compared to in-person consultations.[56] It would be wrong to assume that in the UK we're immune to marketing influence. There are lots of other ways to market drugs to consumers that don't fall foul of our laws, such as disease-awareness campaigns, which seem like innocuous attempts to educate the public about particular diseases.

Such campaigns may do that to a certain extent, but they also reshape how we think about certain conditions. Behind the presented facts, there's often a carefully crafted message framing a health problem in a way that makes a drug seem like the obvious solution – even when other approaches might work just as well.

When it comes to obesity, social media has become a way to combat stigma, and savvy marketers have been capitalising on online body-positivity communities. In 2021, Oscar-nominated actress Queen Latifah became the face of the online 'It's Bigger Than Me' campaign sponsored by Novo Nordisk.[57] Its laudable aim was to transform the societal view of obesity and advocate for more inclusive healthcare that treats people with dignity, regardless of their size. The campaign's content is visible beyond US shores.

The first video evoked scenes from a medical drama. It begins with a gurney being rushed down a hospital corridor. Queen Latifah, dressed in scrubs, questions a worried wife about the patient's symptoms before sombrely delivering the diagnosis: 'It's stigma.'[58] A monitor beeps in the background. 'The only way we're going to beat this is if we talk about it,' she adds. 'What people talk about, how they talk about you, the little words people drop. If people understood it more, then it could change the conversation.'

On Facebook, another video features Queen Latifah, headphones on, listening to a panel of patients recounting their experiences with stigma and shame, much of it reportedly coming from the medical profession. 'Anytime I see a medical professional about something that doesn't have to do with my weight, they make it about my weight,' one says. 'I often feel like I don't want to go to the doctor, for fear of being judged,' another adds. A statistic appears at centre of the video: '66% of participants who reported a history of weight stigma experienced it from doctors.'[59]

Queen Latifah encourages people to seek medical care for their weight. In a caption to the video, she writes: 'Has the fear of being judged ever stopped you from seeking care for your weight? It can happen – and it's not ok.'

All the objectives were entirely reasonable and the sponsorship was declared. Who could oppose more supportive and compassionate care for people living with obesity? But it's all in the timing. The initiative was sponsored by Novo Nordisk and launched months after the FDA approved Wegovy. There was a treatment that people could ask their doctors about.

In June 2021, Doug Langa, Novo Nordisk executive vice president for North America, gave the game away in an interview with industry publication *FiercePharma*. He admitted that the company needed 'more patients to seek treatment'. It's crucial that people living with obesity understand that 'it's not their fault, and that it's not just about eating less and moving more,' he said, adding, 'There's a medical adaptation that they need to understand like any other serious disease.'[60]

The campaigns like those fronted by Queen Latifah are known as 'unbranded' advertising. Free from the restrictions placed on more conventional drug promotion, they're a growing area of investment.[61] I talked to Professor Adriane Fugh-Berman, the director of PharmedOut at Georgetown University Medical Center, which takes a critical look at pharmaceutical marketing practices. 'In a vast number of countries that do not allow direct-to-consumer advertising, drug companies say that it doesn't matter very much because they still have disease promotion, and disease promotion isn't banned in any country,' she explains. These have a different aim to the governmental campaigns to detect untreated health problems at an earlier stage; they're about indirectly promoting approved medicines or those close to market entry.[62]

Lauren Ohlsson, a lead for pharmaceutical video advertising, highlighted the strategy behind unbranded marketing campaigns in the industry publication *Pharmaphorum*:

> Unbranded initiatives are a great way to build up the prospective patient pool prior to advertising the brand name. They also encourage people to build communities and connect with others that have the same condition. Unbranded microsites generally use social connections to build confidence and provide the tools needed to have those important conversations with medical professionals.[63]

Losing weight is incredibly difficult for some people and the GLP-1s are an important aid. But ultimately these campaigns aim to encourage patients to ask their doctors for specific medications.

Dr James Cave, the editor of the *Drugs and Therapeutics Bulletin*, recalls one conversation he had with a drug company sales rep who told him that if people are talking about a condition, the use of drugs for that condition will rise: 'If people are talking about depression, the incidence of depression will rise. And influencers – whether they know it or not – are contributing to this. If they're talking about a condition drug companies go "whoop de doo!"'

Indeed, in December 2024, Baroness Morgan of Cotes, ASA chairwoman, warned that social media is importing American-style drug advertising into Britain's traditionally more restricted marketplace.[64] 'I think because of the health system that we have in this country, for most people, their gateway to getting prescribed drugs has obviously been usually via their GP or potentially via a pharmacist,' she told *The Times*. 'Of course, with the growth of the internet, the growth of social media, the growth of influencers, there are more channels for people who either don't know about the law or choose to ignore the law to push prescription-only medicines' she added.

One way this has occurred is through pharmacies promoting drugs via digital channels. It's something that irks Cave and Dr Alan Black, a former GP with three decades of pharmaceutical industry experience. They've turned themselves into unofficial watchdogs filing dozens of complaints to the MHRA, the official watchdog, about prescription drug content on pharmacy websites. 'The MHRA is relying upon members of the public to do their job for them. They shouldn't be relying on us. They should be the ones monitoring them,' Black complains.

Pharmacies are banned from advertising prescription drugs on their websites' front pages. Nor are they supposed to offer discounts or display images of injection pens when advertising their weight-loss services[65] – a practice I noticed still occurring in May 2025. Equally the regulators take a dim view of syringe and pen emojis, customer testimonials and hashtags like #skinnypen, #weightloss-injection, #flabjab and #skinnypill.[66]

Before April 2023 there were effectively no investigations by the MHRA into weight-loss services at all, Black says. Now, there are several cases every month, 'sometimes three, maybe more' where they're found to be breaking the rules. In December 2024, the *Guardian* reported that the agency had regularly written to online pharmacies that advertise cut-price and multi-buy deals on the drugs to reprimand them for their promotions.[67]

In July 2025, the UK national media reported that an Instagram post by TV personality Gemma Collins, which advertised a weight-loss drug and app, has been banned. In it she said: 'I'm not telling anyone to go on this medication, but it is prescribed on the NHS.' Though the post didn't name a specific weight-loss medication, the ASA said it breached its code. The MHRA had advised the ASA that consumers were likely to be led to request a prescription weight-loss medication. Collins accepted the judgment and said she would follow guidance in future. It was one of nine adverts banned in a crackdown by the ASA.

I asked Charlotte about the news and how it was being received in her TikTok weight-loss circles. Her response was telling. 'I wish I could be more help – I didn't even see the article and I haven't seen anyone speaking about it!' she told me.

Enforcing the rules is an even tougher task when it comes to content creators on different digital platforms. In the US, some drug companies have turned to so-called 'patient influencers'. They can expect to earn anywhere from 'the low hundreds to a few thousand dollars' per social media post.[68]

In a study first published in 2022, Erin Willis, associate professor at the University of Colorado, Boulder, interviewed twenty-six patient influencers with different diseases who collaborated with brands. She approached them via HealthUnion, an intermediary that connects patients with healthcare opportunities.[69]

Eighteen of the influencers collaborated with a pharmaceutical company in some way: serving on advisory boards, speaking to doctors and researchers or communicating with key audiences. All of the influencers considered themselves 'experts' and justified their content as raising awareness by sharing personal experiences. They wanted to help others access information that wasn't available when they were diagnosed and empower others to ask better questions and 'make better choices to improve their daily lives'.

As one participant said, 'Doctors don't know everything'; it is the influencers who are the experts in disease management, as they've lived with their illnesses for such a long time. Others described the loneliness after diagnosis and didn't want others to experience that feeling, referring to their followers as 'family' or 'friends'.

Some of the influencers Willis interviewed pointed to a shortage of resources in certain regions and suggested that social media and online patient communities helped fill the gap. When it came to talking about prescription drugs, only five of the influencers refused to share any prescription drug information simply because they 'thought it was inappropriate and borderline unethical'.

For Willis what makes patient influencers effective is they reach a concentrated audience of patients with similar conditions and that, in itself, can build trust and influence. There's no academic research yet on how social media drug advertising affects consumer behaviour. Previous studies focused on traditional direct-to-consumer marketing via TV and print, leaving a gap in understanding digital marketing's influence, she tells me. 'We don't know how many patients request medications after seeing them promoted by influencers. Yet considering the massive social media user base and influencer following, these promotions must drive medication requests – otherwise drug companies wouldn't invest in this strategy,' she says.

When Willis spoke at a pharmaceutical marketing conference in 2022, she asked the audience to raise their hands if they used patient influencers – nearly everybody did. While patient influencers may have valuable roles in some ways, concerning practices emerged from her research. Some admitted discussing medications they hadn't personally taken and would push messaging further than would be allowed on TV. Others acknowledged having private conversations with followers about medications through direct messages.

This less visible content – including short-form and disappearing video – troubles Willis. She calls patient influencing 'an interactive form of advertising' and says it's difficult to regulate. The problem is we don't know what patients are doing in these messages or what content they're posting, if it's short-lived. Nor do we know if they're disclosing their relationship with drug companies.

Increasingly, there are laws in different countries requiring drug companies to disclose the amount of money they pay doctors. But it wasn't the case for the patients in her study. None of the influencers she interviewed would get into the details of the relationship or their contracts with the companies. The PR companies and agencies won't tell you because of non-disclosure agreements, she says. In her view, if there's nothing wrong, then why don't we know more? HealthUnion has told the *Guardian* that they took Willis's concern seriously and they work 'with all our patient leaders to ensure they follow our best practices and community rules in all online activities'.[70]

Ogilvy has launched a global influencer marketing service to 'bridge the gap between medical expertise and public awareness for pharmaceutical, healthcare, and wellness brands'. It's a clear indication that content creators are not just a fleeting marketing fad but a permanent fixture. The company's client report might tell you why. Across the EU, where direct-to-consumer drug advertising is banned, 37% of TikTok users bought medicines after seeing them on the platform, with 71% of these purchases being on a whim.[71]

Indeed, a 2022 survey of more than 1,500 UK pharmacists by the *Pharmaceutical Journal* found that almost 60% of them had been asked about medicines patients have seen on social media. This included prescription weight-loss drugs, erectile dysfunction medicines, hormone replacement therapy, cancer treatments and statins.[72]

Nor are doctors immune from the influence of social media. One digital agency surveyed 206 doctors in different specialities: 41% said social media influences their prescribing habits; 9% said they change prescriptions frequently based on what they see online; and a further 32% said they do so occasionally.[73]

## WHEN FREE DRUGS COME WITH STRINGS

In the UK, some online pharmacies are relying on the services of influencers rather than drug companies. Charlotte tells me that a UK-based online pharmacy provides her with free weight-loss drugs each month in exchange for creating video content and tagging their business on TikTok. Her videos sometimes include discount codes or affiliate links in the captions, though in others she weaves the pharmacy's name into the content itself. 'I get messages every single day from people wanting me to be their spokesperson for their chemist,' she says, adding that they're often offering commission from each sale their content generates, which she says she's always turned down.

When I ask Black about receiving free weight-loss medications or getting paid commission in exchange for documenting one's journey online, his eyebrows lift. 'I'm not sure that's legal,' he says. The MHRA guidance confirms his suspicions. Such financial incentives are banned. 'You must not do anything like buy one, get one free, or fifty pounds off business,' Cave explains.

The referral system operates as a kind of bait-and-switch. You and your friend both get discounts when you sign up, creating the illusion of mutual benefit. But these promotional rates are a hook. As discounts expire and patients require higher doses, costs surge, sometimes leaving people unable to afford treatment they're depending on.[74]

Social media platforms are flooded with pleas to use personal referral codes as patients scramble for ways to cover the mounting costs of their treatment. 'Can you use my code,' one user begged on a Facebook forum. 'I need it off my second lot please otherwise I can't afford it on top of Christmas.' 'I know everyone is posting these codes but I am really struggling with money this month being a single mother with Christmas coming up… I don't want to stop my journey,' another wrote, followed by their referral code.[75]

What appealed to Charlotte was that the pharmacy she works with wasn't 'overly prescriptive' about what she can and can't say. They told her not to publish videos that seemed promotional. The pharmacist, she tells me, wanted someone who would give 'good, balanced advice that wasn't saying anything too controversial on either side'. Plus they 'do their due diligence' to make sure only eligible people access the drugs, she says: 'With some of the online pharmacies it's quite easy to lie and say "my BMI is 35, I want the medication".'

'I talk about my daily life with the drug. I'm not doing anything different than I would be doing normally,' Charlotte says. Some of her most-viewed posts are those where she describes her struggle with side effects. Perhaps because of her candour, Charlotte's followers are keen to follow her lead. She tells me she gets messages every day from people saying they started a GLP-1 medication because of her TikToks. 'I love it when people just say to me, "Charlotte, I just want to let you know that I'm on a GLP-1 and I'm having a great time and I'm losing a lot of weight, and I feel great,"' she adds.

But it's not all sunshine and light on GLP-1 TikTok. Accusations swirl about weight-loss goals and the pace at which some people shed pounds. Charlotte describes how one influencer faced fierce criticism for not disclosing her starting weight, enduring what she calls 'extremely offensive messages' from a fellow creator who accused her of misleading her audience.

This vicious competitiveness has been commercialised. Some pharmacies have employed dozens of promotional partners, and the atmosphere has become 'very cut-throat' as companies and influencers race to capture the GLP-1 market, she says. Charlotte has seen influencers competing for commissions from online pharmacies with pay-outs tied to the acquisition of new customers. 'The fact that they are getting paid for every single person that they sign up means it's in their interest for more people to be on GLP-1 drugs,' she adds.

From influencers and pharmacies all the way up to manufacturers themselves, financial incentives are geared towards getting these drugs to as many people as possible. Doctors are already seeing harm. Dr Vicky Price, an acute physician at Liverpool University Hospital Trust, routinely treats patients suffering complications from using weight-loss drugs purchased online. Despite prescription criteria limiting access to obese patients, none of her cases have met that threshold. Safeguards for prescription-only medications have failed.[76] 'We are seeing serious, life-threatening complications including inflammation of the pancreas gland and alterations in blood salt levels in patients who were not aware of the risk they were taking,' she says.

There are moves to change this. Pharmacies will be expected to verify height and weight in a video consultation, in person, from the person's clinical records or by contacting their GP. But some are sceptical about the effectiveness of this. There will always be workarounds.[77]

By late October 2024, the MHRA had received 7,228 reports of people experiencing common digestive side effects – nausea, vomiting and diarrhoea – after taking GLP-1s for weight loss.[78] The agency cautioned that this included people who likely didn't meet prescribing criteria and may have used the drugs inappropriately for weight loss.

Yellow card reports have to be interpreted with caution. They do not necessarily establish cause and effect. They also probably represent an underestimate of the true extent of the problem. Across all drugs, the UK government estimates that only 10% of serious reactions, and between 2% and 4% of non-serious reactions, are reported to the Yellow Card scheme.[79]

The surge in demand for GLP-1 drugs for weight loss has created global shortages, putting people with type 2 diabetes, who rely on these medications to manage their blood sugar, at risk of harm.[80] In summer 2023, UK doctors were told to limit prescriptions.[81]

Patients faced limited supplies as pharmacies struggled to stock the medication.[82] Some who were forced to switch to alternative diabetes treatments reported dangerous blood sugar fluctuations after previously maintaining stable levels.

With the shortages, a market for counterfeit medications flourished. A 2023 BBC investigation uncovered unregulated sellers offering unlicensed or knock-off semaglutide online.[83] Lab testing of these 'diet kits' found that while most products contained semaglutide, some had none at all. Nearly all the counterfeit versions contained lower doses than advertised.

Counterfeit drug distribution is a global issue. The United Nations Interregional Crime and Justice Research Institute has pinpointed key channels driving this illicit trade, including unlicensed online pharmacies, social media marketplace listings and messaging apps and forums.[84] Various platforms say they remove posts marketing prescription drugs when they find them.[85]

As the Biden administration intensified its scrutiny of TikTok, the platform responded by announcing new restrictions on the type of content that could be posted. In spring 2024, TikTok said it would clamp down on #weightloss content and the harmful promotion of weight-loss drugs. TikTok announced a ban on content promoting unhealthy body measurements and weight-loss products. The platform also said that posts displaying harmful weight-management behaviours would be removed through a combination of machine learning and human moderation.[86]

Some commentators praised TikTok's new guidelines for being the most thorough and well defined of all the major social media platforms.[87] Notably, however, it was the looming threat of a draconian government ban and not advocacy groups highlighting harmful content that led to a tightening of their policies.

But not everyone was quite so thrilled. TikTok's announcement created fear among some doctor-influencers and content creators sharing their weight-loss drug experiences, as they worried about potential content removal or account bans.

Ironically, those who left careers to monetise their digital presence panicked at the prospect of the platform jeopardising their livelihoods. 'TikTok is my livelihood and how I pay rent,' one UK creator lamented. 'I could lose everything.' Others voiced similar existential concerns: 'If this is how it's going to be, where do we go?' Meanwhile, as TikTok tightened its content policies, some announced they'd go elsewhere as other platforms were felt to have more permissive approaches.

Charlotte describes the panic that swept through the GLP-1 community when creators feared their accounts would be terminated. After reviewing the new terms and conditions, she too began to worry, temporarily removing all her previous videos to prevent strikes against her account. She joined the exodus to Instagram – which she considered 'more lax' – urging her TikTok followers to migrate with her. A few creators did lose their accounts for promoting unhealthy levels of weight loss, she tells me. But enforcement seemed inconsistent. TikTok lacks transparency in their moderation processes, she says.

A unilateral effort by a single platform isn't effective. The centre of gravity for online weight-loss promotion simply shifts. For regulators it's like digital whack-a-mole trying pin down those creating harmful content. In theory, the MHRA's Criminal Enforcement Unit works closely with social media platforms and technology companies to identify and prevent the illegal sale of weight-loss medicines without a prescription.[88] Posts can be removed, accounts suspended and websites taken down. But it's an uphill task.

Determined to maintain their TikTok presence, some creators adopted evasion tactics to sidestep content removal or account flags. They began tweaking spellings in weight-loss hashtags and using coded language like 'chicken' (for Wegovy) or 'turkey' (for Mounjaro) to refer to weight-loss drugs. I saw this on other platforms too. But panic soon turned to relief as creators started to suspect the TikTok guidelines weren't that different from the old ones in practice. 'When the ban eventually came into effect, people put out content as a bit of a tester. Nothing happened,' Charlotte recalls, eventually unarchiving her old content.

Platforms occasionally do crack down, however. A diabetes support group admin urged caution after a member was warned for posting an Ozempic box image. 'To keep you guys and the group out of trouble, PLEASE do not post ANY pics of prescription medications. Likewise we will be removing any we come across,' the group administrator warned.

Prescription drugs have long been marketed directly or indirectly to consumers and patients in various formats. But social media adds a new twist. Here individuals share their personal experiences with conditions, document their health journeys using specific treatments, maintain relationships with online pharmacies through affiliate links or direct partnerships and create communities that coalesce around medication-seeking behaviour.

What might make this particularly effective – and this we can't say yet with certainty because of a lack of robust research – is that influencers are thought of as peers rather than medical authorities. This allows them to make implicit claims about medications that would trigger regulatory action if made by drug companies. It's hard to draw a clear line between personal experience and promotion.

Ozempic perhaps provides a window into the future of prescription drugs and there may be a precedent being set. GLP-1s have a relatively long safety record, but what happens when a similarly attractive drug comes along with far less evidence behind it? We're now seeing how easy it is to bypass traditional medical channels for information, prescribing and access. We're entering into a world where demand may be driven by online trends, not clinical suitability, where those with legitimate needs struggle to access their medication, and where a dangerous counterfeit market exploiting vulnerable consumers can thrive.

# 4

# A DIAGNOSTIC ODYSSEY

Ellie Matthews feels guilty for using TikTok to champion a health test she once reverently described as a 'gift from God' to her followers. Back in 2022, the clean-living content creator and human resources manager from Bedfordshire was struggling with abdominal bloating and bowel issues. 'At the time, I had private healthcare. So I thought: "Well, I might as well take advantage of this,"' she tells me.

During her appointment, the doctor enquired about her diet. 'I was vegan. I don't know if that made a difference or not. They asked me how regularly I exercised too,' she says, adding she was puzzled about the relevance of these questions. An ultrasound, stool test and blood work performed at the clinic all showed normal results. The doctor simply informed her there was nothing wrong. 'Everything came back normal according to them. However, I just knew within myself that something wasn't right,' she says.

Ellie grew frustrated as she grappled with the unidentified health issue troubling her. She began to suspect her experience reflected broader healthcare problems particularly the tendency to dismiss women's pain. She had read countless accounts of women with polycystic ovary syndrome and endometriosis being misdiagnosed or going undiagnosed for years. Her social media feeds were full of stories like these.

Such delays in diagnosis had become headline news. Research published by Endometriosis UK showed that since the Covid-19 pandemic, diagnostic delays had increased. By 2025, it was taking an average of almost nine years to receive a diagnosis, despite one in ten women being affected.[1] 'I thought to myself, "What else are you not diagnosing?"... I had to find out what was going on.'

Medicine is filled with uncertainty. Doctors are trained to think probabilistically, to rule things out methodically and to accept that some symptoms may be unexplained for weeks or even months. But this isn't necessarily what someone wants to hear when their health feels precarious. They want answers. And most of all, they want to feel believed.

The horror stories reported in the news of missed diagnoses, preventable deaths and years in agony before someone would provide an answer struck Ellie. She didn't want that to be her fate. Doctors, it seemed, could not always be trusted to recognise symptoms and treat them. And she wasn't alone in her views: social media has given frustrated patients a powerful voice. Across platforms, the hashtag #doctorsaredickheads was trending, with allegations of patients' concerns being dismissed and misdiagnosed. Amplifying these stories, social media connected people sharing similar unhappy experiences with medical care.

Some doctors pushed back with #DoctorsAreHuman, viewing the flood of complaints as an attack on their profession. 'It's really exposed them [doctors], but they have to play the game,' argues Dr Ronen Rozenblum, a Harvard University researcher. Ultimately, 'this is where we're going, this is where patients and families are going, and this is where the health system is going.' These stories can be a window into people's distress at the hands of healthcare.[2]

In 2022, when Ellie went to her doctor, the hashtag #medicalgaslighting had been trending. Patients used the term 'gaslighting' to describe feeling dismissed by doctors who they said minimised their symptoms as trivial or purely psychological.[3] The term's origin was the play *Gaslight*, from 1938, in which a husband manipulates his wife in order to control her. Today we use it when someone in a position of relative power makes you doubt yourself to the extent that you are then more susceptible to manipulation. The term is all over social media.

One post stood out for its portrayal of medical gaslighting. It was defined by the dismissal of severe symptoms, attributing them to mental illness without providing a referral to a psychiatrist; refusing to carry out key tests, lab work, imaging or specialist referrals; and shaming you for doing your own research into your condition or trying to self-diagnose.

If Ellie wanted relief from bloating, it appeared she'd have to take matters into her own hands. Just like TikTok influencer marketing specialist Alice Bull. 'Social media is such an incredible tool – not just for self-diagnosis, obviously, but for awareness,' she says. Alice tells me about a 'weird patch' of skin, which a podiatrist put down to irritation from her shoes rubbing. 'I knew that wasn't the case because my shoes don't rub there,' she says. Alice then discovered a TikTok video featuring a woman discussing her mother's skin cancer diagnosis on her nose. When her own GP refused to provide a referral, she decided to pay £300 out of pocket to consult with a dermatologist and get a diagnosis. 'If I hadn't seen that TikTok, I'd still be worrying at home about this weird patch on my foot. Social media is so valuable for things like that,' she says. Similarly, when her toddler needed surgery for craniosynostosis, a rare condition when a baby's skull plates fuse prematurely, social media taught her more about it and other families' experiences than any NHS information could, Alice explains.

But people's social media diagnostic journeys aren't always so straightforward. Identifying a disease or a condition can be a complex process. The fact that Ellie's blood tests and scans yielded little is unsurprising. The NHS says that about one in four people who see a GP have unexplained physical symptoms.[4]

Not understanding the cause can sometimes distress patients as, without a cause, it seems a solution is out of reach. But it's easy to forget just how much about our bodies is uncertain and unexplained. Two people can present with identical symptoms yet have completely different underlying conditions. Consider something common, such as fatigue. It might signal iron deficiency in one person, diabetes in another or depression in a third. The same symptom can be the thread that connects hundreds of possible diagnoses. Some diagnoses are only reached by methodically ruling out every other potential cause.

How can a doctor communicate when they don't know something for certain? What do they do when your symptoms can't be put down to one cause, or they can give you a probable diagnosis, not a definitive one? Navigating these thorny questions is an active area of research at Cambridge University's Healthcare Improvement Studies Institute. Speaking from their offices at the university, Dr Zoe Fritz and Dr Caitríona Cox – both practising clinicians – talk me through their work. Fritz tells me:

> Only some diagnoses are given with any certainty, for example pneumonia, where the bacteria has been isolated from the mucous produced from the patient's cough. Much more commonly the doctor puts together information from the patient's history, their examination, and whatever tests they have and makes a probabilistic diagnosis – the most likely one.

It's not unusual for doctors to be uncertain about the exact cause of a patient's symptoms. 'However, there hasn't been much research into how, if at all, doctors should convey this uncertainty to patients,' they wrote in a paper published in 2024.[5]

When doctors are presented with a set of symptoms, they develop a list of potential conditions that might be causing the problem, called differential diagnoses. Sometimes the answer is fairly obvious: a child with an itchy rash whose friend just had chickenpox most likely has chickenpox too.

This is where the medical aphorism 'when you hear hoofbeats, think horses, not zebras' comes from.[6] Coined by US physician Dr

Theodore Woodward, it emphasises prioritising common statistically probable diagnoses over rare or exotic ones when evaluating symptoms – rare diseases are, by definition, rare. But of course, there's a balance to be struck. Zebras do exist. Doctors weigh common versus uncommon possibilities while considering each patient's specific history and context.

Further investigation may be necessary. Part of a doctor's job involves ruling out life-threatening conditions, even when they're unlikely to be the cause. For example, if you visit your GP repeatedly reporting changes in your bowel habits, a doctor may decide to offer testing to rule out bowel cancer even if your overall cancer risk is low.

This principle also holds true in a hospital setting. Take, for instance, a sixty-year-old woman presenting to A&E with sudden chest pain. Alongside her medical history, a series of tests may be conducted to help diagnosis. One such test could measure troponin levels – a high result would indicate acute coronary syndrome, where blood flow to the heart muscle is obstructed or diminished, potentially indicating a heart attack.[7] She may also have an electrocardiogram, a test that monitors heart rhythms and helps identify any irregularities, such as arrhythmias. These could include a D-dimer test, which detects protein fragments indicating or ruling out a potential blood clot, and a CT scan to identify clots in the lungs or blockages in the heart's arteries. She may also undergo blood tests and a chest X-ray to rule out infections like pneumonia.

Sometimes it can take a while to get to a definitive diagnosis. 'Let's say that person who comes in with chest pain hasn't had a heart attack – we have definitely ruled that out. But could they have angina?' Fritz says. Angina is a type of chest pain caused by reduced blood flow to the heart and is a symptom of coronary artery disease. The condition can get worse when doing exercise, for example. One way to see if the chest pain is caused by angina would be to do an angiogram – a scan taken after having an injection of a dye to help highlight the heart and blood vessels.

But diagnostic tests can come with risks. In the case of an angiogram, there might be soreness or bruising; an infection or reaction to the injected reagent; or, more seriously and rarely, damage to the blood vessel or a stroke.[8] These complications might be factored into decisions about whether to go ahead and have one.

For patients who don't have any cardiovascular risk factors, the risk of doing an angiogram may outweigh the benefit, Fritz explains. For instance, subjecting a young athlete with no other health issues to the procedure's one-in-a-thousand risk of stroke, plus the inherent discomfort, simply doesn't make clinical sense, she says. 'If a patient says that they do exercise and don't get chest pain, it would be common for a doctor to say: "You haven't had a heart attack or a clot on the lung, and I don't think it's angina. It's probably musculoskeletal,"' she says.

One of the big questions facing doctors is how much information to give a patient about their differential diagnoses – all the possible reasons for the symptoms they're seeing. Do they tell them everything they're thinking? 'We might say, well, it's probably just musculoskeletal, but we don't know that. It might also be pleurisy [inflammation of the tissue lining the lungs]. But again we don't know that. There aren't really any tests for these things. So we're left with what we call a diagnosis of exclusion,' Fritz explains.

Fritz and Cox were interested in was how doctors communicated this diagnostic process. How do patients respond to uncertainty and are they reassured by more information about the process, or less? They investigated how a chest pain scenario and others were presented by doctors. They recruited doctors from five hospitals and asked them to read the scenarios online, in a randomised order, and then explain to an interviewer what they would tell a typical patient.[9] In their experiment, they found that even when provided with identical clinical information, doctors present their findings to patients in different ways.

Only 36% of doctors in their chest pain scenario explicitly admitted they couldn't explain the pain's cause. Fewer than 30% would directly tell the patient they couldn't rule out angina. When providing 'safety-netting' advice about what to do if symptoms persisted or changed, most doctors wouldn't mention the possibility it could still be a cardiac issue or a diagnostic error, though around 30% did raise these concerns.[10]

But what happens when these patients then consult other doctors who take a different approach, saying something like 'It's possible you have angina, but it's unlikely'? Or when they see a doctor who emphasises cardiac risks while discussing follow-up appointments? 'There's a huge variability in what people say, which we think has a massive impact on trust. If patients are getting very different information depending on which doctor they go to, it can be very hard for them to navigate what to do about their health,' Fritz says. 'One of the biggest things that's come out of our research is that doctors are often focused on wanting to avoid anxiety,' she adds. Rather than explicitly telling someone what they do have, or might have, it's considered more compassionate to rule out what the patient definitely doesn't have.

It's a noble intention, but is it what patients want? Fritz and Cox also created video scenarios for members of the public to watch. In some versions, doctors openly acknowledged their uncertainty about the diagnosis, while in others, they expressed no uncertainty – even when they couldn't be sure. After viewing these videos, participants answered questions about their impressions and preferences.

Of course, this study has limitations. Someone expressing a preference when watching a video doesn't necessarily indicate what they would prefer in real life. 'Essentially, patients preferred the videos where the doctors gave them more information about uncertainty, but these versions also made them very slightly more worried,' Fritz explained. However, patients' understanding of diagnosis differed from doctors'. The study found they generally believed a diagnosis could happen 'in a day' and it was unusual when that didn't occur.

Doctors view diagnosis as a *process* that unfolds over days, weeks and months. Questions about what triggers symptom flare-ups, whether they improve or worsen over time and how much a patient's daily life is affected can only be answered with time. This information can be crucial for diagnosis. For patients, however, silence or vague reassurance can feel like indifference, especially in the face of persistent symptoms. That vacuum is where social media steps in, offering not only explanations but empathy, validation and a community of others who also feel unheard.

## DIAGNOSIS BY TIKTOK

Like many others grappling with health concerns, Ellie Matthews turned to the internet to research her symptoms. Her chosen platform was TikTok. The app is known for its uncanny ability to surface content that feels deeply personal, reflecting users' habits, fears and symptoms. Headlines such as 'The TikTok Algorithm Knew My Sexuality Better Than I Did' and 'How TikTok Reads Your Mind' highlight how users feel it has a remarkable insight into their inner lives.[11]

Some researchers argue that people perceive algorithms as 'all-seeing and all-powerful', believing they understand them better than they do themselves.[12] This stems from the notion that algorithms offer an objective, omniscient perspective – a 'god's eye view' of reality. Beneath this illusion is behavioural targeting. The algorithm boosts content based on engagement, favouring posts that trigger strong emotional responses, such as fear, confusion, relief. The result is a powerful feedback loop.

Once a user clicks on a video about bloating, TikTok serves them more of the same. For users already experiencing health anxiety, the algorithm doesn't just reflect their concerns, it may well escalate them (see chapter 2). As one health psychologist quipped to me: 'The algorithm probably knows your anxieties better than you do.'

Following her own diagnostic pathway, Ellie tells me that she 'just wanted to rule some things out'. One problem with this is motivated reasoning, which refers to our tendency to seek out and believe information that confirms what we already suspect, while ignoring evidence that contradicts it. This, plus a trust in algorithms and a stream of engaging health content that chimes with hopes and fears, can have a powerful effect. In Ellie's case, her TikTok feed served up videos about food intolerances and digestive issues that mirrored her own concerns. It perhaps reinforced her beliefs, but it seemed like diagnostic insight.

Influencers confidently linked symptoms like hers to food allergies and intolerance. Their videos featured symptom relief stories and authoritative-sounding takes on complex immunology. They talked her through IgGs and IgEs (antibodies, also known as immunoglobulins, that are produced by the immune system). This was what it was, she thought. But there's a risk if someone is convinced they have a certain condition, they may be more likely to notice symptoms that fit with their self-diagnosis and dismiss those that don't. This can create a compelling but misleading narrative about their health that encourages them to have unnecessary or even harmful tests or treatments.

In Ellie's case, she encountered a dizzying array of commercial tests promising they would identify the root cause of her symptoms: finger-prick blood tests providing comprehensive food sensitivity profiles, breath tests and even hair strand analyses purporting to show undiscovered intolerances. Convinced she had an intolerance or allergy, Ellie bought a test that was cheap and quick. It only cost £20 – a bargain compared to the others on offer. The company that made it said it could detect which foods were causing 'unwanted reactions in 3 easy steps'.[13]

After a brief review of the website, Ellie was convinced. Hundreds of Trustpilot testimonials claimed the test had helped people feel like 'a brand new person' after eliminating foods flagged in their results. The negative reviews from people pointing out how the test failed to detect their known allergies and sensitivities didn't catch her attention. 'I was like "wow, I need this,"' she says. All she had to do was cut off a few strands of hair, pop them in an envelope and send them by post to a lab.

The company claimed the sample would be analysed by a 'team of experts against a range of food and non-food products.' The test used something called 'bioresonance', which relies on the unproven theory that certain patterns of electromagnetic waves from a hair sample can reveal food or environmental allergies.[14]

This method has never been validated in any clinical trial. But beneath a headline on their website that said 'Research and supporting documents', the company stated: 'bioresonance tests lack sufficient clinical papers'; it went on to say that a 'growing number of people are discovering the benefits' of the therapy and provided around thirty 'research papers'.

Within three to five days Ellie would receive an email with her results, which would enable her to make the necessary changes to her diet and lifestyle. And, as promised, within days of dispatching her hair strands, she received an impressive-looking 36-page PDF report that appeared thorough and scientific.

Excited by this, she turned to TikTok to share her results. In a three-minute video, she guided her followers through each page, flipping through them as she explained what it said. 'At that moment, I thought that was the best test I've ever had over any blood test, any ultrasound I may have had – I thought this was revolutionary. If this test has fixed me, then why wouldn't I share it with other people?' she tells me. 'On TikTok, I have a wide audience. So I just thought, why not? I thought it would be beneficial.'

Ellie's instincts were spot on. The video went viral. Most viewers, with only a handful of sceptics, shared her enthusiasm and announced they had ordered the test themselves. She carefully walked her viewers through the report's traffic light colour-coding system, where red indicated problems requiring immediate attention. Her pages were filled with an alarming sea of red boxes flagging dozens of everyday foods she was apparently highly sensitive to and should eliminate without delay using a 'structured elimination diet'.

'It would just be like "coconut – red". And then you'd be like, "Oh no coconut for me. Okay, I won't eat it,"' she tells me. 'All of my cheese is red… All of dairy is red… I can't have milk chocolate,' she says, unfazed that she can't eat much-loved foods ever again. She reassures her viewers in the on-screen caption that the video isn't sponsored: she genuinely recommends the product. She tagged the company's social media page, joking: 'Never thought I'd be able to sell anything. Seems I can.'

Ellie isn't the only person sharing her journey on social media. Plenty of others have too. In April 2024, UK lifestyle TV programme *This Morning* reported a 250% uptick in people searching online for direct-to-consumer food intolerance testing in the previous year.[15] '"Quick", "easy" and "life-changing" is how they're being sold to us and from anywhere between £30 and £300 for a DIY test kit, food intolerance home tests are big business,' the report said.

Some companies attribute this uptick to the Covid-19 pandemic. For example, the surge in home health testing boosted the turnover of YorkTest Laboratories, a company providing allergy and intolerance tests based on its interpretation of IgG antibody science.[16] The company further projects the home health testing market will reach $8.15 billion by 2030.[17]

Richard Dawson, head of YorkTest Laboratories, put this increase in demand down to limited access to healthcare during lockdowns: 'The challenges of the past couple of years have led to more people than ever taking control of their own health, nutrition and wellbeing,' he said, adding that 'this is reflected in changing buying behaviour and the rise in online sales across our portfolio of home health tests.' He might be right. But when you might have to wait a lengthy time for an appointment, who can fault you for being desperate? And there's always someone willing to provide a service to fill that gap.

'I do understand that doctors now have to deal with a lot of self-diagnosing patients, and that must be very difficult. But if the NHS was doing their job in the first place, we wouldn't feel the weight of having to diagnose ourselves,' Alice Bull tells me. It's not just allergies and intolerances. You can now assess genetic cancer risks, evaluate bowel health or detect vitamin deficiencies, all from the comfort of home. With taglines like 'Your hormones, your way', 'Blood testing made easy' and 'Knowledge is power', these tests promote the idea that endless self-testing is the key to better health.

The ease of home health testing is one potential benefit. Some tests have been around for decades: the positive two lines on a pregnancy test is a pop-culture trope. Most of us will have also tested ourselves for Covid-19 many times over the course of the pandemic. Home testing can be empowering and address gaps in the healthcare system. People report using them when doctor's appointments are difficult to arrange due to costs, travel distances or lengthy waiting times. When patients, like Ellie, feel dismissed by the healthcare system, they may use the results from self-tests to validate their need for medical attention from their doctors.[18]

## THE GREY AREAS OF SELF-TESTING

Clare Davenport, an associate clinical professor at Birmingham University, researches the evidence for medical tests and how they influence diagnostic decision making. She says that the rise in promoted tests is also driven by the consumerisation and medicalisation of normal bodily variations. Changing consumer expectations about healthcare – partly shaped by social media – also play a role.

This shift isn't necessarily bad, she says; the implications are still unclear. Healthcare professionals order tests for several different reasons. They may want to try to diagnose a disease; screen for potential illnesses; monitor how an existing condition is progressing; or assess prognosis.[19] Some tests, like pregnancy and Covid-19 tests, have the potential to answer medical questions or guide decisions with just one result. But at other times, interpreting test results can be tricky.

If, for example, an at-home blood test shows you have an iron deficiency, you might respond by taking iron supplements and adding iron-rich foods like red meat and leafy greens into your diet. However, a doctor might want to know your age, medical history and other symptoms to explore the root cause of the deficiency. They might look at this result alongside other tests. The iron deficiency could be something relatively harmless, like a poor diet or heavy periods. Or it might indicate a more serious issue, such as a stomach ulcer or bowel cancer. The blood test alone doesn't tell you the underlying cause and the information it yields might not be enough to create a full treatment plan.

Nor do tests always give you binary results, such as those that measure things like thyroid hormone levels or haemoglobin. What's considered 'normal' depends on factors like sex, age, pregnancy and other underlying health issues. If a test result falls outside something called the reference range, it doesn't necessarily mean something is definitely wrong. There may even be perfectly innocent reasons: if you ate a cake shortly before you took your blood sugar reading, of course it will be higher than usual. Even the time of day might affect the results of certain tests. And having normal results isn't a guarantee that nothing is wrong – it just means that nothing is wrong that the test can detect.

Dr Margaret McCartney, an academic at the University of St Andrews, explains the challenge of trying to make sense of it all as a doctor. 'If you're trying to test someone with symptoms, you need to work out how to interpret that test result. For example, you can have a negative test result – but still have the condition that you have been tested for,' she says. 'You need to balance the likelihood of the symptoms the patient describes as being caused by the condition versus the likelihood of the test being wrong.'

Moreover, no diagnostic test is 100% accurate. Doctors and scientists look at metrics called sensitivity and specificity. The sensitivity of a test measures how well it identifies people who actually have a disease – does it correctly detect those who are sick, or does it miss them? If a test has low sensitivity, you're more likely to get a false-negative result, meaning you have the disease but the test says you don't.

Specificity measures how well a test identifies people without the disease as healthy – does it correctly clear people who don't have the condition? If a test isn't very specific, you're more likely to get a false positive, meaning you're healthy but the test indicates you have the disease. It makes sense that the more tests you take, the more likely you are to eventually get a result outside the normal range, even if you're perfectly healthy. Sometimes it's just statistical chance.

Tests are most effective when there is already a strong suspicion of an illness. This is similar to criminal investigations. Detectives are more likely to solve cases when existing evidence points towards particular leads. If they follow those leads systematically, they're less likely to waste time on red herrings or circumstantial evidence that ultimately lead nowhere. Likewise, medical tests performed without a clear clinical reason can produce misleading results or false positives that send both doctors and patients down unnecessary diagnostic rabbit holes.

Sometimes building an accurate clinical picture can take time. This is the case with food allergies and intolerances. But that's not what the online marketplace for allergy and intolerance testing would have you believe. It's awash with technologies promising quick results. Some of these tests can accurately measure specific markers, but it doesn't necessarily mean they diagnose any medical condition. Other tests rely on pseudoscientific methods that lack validation from proper research.

Professor Adam Fox, a consultant paediatric allergy doctor at Evelina London Children's Hospital, and who also has a private practice, reluctantly became a content creator in an attempt to cut through some of the noise. He told me he was initially 'completely uninterested' in Instagram, but baby nutrition author Annabel Karmel persuaded him to give it a go. She told him that it was the best way to reach young parents, the audience he felt he needed to connect with. 'She said "you're not going to reach them by talking at conferences and the little bits you might do on the telly. The way you reach these guys these days is through Instagram,"' Fox tells me.

When he started an Instagram account, he had to have his daughter sitting next to him because he found the 'whole thing so unintuitive'. What he found shocked him: 'It's just the Wild West. There's so much dodgy stuff and vested interests on there.' Fox says he uses the platform to explain food allergies, intolerances and sensitivities and to refute misinformed claims about allergies and intolerances.

## NAVIGATING FOOD REACTIONS

The formal classification of these conditions fall under an umbrella term 'adverse reactions to food'. These can then be categorised as toxic or non-toxic. Toxic reactions affect everyone who eats the food, like chicken left out too long causing food poisoning. Only some people experience non-toxic reactions. Their body responds in an unexpected way to a food most people can consume without a problem.

Allergies are a prime example of a non-toxic reaction occurring when the immune system mistakenly sees a harmless substance as a threat. In response, it produces IgE antibodies, which can trigger rapid symptoms like hives, nausea, dizziness, facial swelling and, in severe cases, life-threatening anaphylactic shock. This causes dangerously low blood pressure and breathing difficulties. These IgE-mediated allergies can be diagnosed through skin-prick tests or blood tests that detect IgE antibodies reacting to specific allergens.

A 2024 report by the UK's Food Standards Agency found that approximately 6% of UK adults have a clinically confirmed IgE-mediated food allergy. The severity of reactions ranges from mild symptoms (such as oral itching) to potentially life-threatening anaphylaxis.[20] Around 7% had other types of adverse reactions to food not caused by IgE, such as irritable bowel syndrome (IBS) – which is not related to the immune system at all – and conditions like coeliac disease, an autoimmune condition triggered by gluten.

There are also food allergies which involve the immune system but not IgE antibodies. Symptoms appear later, making it difficult to pinpoint the trigger. One example is non-IgE-mediated cow's milk allergy, which affects about 1 in 200 infants.[21] Symptoms can include reflux, vomiting, skin rashes and eczema. Such allergies, including cow's milk allergy, cannot be diagnosed through tests. Instead, the approach involves removing the suspected allergen from the child's diet and monitoring whether symptoms improve. According to Fox, it's 'massively over-diagnosed in infancy' due to the lack of testing, which contributes to the perception that it is more common that it actually is.

Even detecting IgE antibodies in a blood test doesn't necessarily indicate an allergy or disease.[22] While these tests identify IgE antibodies linked to specific foods pretty effectively, they can't always determine whether they'll trigger allergy symptoms. As a result, people can get false-positive results and eliminate key foods unnecessarily, potentially leading to other health issues. Conversely, the absence of antibodies in a test doesn't guarantee safety. If the test results are taken at face value, someone might wrongly assume they aren't allergic to a food, consume it, and have a serious reaction. Doctors look at the full picture of medical history and symptoms when they use these tests to try to develop a clinical plan.

Intolerances and sensitivities are a whole different ballgame. Food intolerance occurs in the digestive system when the body struggles to break down certain foods.[23] This can result from enzyme deficiencies, reactions to food additives or sensitivity to natural compounds. Many people can consume small amounts without issues. Lactose intolerance is one of the most common examples.

Some people are intolerant to various substances in food, such as salicylates in certain fruits, vegetables, herbs, and spices; histamine in wine and cheese; caffeine; and alcohol. Food intolerances are often dose dependent, meaning symptoms appear when a certain amount is consumed and may worsen with higher intake.[24]

Lactose intolerance can be tested by measuring hydrogen levels in your breath after consuming a solution containing lactose. However, most food intolerances lack reliable tests. Adding to the complexity, how your body reacts to a specific food can be influenced by various factors, including what else you've eaten.

'The only way to find out if you're intolerant is if you cut something out of your diet, your symptoms get better, and if you reintroduce it they get worse,' Fox says. This can be a slow process involving trial and error and some companies market tests as a shortcut. Hair testing and electrode-based methods may seem questionable, but so are tests for IgG antibodies – the most common antibodies in blood. These tests appear more legitimate because they are sometimes presented as similar to IgE testing, which lends them an air of credibility.

IgG antibodies are a normal part of the immune system's response to food and don't correlate with symptoms or intolerances.[25] They're really just a reflection of what you've eaten recently. International medical organisations caution against IgG testing. The European Academy of Allergy and Clinical Immunology says that food-specific IgG antibodies are a typical immune response to food exposure and do not indicate an allergy or intolerance.[26]

'They [websites offering IgG tests] take advantage of the fact that they may be genuinely, reliably and accurately measuring your level of IgG to foods so they can cover their website with all their lab accreditations and all the sciencey stuff to make it look genuine,' Fox tells me. 'But in reality, what they're measuring is meaningless in the context of the problem that the person's got.'

A 2023 Australian study examining online diagnostic tests found that they often target consumers who are on 'diagnostic odysseys'. These are people like Ellie, who are searching for answers to unexplained symptoms or those dissatisfied with conventional medical diagnoses.[27] These companies invest heavily in Google ads for search terms like 'allergy testing' and create Instagram and TikTok content designed to appeal to the anxieties of vulnerable consumers.

There's a large pool of potential recipients: a UK study of around 20,000 people found that 20% believed they had food intolerance symptoms, but the reality was quite different.[28] The researchers focused on eight foods: cow's milk, hen's eggs, wheat, soya, citrus, fish/shellfish, nuts and chocolate. In a controlled, double-blind food challenge study published in the *Lancet*, researchers tested the 20% of people who thought they had an intolerance and gave them food they thought they were intolerant to, but they didn't know if they were actually consuming the suspected food or not. Of this group only 19.4% showed a reaction to a suspect food when challenged. This suggests that true food intolerance in this group was far lower than those surveyed originally believed. Sometimes people may have real symptoms, but it may be a nocebo effect (see chapter 2).

'There is a discrepancy between perception of food intolerance and the results of the double-blind placebo-controlled food challenges. The consequences of mistaken perception of food intolerance may be considerable in financial, nutritional, and health terms,' the authors wrote.[29]

Ellie's experience highlights one of the problems with food tests. After receiving her test results, she diligently cut out everything labelled 'red' – a long list of supposed trigger foods, many of which are considered part of a balanced diet. Rather than easing her health anxiety with definitive answers, the test intensified it. Mealtimes became a source of stress. Nearly every dish seemed to contain a potential trigger.

Her thoughts became consumed with worst-case scenarios. 'What happens if I did have a banana today? Does that mean that I have to be near a toilet? I don't want to have a bad stomach. I don't want to feel unwell…' The test that promised clarity had instead trapped her in a prison of food fear.

But then Ellie started to doubt what she'd done. 'I was like, "this is so stupid, surely we can't live our lives cutting out bananas,"' she tells me. She decided to see whether eating these 'forbidden foods' would actually trigger a bad reaction. 'I was like, let's just try and see what happens if I have coconut or something.' She started her own food reintroduction plan. To her bemusement, nothing happened. No reactions, no stomach problems, nothing of the sort. That's when the penny dropped.

'I don't know why you would want to test hair strands. How do you test that?' she says to me slightly incredulously. 'How does someone know what you're allergic to via your hair… But in that moment of desperation, it doesn't matter because you're thinking: "it's only like £20. You could fix me,"' she says.

## CHECKING THE SMALL PRINT

Ellie was right to be sceptical. What she had missed was a tiny disclaimer on the bottom of their homepage: you wouldn't spot it unless you looked for it. This cautions that hair testing (bioresonance) is categorised under complementary and alternative medicines (CAMs) and results do not constitute a medical diagnosis. The fine print exploits regulatory loopholes. By stating on their website that they fall under the category of 'complementary and alternative medicine', they gain legal protection. Even when the results include dietary recommendations or suggest supplements, often presented in scientific-looking packaging, these companies can disclaim medical responsibility. Their business model relies on consumers believing they're getting a diagnosis. Yet these companies avoid explicitly claiming they provide diagnoses, with their disclaimers denying any such intent.

I ask Ellie about her TikTok video and what she now thinks about her whole experience. She pauses and looks at me. The video extolling the benefits of bioresonance testing still attracted views and comments, even after so many years. By testifying that it worked on camera, she had given it legitimacy. 'I don't know whether to remove it or not. I don't know whether it helped or not. When I changed my diet, my symptoms changed. But I don't know if that was a placebo or not,' she tells me.

Keith Petrie is a professor of health psychology at the University of Auckland. He specialises in illness perceptions, patient beliefs and their impact on health. As we've seen, our minds have a powerful influence over our bodily symptoms. 'Once someone makes the effort to focus on something – like a diet – their attention shifts to the good things happening. It's similar to going to the doctor: we go in focused on our symptoms, and the doctor gives us a diagnosis and a treatment. After that, we often focus on signs of improvement. Shifting our perspective from dwelling on symptoms to noticing signs of progress is a powerful change, and it can happen quickly. Feeling understood and having someone acknowledge where we're at – whether the treatment is excellent or not – reshapes the frame through which we view ourselves. People often underestimate how powerful expectations can be,' he tells me.

Dr David Stukus is a paediatric allergist at Nationwide Children's Hospital in Columbus, Ohio, where he leads the Food Allergy Treatment Center. He also helps families understand and manage allergies, while tackling questionable health claims online. He tells me:

> People are being sold the idea that hidden allergies are everywhere, there are people out there claiming they can cure food allergies. Algorithms prioritise fear-driven messages. Now, everything is seen as a hidden disease or a hidden toxin in our food, and it's making people more paranoid. As a result, more people are turning to non-evidence-based approaches for their health. All it takes is the right influencer or politician to start talking about it, and suddenly, it goes viral. Then we end up spending all this time trying to undo the questionable information.

Because food allergies can have a big impact on quality of life and anxiety, social media can provide helpful peer support. But it can also increase anxiety, as Stukus points out: 'If you end up in an echo chamber where parents are calling up every food manufacturer every time they feed their child – when that's not medically necessary – it can make you start doing the same thing. It becomes a cycle, where social media drives anxiety rather than helping manage it.'

With endless information at their fingertips, many patients arrive having already shaped their opinions based on what they've seen online or on social media. A parent may believe they've identified their child's condition and come in with specific expectations. This might be misguided by social media influencers or advice from well-meaning but medically untrained people, he explains.

The fact she might be misleading people worried Ellie. 'I don't know whether I'm spreading false information with my video still being viral. When I posted it I thought it was true.' If these tests have no scientific basis and no medical validity (by their own admission), how come they are sold to consumers, and how come they can make the claims they do? A key issue with direct-to-consumer diagnostic tests is the lack of regulation before they hit the market. Manufacturers aren't required to prove their tests are effective diagnostic tools or that they offer any real benefit, so long as they steer clear of claims about diagnosing or predicting diseases. This is why food-test marketing often uses the term 'sensitivity' – which has no medical definition. If consumers mistakenly equate 'sensitivity' with 'allergy', as many reviews suggest, the responsibility falls on them.

## WHO'S RESPONSIBLE ANYWAY?

In the UK and Europe, self-diagnosis kits are supposed to be evaluated by largely private organisations called notified bodies and given a CE mark or UK CA mark to show they've been checked. These bodies, spread across Europe, also test household appliances like kettles and fridges to verify performance and safety claims. On the whole, before a medical device comes onto the market, there is not always the same need for clinical trials as there is for medicines.

In my investigations for the *BMJ* and the BBC, I found a lack of transparency in medical device and diagnostics regulation. The evidence allowing companies to enter the market isn't always independently verifiable, meaning we often have to rely on their own claims. Even when evidence is accessible, it may not support the stated accuracy of the tests. Depending on the type of test and its purpose, this can pose risks. Nevertheless, they might still be available to buy.

This lack of transparency troubles Dr Annette Plüddemann, who researches diagnostic tests and technologies at Oxford University: 'You can only rely on what the company has said unless independent researchers have decided to test it themselves and publish their results. There isn't really anywhere else you can find out how accurate the test really is in practice,' she tells me. Much of the time, a consumer can only judge a product on the marketing hype.

There's another issue, one that might seem obvious. When tests are used at home there's no one checking to see if they're used properly. Specialists are trained to do tests correctly, and some people who test frequently – such as those managing diabetes – learn through instruction and practice. But regulators for at-home tests do not require the producers to demonstrate they work in a real-world setting.

'I think we all remember having to do the Covid tests,' Plüddemann says to me. 'You had a leaflet that told you what to do. But I bet you if you spoke to ten people about how they used it, there'd be variation in how people did it; when people took the test; how they interpreted the results; and what they did with the results,' she says. And this is a relatively straightforward test, supported by mass public information campaigns, and largely funded by the state.

Put simply, critics argue there are too few safeguards for private at-home test kits: to check that they do what they say, to check that the consumer uses them correctly and to check they provide any benefit at all. In theory, companies must clinically validate their tests through studies demonstrating accuracy in appropriate target populations. However, Clare Davenport's research suggests this often doesn't happen in practice.[30]

Regulatory evaluations classify tests based on their intended purpose as stated by the manufacturer. Higher-risk tests, like those for life-threatening conditions, face stricter scrutiny. By labelling a test as addressing 'bowel health' rather than 'bowel cancer', manufacturers may lower its risk classification, subjecting it to less stringent assessment, she explains. This test might check for blood in the stool and claim to detect warning signs for multiple conditions like bowel cancer, Crohn's disease and colitis. However, the accuracy varies across these different conditions.

'If I had a negative faecal occult blood test [a test for hidden blood in the stool] and I was sixty-five with a family history of cancer and had never had screening, that's very different from a twenty-four-year-old who's just a bit concerned. In my case, it's much more likely to be a false negative. I should be saying "I still have symptoms, so I should still go to the doctor,"' Davenport tells me. These tests fail to provide crucial context. They don't necessarily indicate that age affects risk, that symptoms increase concern, or whether the test is meant for people with or without symptoms.

With little to stop inaccurate tests coming onto the market, it can fall to the Advertising Standards Authority (ASA) to ensure the claims companies make are backed by evidence. It has ruled against claims that blood or hair analysis tests can diagnose food intolerances. On social media, however, companies can rely on influencers doing their work for them. What duty do influencers have to consumers?

'The fundamental question they need to ask is, are they doing this for the patient's benefit or their own?' asks Fox, who also reviews claims for the ASA. It's never ethical to promote tests that aren't scientifically validated and upfront about what they actually test for. 'But if they are open about the nature of the test – that it's alternative or complementary rather than scientifically validated – then that's people's choice. The problem is duping people into thinking they are getting something they aren't,' he says.

This issue is vexing the medical profession. In September 2023, a group of medical organisations penned an open letter to the government calling for changes to how diagnostic tests are regulated and advertised. 'Capacity issues within the NHS are enabling the exploitation of the "worried well" – selling anxious people data without providing them with any professional support, and often no interpretation of their data. In turn, this often leads to further strain on capacity as the patient seeks support or interpretation,' they wrote.[31]

Professor Michael Osborn, former president of the Royal College of Pathologists, was one of the signatories. He tells me about his colleagues who have patients come to them with 'files full of results' from various companies, saying how worried they are. When GPs are stretched more than ever, it's difficult to spend time wading through unverified tests that may well be meaningless. There's a narrative around patient choice that needs discussing, Osborn tells me. With some frustration he adds: 'There's a fantasy of patient choice because you just end up with the same questions further down the line that the NHS has to follow up.'

Dr James Cave, editor-in-chief of the *Drug and Therapeutics Bulletin* and a practising GP for over twenty-five years, recalls experiences at his Berkshire practice. Patients have come to him convinced they have bowel cancer based on the bowel health tests that the NHS doesn't use. When he referred them to a gastroenterologist, the specialist had to test them again, only for the same test to come back negative. But when presented with two conflicting sets of results, patients don't necessarily know which to believe: 'They might say I got a positive result… Your test could be wrong, and my test could be right,' Cave tells me.

In one case, another test was ordered, which again returned a negative result. Cave contacted the company who had provided the original test. 'What was fascinating is we could not get out of the company any information about what standards they had, what were their criteria for positive and negative?' Cave says.

Several years on, Ellie is still trying to resolve her symptoms, still attempting to work out what foods might prompt her bloating and discomfort. 'These symptoms are definitely physical, as well as mental, like with anxiety it just flares up. But still to this day, I don't really have an answer. It's just whatever happens, it happens, you know?' she says.

Ellie's experience may be a reflection of a broader trend – people turning to social media when healthcare feels inaccessible, dismissive or slow. Her expectations were shaped by compelling online narratives of misdiagnosis, gaslighting and unexplained pain.

Doctors communicate diagnostic uncertainty in different ways. While medicine sees diagnosis as a probabilistic process over time, consumers may be led to expect instant, binary answers – an expectation reinforced by online content. There's a commodification of this uncertainty: the self-testing industry exploits desperation. Companies capitalise on regulatory grey areas, selling scientifically unsupported diagnostics under the guise of empowerment and personalised health. The result is that profit being made by exploiting people's fears. Content creators telling compelling stories – regardless of how sincere they are – help drive a market for tests that have no medical utility.

Empowerment is important. But it can only go so far when tests are inaccurate and misleading. Mainstream medicine might be left to clean up the fallout. Patients arrive with dubious test results and fixed beliefs, putting additional pressure on already stretched services. Far from being empowered, patients are left in the troubling position of not knowing who to trust. They are left in a quandary with no easy solutions. But Ellie's experience, and that of countless others, makes it clear that inappropriate testing might do more harm than good. There are perhaps things to consider before buying a test.

## WHAT TO ASK BEFORE BUYING A TEST/DOING A TEST:

**Why am I buying this test?** What is the specific reason or concern driving your decision?

**What will I do with the results?** Will the results lead to a clear action plan? If you would consult a GP regardless of the outcome, consider whether self-testing is necessary.

**Do I understand the potential harm of testing?** What seem like abnormal results might not actually be a problem for you, and 'good results' do not necessarily rule out a serious problem.

**Will I have support to interpret the results?** Not all results are easy to work out, Interpreting 'bad' results can be stressful and overwhelming, especially if you don't have a professional to explain what they mean in terms of your life and health going forward.

**How accurate is this test?** Do not simply look at what the company says about the test. Check whether its technology has been proven in clinical trials, and see if it's recommended for use by the NHS or a relevant professional body.

**Who's promoting the test, and why?** It's easy for social media influencers to present themselves as people like you, in search of answers. And often a viral TikToker is simply someone who thinks they've found something that helps them. But these tests are big business, and companies can and do put money into advertising them on social media, and target their adverts to people like you: worried something is wrong, but not sure what to do about it.

# 5

# SICK UNTIL PROVEN HEALTHY

Tired of getting repeated, worsening migraines and failing to get reassurance about any underlying causes, Elle Oglesby took her health into her own hands. The Texan realtor and business owner had seen the buzz around full-body MRI scans on Instagram. It was 2023 and celebrities had started to promote them as the ultimate in preventive care. The algorithm had detected her unease and her need for answers. Her Instagram feed, once filled with luxury listings and interior-design inspiration, now served her an endless stream of wellness content. 'If you want to take control of your health, book your Prenuvo scan today!' one influencer enthused.

She had watched an old acquaintance, now a lifestyle content creator, document her own experience with the scans. Once she'd lingered on the video, her feed became inundated with posts extolling their benefits. The testimonials were compelling, particularly one from an actress who credited the company with detecting pancreatic cancer early enough to save her life. Elle, who admits she has 'health anxiety', found the promise irresistible. Her previous MRIs had come back clear, but Prenuvo was promising superior technology and revolutionary machines. It could spot trouble before it made itself felt.

Elle says that the idea of seeing a detailed image of her body – confirming she had no cancers or other health concerns – would bring her peace of mind. What really sold it to her in the end, however, was having a radiologist explain the results of her scan just like she'd seen in influencers' posts.

For Elle, the cost of $2,500 for a scan was expensive but a price worth paying for a clean bill of health. As a divorced mother of four young children, she says she's even more proactive about her health. 'I just want to make sure everything's okay.' She booked her appointment at Prenuvo's Dallas location applying the $300 discount code that her influencer friend had shared. The overlap of medical care and social media marketing struck her as strange, she admitted, but no stranger than many other aspects of contemporary wellness culture.

Two weeks after her scan, Elle got a call from a Prenuvo customer service representative. But it was not the reassurance she'd hoped for. To Elle's dismay, her scans hadn't come back clear. Adding to her anxiety, the representative couldn't provide any specifics about what the scans had detected or what the findings might mean for her health. Instead they advised her that a nurse practitioner would call to review the results the following week.

Elle says she started to freak out and tried to press for more information. 'I'm like, well, what kind of findings? Are they serious?' After an excruciatingly tense five-day wait, the call finally came. The nurse delivered unsettling news. The scan had picked up a lesion on her kidney, but more urgent was a round, 'quarter-size' circle on the cerebellum on the left side of her brain. For someone already plagued by migraines and anxious about their cause, this particular piece of news was what she dreaded most. 'An indeterminate lesion of the brain can potentially be a benign or a malignant lesion,' the scan results said. 'Unfortunately we are unable to determine the exact nature of it.' The nurse concluded the call by advising Elle to consult her own doctors for further testing. It was then that panic truly set in, as she was confronted with the fear of dying and the thought of leaving her children motherless.

She'd expected to see one of Prenuvo's radiologists. But the reality fell short of the glossy social media promise. The consultation with a radiologist that Elle had watched in promotional videos wasn't included in her $2,500 package. That conversation would cost thousands more, which led her to suspect those influencer consultations might have been more marketing than standard practice.

MRI – or magnetic resonance imaging – is a type of test that can create detailed three-dimensional images of our internal organs using powerful magnets and radio waves. Doctors typically use these scans to focus on specific areas where they suspect trouble: a worrisome mass, a damaged knee, an inflamed organ. But it's the full-body version, promising a comprehensive portrait of what's happening internally, that has captured the imagination of enthusiasts on social media.

Prenuvo has been at the vanguard of this. Founded in 2018, it began as a joint venture between co-founders Andrew Lacy, the CEO, and radiologist Dr Rajpaul Attariwala in a small office in Vancouver.[1] Using Silicon Valley buzzwords about cutting-edge software and AI technology to 'reimagine preventive healthcare', Prenuvo attracted investors such as billionaire 23andMe co-founder Anne Wojcicki. Now based in California, the start-up promised it could 'screen for and diagnose more than 500 conditions at a fraction of the cost of traditional MRI screenings'. All of this in under an hour.

The appeal to the titans of tech is obvious. Fundamentally, these ideas are rooted in logical, predictable input–outcome systems that prime people to apply the same mechanistic thinking to the complexities of human biology. Tech enthusiasts, driven by a relentless march of progress in processing power and engineering, risk harbouring blind faith in cutting-edge medical technologies.

The company then turned to social media with a savvy campaign. It secured endorsements from celebrities and influencers and shaped a narrative suited to the digital age: that these scans can catch the hidden health risks that might otherwise kill you, accompanied by phrases like 'peace of mind and reassurance', 'be in control of your health', 'know your body' and 'be proactive'.

Content creators use hashtags like #ScreeningSavesLives, #EarlyDetection, #EmpowerYourself, #KnowledgeIsPower and #CatchItEarly. On TikTok and Instagram, content creators share their MRI journey. Lying on beds, they're fed through the Polomint-shaped tube in spa-like surroundings and enthuse that you can even watch Netflix during the scan to pass the time. Less an inconvenient health test, more of a bougie experience – a status symbol akin to a first-class flight.

Kim Kardashian, who has made an art form of transforming medical procedures into social media moments, has predictably embraced the trend. This is, after all, the woman who once submitted herself to an X-ray on camera to authenticate the naturalness of her famous posterior. In 2011, Kim posed by the resulting X-ray images, while her sister Khloe tweeted the picture. 'Hey dolls. The PROOF is in the X-ray. Kim's ass is 100% real!!!' she quipped.[2]

Kim Kardashian posted a photo to Instagram dressed in Prenuvo's dark grey, branded scrubs, leaning against the 'life-saving' scanner.[3] 'It was like getting a MRI for an hour with no radiation. It has really saved some of my friends lives and I just wanted to share #NotAnAd,' she told her hundreds of millions of followers, while also announcing that it could find aneurysms and cancers before they turn deadly.

Kardashian's post was certainly helpful for the company in terms of publicity. It generated newspaper headlines worldwide, while Prenuvo reportedly acquired a hundred thousand more followers in a week. The post itself garnered almost 3.5 million likes.

Recognising the power of aspirational branding on platforms such as Instagram, company execs invited celebrities for a scan at New York Fashion Week in September 2023. Some accepted their invitations and rushed to get their bodies checked between shows, posting pictures on the platform – high fashion meets clinical utility chic. It was a deft manoeuvre that pushed Prenuvo's brand beyond the confines of social media and into mainstream news coverage.

Using similar language to Kardashian, US designer Zac Posen told his followers about Prenuvo's ability to detect cancers and diseases such as aneurysms in its earliest stages. Relieved that he was 'all healthy', Posen shared a personalised Prenuvo link citing his name and offering a $300 discount so others could get the help he had too. The post has since been taken down.

Lacy, the Prenuvo CEO, told the *New York Times* that the company doesn't pay anyone to promote its products. But it does offer free scans to influencers and prominent figures in the wellness industry 'in exchange for an honest review if they feel like it'.[4] This health trend isn't confined to the US. Prenuvo now has a clinic in central London just off Oxford Street, but before it had even opened the hype had led to a waiting list.

It's a growing market. Spotify's founder, Daniel Ek, has set up Neko Health, which launched in Stockholm in 2018. He claims he is addressing a gap in the availability of preventive care. The solution, he says, are full-body MRIs that are accessible to 'real people'.[5] His goal is to make early diagnosis affordable, so that full-body scans become 'as routine as an annual check-up.'

With NHS waiting lists stretching into years, Neko Health has opened its first clinic in London's Marylebone in a blaze of publicity offering tests billed as 'a health check for your future self'. All curved cream chairs and pastel walls, with equipment designed to look more like sculpture than machinery, Neko Health's clinic could easily be mistaken for a high-end spa. The scanning rooms, bathed in soft light, bear little resemblance to the institutional fluorescent lights of a typical hospital – they're designed not just for diagnosis but for Instagram. Neko's scans cost £300 a pop and come with some big claims about what the firm can do: Neko claims their scans have led to 'potentially life-saving' healthcare.[6]

Vista Health, a UK provider of private diagnostic scans, has taken cues from its American counterparts, enlisting reality TV star Chloe Ferry – known for *Geordie Shore* and *Celebrity Big Brother* – with a complimentary scan in exchange for exposure to her massive social media audience. Ferry, who told her millions of Instagram and TikTok followers that she's a 'massive overthinker' seeking 'peace of mind', documented the experience in a video that transformed the medical procedure into a curated lifestyle moment.

Draped in a plush spa robe, she was surrounded by serene imagery of rose blossoms drifting across azure skies. The finale showed her emerging from the scanner beaming, arm linked with her best friend as they departed the clinic – less a medical visit than a girls' day out. And why wouldn't you want to share details of a scan you'd had if you felt it could provide reassurance and could save lives? The repercussions, however, are far less glamourous and likely to appear on the pages of the glossy magazines.

## PREVENTION BETTER THAN CURE?

Prevention – as we've been told for centuries – is better than cure. Avoiding conditions like heart disease through lifestyle changes is preferable to requiring long-term treatment. If illness does develop, then it's best to detect it as early as possible and treat it as aggressively as possible – the inconvenience and cost of testing is a small price to pay if the test picks up a deadly illness. Perhaps the Kardashians and Ferrys of the world have fallen into the same seductive trap: the belief that 'earlier is better' must inevitably lead to better health.

A complimentary scan seems like a win–win situation for influencers. They get to produce content for their followers and get peace of mind for themselves. But this doesn't account for the complexity of medical screening, where good intentions can lead people down unexpected paths. Full-body MRI scans belong to a specific category of testing called screening. Unlike diagnostic tests, which follow a trail of existing symptoms, screening aims to pick up problems in seemingly healthy bodies. When doctors diagnose, they're responding to specific complaints – a nagging cough, unexplained fatigue, troubling weight loss. They form hypotheses based on these symptoms, ordering targeted blood work or imaging to confirm or rule out their suspicions (see chapter 3).

The difference may seem subtle but it's crucial. The distinction between the two lies in what statisticians call 'pre-test probability' – the likelihood that someone has a condition before any testing begins. When a doctor examines a patient with symptoms, the presence of those symptoms already increases the probability of finding something specific. Like a detective with promising leads, they're working with more favourable odds. But screening healthy people changes this equation. Without symptoms to guide the search, the likelihood of finding meaningful disease drops, while the chance of discovering ambiguous or misleading findings rises.

Despite these caveats, companies and private clinics have created a market for pricey tests, scans and screenings targeting the 'worried well'. Screening isn't limited to high-tech machines – it can involve blood tests, urine analysis or monitoring blood pressure. Essentially, it's any test done when a person is symptom-free. A scroll through social media throws up endless screening choices often at eye-watering prices: 360 health assessments, biometric screenings, well woman and well man check-ups, full-body MOTs and general wellness scans.

For the purposes of explaining how screening works, we'll focus on full-body scanning because it touches on lots of central themes. As a health journalist, I've found few topics in medicine harder to write about than screening. There's a sense that even if screening saves just one life then it's worth doing. The person whose life was 'saved' by a scan makes for a compelling story: the thousands who underwent unnecessary procedures because of false alarms do not.

It's hard to imagine how lying in an MRI machine watching Netflix could lead to problems, particularly when compared to taking medication, with its obvious potential for side effects. Yet screening tests, seemingly so benign, come with their own hidden risks. The scanner itself may be radiation-free, but no screening test, even the most sophisticated, is 100% accurate. The images might reveal shadows that turn out to be nothing, miss real problems or uncover ambiguous findings that launch people into a spiral of worry and further testing – all without clear answers.

Unlike prescription drugs, which must be tested in randomised trials before reaching the market, medical screening tests face far fewer regulatory hurdles. The bar for marketing a full-body MRI scan is far lower than for new medications. Companies can advertise these screening services to the public without first showing, through controlled studies, whether they help more than they harm.

Before offering screening programmes to the public, health authorities like the UK's National Screening Committee demand scientific evidence. It relies on a framework developed over fifty years ago.[7] In 1968, Scottish doctor James Maxwell Glover Wilson and his Swedish colleague Gunnar Jungner published a pivotal World Health Organization report that reshaped the approach to disease screening. Their criteria emphasise that screening should target major health issues and rely on well-researched tests that show the benefits outweigh the harms.

There are other factors to consider. Will this test prevent deaths by catching treatable diseases early? Can it identify conditions that would otherwise be hidden until too late? The test's accuracy must also be considered. How often does it raise false alarms or miss real problems? What is the cascade of consequences that follows each result? Detecting disease early to save lives seems like a simple goal. But in reality, it's a balance of probabilities and trade-offs.

The NHS has implemented eleven national screening programmes covering more than thirty different conditions. Other countries have similar bodies. In the US, it's the Preventive Services Taskforce. Their recommendations are a more reliable guide through the increasingly commercialised landscape of preventive medicine.

When it comes to having a full-body MRI, however, neither of these organisations recommend it. The American College of Radiology – a professional society representing more than 40,000 radiologists, radiation oncologists and medical physicists – doesn't endorse these scans either, despite their members being the ones who could profit from offering them.[8] So why do people have them?

Like many others I interviewed for this book, Elle Oglebsy waved away the official recommendations. 'I know what the authorities say', she tells me. 'But I just don't trust the healthcare system to do the right thing anymore.' Her distrust of traditional healthcare runs deep. 'In America, preventive care isn't even a thing,' Elle says. 'They want you sick. They want you unhealthy because that's how they make money. They keep you on medication.'

There is a slight irony of turning to Prenuvo – itself a profit-making enterprise – but perhaps that's beside the point. In her view, taking control of her health means stepping outside the traditional medical system, even if it means paying thousands of dollars for a scan that medical authorities don't recommend.

## WHAT DOES THE EVIDENCE SAY?

The American College of Radiology says there is no documented evidence that full-body screening is cost-efficient or effective in prolonging life.[9] Their concern centres on what radiologists call 'incidental findings' – the medical equivalent of false leads. This can launch patients into a cascade of follow-up tests and procedures leading to great expense and anxiety without necessarily improving health outcomes. In essence, technology's ability to peer inside the body in such fine detail may reveal too much, finding abnormalities that would never have caused harm but cannot, once spotted, be ignored.

This is what happened to Elle Oglesby. After Prenuvo spotted 'indeterminate' lesions on her MRI scan, she consulted her own neurologist for a brain scan. This cost her another $2,500. She also saw a urologist who scanned her kidneys. More money left her bank account. After more anxious days of waiting, the follow-up tests brought unexpected relief. The kidney scan showed only scar tissue, while the brain scan came back all clear.

When Elle questioned Prenuvo about the discrepancies between their findings and her doctors', the customer service representative offered no explanation. But rather than feeling reassured by the follow-up tests, she found herself with a new dilemma. The company had claimed their machine could pick up things that other MRIs don't, she says. What if Prenuvno was right and her neurologist's reading had been wrong?

After voicing her concerns on social media, Elle received an invitation from Prenuvo for a complimentary second scan. This time, when they imaged her brain, a radiologist reviewed the results: there was nothing of concern to be found. The shadow from her initial scan turned out to be a mere distortion. It was an artifact of the test caused by external factors or the imaging technology rather than anything within her body. It was a false alarm or what doctors call a false positive. In essence, an expensive flaw of the test.

When machines are as sensitive as Prenuvo's – which the company promotes as beneficial – they can detect numerous lumps and bumps that eventually prove insignificant. Even with standard full-body MRIs this is a problem. A 2019 meta-analysis in the *Journal of Magnetic Resonance Imaging* looked at twelve studies involving over 5,000 people who did not have any symptoms of diseases like cancer but had full-body MRI scans. Among the six studies that had complete data, the researchers found that 16% of people who were scanned ended up having false-positive results.[10]

When a scan reveals an ambiguous shadow, the natural response is to investigate further. What appears as a 'blob' could, after all, be cancer. This is where the clinical cascade begins: additional scans, costly work-ups, perhaps even surgical biopsies, each carrying its own set of risks. Elle tells me her scan had put her 'down a rabbit hole of all this additional testing' that she didn't necessarily need to have done. People can be drawn into a cascade where each test leads to another, and where the drive to know or to be certain can itself become a source of harm.

For Elle, the initial scan triggered a cycle of anxiety and testing that shows no sign of stopping. After her follow-up MRI, she scheduled another brain scan 'just to be sure', and plans to continue monitoring. The tech that promised peace of mind has in fact made her highly vigilant.

Companies claim that a national roll-out of preventive full-body MRI scans would not only save lives but also billions of dollars for healthcare systems.[11] However, Elle's story demonstrates why this might not be true. Each follow-up for an incidental finding requires time and resources – each new scan requires a radiologist to review it. These costs add up.

David Ropeik is a former journalist who worked at Harvard's University's Centre for Risk Analysis. 'False positives cause psychological harms, which are easy to dismiss because they're just emotions', he tells me. But he points to research on the long-lasting psychosocial cost of a false positive. It stays with you and this in itself is bad for your health, he tells me.

Professor Ishani Ganguli started out as a journalist, writing for Reuters, the *Boston Globe* and the *Washington Post* while pursuing her medical degree. Now at Harvard, she studies what the healthcare industry calls 'low-value care'. These are medical interventions that offer minimal benefit to patients while often causing harm and incurring disproportionate costs. This isn't just a private healthcare problem; even tax-funded health systems, despite their presumed fiscal prudence, frequently provide treatments and tests that do more harm than good.[12, 13]

In 2019, Ganguli published a survey of 376 US doctors that found almost all respondents had patients who experienced cascades after incidental findings that did not lead to clinically meaningful outcomes yet caused harm.[14] Nearly 90% reported that these cascades had harmed their patients – psychologically, financially and sometimes physically. The doctors themselves weren't immune, describing hours lost to unnecessary procedures, mounting frustration and their own anxiety as they followed these diagnostic trails to nowhere.

Ganguli tells me this is something she has experienced herself in her busy Boston clinic. Prenuvo says their scanner can detect aneurysms and she's seen patients who have had these picked up on scans. 'It's a medical issue that can be very scary,' she says. But there are a lot of small aneurysms that may be there that won't cause problems. The real harm, she explains, comes from the knowledge itself. Once patients learn they have an aneurysm, every headache becomes a potential crisis, sending them rushing to emergency rooms. These aneurysms are very unlikely to have any medical effect, she tells me, but knowing they're there fundamentally changes people's lives. It can be devastating and has a big impact on the quality of their lives, she adds.

The UK National Screening Committee does, in fact, recommend that some people have a scan for an aneurysm.[15] They recommend scanning for just one specific type: the abdominal aortic aneurysm. This is a potentially dangerous bulge in the body's main artery. If not spotted early, it could get bigger and eventually rupture. The programme has been adopted because it fits one of the fundamental criteria for effective screening: that when an aneurysm is found, there is something you can do. These aneurysms can be monitored and managed. Small bulges warrant yearly checks and lifestyle changes. Medium ones require more frequent monitoring.

For the largest aneurysms, surgery becomes an option, though this decision involves its own careful weighing of risks. The procedure can damage kidneys or the spinal cord, and in rare cases prove fatal. However, for large aneurysms, these surgical risks are generally outweighed by the greater danger of doing nothing.

But not everyone is offered a scan. In the UK, only men over sixty-five receive this service through the NHS. This is the population most at risk and therefore most likely to benefit. Having a scan is thought to be worth the cost. By focusing on the population most likely to benefit, the programme maximises its public health impact while minimising unnecessary testing. It's a far cry from the indiscriminate scanning promoted by commercial services.

However, the influencers marketing these full-body MRIs are *not* targeting men over sixty-five; they're promoting full-body scans to an entirely different demographic. Their content is aimed at the young, aspirational, fit and healthy, often in their twenties, thirties and forties. Those least likely to need them.

We all know influencers may paint a rose-tinted picture. This matters less when it comes to hair and beauty or a holiday destination. But in medicine, an overly optimistic pitch doesn't just leave your followers' wallets lighter. It can cause a new kind of stress – opting into tests that you feel you *have* to have, and all the worry that comes alongside that.

Over in Australia, Dr Brooke Nickel and her team at the University of Sydney set out to understand how medical testing is being sold to the public. They focused on five screening tools, such as anti-Müllerian hormone, prostate-specific antigen, testosterone, multi-cancer tests and full-body MRIs, and began asking a series of questions.[16] Who are the people promoting these tests? What hidden financial ties might influence their message? And perhaps most crucially, are they telling the whole story – about both the promise and the potential harms of these technologies?

What they found was that, across the board, the posts 'overwhelmingly' discussed benefits and very few discussed harms. 'If there is any harm that comes up it always had a positive spin in the sense that "at least I know about it now",' she tells me. Most of these posts were highly promotional, Nickel says. Influencers framed the scans not as medical procedures but as essential elements of a wellness lifestyle, alongside juice cleanses and meditation apps. They're just another tool for 'living your best life'.

This is a savvy spin. Research shows that fear-based health messages have complicated effects. Studies have found that simply scaring people isn't very effective at changing behaviour. The most effective health messages combine a clear sense of threat with specific, achievable actions people can take. They make health threats personally relevant while emphasising practical steps for prevention.[17] In other words, 'Worried about cancer? Here's a scan that will help catch it early.'

But some influencers take it a step further, generating health anxiety among the well. Nickel suggests the messaging implies that those who can't afford scans aren't just missing out on a medical service: they're being irresponsible. In one particularly troubling finding, Nickel's research revealed that medical professionals were engaged in promotional excess and going beyond evidence. Her team discovered one doctor who repeatedly posted about the scans. 'He was saying things like: "If you can't catch these things early, what's the point of having all this money?"' she tells me. But it's one thing to feel you can't afford a handbag and another entirely to think you can't afford something that might be critical to your health.

Using coercive marketing tactics to sell medical procedures, contrasts with the decades-long effort to ensure informed decision making in public health screening. Years of research have focused on preventing people from feeling pressured into undergoing screening. When people are offered a screening test by the NHS, the invitation comes with a lengthy booklet describing the benefits and harms. It includes the chance of false positives and negatives and gives a guide about what might happen when the results come back.

But this hasn't always been the case. In 2006, Danish researchers Karsten Juhl Jørgensen and Peter Gøtzsche published a review of breast cancer screening invitations sent by public health authorities in seven Western countries in the *BMJ*.[18] It found that while screening can cause harm, including over-diagnosis and overtreatment, public campaigns didn't reflect this. Doctors cannot always accurately predict whether a cancer will become life-threatening. So some cancers that are detected and treated may never have posed a serious risk, leading to overtreatment, as we'll explore.

In some of the invitations issued that came with an assigned appointment for a mammogram, screening seemed more of a public duty than a personal medical decision. For example, a majority of American women aged fifty-five believed it was irresponsible not to attend screening, the researchers suggested. Jørgensen and

Gøtzsche argued that information included with invitations should be more balanced.

The information provided on the invitations at the time failed to meet the best practice for informed consent. Informed consent is not only the cornerstone of modern healthcare; it's a legal requirement in many countries. But informed consent may be overlooked when targets are at stake, Jørgensen tells me. It took several years for invitations to reflect the benefits *and* harms. Many are still far from good enough, he adds.

Unsurprisingly, people will go to great lengths when it comes to cancer prevention. Despite warnings from her doctor, general medical recommendations against full-body MRIs and her own stressful and costly experiences, Elle Oglesby is undeterred. She'd told me she'd have another full-body MRI in the coming years, and she'd also persuaded her new husband to have one too. 'I just want to stay on top of it,' she maintains. The seed of doubt that she *might* prevent something serious has only grown.

David Ropeik has spent decades looking at the fear of cancer. It's a disease people in rich countries fear more than any other, he tells me. There are two key reasons why cancer has the place it does in people's psyche, he adds. 'We are more afraid of something that will kill us in a really painful way, regardless of the odds that it will or won't,' he says. To demonstrate his point, Ropeik asks me what sounds worse: dying of heart disease or a shark? Burning alive or heart disease? Cancer or heart disease?

Shark, burning alive and cancer, I reply.

Cancer often involves pain. As Ropeik explains, it's not the likelihood of death but rather how we die that has the most profound impact. A risk that's imposed on us also feels worse. It's scarier and evokes more fear than a risk we engage in voluntarily, he tells me. Powerlessness compounds the problem. He says that the feeling of having no control over the situation intensifies the distress. Cancer is widely thought of as a 'vicious, unpredictable, and indestructible enemy'.[19]

We all know people who have been affected by cancer: it's the cause of one in four deaths in the UK.[20] We have witnessed them going through chemotherapy, surgery and radiotherapy, and witnessed the side effects and agonising waits for results. When the illness has a face to it, it becomes much more personal. Media coverage intensifies our cancer fears, especially through high-profile cases. When public figures like Kate Middleton, Steve Jobs or Hugh Jackman are diagnosed with cancer, their stories dominate headlines.

The more we're tuned into it, the more emotional power it has, the bigger it feels in terms of risk, Ropeik explains. Social scientists call this the social amplification of risk. This describes how our minds process repeated exposure to frightening possibilities. Each news story and each conversation with friends adds to our perception of threat, until the risk feels not just possible but probable.

Writing in *Harvard Public Health*, doctors who study social media reported that one young female TikTok user commented, 'I see so many poor people of all ages on this app dying of stage 4 cancers.'[21] Without her realising it, the platform algorithms fed her more stories of dying cancer patients the more time she spent watching them and it was scaring her.

There's a fine line between raising awareness and exploiting fears. As Ropeik points out, some companies capitalise on cancer anxiety, turning 'cancerphobia' into a profitable business. But the ripple effects can be insidious and far-reaching. Perhaps most perversely, intense cancer anxiety can paralyse some people into avoidance, making them reluctant to acknowledge potential symptoms until their disease has progressed. This can lead to 'delayed presentation',[22] that is, people not seeking timely medical help after symptoms begin, which can negatively impact outcomes.

At this point, it is worth noting that recent research suggests survival in the UK has fallen behind countries like Australia, Canada and Norway across several different cancer types, including colon, lung, pancreatic and stomach cancer. The reasons for this are complex.[23] But there are concerns that people are not seeking medical care when they have symptoms.

In 2023, when England's NHS asked people how they would respond to potential cancer symptoms, 40% said they would avoid seeking medical care entirely and 25% would wait and hope the symptoms would disappear on their own. In response, the NHS deployed a double-decker bus campaign across the country urging people to consult their GP about unusual symptoms.[24] They are those with signs that warrant investigation.

For the worried well, however, research has repeatedly shown that screening gives people the sense that there is something they can do. It makes them feel like their hands are on the steering wheel, 'Screening equals empowerment and is seductive because of that,' Ropeik says. In an increasingly unstable and uncertain world, there's a power in 'solutions'.

As you'd expect, the fact you might be able to control your health by getting techy scans appeals to the science podcast bros too. They've taken to social media and their podcasts to comment on the utility of the scans. For them, money is no object.

In January 2024, Stanford neuroscientist and podcaster Andrew Huberman discussed his personal experience with full-body MRI scans to his millions of listeners on his *Huberman Lab* podcast. He found it 'informative and reassuring' to not see any tumours on his kidney or liver and said it allowed for a deeper understanding of human biology. During his podcast, Huberman suggested listeners might want to remove even benign tumours if non-invasive options existed. But he acknowledged that 'some people don't want to know what's going on under the hood.' Then came the twist, delivered in his measured tone. 'Could we be walking round with tumours on the brain without even knowing? Yeah absolutely.'

I read Huberman's tumour comment to Dr Barry Kramer, former director of the Division of Cancer Prevention at the US federal government's National Cancer Institute – the Congress-funded agency dedicated to enhancing cancer prevention, detection, diagnosis and survivorship. He stared at me in stunned silence – a look of bemusement on his face. 'This feeds into the notion that we're sick until we're proven healthy,' he tells me. 'Many years ago, it used to be that we were healthy until proven sick.'

While Elle Oglesby might have had reservations about the motives of authorities, Kramer, having been at the heart of government-backed cancer research for decades, also harbours his own doubts. His scepticism, he tells me, may be partly inherited from his father, but it crystallised during his medical oncology training as he delved into medical history. He says he learned that the thought leaders of the past were frequently wrong, and that many interventions turned out not only to be useless but actually harmful. He points to the fact that some of social media's doctor proponents of full-body MRIs also run private clinics that offer them.

Kramer knows there's money to be made by convincing well people they may be sick and this, he says, carries with it ethical implications. Offering your best guess to relieve the suffering of someone with cancer is fundamentally different from promoting interventions to healthy individuals. The threshold for the latter ought to be that the evidence suggests that the benefits for the few outweigh the potential harm to the many subjected to unnecessary testing, he argues.

Matt Kaeberlein, an American biologist and biogerontologist, is known for his research on ageing mechanisms. He is a professor at the University of Washington School of Medicine. For him, it's all about individual decisions. 'This is where informed people can have differences of opinion about what's right for them,' he tells me. He says he believes that the healthcare system in the US, the UK, and most other countries operates with a culture of waiting – essentially, a mindset that says, 'Let's hold off until we absolutely have to act.' This thinking is deeply ingrained, he argues, and it consistently skews toward inaction. He tells me:

> My personal view is that there's a middle ground – one that leans more toward proactive health management rather than waiting

until people are already sick. Philosophically, I align more with that perspective rather than the conservative approach of current medical boards and regulatory committees. And ultimately, that influences how different people interpret the same data and shape their conclusions.

But there's another question that those assessing screening programmes ask. How do we know if spotting a tumour early and treating it saved someone's life? Again, it's more complex than it seems.

Ryan Crownholm is a trim ex-military veteran turned business owner from California, and he is willing to do and spend whatever it takes to stay healthy for his kids, just like Elle Oglesby. An avid Huberman podcast listener, he heard about Prenuvo and booked in for a scan. Ryan wasn't worried about anything in particular. He leads an ultra-healthy lifestyle and was already tracking his health using all sorts of tech. But he was curious to see if there was anything 'hiding inside me undetected', he tells me.

His scan flagged a three-inch-long mass in his right kidney, he says. 'That curiosity saved my life.' He went to his doctor for a second opinion, who decided to take it out. The pathology came back as renal-cell carcinoma, a treatable cancer that, in some cases, can be fatal.

Crownholm, one doctor wrote rather sceptically in the *New Yorker*, is an ideal Prenuvo patient.[25] What's unusual is that his tumour was, he says, totally asymptomatic, small enough to be removed but big enough to be detected by a full-body scanner. In the US, renal-cell carcinoma screening is not recommended by the authorities unless there is a known hereditary syndrome linked to its development.[26]

The company recruited Ryan as a poster boy and he is pleased that it was found. But for every Ryan who has had cancer detected by a full-body MRI, how many Elles are there who have pursued a cascade of unnecessary care? The findings from the aforementioned

2019 meta-analysis found that about 32% of full-body MRI scans detected potentially significant abnormalities.[27] But would these detected abnormalities ever have developed into harmful conditions or caused death? We don't actually know.

The discovery of tumours or lesions isn't the main goal of screening. What matters is identifying those that pose a genuine threat – specifically, asymptomatic illnesses that can be treated effectively at an early stage, which would otherwise progress to symptomatic or fatal disease if left undiscovered.

We often think finding any tumour is a life-saving discovery, but the reality is more complex. We've heard about false positives – all those screening test results where follow-up tests show that it was nothing to worry about. But we don't often hear about the true positives in which treatment wasn't necessary, because the condition would never have caused problems.

This is how it comes about. A screening test might raise a red flag then follow-up tests confirm the presence of disease – perhaps even cancer. We've seen this in breast cancer screening, even though the UK National Screening Committee says this is a programme where the overall benefits do outweigh the harms.

Between 15% and 25% of all breast cancers detected are known as ductal carcinoma in situ (DCIS).[28] But for most women, as autopsies indicate, these lesions do not progress to invasive cancer. Writing in the *Lancet*, cancer specialists argue that widespread screening has led to more cases of DCIS being diagnosed, even though not all will develop into invasive cancer.

But once they are detected, the recommended treatment is surgical removal, even a mastectomy, and possibly radiotherapy or hormone therapy.[29] All of these treatments come with side effects – worth it if they are life-saving, but detrimental if they were unnecessary. The trouble is that there's no cast-iron way of predicting which DCISs would develop into invasive cancers within someone's lifetime. It's a tricky balance between overtreatment and undertreatment,[30] and this is an active area of research.

It can be hard to spot individual cases of over-diagnosis because it's not always clear what would happen if someone wasn't treated. The main way to spot it is at the population level. Over-diagnosis is exactly what happened in South Korea, and it offers a lesson in the pitfalls of overzealous screening. In the late 1990s, the government launched a national cancer screening programme and, while thyroid cancer wasn't officially included, people could add a thyroid ultrasound scan for a modest fee. Thyroid cancer diagnoses began creeping up in the 1990s, then skyrocketed after 2000 when screening became widespread. By 2011, doctors were finding thyroid cancer at fifteen times the rate they had in 1993 – a surge that should have raised red flags.[31]

Despite increased diagnoses, thyroid cancer death rates barely changed. Most detected cases were papillary thyroid tumours, which are found in up to a third of adults and rarely pose a serious health risk. Instead of saving lives, the screening programme had transformed thousands of healthy South Koreans into cancer patients. This ultimately condemned them to unnecessary thyroid removal surgeries and a lifetime of hormone supplements.

We minimise these harms of overtreatment too easily, yet they can have a major impact on people's lives. Surgery carries real risks, from anaesthesia complications to infection. Thyroid hormone replacements, meanwhile, may be associated with a second primary cancer appearing in patients who had their thyroid taken out.[32] You risk setting off a medical cascade for something that wasn't going to kill you in the first place, Ropeik says.

The promotion of full-body scans by private UK clinics turned Glasgow-based GP Dr Margaret McCartney into a writer. Some twenty years ago, McCartney was on maternity leave when she read a feature in the *Independent* that incensed her. The article featured a journalist who had received a complimentary full-body CT scan. She breathlessly promoted it as an amazing window into one's health and questioned why the NHS wasn't providing such services. To McCartney, it read like nothing more than thinly veiled marketing.

CT scans carry an inherent risk that MRIs don't – they use ionising radiation. Studies suggest that for every 2,000 people who undergo certain full-body CT scans, one may develop a fatal cancer as a direct result of the radiation exposure.[33] The journalist discovered apparent abnormalities that required follow-up testing all of which turned out to be harmless. Speaking to me, McCartney expressed disbelief that the journalist felt grateful rather than frustrated about the wasted time, money and needless anxiety caused by these false positives from an unnecessary scan.

Starting with phone calls to complain about the article, McCartney unexpectedly found herself writing her own piece. She was determined to provide a balanced view of commercial health screening. 'I think they got mixed up and thought I was actually a journalist,' she recalls. She took to shoe-leather journalism, pounding the streets of central London, gathering promotional leaflets from clinics in the hallowed environs of Harley Street. Asking questions to obtain clarity about healthcare and evidence for claims should be part and parcel of decision making, she says. But she found some clinics were hostile to this basic inquiry.

The clinics were presenting only the positive side of the story. 'This wasn't designed to help people make an informed choice,' McCartney explains. 'It was designed to get people to get the scan.' In a series of heated social media exchanges, clinics offering these tests lashed out at McCartney. One even resorted to thinly veiled defamation threats and, ironically, accused her of spreading 'misinformation' for questioning their claims.

In her top-floor study there is a drawer full of documentation – pages of complaints she's filed with the Advertising Standards Authority about companies' misleading websites and advertisements, alongside letters confirming that her concerns were justified. Two decades after her initial article, McCartney says little has changed. As with diagnostic tests, there's an emerging theme – an inability of the regulatory authorities to keep on top of the claims about what is sold to us. If it is hard to keep a watchful eye on clinics, then social media has made it even tougher.

With social media being particularly hard to tame, McCartney has taken her fight to the Competition and Markets Authority, urging them to investigate the entire sector. 'It's only got worse,' she says. The private screening industry has systemic problems, McCartney tells me, from the absence of independent information to a lack of informed consent and aggressive overselling. Challenging individual organisations one by one is futile. This is a system-wide failure, she adds.

She hopes that reforming the entire sector could help curb the excessive promotion of screening on social media and prevent people from making costly, potentially harmful decisions based on marketing, rather than medical evidence. You can't, of course, stop the practice of full-body tests entirely. Some, like Elle Oglesby, having been informed of the risks, will go ahead anyway. Consumers are free to choose how to spend their money. But they clearly need to hear from both sides in order to be make genuinely informed decisions.

While Americans pay for follow-up tests after private scans, in Britain these costs likely fall on an already overburdened NHS. However, a poll of 500 doctors conducted in 2018 via social media (and therefore subject to sampling biases) found that 91% of responding doctors had visited them to discuss private health screening. Only 13% of the time professionals thought this was a reasonable use of NHS resources. But 75% of the time, further resources within the NHS were allocated, like follow-up appointments, blood tests, or imaging.[34] The NHS is essentially left to pick up the pieces once the private sector has profited, leaving those who are symptomatic but poor at the back of a lengthening queue.

As the NHS struggles under mounting pressures, companies like Neko Health and other screening companies position themselves as solutions to healthcare gaps. Their interventions impact the NHS by extending wait times, draining resources and deepening healthcare inequalities. We are sleepwalking into a two-tier system, in which the affluent worried well have access to all the tests their hearts desire, while the poor and sick inherit a broken system in which they can't get seen.

## WHAT YOU NEED TO ASK

Amid the slew of conflicting advice, Danish researcher Professor Jørgensen, whose research into mammography screening was mentioned earlier, outlines key questions everyone should consider. First, be wary when no downsides are mentioned. Every medical intervention has potential harms. If a company or content creator only presents benefits, they're not telling the whole story. This selective presentation should raise immediate concerns about their motives and transparency.

Next, look for clear, comparable numbers about both benefits and harms. Companies should provide solid evidence backing their claims – not just about detection rates but about meaningful health outcomes. 'We are talking about real benefits and not just that it detects there's something there,' Jørgensen says. They should demonstrate how the screening reduces illness and death from targeted diseases. If they can't or won't provide documentation supporting these benefits, that's a warning sign.

Finally, consider the 'clinical cascade' – all those downstream costs and consequences that follow an initial screening. What additional tests, procedures or treatments might be needed? What are their costs, both financial and personal?

I don't believe all influencers are cynics, preying on people's anxieties. Many sincerely think that the scans they've done have helped them and can help their followers. If they've not experienced the anxiety of an uncertain finding, or further investigations, they won't see the harm. But when it comes to screening, we need to ensure that evidence triumphs over influence. That's much easier said than done.

# 6

# EXPANDING THE SYMPTOM POOL

'Bieber, Muhammad Ali, Miley Cyrus. And then there's murderers, rapists, arsonists. I probably have seen more brains than anybody in the world. And now your brain. So this is going to be really hard for you. You have ADHD.' This dramatic revelation doesn't come from a medical melodrama. It's the slightly unconventional way Steven Bartlett, host of *The Diary of a CEO* podcast with millions of followers, chose to share his ADHD diagnosis with his audience.

In an accompanying viral LinkedIn post, he linked his condition to success, citing entrepreneurs and creatives like Bill Gates, Richard Branson and Emma Watson, who reportedly share his diagnosis.[1] He described his diagnosis as empowering. It made him more productive and ambitious by helping him recognise and leverage ADHD as a 'powerful gift', he wrote.

Bartlett described never being typical, failing academically except in subjects that fascinated him. His school experience was blighted by disciplinary action, with him spending a lot of time in the exclusion unit.[2] Yet for subjects he found interesting, he was so engaged he 'literally stole the textbooks and took over the lesson'.

Following other celebrities, Bartlett travelled to Los Angeles to visit high-profile psychiatrist Dr Daniel Amen, who delivered his diagnosis on camera. Amen has his own sizeable social media presence, delivering daily mental health content to millions of followers. His posts on diagnostics, treatments and brain 'hacks' reach viewers hungry for accessible mental health information. This social media presence fuels his business empire. Eleven US clinics drawing international patients, a supplement line, 'Amen University' for practitioner certification, bestselling books and TV specials are all marketed through his massive digital platform.

At the California clinic, Bartlett completed standard ADHD questionnaires followed by a fifteen-minute computerised attention test measuring impulse control. 'They made me do a test on a computer…a speed test of sorts,' Bartlett tells his viewers.

What distinguishes Amen's approach is his use of SPECT scanning. This is a technique that uses radioactive injection to produce colourful brain blood-flow images. Examining Bartlett's scans, Amen identifies 'decreased activity' in the left temporal lobe and a 'flat' left prefrontal cortex, prompting him to enquire about past trauma, concussion and toxin exposure, particularly mould. Bartlett reveals he grew up in a mould-infested home with constantly fighting parents and suffered several football-related head injuries during childhood. Amen confirms the diagnosis based on these findings, plus Bartlett's boredom, poor handwriting, disorganisation, academic difficulties and his 'scatty' mother – possibly indicating a family history of ADHD.

Beyond celebrities, Amen's approach appeals to those disillusioned with conventional healthcare and those who feel overlooked by traditional mental health services. People like Alyssa Brown, a Chicago-based TikTok creator and Microsoft researcher, who reports lifelong struggles with reading, following TV shows, making even simple decisions and starting everyday tasks. She meticulously documents her symptoms in a notebook. Alyssa's diagnosis wasn't straightforward. Her first psychiatrist dismissed ADHD, claiming she was simply 'in the top 1% of intelligence and was bored all the time', she says.

Social media has exposed her to 'more holistic and progressive' approaches – which is something she praises the platforms for. It allowed her to find Amen and have her ADHD diagnosed at his Chicago clinic. The SPECT scan made her diagnosis feel real. Alyssa explains that seeing her brain physically validates her experience. It proves her condition is not imagined. It's down to a tangible, inherent trait rather than a personal failing. She emphasises:

> It's not just you making things up. It's literally a physical thing that you are born with or that you develop over time that's not your fault. And that in itself is extremely validating. When you share that with other people, I think it's easier for them to understand when they see a scan.

Brain scans appear to provide concrete proof for conditions that might be hard to comprehend. For example, one study found some people find articles with brain images more scientifically credible than identical content with other visuals or no images.[3] People like to be able to 'see' abstract mental processes; this satisfies our desire for simple, tangible explanations of cognition.

SPECT scans are undoubtedly appealing and Amen claims to have validated their use through tens of thousands of scans. His approach, however, has come in for widespread criticism from psychiatrists. Not only do they expose people to radiation, they lack FDA approval for ADHD diagnosis and aren't supported by robust scientific evidence demonstrating their effectiveness or accuracy.[4] In essence they're not necessary in the diagnosis of ADHD and they cause harm. As we saw in earlier chapters, this balance is a key consideration in the appropriate use of diagnostic tests.

This is just a snapshot of ADHD on social media. Content creators like Bartlett, Brown and Amen join countless others in sharing personal experiences, daily challenges, potential symptoms and diagnostic pathways. ADHD is one of the most-discussed health conditions on social media, with over 3.5 million posts and tens of billions of views under the hashtag #adhd on TikTok alone.

YouTube, Instagram, Facebook support groups and Reddit forums are no different. In 2023, ADHD was the second most-viewed condition on the NHS website, after Covid-19.[5]

But should this explosion of online ADHD content be celebrated or viewed with caution? Many people with ADHD are finally finding recognition and community, but are we also medicalising ordinary human struggles? Everyone occasionally finds it difficult to be punctual, manage paperwork or maintain focus on long-term projects. But at what point do these challenges transform into a condition requiring medical intervention?

In this environment, where diagnostic and treatment advice circulates freely online, how do we shield vulnerable people from those profiting from their concerns? Years after a new disease has been described, those diagnosed in later years might not look anything like those at the start. How are these digital discussions and viral testimonials transforming our fundamental understanding of ADHD itself?

In the UK, between 2000 and 2018, ADHD diagnosis and treatment rates increased across most age groups.[6] Adults had the largest proportional growth. Men between the ages of 18–29 had twenty times more diagnoses and fifty times more prescriptions by 2018. Despite these increases, absolute numbers remained lower than perhaps estimates would suggest might be expected: 2.6% of boys and 0.7% of girls had ADHD diagnoses, with lower rates in adults. Some suggest these figures suggest ADHD was under-diagnosed rather than over-diagnosed in the UK in this time. But both of these phenomena can happen at the same time.

Since the pandemic, however, between 2020 and 2023, there has been a 400% rise in adults seeking ADHD diagnoses.[7] Professor Anthony David, a neuropsychiatrist with four decades of experience and director of the Institute for Mental Health at University College London (UCL), describes the online ADHD movement as an 'amazing social phenomenon': 'It's a reflection of people becoming more interested in their mental health. They want to better understand their difficulties and connect with others who share similar struggles – that's a basic human need,' he explains.

But for adults seeking diagnosis in the UK, NHS access is virtually impossible. A 2024 BBC investigation revealed waiting times of up to eight years, with approximately 196,000 adults on waiting lists and some NHS trusts closing their lists entirely.[8]

The effective disappearance of psychiatric assessments within the free, regulated healthcare system has effectively allowed a booming online industry to flourish. ADHD influencers, informal support groups, coaches, private clinics and therapists now market services from diagnostic facilitation to fidget toys, workbooks and system navigation guidance.

In the UK, 'therapist' and 'counsellor' aren't legally protected titles. Anyone can use them without qualifications. In this unregulated environment, people must rely on their own judgement to determine which authorities to trust. 'You have to feel for individuals trying to make sense of themselves while being bombarded with conflicting information,' David says.

## HOW MEDICINE FIRST MADE SENSE OF INATTENTION

Attempts to explain why some people struggle with attention and impulsivity date back over two centuries. One of the earliest descriptions of what we now call ADHD comes from Edinburgh-born Sir Alexander Crichton. After receiving his medical degree, he travelled across Europe before returning to London in 1788. During this time, he immersed himself in continental literature on mental illnesses.

A decade after his European tour, he published *An Inquiry into the Nature and Origin of Mental Derangement*. In a chapter titled 'On attention and its diseases', he described 'the incapacity of attending with a necessary degree of constancy to any one object'. Crichton described sufferers experiencing 'mental restlessness' from minor stimuli like doors closing or temperature changes, noting they 'have the fidgets'. He observed this condition primarily affected the 'more affluent' portion of mankind whose attention was under-exercised, particularly schoolboys struggling with Latin and Greek.[9]

A century later, as more children were in school, clinicians revisited attention problems. In 1902, Sir George Frederick Still of King's College Hospital in London described twenty children who showed 'violent outbursts, wanton mischievousness, destructiveness and a lack of responsiveness to punishment'. These children, predominantly boys, displayed 'quite abnormal incapacity for sustained attention', causing school failure despite normal intelligence.[10]

With this new interest came a formal description of what later became ADHD. In 1968, the American Psychiatric Association's second edition of the *Diagnostic and Statistical Manual of Mental Disorders (DSM)* – which health professionals use to research and make diagnoses – included 'hyperkinetic impulse disorder', described as 'overactivity, restlessness, distractibility, and short attention span, especially in young children'. Unlike today's focus on adult ADHD, the manual claimed 'the behaviour usually diminishes by adolescence' – echoing Crichton's centuries-old observation that the condition 'is generally diminished with age'.[12]

How is it that some conditions can seemingly vanish with a stroke of a pen, and others can be created? Diagnostic criteria are established by mental health expert committees who evaluate current research and determine disorder classifications. They incorporate feedback from patients, families, clinicians and advocacy groups.[13,14]

Throughout this process, these experts confront challenging questions about distinguishing between normal human variations and genuine disorders, while considering how cultural differences influence mental health understanding. A notable example occurred in 1973, when 'homosexuality' was removed from *DSM-II* as a diagnosis. This change followed the evaluation of competing theories – those that pathologised homosexuality versus those recognising it as a normal variation of human sexuality.[15] But on the whole, new diagnoses are more likely to appear in the *DSM* than be struck out.

'In the end, it comes down to consensus, rather than objective answers. Clinical needs are considered, and in the US, administrative needs like funding and reimbursement also play a role in what appears in the *DSM*,' David says. He goes as far as to suggest that 'it's not a very edifying process'. 'It's more like horse trading and compromise,' he says.

In an ideal world, the *DSM* and the World Health Organizations's *International Classification of Diseases (ICD)* conduct their own research. These are called field trials, which aim to assess how criteria work in the real world.[16, 17] It's comparable to beta-testing an app. Developers want to confirm if it works as intended, provides user value and identify any bugs needing correction. For example, researchers may ask if it's clear what counts as ADHD and what doesn't? Or did different doctors looking at the same patient reach the same conclusion? Or was it practical to use these guidelines in a busy clinic?

These trials identify issues that might be overlooked during theoretical discussions. They might reveal that certain symptoms are too ambiguous for reliable diagnosis or that criteria apply differently across age groups. Based on findings, final adjustments are made before publishing the official diagnostic manual used by clinicians worldwide. However, David explains this process demands substantial resources, and there's no straightforward path from research to criteria development.

Since hyperkinetic impulse disorder, what we now call ADHD, entered the *DSM-II* its treatment and diagnosis has been mired in controversy.[18] Issues around medication use came first. In the 1970s, widespread Ritalin prescriptions for 'hyperkinetic impulse disorder' sparked nationwide debate in the US. A 1970 *Washington Post* article claimed that 5–10% of Omaha schoolchildren were taking 'behavior drugs', triggering media outrage and government restrictions on Ritalin.[19] Critics questioned the legitimacy of the diagnosis and dismissed the medication as a 'chemical straitjacket'.[20]

Despite opposition, research progressed, shifting focus from hyperactivity to attention deficits. This led to attention deficit disorder (ADD) being included in the 1980 *DSM-III*, recognising the condition could exist with or without hyperactivity.[21] Nonetheless, the definition of the condition continued to evolve. In 1987, the revised *DSM-III* renamed it attention deficit hyperactivity disorder (ADHD), combining inattention, impulsivity and hyperactivity under one term.

Research in the 1990s showed ADHD symptoms could persist into adulthood, leading to the first appearance of adult ADHD in *DSM-IV* (1994). Adult diagnosis required at least six hyperactivity and impulsivity symptoms present for six months before age seven that caused impairment across multiple settings. But for some commentators, commercial interests muddied the water.[22] Throughout the evolution of diagnostic criteria, drug companies had a behind-the-scenes presence, perhaps influencing how we come to see and treat ADHD.

When *DSM-IV* was published, no drugs were approved for adult ADHD. But the expansion of diagnostic criteria opened new markets, simultaneously drawing pharmaceutical industry interest and raising concerns about medicalising normal challenges in life. Eli Lilly's Strattera (atomoxetine), approved in the US in 2002 and UK in 2004, was the first licensed adult ADHD medication.[23] Lilly's US advertisements blurred boundaries between ordinary stress and clinical symptoms: 'Distracted? Disorganised? Frustrated? Modern Life or Adult ADD?' Media stories quickly promoted the drug as 'new hope for coping with distraction and anxiety'.[24]

Lilly wasn't alone in aiming for this emerging market. Shire also targeted adult ADHD with their drug, Adderall. At a New York investor meeting, the company's CEO highlighted 8 million potential adult US patients, most untreated.[25] A marketing campaign targeting healthcare professionals through medical education, societies and patient groups ensued.

Because of ongoing controversy and evolving diagnostic methods, the UK had no formal ADHD guidelines until 2008.[26] Their recommendation for nationwide diagnostic and treatment services across England and Wales triggered rapid expansion of clinics.

Five years later, *DSM-5* (and its 2022 revision) expanded ADHD diagnostic criteria, generating controversy among psychiatrists and beyond. Key changes lowered diagnostic thresholds: adults now needed only five symptoms instead of six, and symptom onset age was raised from under seven to under twelve years.[27] Impact requirements changed from 'clinically significant distress or impairment' to symptoms that 'reduce the quality of social, occupational, or other important areas of functioning'.[28] The differences in language seem subtle. But they can have a large effect in clinical practice.

Some welcomed these changes because they are more inclusive and reflect the different ways ADHD can appear in someone's life, as well as reducing stigma in seeking diagnosis. They argued that more people will get diagnosed and treated properly because of these changes. The new criteria would better match what we now know about how ADHD affects people throughout their lives, while keeping the idea of what ADHD is from the older guidelines.[29, 30]

Critics, however, questioned the evidence base. Researchers at Australia's Bond University's Institute of Evidence Based Healthcare evaluated the research underpinning these changes and found it 'limited' and at 'high risk of bias'.[31] The age criteria modification was based on just one British twin study. No research had examined potential benefits or harms from changing impairment and age-of-onset criteria, nor their impact on diagnostic precision, they argued. 'Changing the definition of health conditions places many people at risk of unnecessary diagnosis and treatment,' they wrote.[32]

What's more, these changes have occurred 'alongside society's progressively narrowing standards of normality', one Danish social anthropologist wrote. We're less tolerant of anything. A growing number of people receive diagnoses not because of genuine pathology, but because they no longer fit within these ever-tightening boundaries of normalcy, she argued. The more behaviours and deviations are pathologised, the narrower the definition of 'normal' becomes.[33]

Another high-profile critic is US psychiatrist Professor Allen Frances who chaired the *DSM-IV* task force. He made his ire very public about its successor. 'DSM-5 will likely trigger a fad of adult attention deficit disorder, contributing to the already large illegal secondary market in diverted prescription drugs,' he told *Mother Jones*.[34] In a separate interview, he pointed the finger at drug companies 'selling the ill to peddle the pill' as well as 'intellectual conflicts of interest', with experts in the field 'expanding their pet diagnosis'.[35] 'If I've learned anything during these forty years I've worked on *DSMs*, it's that if anything can be misused, it will be misused, especially if there's a financial incentive,' he said.

A study in the *BMJ* subsequently found that 60% of panel members received industry payments totalling $14.2 million. For the ADHD diagnostic criteria panel specifically, 78% had industry connections.[36]

## HOW ADHD GETS DIAGNOSED

Even with these concerns, the current diagnostic practices are a world away from Amen's SPECT scans. *DSM-5* notes that no biological marker is diagnostic for ADHD and that 'no form of neuroimaging can be used for diagnosis of ADHD'. It is diagnosed through a series of assessments and validated questionnaires, as Dr Charlotte Hall and Professor Maddie Groom, neurodevelopmental researchers with an interest in ADHD, explain.

In the UK, ADHD is diagnosed through a thorough assessment by a specialist – typically a psychiatrist, psychologist or paediatrician, depending on the patient's age. For children, parents or teachers may raise concerns with a GP, who can then refer them to a specialist. Adults going through the NHS follow a similar process, with GPs referring them to an adult psychiatrist. The diagnosis involves an assessment that varies by clinic but usually includes an interview to gather information on behaviour across different settings such as home, school or work. Adults are normally asked to provide details of someone who can give evidence of how it's affecting their life. Standardised questionnaires may be used to assess symptom severity. Many rely on self-reported symptoms.

Many ADHD symptoms exist on a spectrum throughout the general population and identifying impairment and frequency of symptoms as defined in the *DSM* is a judgement call. These symptoms often overlap with anxiety, depression and learning disabilities. Responsible clinicians should rule out alternative explanations before diagnosing ADHD and prescribing medication.

This nuance sometimes goes out of the window when you go online. Viral videos on Instagram and TikTok list 'common signs' of ADHD describing their impact on daily life. Megan McHugh, a UK DJ and radio host, is one content creator who has gone viral on TikTok after listing 'lesser known' tell-tale signs of the condition with a video captioned: 'Six ADHD behaviour traits you might not have known about'. She cites overpromising and wondering: 'Why the fuck can I not just say no?' 'Your long-term memory is fucking shocking... You have some sort of subconscious tic, usually, whether it's pressing your lips or scrunching your nose,' McHugh told her followers.

She's far from alone in sharing her experiences in this way. Others point to indicators of ADHD that include trouble getting up in the morning, problems choosing what to eat in a restaurant, missing deadlines, and being unable to finish a book.

A study by Vasileia Karasavva from the University of British Columbia and a team of researchers question the way symptoms are described on social media. When researchers examined the top 100 ADHD TikTok videos on a single day, 10 January 2023, clinical psychologists found only 48.7% of claims accurately reflected *DSM*-5 symptoms.[37] Of those inaccurate claims, nearly 70% depicted experiences that many people without ADHD would have; about 50% showed symptoms common across multiple disorders as being specifically ADHD; and almost 20% better matched different conditions entirely.

Videos often portrayed behaviours like bumping into furniture, repeatedly playing the same songs or craving sweets as ADHD symptoms. Content typically lacked nuance – only 4% acknowledged their claims might not apply universally, and less than 2% mentioned that these experiences could occur in people without ADHD. Of creators sharing credentials, 84% claimed 'lived experience' while 13% identified as life coaches. Not one top video came from a clinical psychologist or psychiatrist.

When researchers showed these videos to 843 psychology students – which may limit the applicability of the study to the general population – they generally rated scientifically inaccurate videos much more positively than experts did, while slightly downgrading expert-approved content. The students either did not have ADHD, had a formal diagnosis or had self-diagnosed ADHD. Overall, self-diagnosed students rated all videos the highest, giving even expert-rejected content higher marks than those with formal diagnoses. This, the researchers say, suggests that young people prioritise relatability over clinical accuracy.

## SEEING YOURSELF IN THE FEED

For self-diagnosed people especially, previous painful and frustrating experiences of being dismissed may make TikTok's validating content particularly appealing: people like Alyssa Brown, who found that these ADHD descriptions matched many symptoms she had documented. She speaks warmly about discovering an ADHD community on social media after her experiences were disregarded by conventional healthcare. 'I always assumed everyone experienced the world like I did. Finding out that's not true was eye-opening. It's deeply reassuring to connect with people who share similar experiences,' she explains.

One of Alyssa's favourite accounts features quirky conversations between a husband and his wife who has ADHD. She and her fiancé bond over these videos. Some of these creators also have merchandise to sell, including t-shirts with slogans such as 'What if you're not a lazy useless loser' and 'Caution: mid hyperfocus'. 'We both just laugh about it because it's super-relatable,' she says.

Mental health specialists are divided on viral ADHD content. Some value its destigmatising effect, while others worry it trivialises a serious condition or blurs diagnostic boundaries. Celebrity advocates like Steven Bartlett have shaped public perception further. For instance, the most decorated gymnast in history, Simone Biles, announced her diagnosis on X in 2016.[38] 'Having ADHD, and taking medicine for it is nothing to be ashamed of nothing that I'm afraid to let people know,' the US athlete said. Similarly, UK singer Jessie J shared in a July 2024 Instagram post what her ADHD diagnosis evoked: it both 'empowered' and 'overwhelmed' her.[39] Like Bartlett, she described her condition as 'a superpower', given proper support. 'If there is one thing social media has given me', she wrote, 'it's the chance to relate, connect and heal with strangers that have kind hearts and are going through a similar thing.'

But this celebrity endorsement sits uncomfortably with some researchers. Oxford University psychologists Drs Lucy Foulkes and Jack Andrews caution that, despite good intentions, celebrity disclosures might inadvertently elevate certain conditions into 'prestige items'. This social value can make diagnoses seem desirable, particularly on social media platforms. The resulting glamorisation focuses attention on high-profile cases while overlooking those suffering in less privileged circumstances.[40]

This chimes with Professor Susan Young, a clinical psychologist who set up the first national adult ADHD service at London's Maudsley Hospital in 1994 and co-authored the 2008 NICE guidelines. She objects to the 'glib' tone of some content online. 'If you look at TikTok in particular, it's all about entertainment. I feel uncomfortable with having a condition that people can really struggle with being used for entertainment purposes,' she tells me. Having worked extensively in the penal system, Young knows that the reality of ADHD for many does not involve Olympic gold medals, multi-million-dollar record deals or TV stardom.

Her 2015 study found that ADHD prevalence in prison populations significantly exceeds that of the general population; in youth prison populations five times as many young people (30.1%) and in adult prison populations ten times as many people (26.2%) have ADHD than in the population as a whole globally.[41] The outlook is bleak for prisoners with ADHD: they are more likely to be involved in violent incidents, engage in self-harm and have substance abuse disorders. Yet in this environment, far removed from TikTok's portrayal, the condition remains under-diagnosed, with sufferers unlikely to receive support, making rehabilitation substantially more difficult.[42]

'People talk about, "ADHD is my superpower! I love having ADHD! I'm zany and I'm fun." It can undermine the condition,' Young adds. This glosses over all those, predominantly from marginalised backgrounds, for whom the condition has wreaked havoc on their already fragile lives.

US research – also replicated in other countries – shows children from low-income backgrounds are more likely to meet the criteria for ADHD but are less likely to receive treatment.[43] David agrees. The 'ADHD is a superpower' idea really bothers him too. 'I honestly can't see any true advantages to having ADHD itself. For someone to be diagnosed as having ADHD, it has to actually cause problems or impairment in your life – that's a medical requirement – but we rarely talk about what "causing problems" really means,' he says. That isn't to say people can't adapt to their challenges or develop strengths in spite of their difficulties. But it doesn't mean the condition itself is beneficial, he explains.

Social media awareness campaigns about mental health walk a fine line between reducing stigma and trivialising conditions to the point where they lose credibility. This can lead people with diagnoses and difficulties brought on by ADHD to question their own experiences.

Twenty-one-year-old Alex, from a middle-class family, had struggled throughout his school years with disruptive behaviour, frequent outbursts, detentions and multiple suspensions. When his school initiated an ADHD assessment through the local authority, Alex initially refused.

As a regular social media user, his algorithms had exposed him to numerous ADHD-related posts. But he couldn't identify with social media portrayals of ADHD. He thought the condition was a fashionable fad for influencers. He didn't possess the celebrated 'superpowers' these posts described, he tells me. Instead of being successful and creative, he felt he was disruptive and constantly in trouble – that's what he'd repeatedly experienced. The light-hearted memes failed to reflect reality for him, which was incredibly difficult at times. Though he eventually received an ADHD diagnosis after specialist consultation, Alex is still sceptical about its validity.

## WHEN TIKTOK SPEAKS BEFORE THE TEXTBOOKS

But there's another view. Dr Jessica Eccles, a reader in brain-body medicine at Brighton and Sussex Medical School, welcomes the social media conversations. Rather than viewing ADHD as trendy, she's concerned that too many people with the condition lack proper support. She says social media provides community for those with under-recognised conditions – connections often absent in clinical settings. Many turn to platforms like TikTok because they feel misunderstood by healthcare providers.

'That's not necessarily a criticism of doctors – there's so much to learn, and we are discovering new things all the time,' explains Eccles, who treats adults with ADHD in her Brighton clinic. She finds social media useful for understanding patient concerns and community discussions. 'If everyone's talking about something, it helps me reflect on my clinical practice. It doesn't mean I spend all my time on social media instead of reading journal articles, but it can be really helpful.'

Patient communities often identify connections faster than researchers. The same kind of information, when researched through field studies, might take ten years to appear in textbooks or inform clinical guidelines, Eccles says. 'Naturally, discussions on social media about these topics happen long before they're fully adopted by the medical community,' she adds.

'We think about ADHD as having these core features of inattention, hyperactivity and impulsivity, but there are loads of other features that aren't captured very well in the diagnostic criteria,' Eccles explains, citing 'time blindness' – an ongoing struggle with sensing and managing time – as an example discussed online. 'A lot of the memes on social media explore that… It can be pretty useful to start conversations,' particularly for groups traditionally overlooked in diagnostic frameworks, such as women and people of colour. One US study found that Black, Hispanic and Asian children were substantially less likely to be diagnosed with ADHD than White children and less likely to receive medical treatment.[44]

The ADHD self-discovery journey on TikTok has become so widespread it's evolved into its own meme.[45] The platform abounds with grateful comments: 'This platform actually helped me get diagnosed' is a typical comment. Older adults are similarly grateful: 'Finally, in my 50s and after finding you on TikTok, I was finally diagnosed with ADHD.' Others echo this sentiment: 'Thanks to this community, I was recently diagnosed with ADHD! Grateful for the posts on here that were relatable and made me realise I potentially had ADHD.'[46]

Like Alyssa Brown, social media agency owner Alice Bull discovered her ADHD through TikTok. During the 2020 pandemic, the platform's algorithm began showing her videos about undiagnosed women with ADHD. 'Over about two weeks, I went from thinking "this is interesting" to "Oh shit, this is me"' Previously, she had assumed ADHD only affected hyperactive young boys.

While Alice had a history of various mental health diagnoses, TikTok gave her an alternative explanation: its algorithms know you better than you know yourself, she tells me. Alice had previously thought she 'just a bit shit' sometimes at doing grown-up life. What resonated for her were the descriptions of the hyperactivity in the brain. 'I have probably sixteen simultaneous conversations going up there at any one time... always thinking, always tabs open, it's exhausting.' She also identified with 'task paralysis' – knowing what needed doing but feeling overwhelmed by it.

Captivated by what she had seen, Alice tried to seek medical help on the NHS. It took her three and a half years. 'I had to fight doctors,' she recalls, one of them asking if she wanted an assessment because 'it's trendy'. The comment upset her, so when she finally got an NHS assessment Alice approached it like she was preparing for an exam, she tells me.

Online content creators provide guidance on the diagnostic process, explaining how to navigate clinical appointments and paperwork. 'I studied for this appointment. I'd done a lot of reading about what might happen and what they might ask me. I'd overprepared,' she says. 'I didn't need to go into all the detail that I'd gone into – my entire backstory. I didn't need that, but I had it ready.' Alice was finally diagnosed in 2023. 'At the end of the appointment, he said: "Yeah, you scored pretty highly."' Knowing what was wrong brought her enormous relief.

Vancouver psychiatrist Dr Anthony Yeung analysed TikTok content after noticing increased ADHD referrals and his patients specifically mentioning social media as prompting their requests for assessment. 'There was this clear reflection: growing interest in ADHD on social media was paralleled by increased clinical referrals,' he states.

During the pandemic, Yeung was also exposed to ADHD content on TikTok. He was concerned about what he observed. He systematically reviewed the top 100 #ADHD videos on 18 July 2021, which collectively garnered 283,459,400 views (averaging 2.8 million per video). Unsurprisingly, personal experience videos proved most popular.[47] Lived experience increasingly carries such weight across health conditions that some therapists in the UK and US now use their own diagnoses to advertise their services.

Three psychiatrists evaluated each video, categorising them as misleading, useful or experiential. One aspect they looked at was how ADHD was explained: 15% of TikTok videos misrepresented

ADHD's mechanisms, reducing the complex disorder to a simple dopamine deficiency or chemical imbalance.

## IS IT JUST BIOLOGY?

David explains that biological explanations offer comfort. In his practice, patients prefer physical rather than psychological explanations for their symptoms. In his clinics, he found that people didn't want to be told they might have anxiety, for example – something it's implied can be surmounted by power of will. 'There's a sort of hierarchy of stigma. If you have ADHD, it's a brain condition. It's not your fault. You're not unreliable or impulsive – you've got ADHD. So it takes away any moral taint,' he notes.

This hierarchy of stigma creates its set of own problems. If you're diagnosed with ADHD when your symptoms stem from something else, you may miss effective treatments for your actual condition. David says we have established methods for managing anxiety. 'You can habituate yourself to overwhelming situations through gradual exposure. But if you assume it's ADHD, you may just avoid the trigger,' he says, making your difficulties unnecessarily life-limiting.

One issue with the rise in adult ADHD diagnoses is that it misses out recovery. When someone only gets diagnosed as an adult, there's no chance to see if they might have outgrown it naturally over time, as per earlier iterations of the *DSM*. 'We know many children with ADHD see their symptoms get better as they mature. But adults getting diagnosed for the first time are basically told they have a lifelong condition, perhaps needing lifelong treatment instead of seeing some of their "symptoms" as simply traits, part of who they are,' David says.

As we've seen in other chapters, diagnosis isn't always harmless. There are other risks to consider in having a diagnosis of ADHD. If you're led to believe that you *can't* do something as a result of a legitimate disability, you may stop trying to improve things for yourself. For instance, if you struggle with the planning required to cook meals, you might, as some TikTok ADHD influencers claim they do, rely on takeaways, ready meals and snacks, instead of working out ways to manage cooking nutritious food to the extent you can.

Nor is the relationship with dopamine as simple as it seems: there isn't enough evidence to say low levels are the actual cause. There are many theories about what causes ADHD, including underdevelopment of particular parts of the brain, environmental factors like nutrition and brain injuries, and perhaps the thorniest issue of all: whether social environments might aggravate particular symptoms or make them more clinically significant.

Yeung explains the complexity. 'Right now, with the way ADHD is being presented, we're overly focused on the biological aspect – this idea that it's purely a matter of lacking dopamine and requiring stimulant medication. We need to think more about the psychological factors – why someone might be struggling, what psychological reasons might lead them to seek a diagnosis and also the social factors. What's happening in our environment and society and how is that affecting our attention?'

The *DSM-5* itself says that signs of ADHD might be absent if someone with ADHD gets 'frequent rewards for appropriate behaviour, is under close supervision, is in a novel setting, is engaged in especially interesting activities, has consistent external stimulation (e.g., *via* electronic screens), or is interacting in one-on-one situations (e.g., the clinician's office)'.[48] But these difficult questions don't sell custom t-shirts, mugs and other merch with memes like 'Dope' and 'Chasing Dopamine' written on the front.

Indeed, Karasavva's Canadian study found that the creators of half of the videos they analysed were monetising their content, either selling products or soliciting funds through donations to payment platforms or wish lists. They suspect this is an underestimate given lack of transparency around promotional ties.[49]

'Good morning my dopamine-deficient darlings!' Simone Saunders, a Canadian therapist, calls her TikTok followers in a 'low-dopamine morning routine' video. Content creators regularly discuss managing 'low-dopamine days'. TikTok motivational speaker Ricki Friedman describes feeling 'anxious, underwhelmed, overwhelmed, understimulated, etc.'. Her solution includes avoiding her phone, listing stressors, morning exercise and yoga because 'stretching helps'.

I even get emails telling me how to dress for a dopamine boost. This need to attribute enjoyable activities to dopamine boosts puzzles David. 'Why not just say, "Do things you enjoy, things that are healthy and make you feel good"? Why put a chemical label on it? How does saying, "I went for a swim and came out feeling great because my dopamine levels shot up," add anything to the experience?' he asks.

A cynic might answer that there's not much money to be made from the advice 'get some fresh air'. Medical terminology lends the same advice a sense of specialist knowledge, something worth shelling out for. This has spawned an industry of dopamine coaches, 'dopamine-boosting' supplements (from vitamin B to ashwagandha) and creators sharing hacks, routines and customised 'dopamine menus'.

Those promoting complex treatment protocols sometimes push additional services. When clients report no improvement, specialised classes are offered, so too are books and bespoke supplements. Amen promotes the dopamine deficiency theory, making it central to his treatment approach. His website offers 'nine natural ways to balance dopamine in the brain' while marketing 'dopamine-boosting' supplements alongside conventional ADHD medications.

Alyssa Brown vividly describes her treatment plan from Amen Clinics that involves numerous medications and supplements. 'I'm taking fifty pills a day,' she says, listing four multivitamins, two vitamin D pills, an iron pill and two omega-3 capsules. She even had to search Amazon for a pill organiser large enough to hold everything. 'There's a giant box full of all the different supplements that I take daily. I call it my pharmacy,' she explains.

Amen is far from the only person selling supplements. Some content creators have exploited medication shortages. When the UK government announced ADHD medication supply issues in autumn 2023 due to manufacturing problems and increased demand, a crisis emerged. A UK ADHD survey published at the end of November 2023 found that 27% of patients had received no medication since September 2023, while 33% had had their treatment interrupted.[50]

As the supply problems hit the headlines, the panic was amplified: 'My ADHD medication ran out – then my life fell apart,' one person wrote in the *Sunday Times*.[51] At the same time, an illicit market for prescription drugs and unproven alternatives flourished online. 'Natural' supplements were marketed as substitutes.

In a sponsored post on TikTok, the *Observer* reported that a woman held up three bottles of pills – it's not clear what they were – saying: 'There is a national shortage of ADHD medication but I'm extremely grateful I have these.' She added, 'If you're struggling like me, these are literally going to be your best friend.'[52]

ADHD influencers also promoted unproven supplements in Facebook support groups, claiming they improve focus and memory and reduce brain fog. Choline and guarana seed (two popular supplement ingredients) might not help you at all – there's a lack of robust evidence to say they can – but at least they will be excreted by the body naturally, and all you will have done is lose your money. Other supplements are not necessarily so innocuous and some may even interact with ADHD medicines.

The shortage contributed to the already thriving illicit market for ADHD drugs, some of which are sold in 'potentially lethal' doses. Some capitalised on the national shortage by offering controlled prescription drugs through a mail-order service. These drugs may not even be real ADHD medications but counterfeits that could cause unexpected reactions. Those involved were condemned by charities for being 'irresponsible' and 'exploitative'.[53]

## WHEN EVERY SYMPTOM FEELS LIKE YOURS

Against this backdrop, as he scrolled through TikTok videos, Yeung noticed they often contained 'a grain of truth' and offered 'something validating and relatable' to viewers. Like Vasileia Karasavva's team, he found everyday experiences being misinterpreted as ADHD symptoms.

He observed creators saying things like 'I'm a sensitive person' or 'Sometimes I feel bad if I don't meet my standards' – normal traits presented as indicators of ADHD. He compares these to 'horoscope statements' – those predictions for your zodiac signs in the papers and magazines that are so broad that any event could validate them as true. This taps into a psychological phenomenon known as the Barnum effect, where people believe general statements that could apply to anyone are specifically relevant to them.[54]

This technique flourishes on social media. It fosters more engagement, more clicks and ultimately more money. When belief in the algorithm's infallibility meets the Barnum effect, it creates a powerful psychological cocktail. It might feel like your feed is speaking directly to you, unveiling hidden truths about yourself.

This is reflected in Karasavva's study.[55] At the start of the experiment, non-ADHD participants were more certain about not having ADHD than self-diagnosed people were about having it. After watching just ten ADHD-related TikTok videos, this pattern changed. Non-ADHD participants became less certain, while self-diagnosed individuals grew more confident. Everyone trended in the same direction.

Only after a psychologist explained which videos accurately represented ADHD did non-ADHD participants regain confidence that they did not have it. However, self-diagnosed individuals maintained their conviction, despite professional clarification. The authors suggested social media may reinforce existing beliefs more effectively than clinical expertise can modify them. The study couldn't confirm whether TikTok videos directly caused more self-diagnoses.[56]

But this was just an experiment and it's not clear how it plays out in real life. For example, people who don't suspect they have ADHD may not see any ADHD-themed content. On the other hand, Yeung also notes that algorithms serve far more than ten videos and, with misleading content appearing regularly on TikTok, it can create a distorted view of the condition. 'You start seeing a distorted view of ADHD – an accurate video, then a misleading one', creating 'a sort of parallel reality of ADHD.'

Understanding ADHD and other mental disorders 'becomes more about understanding oneself through the lens of social media than aligning with clinical reality', Yeung suggests. This aligns with David's clinical experience. Patients arrive with predetermined diagnoses based on social media content. 'People come up with a narrative that seems to explain their life. You're not really in a position to challenge it and that can be quite awkward. You find yourself saying, "Well, you know, I disagree. I don't think the medication is going to help you. I don't think it is ADHD,"' he explains.

Being able to determine that ADHD is the root cause of your problems is an important part of the diagnostic process. ADHD medication is largely safe, with research over decades showing efficacy in people with the condition. However, there are grounds for caution in prescription: they can cause high blood pressure and sleeping problems and can exacerbate particular mental health conditions. 'You wouldn't want to treat someone with ADHD medication if, in fact, they had bipolar disorder, where manic symptoms could be mistaken for ADHD,' Eccles explains.

Before receiving a prescription, it's important to have blood pressure readings, and speak to your doctor if you have a history of heart problems or mental illness. In practice, the extent to which these guidelines are followed can vary. This raises important questions about how social media-influenced diagnostic beliefs affect doctor–patient relationships, particularly when medical opinions contradict what patients have learned online. But ultimately, if you think you have ADHD, it's possible to find a professional who will diagnose the condition if you have the financial means.

In 2023, a controversial BBC *Panorama* investigation featured an undercover reporter being diagnosed with ADHD by no fewer than three private clinics. In one egregious case, a psychologist delivered the diagnosis after a forty-five-minute video call.

This is different from the process in the NHS, during which a person and those close to them are asked to fill out questionnaires about the person's childhood and current habits before a three-hour long psychiatric assessment. A clinician also needs to be sure the symptoms have a serious impact on the person's life and are caused by ADHD before they can give a diagnosis. The private sector's threshold for diagnosis may be lower than this; this is why NHS guidance says that an NHS clinician can reject a diagnosis obtained privately.[57]

The mainstreaming of ADHD points to evolving ways people seek to understand and explain their mental health. Clinical terminology 'has taken on a life of its own online', with creators repurposing established psychological concepts, Yeung says. One example is 'object permanence'. TikTok creator Mr Impulsiv (real name Eric Bzink), a mental health advocate with over a million followers, claimed in a popular video that people with ADHD forget others when they're not present due to their not having developed object permanence.

'People with ADHD do not miss other people… It's out of sight, out of mind. We have [not developed] what's called object permanence. If you are not in front of us or engaging with us, our brain literally files you away and we forget about you,' he told followers. Owen Chevalier, a researcher at the University of Western Ontario studying 'digital psychiatry', says this is a classic case of concept redefinition through social media.

The term was originally defined by Jean Piaget in the 1950s to describe infant development – babies not understanding that objects continue to exist when out of sight. This definition remained consistent in scientific literature for decades.[58] Chevalier traced the origin of the new use of the concept to June 2020, when TikTok creator @peterhyphen first suggested that adults with ADHD struggle with object permanence. Peter began with Piaget's definition but applied it to adults with ADHD forgetting food in the fridge or struggling with relationships when people aren't physically present.

After obtaining ethics approval, Chevalier attempted to interview other creators using the term, though many demanded compensation – up to $300 hourly – to participate, and as a result did not take part. This will perhaps influence the kind of people included in research and the ability to draw generalisable conclusions. Chevalier's research showed the real-world impacts of expanding ADHD definitions on social media. Study participants reported that regularly consuming and creating ADHD content made their diagnosis more central to their identity. They increasingly looked to other creators to determine which aspects of ADHD to highlight, creating a self-reinforcing influence cycle.

This exemplifies what Canadian philosopher Ian Hacking calls the 'looping effect', where mental health classifications evolve as people respond to diagnoses. When diagnosed, people reinterpret experiences through that diagnostic lens, potentially developing new behaviours not originally associated with the condition. As new ideas about ADHD and stories from the community spread, the way the condition is defined and understood keeps changing.

Hacking used ADHD as an example. A child told his distractibility stems from ADHD begins interpreting looking out windows not as noticing something interesting but as 'a symptom of my ADHD', redefining both his identity and the concept itself. Those Chevalier interviewed confirmed this effect. Peter, diagnosed as a child, rarely considered his ADHD significant until TikTok prompted him to 're-evaluate his entire life through an ADHD lens'.[59]

Olivia found that social media elevated ADHD from tenth place in her self-description to among her top three identifiers, noting, 'I'm a lot more open to say it's a good thing now.' Emma's journey was different. Social media led her to seek diagnosis. Initially treated for anxiety, she recognised herself in ADHD content on Instagram, which encouraged her to pursue formal evaluation. Her experience creating content shows how the algorithm shapes the ADHD narrative. Poorly performing videos make her question whether her experiences truly resonate with the community.

This suggests the algorithm does more than just determine which ADHD topics go viral. It shapes how creators understand and present their own experiences with the condition. Peter, now believes his initial video was incorrect and tries to verify future videos in light of peer-reviewed research before publishing. Olivia insisted her explanation of object permanence was research-based but couldn't provide sources. Others believe the term isn't being used correctly but describes a real phenomenon not covered by *DSM* criteria – a view shared by other creators. Some hope experts will take the described symptoms seriously, even if they use different terminology.[60]

Dr Naomi Fisher, a clinical psychologist with decades of experience working with ADHD and autistic children in both NHS and private practice, highlights 'rejection sensitivity dysphoria' (RSD) as another emerging concept. As one TikToker describes it: 'RSD is like having your emotional volume turned up to eleven when facing criticism or perceived rejection.' Fisher first noticed RSD appearing in referral reports from other psychologists a few years ago: '"As part of her ADHD, Amelia also has RSD", a typical report might say,' she tells me.

Fisher had never been trained in RSD, nor could she find it in any diagnostic manuals. But, nonetheless, referrals she got from schools and assessment reports talked about it officially as if it had been established in the *DSM* for decades. When she asked the children's parents about it, they were confused by her question. 'Didn't I know about RSD? To them, it was no different to ADHD or GAD [generalised anxiety disorder],' she recalls.

Parents described RSD as an integral part of ADHD, explaining their child's distress when friends didn't respond to text messages. 'One of them told me that this was the way their child was wired and always would be – it's neurological,' she says.

Wanting to know more, Fisher looked online. Her research revealed that American psychiatrist William Dodson had identified heightened rejection sensitivity in adult ADHD patients during the 2010s. He reached this conclusion by asking: 'For your entire life, have you always been much more sensitive than people you know to rejection, teasing, criticism or your own perception that you failed?' 'Many clients answered yes, leading Dodson to create the term "rejection sensitivity dysphoria" or RSD,' Fisher explains.

Eccles, for example, suggests that RSD does seem to be part of ADHD. Her patients tell her they struggle with it in her clinics. One 2023 study involving forty-three young adults (mostly women from the US and Canada) found that current ADHD diagnostic criteria don't fully reflect their experiences.[61] Participants reported issues with attention and emotional regulation, including RSD, which was described as intense negative emotions and physical distress after feeling rejected. Some suggested that RSD might be a conditioned response to social rejection rather than an inherent ADHD characteristic. As yet, there's no clinical consensus about RSD. More research is needed to understand its relationship with ADHD.

Nevertheless, Fisher observed a proliferation of TikTok and YouTube videos about RSD, explaining it as an established fact and how to identify it. 'The list of ways in which RSD manifested itself spread way beyond the original question,' she adds. Fisher worries that TikTok is expanding ADHD's 'symptom pool' by incorporating new behaviours into the condition without solid evidence that these traits are actually caused by ADHD or even occur more frequently in people with ADHD than in the general population.

'It's showing people, "look, this is another thing that you could have". When you do that, you get more and more people identifying with those symptoms,' she says.

## QUESTIONABLE QUESTIONNAIRES

There's a profit motive for persuading people to view themselves in medical terms – as individuals who need extra help and professional support to manage their lives, Fisher adds sceptically. These expanding definitions already feature in online self-diagnosis questionnaires and checklists, some of which are being given a credibility boost by being promoted by health professionals with large social media followings. Many of them have services to sell.

According to Australian clinical psychologist and social media influencer Steph Georgiou (@mindfoodsteph), RSD is 'an emotional unbearable pain that people with ADHD experience.' She presents a checklist covering a wide range of emotional issues. It includes being a 'people pleaser' who 'will do anything to avoid disapproval', someone who gets 'embarrassed and self-conscious' or who doesn't 'quite believe in' themselves, and having difficulty managing emotions when feeling 'rejected.' Her profile contains links to adult ADHD assessments and retreats that cost several thousand dollars each. She's joined by many qualified clinicians, and some unqualified, in hawking their services to TikTok users worried about their mental health.

Another quiz comes from London-based private psychiatrist and TikTok influencer Dr Ali Ajaz, who targets women and girls. In a video that has had approaching 1 million views, formally dressed Dr Ajaz sits in front of a bookshelf saying 'current ADHD diagnostic criteria is biased against women'. That might well be true. His eleven-point questionnaire includes unconventional questions not found in standard NHS assessments, such as whether you've been considered selfish for not sending thank-you notes, if you feel like an imposter passing as 'normal' or if you despair about unfulfilled potential. He suggests that scores above a certain threshold indicate

ADHD, recommending that viewers seek specialist referrals through their doctors. Indeed, he offers a range of unconventional treatments for various psychiatric illnesses. The comments section reveals how readily users accept these conclusions, with one writing: 'I scored 45, watching these TikToks, I know I've found the problem to my life now.'

And, predictably, a US-based supplement company with over 1 million TikTok followers offers a 49-second adult ADHD test with six generic questions. They claim it is 'proven to reveal whether or not you might have ADHD'. Not coincidentally, the company sells supplements marketed for 'brain health' and 'focus'.

Some clinicians like Eccles welcome the broadening understanding of ADHD, suggesting this will help more people who need help to pursue diagnosis. If you believe ADHD is the preserve of boys acting disruptively in school, you're unlikely to go to a doctor if, even if, as an adult, you are perpetually late to appointments, untidy, unable to concentrate and lose your wallet several times a year.

However, if a young professional just like you talks about ADHD as chaotic and being overly chatty, you might see it as condition you could plausibly have. But despite Eccles' support for the ADHD community online, she cautions against using the online questionnaires that circulate on social media. They fall short, she says, because symptoms are taken and interpreted out of context: 'You might have a list of symptoms, but not all of them necessarily reflect the broader experience of ADHD – ticking a set of boxes doesn't necessarily mean you have a particular condition.'

This raises the question: what role should social media platforms like TikTok have in defining and discussing mental health conditions? You can't, of course, stop people talking about their mental health online – and nor should you. Finding support, dismantling stigma, finding out about treatment options and even receiving care are incredibly important for many people. Digital platforms are far from all bad.

While medical experts traditionally defined terminology through research, social media now allows ordinary users to shape these meanings too. When millions adopt a term like 'object permanence' to describe their ADHD experiences, it gains new meaning through usage, regardless of its original definition.

Yeung says the influence of social media often extends to clinicians, impacting the diagnostic process. 'There is a lot of subjectivity in psychiatric diagnoses, and there are clinicians who may be more aligned with what patients identify with online.' This raises challenging questions: is the use of this term 'object permanence' identifying a new symptom, relabelling existing ones or simply providing a helpful metaphor?

On one hand, it could provide valuable insights into lived experiences. If many relate to TikTok's description of 'a lack of object permanence' in ADHD, this might spark research into previously overlooked symptoms. But other professionals worry that if you stretch the diagnostic remit too far, more and more people will be captured by the ADHD diagnosis and the treatment pathway, when they actually need other forms of help. Perhaps, the argument goes, you shouldn't need a diagnostic label to access support if you're struggling with life.

A term's popularity might stem more from TikTok's algorithm than its actual usefulness. The algorithm sends new interpretations to potentially interested users, who then adopt and modify these terms, often unconsciously. As psychiatry incorporates more patient perspectives into diagnostic criteria, understanding this dynamic becomes crucial – especially since patient testimony may be shaped by social media discourse. The situation grows more complex when content creators monetise or gain followers through viral videos. They may promote terms that ultimately serve to boost their content.

However, the risks aside, the question isn't about whether we engage in the social media discussion about mental health and neurodiversity, but that we need to learn how to do so responsibly, so we can maintain scientific rigour and incorporate patients' lived experience, not simply that of those with the most monetisable symptoms.

The debate around ADHD and how to define it has gone on for decades. What the condition consists of, how to diagnose it and how to treat it have always been influenced by conflicting interest groups, as well as research. Today, our understanding of ADHD is different from what it was even ten years ago. But as more people seek diagnosis, and expensive prescriptions, we have a responsibility to ensure that our research into treatment and outcomes keeps up with the ways the diagnostic remit is perhaps changing. A diagnosis is not simply another thing to add to your bio on X or TikTok.

# 7

# THE OPTIMISATION TRAP

Sleep has become a competitive sport. At least that's how Kim Kardashian treats it, sharing screenshots of her Oura Ring sleep scores on Instagram – proudly displaying an impressive 93 out of 100. The post drew an envious reaction from Gwyneth Paltrow, the wellness entrepreneur and Oscar winner, whose modest seven hours and seventeen minutes paled beside Kardashian's superior eight hours and fifteen minutes.[1]

The Oura Ring itself, a minimalist band of metal packed with sensors, had become the latest totem of celebrity wellness culture. Jennifer Aniston wears one on her finger, as do Prince Harry and Will Smith. Gucci, never one to miss a luxury opportunity, released its own limited-edition version emblazoned with interlocking Gs, priced just shy of a thousand dollars – because even sleep tracking can be couture.[2]

Recognising a golden marketing opportunity, Oura Ring's promotional team seized the moment. They expanded the celebrity sleep face-off into a mass participation event, instructing followers on Instagram to tag @ouraring and three sleep-deprived friends. What began as a dispute between A-listers became the '#OuraChallenge', encouraging ordinary users to benchmark their rest against the stars'.

Oura is a smart ring that tracks various bodily metrics like your heart rate, body temperature, blood oxygen and more. The Finnish company that makes it claims it provides daily scores for sleep, readiness and activity, and offers personalised insights and recommendations to help you improve your health and wellness.

Oura is just one example of wearable technology that has thrived through influencer marketing. The rapidly growing wearables market offers an array of smartwatches, bracelets, rings and patches. Tech companies increasingly promise ever more data, with AI posited as the solution for processing this information overload. Their sales pitch promises more insight and mastery over our personal health. And it's not just on social media. This is reflecting a broader trend. The UK government's *Fit for the Future: 10 Year Plan for the NHS*, launched in 2025, promised the use of biosensors in the home, and even the workplace, providing a more constant flow of information. Using AI, people will be able to monitor glucose, the heart, stress and other biomarkers to prevent ill-health and detect early disease. It all sounds remarkably sensible. But as you've possibly seen from other chapters, some caution may be needed.[3]

Already, some estimate that around 35% of adults in the UK use a wearable device,[4] with similar numbers in the US.[5] It's a lucrative market and an expensive investment, with some setting you back by hundreds of pounds, plus monthly subscription fees.

Professor Gina Neff, a sociologist at the University of Cambridge and head of the Minderoo Centre for Technology & Democracy, examines how digital technologies reshape society, focusing on the impact of data, metrics and AI on our work and lives. 'From the Apple Watch to the designer cuff, many self-tracking consumer devices attempt to appeal as luxury goods. They are designed to help relatively wealthy people have more fashionable bodies, flaunt a technology insider's knowledge or show the world a status symbol,' she says.

Wearable devices designed to monitor patients in clinical settings have become a billion-pound wellness market, complete with celebrity endorsements, TikTok routines and daily scores. Apps promise sleep efficiency. Rings measure recovery. Patches track glucose spikes from your morning toast. The body is now a dashboard to be monitored and gamified.

## THE RISE OF THE MEASURED SELF

The desire to measure and improve ourselves has historical roots. Long before modern fitness trackers, the Puritans practised self-examination, and Benjamin Franklin meticulously tracked his progress toward 'moral perfection', logging virtues in a daily ledger. In 2007, the Quantified Self movement took self-measurement to another level. Founded by *Wired* editors Gary Wolf and Kevin Kelly, it championed 'self-knowledge through numbers', attracting tech enthusiasts and athletes alike. Members used wearables to monitor metrics like sleep and heart rate, believing that precise tracking empowered them to make meaningful changes. They built a community to share their tracking experiences. The movement has waned in recent years, but its legacy endures in the popularity of wearable technology and health-focused apps.

Fitness tracking is one of the most popular uses for these devices, helping everyone from beginners dusting off their running shoes for the first time, to amateur cyclists and elite athletes perfecting their training. 'What gets measured gets improved,' says personal trainer and TikTok personality Tim Helton. 'If you're not measuring it, you cannot improve it.' This principle is especially crucial in elite sports, where small improvements can make the difference.

Fitness trackers can provide users with a sense of accomplishment, community and friendly competition, but evidence on their health effects is mixed. A systematic review of nearly 164,000 participants across all ages and health conditions found that activity trackers led to meaningful improvements in physical activity. Users typically added 1,800 daily steps and forty minutes of walking, along with modest fitness improvements and 1 kg of weight loss. However, the devices showed little impact on blood pressure, cholesterol or quality of life, with any benefits plateauing after six months.[6]

The relationship between tracking and lasting health improvements isn't as straightforward as device makers suggest, Dr Lukasz Piwek, a data scientist at the University of Bath, tells me. What works for the elite athlete doesn't necessarily work for the ordinary user trying to increase their activity levels. In research, they call this 'generalisability' – essentially, how well findings from one group apply or set of circumstances applies to another. His research suggests that while fitness trackers often create initial excitement and short-term changes, their long-term impact is less certain.

There's a 'hype' element when you first start using a new technology strapped to your wrist, feeding you data, Piwek tells me. But this novelty can wear off. Device manufacturers claim 'you can't manage what you don't measure', suggesting that simply showing people their health data will automatically lead to behaviour change. But this oversimplifies things somewhat. 'It's like a weighing scale. Just giving someone a scale and asking them to lose weight isn't going to work very well on its own,' Piwek says. Tracking tools can be helpful, but they are only a part of the broader picture. Achieving lasting health improvements typically requires support beyond gathering data. One systematic review of the literature found that while weighing yourself daily can help, it's much more effective when combined with goal-setting. Full weight-loss programmes that include self-weighing have the biggest impact.[7] It's a principle that applies to other health monitoring wearables too.

Even the sceptics aren't immune to the allure of self-tracking. Dr Margaret McCartney, a Scottish GP who holds little truck for poorly evidenced interventions and the medicalisation of life, finds herself caught up in it all. As an avid cyclist, she's developed a love–hate relationship with fitness tracking devices. 'I know before I set them off they're not good for me. I know when I'm charging them up, they're not good for me and yet I do it anyway because I'm completely addicted to them and I hate myself for it,' she tells me with a chuckle.

Rather than embracing the simple joy of cycling and running in the beautiful Scottish countryside, McCartney finds these activities end up turning into data-driven challenges. 'Instead of just enjoying that lovely experience, I make it into this battleground with my stupid apps and wearables,' she says. 'The whole thing becomes a festival of competitive misery, which I know is not good for me.'

Exercise is one thing, but devices once confined to the clinic – pulse oximeters, blood pressure monitors, glucose trackers – have been repackaged and rebranded for the consumer market, promising us better health. They now appear everywhere, from Instagram feeds to glossy magazines, blurring the boundary between medical monitoring and wellness. As one content creator put it to me, 'Whatever metric you want, there's a device out there to track it for you.'

Perhaps it's no bad thing. Over the years, numerous government health campaigns have encouraged healthier eating, increased exercise, reduced alcohol consumption and quitting smoking to prevent ill health. But how much of our health is within our power to change through personal choices, and how much is determined by the wider world in which we live? Our health is shaped by a mix of interconnected factors, creating a tension between personal responsibility and the state's role in tackling broader health influences, such as economic inequality, environmental factors and social circumstances.[8]

While we make personal decisions about diet and exercise, government policies influence our ability to make healthy choices by affecting healthcare access, service quality and basic needs like housing, education and income. Smoking, poor diet, physical inactivity and harmful alcohol use, along with most chronic diseases, all follow a socioeconomic trajectory. The less money you have, the worse your health outcomes.

Beyond the polished ads featuring toned models flaunting Insta-friendly gadgets, Professor Amitava Banerjee's experiences are quite different. As a cardiologist at University College London and a professor of clinical data science, he treats the NHS's sickest heart patients – often from the poorest backgrounds, where health monitoring isn't a lifestyle choice but a medical necessity. Health professionals like Banerjee might put a probe on your finger to check your oxygen levels; or use an ECG to check your heart rhythm; or they may monitor your fluid intake. This careful monitoring takes place in medicalised healthcare settings and may be the result of years of research. Can we have the same confidence when we strap on a wearable device after listening to an enthusiastic influencer?

'Healthy, wealthy people could build an entire intensive care unit at home if they wanted to', Banerjee says, 'but that doesn't mean they should.' He's critical of the narrative driven by some influencers and industry leaders that achieving optimal health demands relentless body monitoring. True health, he contends, isn't about tracking every detail of your physical state. 'Frankly, I'd rather go river rafting,' one US doctor quipped in *The Atlantic* when asked about tracking metrics.[9] Others I've spoken to take a different view. They've told me this approach is old-fashioned and they place great faith in the role of measurements and data.

Banerjee notes that wearables users don't include his Whitechapel patients from deprived London areas. Digital health tools typically reach those who need them least, while high-risk people in poorer areas lack the money or resources for such devices. That's clearly not the case for Steven Bartlett, whose influence has soared alongside his chart-topping podcast, *Diary of a CEO*. Alongside his business ventures, he says that his true passion is maintaining his health. 'Contrary to popular opinion, the most successful people sweat the small stuff, they obsess over the details,' he says. 'Without our health, we have nothing,' he declares in a TikTok video for wearable WHOOP. The product 'allows him to obsess over the details so he can perform at his best', it says.[10] It's one of several wearables he endorses: he advocates all sorts of such devices to manage his health.

## BEFORE YOU STRAP IT ON

But just collecting data does not guarantee improvement. If you can't influence or change what you're measuring, it might not be worth tracking at all. Before strapping on a wearable device, there are some questions worth asking.

- What exactly am I measuring and why does it matter?

- Will changing these numbers actually improve my health, either now or in the future?

- Are the methods I'll use to improve these metrics genuinely good for my overall health?

- Do the potential benefits outweigh any downsides of tracking and trying to change these measurements?

- How accurate and reliable is this device?

- Are the people promoting this product being paid to do so?

Many wearables clearly do bring a benefit for their users, because the metrics are useful, and users can take action on them. They're increasingly used in healthcare to monitor people with certain conditions. But there has long been a temptation in medicine to assume that the more biological parameters we monitor, the better. There are lots of functions you can measure, from external traits like temperature and weight to internal biomarkers found in the blood and tissues. But not everything you can measure can tell you much about your health. Some changes in bodily metrics may mean little, while others are a warning signal for current or future health problems. Understanding which changes matter and why typically takes careful long-term scientific study.

Blood pressure is one example of why some health measurements matter. We have good evidence that high blood pressure leads to serious health problems and, importantly, we have effective ways to treat it. High blood pressure damages blood vessels and organs throughout the body, increasing the risk of heart attacks and strokes. That's why health professionals take this measurement seriously, sometimes asking patients to wear monitors for twenty-four hours to get a better picture.

Evidence collected over decades of research suggests that lifestyle changes such as losing weight or stopping smoking can lower blood pressure. If it stays high, doctors may prescribe different kinds of medicines to reduce it. This is what makes a measurement worthwhile: it serves a meaningful predictor of a health problem, and there is action you can take to change it.

French influencer the Glucose Goddess, real name Jessie Inchauspé, has built a global following sharing graphs. Her book, *The Glucose Revolution*, is an international bestseller, and she's now made the leap to television, hosting a series on Channel 4. Inchauspé is a biochemist and her Instagram feed seems reassuringly scientific. It's full of metrics about blood sugar. Inchauspé warns against the dreaded 'spikes' in glucose, which she says can lead to a host of health problems. She offers lifestyle 'hacks' to keep blood sugar levels stable, an approach that fashion and lifestyle magazines have described as being 'more of a philosophy than a diet.'

Like many influencers, Inchauspé has turned her health advice into a thriving business. Alongside her book, she markets supplements designed to counter the glucose spikes she cautions against. Her content draws heavily on data from continuous glucose monitors (CGMs), which have surged in popularity, with the hashtag CGM amassing billions of views across social media platforms. Inchauspé says:

> This simple device gave me insight into one of my most important biomarkers, and with that data came agency. I could observe what

foods and situations would cause my levels to spike and what protocols lowered levels and evened out naturally occurring ups and downs. We want our blood glucose readings to resemble the rolling hills of Georgia, not the Swiss Alps.[11]

CGMs are small devices that track your blood sugar levels around the clock. They work through a tiny sensor inserted under your skin, usually on your arm or stomach, held in place by a sticky patch. This sensor measures glucose levels in the fluid between your cells, which closely matches blood sugar levels, and sends regular updates to an app on a smartphone. CGMs have become a booming industry with companies offering premium subscriptions, which can cost hundreds of pounds annually, that pair them with personalised advice.

Adding his hefty social media weight behind the need to continuously track glucose is Stanford neuroscientist, Professor Andrew Huberman, one of a cadre of 'science bro' podcasters. Millions tune into his podcast, *The Huberman Lab*, and YouTube channel to find out about his ambitious morning and evening health routines all dressed up in scientific patter.

Predominantly male devotees, who religiously follow his advice, have been dubbed 'Huberman Husbands'. Swathes of long-suffering partners have turned to social media to share their fascination and bewilderment with their husbands' obsession with the Huberman 'optimisation' and 'biohacker' lifestyle. It's quite a toll to place on someone's partner and family – who is doing the dishes and laundry and taking care of the kids when someone goes to bed at 9 p.m. and gets up at half five: 'Not only do I have to live with him my whole life, but I'm also going to live forever,' one bemoaned.[12]

With his academic affiliations, Huberman is credible. As one magazine columnist said, after listening in with her husband: 'Huberman shares scientific data with his listeners, not subjective opinions passed off as the former.' Citing science is persuasive and appears to offer objective, unassailable truth. While Huberman has been sceptical about health tracking devices in the past, he has promoted blood glucose monitoring, claiming it has 'led to permanent shifts in what I eat and when I eat, and in doing so, vast improvements in some critical health metrics.'

When scientists publish research papers, they must disclose conflicts of interest, where external factors like financial gain could compromise their judgement in patient care, research or advice to the public. Such conflicts often stem from financial ties but may also involve career ambitions or other influences. These conflicts aren't just buried in journals; they're ever present on social media too.

Huberman has a sponsorship deal with Levels, a company offering continuous glucose monitoring subscriptions, promoting them on his platform and providing a 'Huberman discount code'. This affiliate marketing strategy benefits both the company and himself financially. Huberman says that he only collaborates with brands whose products he 'personally use[s] and love[s]'. It's a justification that's a familiar refrain in influencer marketing.

He may genuinely use the product. But these financial incentives can still introduce bias, whether intentional or not. Such sponsorships align the influencer's financial interests with the success of the product, potentially raising concerns about the objectivity of the advice.

Ryan Crownholm, an advocate for Prenuvo after his renal-cell carcinoma diagnosis, epitomises the 'Huberman Husband' trend. 'You get some data and then you want more data,' he tells me. 'If I can't put a number on it, it doesn't mean anything to me.'

Ryan embodies Silicon Valley's fixation with health optimisation. His bright, airy California home features both a cold plunge and sauna. He employs a personal concierge doctor and gets his blood tested quarterly. Ryan has tried all manner of health interventions, from hyperbaric oxygen treatment to full-body MRIs in pursuit of peak wellbeing. During the pandemic, he added continuous glucose monitoring to his health tracking repertoire, driven by curiosity and a desire to boost his immune system. 'I wanted to know what's going on inside my body,' he explains.

The device uncovered 'awesome things' about his metabolism, particularly the impact of various foods on his blood sugar. This insight led to tangible changes. He now eats more protein after observing his glucose spikes. 'It was really eye-opening,' he remarks. That all seems sensible. But do changes in glucose fluctuations translate into meaningful improvements in overall health?

## FROM LIFE-SAVING TO LIFESTYLE

For people with diabetes, the short answer is yes. Diabetes is a condition that causes a person's blood sugar or glucose level to become too high or too low, which can cause fatal complications very quickly. People with type 1 diabetes and some people with type 2 diabetes need to use insulin to control their glucose levels. Readings can help to adjust insulin doses and improve control. There is a good body of evidence to understand the long- and short-term effects of glucose levels in diabetes. But a fundamental principle in medicine is that evidence supporting a medical intervention in one population doesn't necessarily translate to benefits in another.

For people without diabetes, the body has a sophisticated system for managing blood sugar. The pancreas produces hormones that adjust glucose levels by releasing or storing sugar to keep it within normal parameters. When you eat, your blood sugar naturally rises. These 'spikes' are a normal part of digestion. In healthy people, the body responds by releasing insulin, bringing glucose levels back down to normal baseline levels usually within about two hours.

We're just learning more about what these spikes mean. For example, in one large 2024 study, researchers tracked blood sugar patterns in over 1,000 people using continuous glucose monitors.[13] They found that even people with healthy blood sugar control regularly experience what might look like concerning spikes on these devices. In fact, they typically spend about three hours each day above what some consider the 'ideal' range.

Dr Peter Attia, with his impressive credentials from Stanford Medical School and degrees in engineering and mathematics, has built a large following by challenging traditional medicine. Through his podcast, *The Drive*, and social media, the Canadian-American physician advocates continuous glucose monitoring in healthy people, suggesting that the 'magnitude of glucose swings is related to health'.[14] He recognises he perhaps takes a heterodox view that clashes with many in the medical establishment and explains his reasons in densely written posts on his website.[15]

Attia's support for Dexcom's glucose monitors began with a chance meeting on a flight with Kevin Sayer, the company CEO. Bonding over watches, they formed a professional connection. Attia then became a vocal advocate for the company's monitors, which he uses and discusses frequently. He even hosted Sayer on his podcast.[16]

'Today's normal individual is tomorrow's diabetic patient if something isn't done to detect and prevent this slide,' Attia warns his audience.[17] This statement sounds logical: since diabetes involves high blood sugar, wouldn't tracking and controlling glucose spikes help prevent the disease? However, it oversimplifies things somewhat. While it's true that type 2 diabetes involves problems with blood sugar regulation, there's no robust scientific evidence that monitoring your readings on a CGM and reducing normal glucose fluctuations prevents the disease. This is in part because the relationship between glucose and type 2 diabetes is complex; sugar does not cause it directly, but you are more likely to get it if you are overweight.[18, 19] This is because the body becomes less sensitive to insulin with increasing weight, though insulin levels may be quite high in those with type 2 diabetes.

Despite their large followings and scientific credentials, influencers promoting glucose monitoring overlook the fact that scientists are still trying to understand what these measurements mean for healthy people. For example, do those natural spikes after meals affect our future health? Should we worry when our glucose rises after eating certain foods? Do different people's varied responses to the same foods matter?

We don't have good answers to these questions yet. There's a lack of evidence that normal blood sugar fluctuations either signal current health problems or predict future ones.[20] Without fully understanding these numbers, tracking them may create a false sense of control. We could begin to view normal blood sugar responses to meals as issues, unnecessarily treating natural processes as problems to fix.

Nonetheless, companies are eager to offer their proposed solutions. Major medical device manufacturers are shifting their focus from the clinical setting to tap into the profitable and growing wellness market. Abbott, the US healthcare giant that makes glucose monitors for people with diabetes, exemplifies this trend. After the Covid-19 testing boon that had brought in tens of billions of dollars, the company's profits had dropped.[21]

In a 2023 earnings call, CEO Robert Ford pointed to the 'revolution ongoing right now between health care and tech'. 'We always believed that we could take this platform [their CGM] that we developed for diabetes and expand it beyond diabetes,' he said. 'There's a much larger population in the world that is actually healthy,' Ford added. 'We're going to continue to solve medical problems, but I think we also need to look at the healthy that want to stay healthy, and develop products and solutions and services for them.'

Expanding access to health technology isn't inherently problematic. But do these devices help or harm our health? Dr Nicola Guess, an Oxford University dietician, uses her Instagram account to challenge misconceptions about glucose monitors. Most of what we 'know' about these devices' benefits for healthy people comes from social media anecdotes rather than scientific research, she tells me.

Companies saying they're scientifically driven are now using wellness influencer tactics, relying on personal transformation stories to market products, often without solid evidence of their effectiveness.

ZOE is one such example. The company offers what it calls a personalised health package: blood analysis, a microbiome test that examines the mix of bacteria in your gut and a period of continuous glucose monitoring. They use these results to create customised nutrition recommendations. The company says this personalised approach can improve energy, reduce hunger, leads to better weight management, less bloating, improved sleep and protection against chronic disease.

ZOE has perfected social media marketing, turning their bright yellow glucose monitoring patches into a status symbol. Across TikTok, Facebook and Instagram, celebrities and influencers speak about it in glowing terms, encouraging followers to join what feels like an exclusive club. The company's rise in profile owes much to endorsements from figures like Steven Bartlett and Davina McCall. Bartlett, who invested £2 million in ZOE,[22] credits it with optimising his diet for peak performance, while McCall says it helped her to live 'her best life'.[23] These celebrity endorsements boosted ZOE's commercial success, even as scientific validation of its benefits was a work in progress.

## WHEN TECH OPTIMISM MEETS MEDICAL CAUTION

Throughout the book, we'll hear more about the differences in the way some tech innovators and medical researchers think about new ideas. In the world of technology and start-ups, and even doctors in some clinics, Carl Heneghan, professor of evidence-based medicine at Oxford University, says many start with the 'alternative hypothesis'. It's the belief that a new product or intervention works and should be rolled out on that assumption. The thinking is get it into people's hands, let it prove its value in real time and adjust only if something goes wrong.

Heneghan compares it to the legal principle of 'innocent until proven guilty'. In this view, the innovation is assumed to be beneficial until there's clear evidence it isn't. It's also deeply embedded in

Silicon Valley's culture of moving fast and breaking things. But in medicine, Heneghan argues, that approach might not just be costly but even harmful.

In healthcare and science, researchers start from the opposite assumption. They start with the null hypothesis. This is the idea that a new intervention doesn't work until it's been rigorously tested and shown to be effective. Until data from rigorous studies can show otherwise, the assumption is that a new treatment has no benefit or could cause harm. It's a 'guilty until proven innocent' stance that prioritises caution and safety. Only after testing do they accept the alternative hypothesis.

In consumer tech, the cost of failure is often measured in inconvenience or money. In medicine, the cost can be measured in lives. Unproven interventions may not just be ineffective: they can cause serious harm. That's why, Heneghan insists, when it comes to health, the belief in something working isn't enough. Robust evidence should guide what we use or recommend.

ZOE, named after the Greek word for life, positions itself as a 'science-first' company under the leadership of Tim Spector, a professor of genetic epidemiology at King's College London. Its website is filled with links to studies in esteemed journals like the *Lancet* and *Nature Medicine*. Other science influencers do this too but these acts of transparency can seem rather performative. Not all of the studies such influencers cite are accessible without expensive journal subscriptions or university access.

This creates what some call an 'information asymmetry' – a situation where the provider knows far more than the consumer.[24] The imbalance in knowledge can be exploited by healthcare providers, potentially leading consumers to spend money on health products and services they may not actually need.[25] It's a marketing tactic that genuflects to scientific authority while keeping the actual evidence behind a paywall.

One other issue is that several of the studies ZOE references are observational. These highlight associations, but they are not designed to establish a cause and effect. Spector has highlighted the problems in relying on observational studies in isolation, without also conducting short-term human trials, in the *BMJ* – which to be fair the company has gone on to do.[26]

Spector is what academic Rachel O'Neill, based in the department of media and communication at the London School of Economics, calls a 'wellness medical influencer', essentially a new breed of doctor reshaping how medical expertise appears on social media. With his greying hair and impressive academic credentials, he may not fit the typical influencer mould, yet he has seamlessly made the leap from traditional medical authority to wellness advocate. Along the way, he has gained hundreds of thousands of followers, appeared on television (similar to Inchauspé) and launched a range of ZOE-branded 'health food' products.

'They often use the established playbook of conventional wellness influencers to gain visibility but add the weight of their credentials to the messaging,' O'Neill tells me, having studied the rise of this phenomena. Spector's story, like that of many wellness influencers, begins with a personal crisis, she says. A health scare while skiing in the Alps was the origin story that led to his 'personal odyssey'. Prescribed a course of aspirin and blood pressure medication, his sense of self was undermined. 'I had gone from a sporty, fitter-than-average middle-aged man to what felt like a pill-popping, hypertensive, depressed stroke victim,' he has said. He then discovered 'the truth about food'.[27]

This narrative arc – crisis, revelation, transformation – mirrors the classic wellness influencer playbook and is similar to that of Ella Mills, daughter of politician Shaun Woodward and Camilla Sainsbury. Mills launched the blog Deliciously Ella, where she documented her journey of learning to cook plant-based meals so as to manage her health conditions, including postural tachycardia syndrome, Ehlers-Danlos syndrome and mast cell activation disorder.[28] Her blog quickly grew in popularity, amassing over 100 million hits in its early years. Now Deliciously Ella products are readily available in supermarkets, with a product sold every second.[29]

But Spector can count on something even more potent than personal testimony. He has a compelling story backed up by medical authority. He highlights his credentials, prominently listing 'MD' and 'FRCP' (Fellow of the Royal College of Physicians) on his Instagram profile, while also challenging mainstream medicine, criticising doctors as 'ignorant' and 'out of touch' when it comes to nutrition.

Where a typical wellness influencer might say 'conventional medicine failed me', a doctor-influencer can say, 'Trust me, I know what's wrong with conventional medicine – I'm part of the system.' This positions him as both insider and outsider, profiting from his credentials while simultaneously challenging the medical establishment. Spector is far from alone in doing this.[30]

One critic told me the glucose fad is just the latest iteration of Big Diet – or Big Nutrition. It's a classic playbook. XYZ doesn't work; the experts are wrong; read my book and find out the truth. The next step is to then buy my product, which will FINALLY fix everything.

This poses a challenge for those who see doctor-influencers as a purely positive development. In the wake of the pandemic, many welcomed these medically qualified voices online, seeing them as a digital safeguard against dubious health claims. However, Spector's navigation between evidence-based medicine and wellness influence raises questions about the evolving nature of medical authority in the Instagram era.

Some influential doctor-influencers have argued that it's a 'grey area' and that there's nothing inherently 'bad' or 'wrong' if medfluencers monetise their platform. While they may lean on authority bias, there are countless others without credentials providing outright bad information. On the whole, they tend to do good, particularly when it comes to highlighting problems with food policy and nutritional awareness.

## THE FINE LINE BETWEEN EDUCATION AND MARKETING

At what point does education blur into marketing? With Spector promoting his own product line, this question becomes especially relevant. It's a long-standing issue within medicine, where drug and medical device companies have played a role in shaping professional training, after doctors are qualified and practising. In the UK, the doctors' regulator, the General Medical Council (GMC), says doctors 'must remain competent and up to date in all areas' of their professional practice. This will involve spending time doing what's known as continuing professional development (CPD).[31]

This can take different forms: events and seminars facilitated by universities, medical societies or the Royal Colleges can count towards it. But the costs aren't always borne by these institutions. Some accept industry sponsorship, a welcome reprieve for their budgets. Yet hidden within this convenience is the quiet power of sponsorship.[32] Some commentators argue that industry-sponsored medical education tends to favour the sponsor's medications over alternatives, directly affecting prescription patterns.[33] In one study, doctors who participated in a drug maker's educational programme doubled their prescriptions for that company's medications – a shift in clinical behaviour traced directly to industry-sponsored learning.[34]

The most notorious example of this was the enthusiastic promotion of opioids. Between 1996 and 2001, sales of OxyContin by Purdue Pharma grew from $48 million to $1.1 billion.[35] In that same time period, Purdue hosted more than forty pain management and speaker training symposia, attracting 5,000 attendees, all expenses paid. It didn't stop there. Purdue also provided funding to more than 20,000 pain-related educational programmes.[36]

Medical wellness influencers are clearly not peddling highly addictive controlled drugs in the style of Purdue Pharma. But they do need to get their message across. To stand out in the deluge of content, they may feel compelled to use attention-grabbing tactics – even when they know these approaches might oversimplify complex medical topics. The core difficulty for healthcare communicators is that nuanced, balanced information rarely achieves the engagement needed to reach mass audiences on today's algorithm-driven platforms.

Spector and his team at ZOE are clearly conscious of the risk of being seen as product promoters rather than health professionals dispensing evidence-based health advice. To their credit, they conducted a randomised controlled trial, published in *Nature Medicine* in 2024. They told customers that: 'Compared with the control group, ZOE members saw greater improvements in a range of health measures. For instance, they had increases in "good" gut bacteria linked to better health outcomes. They also reported feeling less hungry, sleeping better, and having more energy.'[37]

However, flaws in the study's design undermine the strength of its conclusions, highlighting that not all trials are created equal. In the eighteen-week trial, 347 participants either received ZOE's personalised nutrition plan or got standard US dietary advice via a leaflet, video and weekly generic emails. But this set-up created several problems.[38]

First, the big difference between the groups' experiences makes it impossible to tell what caused the reported improvements. We couldn't say for sure that it was ZOE's specific algorithm that suggests specific foods that led to changes. The ZOE group received extensive attention and monitoring, while the control group got basic materials. Research shows that increased attention alone can heavily influence outcomes in dietary studies. This is known as the Hawthorne effect, where people alter their behaviour simply because they're being observed.

A more robust test would have ensured both groups received equal monitoring and attention. Both should undergo blood tests and stool analysis, believing they were getting personalised advice, while only one group would receive ZOE's algorithm-based recommendations.

The study may have been affected by expectation bias. When participants believe they are receiving a ground-breaking treatment rather than standard guidance, they tend to put in more effort and anticipate better outcomes, which can influence the results. This means we don't know if it was ZOE's specific algorithm and measurement of all the metrics that made the difference or something else.

Finally, there's the issue of independence. The trial was funded by ZOE, and every author had financial connections to the company – as founders, consultants, employees, option holders or scientific board members. While industry-funded research is not inherently flawed, this study seemed focused on highlighting ZOE's benefits, not rigorously evaluating whether personalised nutrition advice outperforms standard recommendations.

Sarah Berry, chief scientist at ZOE, says they were testing to see if the 'entire ZOE program experience works compared with standard care'. Highly adherent participants had a significant improvement in 'hard' metrics, such as cholesterol, blood pressure and weight.[39] Publicly funded research has played a role here, or at least in the past. At the National Institutes of Health (NIH) near Washington DC, Dr Holly Nicastro has been tackling a question that fascinates wellness influencers and tech entrepreneurs: can nutrition advice truly be personalised?

## SLOW SCIENCE IN A QUICK-FIX WORLD

Unlike the quick fixes of some gurus and start-ups, Nicastro's $170 million study, launched in 2022, takes a methodical approach to explore how factors like genetics, gut microbes and environmental factors shape individual responses to food. While free from commercial pressures, this research faces its own hurdles, including proposed 2025 budget cuts under President Trump, which threaten its progress.[40]

Known for his important work on ultra-processed food, one of the lead nutrition and metabolism scientists at the NIH, Dr Kevin Hall, is retiring early aged fifty-four. In an interview with the *New York Times*, he'd hoped his work 'might accelerate' under RFK Jr, who has said one his priorities was to improve the nation's diet.[41] Instead, Hall alleges he'd 'experienced what amounts to censorship and controlling of the reporting' of his science

In February 2025, Hall alleged that NIH officials told him that he would have to modify a section about 'health equity' in a scientific review on ultra-processed foods that he had written with other scientists. The paper suggested that some people in the US don't have access to healthy food, a point which may not have chimed with President Trump's views on diversity, equity and inclusion. Hall took his name off the paper. He'd never had to do that before as a government scientist. Hall said he was worried that, if he stayed, officials might also interfere with his studies. An NIH spokesperson told the *New York Times* that they were 'committed to promoting gold-standard research and advancing public health priorities'.

I spoke to Hall before this happened. Hall has conducted experiments at the NIH Clinical Center in Maryland. In this 'scientific monastery', participants spend a month living under strict conditions, consuming precisely measured meals and following a carefully structured exercise regimen. His team isolates individual factors by altering just one variable at a time – such as meal timing – while keeping exercise, sleep, and food content constant. This provides insights into how each factor impacts blood glucose levels, free from the noise of multiple simultaneous changes. Their controlled experiments have shown that blood sugar responses are shaped not only by what you eat but also by factors like prior meals, exercise, stress and sleep.

In one study, Hall's team found inconsistencies when testing different glucose monitors under tightly controlled conditions. Publishing their findings with the title 'Imprecision nutrition?' – an overt dig at the 'precision medicine' genre – they found that two devices on the same person often showed different readings for the same meal, one indicating a spike, the other showing normal levels.[42]

When participants ate the exact same meal in different weeks, their glucose responses varied as much as if they'd eaten completely different foods. 'A banana might trigger very different readings from one week to the next', Hall explains, 'even when we controlled for other variables like exercise and other meals.'

These findings cast doubt on the reliability of these devices for precise dietary decisions. The only consistent result mirrored what scientists have known for decades: reducing carbohydrate intake leads to lower glucose readings. 'There are hundreds of books about low-carb diets already,' Hall says.

Even if we can alter our glucose metrics, does it truly impact our health? Long-term, detailed studies, across multiple populations, are required to find an answer. You might say, 'I know I'm experiencing a sugar crash because I feel it. I lose energy or feel tired.' That's what Steven Bartlett says happens to him. He says he's noticed a *correlation* between what he's eaten, his blood glucose levels and how he's feeling. The last thing he wants to do is have his 'blood glucose crash' in the middle of a podcast recording.

So what do we really know about these subjective measures of symptoms, such as energy levels and feeling a lethargic 'crash'? It's easy to assume the cause of our symptoms. For instance, a friend feeling awful after exercising on an empty stomach might blame it on not eating. However, other factors could be at play, such as a stressful commute, dehydration, a hotter workout space or poor sleep. Without a 'counterfactual' – an identical scenario where the only difference is eating beforehand – we can't pinpoint the exact cause.

Throughout his years of research Hall found the more data people have about their bodies, the more likely they are to make these cause-and-effect assumptions. In his studies, participants sometimes had low blood sugar but felt fine, while at other times they felt awful with normal readings. Our subjective feelings of energy crashes or lethargy perhaps might not correlate with glucose levels as neatly as we think.

This highlights a broader issue with self-tracking. Having more measurements doesn't necessarily mean we understand our bodies better. We might actually be creating connections that aren't really there. Dr Shivani Misra, a consultant in metabolic medicine at Imperial College London, sees this in her NHS clinic. When researching continuous glucose monitors, she has noticed how people often blame their symptoms on blood sugar levels, even when the numbers don't show it. Many report feeling signs of low blood sugar, yet their readings are completely normal.

'It's human nature, when you're monitoring something you become hyper-vigilant about that,' she explains. People wearing glucose monitors tend to attribute every feeling to their blood sugar, such as stress, mood changes or energy dips. This hyper-awareness can lead them to see glucose connections everywhere, even when other factors might better explain how they're feeling.

One of the biggest risks of wearable devices is the tendency to fixate on a single metric, losing sight of the bigger picture of our health. Constantly tracking glucose levels or any other data can lead to an obsession with real-time fluctuations. We may then modify our behaviour, even when those changes might not matter or even be harmful for our overall wellbeing. We risk missing the forest for one very closely monitored tree.

Obsessing over glucose levels can lead to unhealthy eating habits, Guess suggests. Some of her patients have avoided nutritious foods like fruits, milk and nuts just to keep their smartphone screens showing steady, flat glucose lines. They may have fallen into what might be called the optimisation trap. In their attempt to perfect one biological metric, they've eliminated foods that are associated with reduced blood pressure and improved cardiovascular health.

Guess recognises that some people genuinely enjoy monitoring their health – tracking sleep, food, exercise or glucose – and this isn't inherently an issue. However, problems arise when people make dietary and lifestyle changes based on data they can't interpret clearly, because the evidence isn't there. By trying to stay healthy, they may inadvertently turn themselves into patients seeking medical care.

In her clinic, she has encountered people who became depressed after unnecessarily restricting their diets. Some even distanced themselves from family mealtimes, avoiding the temptation of shared foods. Doctors have been expressing concern on social media about the surge of otherwise healthy patients scheduling appointments for diabetes testing due to worries over readings from their wearable devices. Health professionals have also told me about patients opting for burgers over oranges, as the fruit raises glucose levels while the fatty burger doesn't register a 'spike'.

We don't yet know the full impact of these devices and the changes they foster in our behaviour. In order to market wearable devices for wellness purposes, no one has to demonstrate that they lead to measurable improvements in overall health. Put bluntly, we don't yet know if the rolling hills of Georgia might be quite the desirable destination the Glucose Goddess suggests.

For the sake of argument, let's make some assumptions about these devices. Let's suppose that every metric they track carries genuine significance, that the data they generate guides us toward better health decisions, and that their use leads to meaningful lifestyle improvements. But who's tracking the trackers? Are they accurate?

## ARE THE TRACKERS ACCURATE?

Over a period of ten years, I have broken multiple global stories exposing the shortcomings in the regulation of devices in clinical medicine, including those that are inserted directly into your body, such as pacemakers, hip implants and spinal rods. But there's even less oversight from government regulators, such as the MHRA in the UK and the FDA in the US, when it comes to devices used in the wellness space.

Rob ter Horst, a scientist turned YouTuber, has concerns. 'The algorithms – the computer programs that interpret our biometric data – are very much a black box,' he explains. His unease with the lack of regulation and potential inaccuracies has driven him personally to test over eighty wearables, sharing his findings with his quarter of a million YouTube subscribers.

Ter Horst evaluates consumer devices by comparing them to 'gold-standard' medical-grade equipment, typically used in clinical research. He follows a carefully choreographed routine designed to eliminate variables that might compromise his results.

For heart rate monitoring evaluation, for instance, he cycles for four-minute intervals over thirty minutes, with carefully timed rest periods. His experiments have shown inaccuracies in different wearables, casting doubt on the reliability of the data that consumers rely on for their health decisions.

Naturally, ter Horst's testing of these devices appears scientifically rigorous but has methodological constraints. His insights, while valuable, are just one data point. Bigger datasets are needed to make definitive claims about device reliability. However, ter Horst's concerns about wearable technology echo those of the scientific community, with some researchers describing the market as the 'Wild West'.

One class of wearable device that has come in for scrutiny is that beloved by celebrities and CEOs alike – sleep trackers. Chicago-based Alyssa Brown, whom we met as she pursued an ADHD diagnosis, tells me she's a fan of wearables and regularly publicly dissects her sleep data. Her insomnia is 'a problem with a capital P', she says. She's transformed her sleep patterns into TikTok content, complete with before-and-after visualisations of her prescribed sleep medication's effects.

I asked her why she does it. 'A lot of people struggle with sleep,' she tells me and she's spoken to people who have approached the issue in different ways. Her bedroom has become a laboratory of sorts, filled with an arsenal of sleep aids – specialised pillows, whirring fans and an array of devices that promise salvation from sleeplessness.

'I wish I could get to sleep faster because I lay there for hours staring at the ceiling just wishing I was unconscious. Can anyone help me?' she asks TikTok followers. In one post, Alyssa contrasts her sleep metrics with those of her fiancé. His data suggest efficient sleep. He went to bed after midnight and woke up at just after seven in the morning. That wasn't the case for her. 'I was in bed two extra hours more than him,' she reports, breaking down the architecture of their respective nights' sleep. 'I got an hour and half worth of REM and an hour and ten of deep sleep... even though he goes to bed later than I am, he is getting higher quality sleep,' she says with sigh.

Trackers use a variety of measurements to tell us about our slumber habits, but they don't measure sleep directly. They track proxy measurements to make educated guesses about our sleep patterns. This might include periods of stillness, movement patterns and lifestyle factors like caffeine or alcohol consumption. Some also track other physiological parameters, such as heart rate, skin temperature and respiratory patterns.

But these don't tell you what's going on in your brain. The gold standard for measuring sleep is a polysomnogram, a specialised electroencephalogram (EEG) that monitors brain waves directly. Data from these show the sleep stages we cycle through during the night.

Neuroscientists at West Virginia University (WVU) assessed consumer sleep trackers, comparing nine devices to medical-grade EEG equipment. Analysing data from five healthy adults over ninety-eight nights, they found Fitbit and Oura devices were most accurate for total sleep duration, time awake and sleep efficiency. However, none of them 'appeared to accurately quantify sleep stages' and nor should be they used in sleep research for these purposes, the authors said.[43]

A 2024 editorial in *Sleep*, by Stanford professor Jamie M. Zeitner put it more boldly:

With increases in the amount of data being collected and the number of physiological signals being recorded with high fidelity, as well as fancier machine learning algorithms being applied to these data, one might imagine that determining sleep and wake with a wrist wearable has improved substantively in the past forty years. One holding such a notion, however, would be sorely disappointed... while improvements have been made, the gains in accurate detection of sleep and wake are closer to marginal than magical.[44]

Dr Matthew Reid, who researches sleep medicine at Johns Hopkins University in Baltimore, Maryland, has dedicated years to examining sleep trackers and their outputs. He's concerned about their potential impact on people struggling with insomnia. We've seen how companies and influencers weaponised the fear of cancer to promote unnecessary full-body MRIs. In the case of sleep, Reid tells me, an industry has grown out of scaring people into getting better sleep.

Despite social media's obsession with granular sleep metrics – REM cycles, deep sleep percentages and slow-wave patterns – Reid cautions against overinterpreting these data: 'We don't really know how day-to-day fluctuations in these sleep stages affect you.' We know about the effects of complete sleep deprivation or the selective elimination of specific sleep stages. However, Reid says that these sleep stages are naturally self-regulating processes controlled by the body.

If you get more slow-wave sleep one night, you might get less the following night but that doesn't mean you've had a bad night's sleep. People are putting too much emphasis on physiological sleep quality without there really being a good scientific understanding of what it means, or what it means to have good sleep quality, he tells me.

Once again, marketing fervour has outpaced scientific understanding. In clinical practice, the sleep tracker metrics play virtually no role in diagnosis. 'It's all about subjective sleep; how you feel,' Reid explains. Sleep specialists focus on human factors, such as morning fatigue levels, perceived sleep duration and daytime impact. 'An essential criterion for pretty much any sleep disorder is that it has to affect you during the day,' Reid says. 'You can have the worst fragmented terrible sleep, but if it doesn't affect you on a daily basis you don't meet the criteria for insomnia disorder.' You might have a 'perfect' sleep score but wake up feeling unrested, or have terrible metrics after a night that felt restorative. Your subjective experience matters more than any algorithm's assessment.

According to Reid, strapping on a sleep tracker might be the worst possible intervention for someone with insomnia. They risk amplifying the anxieties that contribute to sleepless nights. 'One of the most important parts of treating insomnia is addressing somebody's dysfunctional beliefs about sleep. If you never do that, they will never get better, because that's the thing that generates insomnia: they're worried about sleep,' he says.

'Orthosomnia,' though not classified as a medical disorder, has been coined as a term that reflects on data-driven wellness culture – a fixation on achieving perfect sleep. In a series of case reports, some clinicians suggested that that sleep trackers contributed to harmful behaviours, such as excessive time in bed or rigidly managing night-time routines to optimise sleep metrics in certain patients.[45] But again, there's a lack of robust data about their downstream effects.

Much like the obsession with glucose monitor readings, constant tracking of sleep data may turn healthy awareness into an unhealthy pursuit of numerical perfection. One doctor said that she's seen patients who lie awake anxiously checking their sleep scores, creating a feedback loop where worry about sleep metrics prevents actual sleep. A patient described checking her app multiple times nightly, then spending the next day analysing why her deep sleep percentage was only 18% instead of the recommended 20%. During her battles with insomnia, Alyssa has brought her sleep tracker data to medical appointments, hoping to 'speak the same language' as her doctor. The metrics, she believes, help validate her subjective experience. But Alyssa acknowledges the limitations. While her doctor finds the data 'curious and interesting', she notes that they don't consider it reliable enough for diagnosis. 'It's just an additional data point at the moment,' she concedes.

Some doctors are uneasy about patients bringing wearable data. NHS clinicians I've spoken to question both how to address such metrics and whether they should interpret them at all. 'We're not wellness gurus,' one told me. Beyond the practical challenges, they worry about the impact of the creeping medicalisation of everyday life. 'Where does it all end?' another asked.

But one particular podcast host's use of sleep trackers further reveals the complex ties between health companies and medical influencers on social media. There's been an evolution in Attia's stance on wearables. While he once dismissed the 'vast majority' of such devices as useless, he's made a notable exception for Oura – a company he joined as an investor and advisor in 2018 (a relationship he acknowledges in his posts). 'Sleep quality matters,' he tells his followers, encouraging them to 'act on the accurate data' provided by the Oura Ring.

Now, though, it looks like the relationship between Oura and Attia has turned sour. In 2023, he sued Oura claiming that it owes him $1.3 million in unallocated stock options.[46] This is not a run-of-the-mill lawsuit to collect on an overdue bill. It reveals the blueprint for the relationships between medical companies and medical influencers. And it offers us a rare peek into the money that moves around behind the scenes, affecting the way health information is communicated, YouTube investigative journalist Scott Carney says.

Documents from the lawsuit outline the payments Attia was set to receive, how he followed Oura's guidance to secure mainstream media coverage, and the efforts he made to position the fitness tracker in scientific studies for marketing purposes. These are the types of details that large companies and public figures had hoped to keep private but are now becoming part of the public record, despite the existence of non-disclosure agreements.

The podcast host's connection with Oura went beyond endorsement. The filings show he offered technical advice and leveraged his large social media presence, all while holding prominent roles such as an editorial board position on the journal *Aging*. The partnership began in December 2016, when Harpreet Singh Rai, then-president of Oura, spotted Attia's value. As a medical expert with a widely followed podcast and substantial social media influence, he brought credibility. Strengthening his profile further, he was listed among the top thirty most influential figures in public health.

'Dr Attia is very well connected, not just in medicine, but with all type of influencers as well,' Rai noted to Oura's leadership. He could provide awareness in the US market through social media to hundreds of thousands of people specifically interested in products of this nature and also introduce the company to potential high-profile influencers, partners, or investors interested in wearable technology.

This came to pass. As detailed in legal documents, Attia's advisory agreement included creating content, introducing the company to potential investors and partners and helping to 'prove certain use cases of Oura' through peer-reviewed studies. At that time there was no clear market leader in the fitness tracking space. It could have turned into a winner-takes-all situation, where the recommendations of influencers in the medical field really mattered, Carney says. The compensation structure for all this included stock options worth a substantial sum – options which now form the basis of a $1.3 million lawsuit against the company.

The partnership proved profitable for Oura. Court records show that Attia's promotion of the rings through his newsletter, using a discount code vetted by Oura's brand and marketing teams, led to the sale of over a thousand devices. He frequently showcased the product in his popular newsletter and on social media, consistently disclosing his advisory role and investment in the company. Court documents also reveal that the launch of the second-generation

Oura Ring boosted sales, driven largely by social media endorsements from prominent influencers, including Attia.

Dr Rohin Francis is an NHS cardiologist and YouTuber who has watched the rise of people like Attia. 'If you are making your reputation by being some kind of health authority, some kind of reputable credentialled authority figure, but you are taking money from a company in the exact space where you are making your content and giving advice about products or interventions, then that is an absolute, direct financial conflict of interest,' he tells me.

The web of commercial relationships between tech companies and influential voices in medicine adds another layer of complexity to an already confusing landscape. Which metrics matter? What constitutes 'normal'? When does measurement become excessive?

Some take great comfort in seeing their data, feeling more in control, reassured and encouraged. But while this is sold as empowerment, data may fuel anxiety, obsession and over-medicalisation. The wellness market exploits medical language and authority, repackaging tools meant for patients with chronic disease for the healthy and wealthy. Influencers, including doctors, blur the line between education and promotion, and sometimes have financial ties to the products they endorse. In certain instances, marketing has outpaced science, with companies pushing devices to healthy consumers based on shaky evidence and anecdote.

The result is a new health paradigm. It's hyper-personal, algorithmically guided and sometimes self-defeating – tracking for tracking's sake. The language is clinical. The branding is sleek. But it's not always obvious we're getting any healthier.

# 8

# WHO'S REALLY EMPOWERED?

In 2016, a routine Facebook comment by Dr Chelsea Polis would turn out to be life-changing. The algorithms had tuned in to her work as a reproductive health researcher, turning her feeds into a stream of fertility and reproductive health content. One day, while mindlessly scrolling through her feed, she noticed several influencers enthusiastically endorsing Daysy, a fertility tracker by Swiss company Valley Electronics. It was being marketed as a groundbreaking tool for understanding the reproductive cycle.

Daysy is a thermometer that purports to help women identify the time of the menstrual cycle when a woman is most likely to ovulate and so conceive. It's called the fertile window. Users measure their basal or resting temperature with the thermometer, which tracks natural fluctuations during the menstrual cycle. By combining these readings with menstrual data, Daysy claims to identify ovulation and fertile windows, using a simple colour-coded system: green for non-fertile days and red for fertile ones.

But Polis soon found herself fearing for her career. She had come across a Valley Electronics social media post about the impact of contraception on women's lives, which was based on the company's own survey. As an expert in reproductive health research methodology, she was alarmed by what she viewed as scientifically flawed interpretations of the data.

The company had used dubious survey methods. They hadn't clarified participant selection, yet made broad claims about women's contraception experiences. Their conclusions included the assertion that natural birth control was key to enhancing romantic relationships.

Polis, then a senior scientist at the Guttmacher Institute, a non-profit sexual and reproductive health research organisation based in New York, posted a comment underneath Daysy's Facebook post. '"Statistics" from "surveys" that are not accompanied by a clear presentation of the survey methodology are uninterpretable. We do not know who was included in the survey or how they were recruited for participation, although this will strongly impact results,' she wrote. She added:

> If I did a survey on attitudes towards race in the United States, surveying a KKK group would produce different results from surveying a Black Lives Matter group. It should be clearly explained who was surveyed; what methodology was used; how many individuals were surveyed; who the results are intended to generalize to; what the error bounds are, etc. – otherwise the numbers presented are useless.

Her comment was removed soon after posting. When she contacted the company for an explanation, they acknowledged that her feedback was 'absolutely correct' but stated that 'by default, anything we post is intended to promote the use and sales of our fertility monitors'.

Valley Electronics' social media activity piqued Polis's researcher instincts. Her unease grew as she monitored their posts more closely. Their marketing claims about Daysy went beyond the science, all while leveraging social media's reach to promote their tracker.

As she looked into the issue further, she realised there was a trend happening in reproductive health: women, disheartened by doctors dismissing their concerns about contraception and fertility, sought answers on social media. And, as we've heard in earlier chapters, it's a place some young women – in other words, the most frequent users of contraception – say they turn to for information. The platforms provide them with emotional support and practical guidance, drawing on the first-hand experiences of others.

US-based doctor and content creator Dr Danielle Jones, with millions of followers across TikTok, Instagram and YouTube, initially used social media to listen to patients' stories.[1] She noticed that patients felt dismissed when sharing gynaecological concerns with their doctors, and this showed just how many women had unanswered questions and uncertainties about their health. 'More and more we're seeing that people go to [their doctor] to talk about women's health or gynaecology problems and that they're ignored or no one is listening to them,' she said. 'It's not popular to say that, but people are telling us that they're not being heard and we have to listen to that.'

There's a body of health literature that suggests building trust in healthcare requires genuine two-way communication.[2] This is more than doctors just providing information. True communication requires understanding where patients get their health information and how personal experiences shape their decisions. This is what some influencers have mastered. They excel at creating connections through shared experiences and cultural understanding. When health professionals fail to listen or acknowledge people's experiences so they feel 'unheard' or 'unseen', patients often turn elsewhere for information and that can be to unreliable sources.

A 2024 survey by Brook, a UK sexual health charity, showed that this frustration is widespread among young people between the ages of 16–24.[3] Of the 2,700 mainly female respondents, recruited via social media at Brook clinics and partner organisations, over half shared negative experiences with healthcare professionals regarding contraception. Complaints included feeling rushed during appointments, receiving insufficient or inaccurate information and having their autonomy compromised in contraceptive decisions.

Brook's survey suggested that social media fills an information gap for young people exploring contraceptive options. Many respondents valued platforms like TikTok and Instagram for offering insights into birth control and the difficulties of accessing sexual health services. While they appreciated first-hand accounts, they acknowledged that social media content could lack accuracy and balance.

Lisa Hallgarten is head of policy and public affairs at Brook. 'Young people are trying to triangulate information from sources that they know are reliable, with anecdotal information from influencers and other online sources that resonates with them even though they know it may not be accurate,' she tells me. With questionable claims circulating through these networks, social media's promise of empowerment can potentially lead people down precarious paths.

## OLD METHODS, NEW DEVICES

One of these is the use of certain digital technologies. By relying on temperature changes and menstrual cycle start dates, Daysy is what is known by those working in the sexual health space as a 'fertility awareness-based method' (or FABM). The underlying concept behind Daysy isn't entirely revolutionary. Women have used fertility awareness-based methods for generations to either get pregnant or avoid it by monitoring various biological markers of fertility. Some track menstrual cycles, while others observe basal body temperature, cervical fluid changes or a combination of these. Each FABM has its own specific way of interpreting these biological markers to predict fertile windows.

The rhythm method, a widely known FABM, estimates fertile windows by analysing the start dates and lengths of a woman's last six cycles. Couples avoid pregnancy during these periods by abstaining or using barrier methods like condoms. FABMs typically predict more fertile days than the actual biological six- to nine-day window because pinpointing the start and end of fertility isn't an exact science.

Daysy is part of a growing fertility tracking tech industry rooted in FABM principles. Various apps and devices, including wearable watches, bracelets and rings like Oura, monitor changes in basal body temperature aiming to forecast menstrual cycles, ovulation dates and fertile windows. On Facebook and Reddit, large communities focus on contraception, including FABMs. Users share readings from fertility monitors posting charts and seeking help interpreting their data. These products are what has been dubbed 'Femtech', a term coined in 2016 by Danish internet entrepreneur, Ida Tin, co-founder of period tracking app Clue.[4]

Tin had spotted a gap in the market: health technology designed for women. The launch of the iPhone, together with wearables, meant there was an opportunity to give women a 'powerful insight into their bodies' by collecting their own cycle data.[5] This industry is projected to hit $100 billion by 2030 and includes cycle apps, menopause platforms and AI-driven diagnostics.[6] The tools are often marketed as empowering women.

The pandemic fuelled rapid growth in digital health solutions as Covid-19 restricted access to routine care.[7] With traditional women's healthcare becoming harder to access, tech-based alternatives gained momentum and filled the gap. The neglect of women's health and family planning research sparked something in Tin. She saw technology as a solution to these unmet needs, addressing gaps left by traditional healthcare.

As one UK consultancy put it: 'Femtech takes a stand against poor healthcare for women – giving women the access to apps, platforms and other resources to look after and monitor their own health. But it's also a great opportunity financially, with women representing 49.58% of the world population.'[8] This statistic brings home the frustration over the lack of investment in women's health globally.

Dr Rebecca Mawson is a GP, researcher and lecturer in women's health at the University of Sheffield. 'One of the big problems is that we've been stuck in the dark ages when it comes to gynaecology and gynaecological research, because it's been so underfunded,' she tells me. The statistics paint the picture. According to one online anonymous government survey of women over sixteen, one-third of British women 'had experienced severe reproductive health symptoms'.[9] Reproductive health – including contraception, menopause and gynaecological conditions – receives only around 2% of UK public health research funding.[10]

A 2025 analysis by the *Guardian* found that, of all the clinical trials submitted to the MHRA between 2019 and 2023, 'male-only trials (6.1%) were nearly twice as common as female-only studies (3.7%)'.[11] Indeed, reproductive and childbirth trials made up only 2.2% of the total. Professor Andrea Manfrin, the MHRA's deputy director of clinical investigations and trials, told the *Guardian*: 'When specific groups are not adequately represented in trials, it creates evidence gaps about how medicines work for them.'

Polis says it goes beyond research funding. Historically, women have often been excluded from studies altogether. In the US, the National Institutes of Health, a leading public research organisation, did not mandate the inclusion of women in clinical trials until 1993.[12] This exclusion was partly justified by the perception that women's fluctuating hormones made their bodies too complex to study.

Yet men and women may experience diseases differently.[13] Some conditions hit women harder – for example, women who smoke are more likely to get lung cancer than men who smoke the same amount.[14] Women can also show different symptoms for the same disease, such as heart problems, and their bodies may react differently to medications.[15] These differences mean that medical research and treatment need to account for sex-specific factors, rather than treating men and women as medically identical.

In contraception, different ideologies and powerful trends have emerged on social media. Two big movements show just how messy things can get. A wave of women sharing their experiences of quitting hormonal contraception swept across social media, giving rise to the #offthepill movement. Researchers have labelled this phenomenon either 'hormonophobia' or, more sympathetically, 'hormone hesitancy', reflecting a growing wariness of synthetic hormones. Femtech has seized this opportunity, with influencers promoting fertility wearables as modern, 'natural' alternatives to hormonal contraception, positioning them as digital-age solutions to counter 'big pharma.'

At the same time, the #deletetheapp movement gained traction as a reaction to America's changing abortion laws. With the erosion of reproductive rights, fears rose over the sensitive data fertility apps gather – detailed menstrual and reproductive health records that, in the wrong hands, could act as evidence instead of empowerment.

*Roe v Wade*, a landmark 1973 Supreme Court decision, established a constitutional right to abortion in the United States. The case started when Norma McCorvey, under the pseudonym 'Jane Roe', contested Texas laws that prohibited abortion except to save a woman's life. In a 7–2 ruling, the court held that the constitutional right to privacy included a woman's choice to terminate her pregnancy, while states could regulate access to abortions in the second and third trimester. For nearly fifty years, the *Roe v Wade* judgment upheld abortion rights in the US. However, in 2022, the Supreme Court overturned it in *Dobbs v Jackson Women's Health Organization*, stating that abortion could not be a constitutionally protected right.

Twelve states moved to make abortion illegal in nearly all circumstances, while eleven states imposed more restrictions.[16] Ten states, mostly on the East and West Coasts, passed laws to expand access and protect abortion as a right within their state. American women are faced with a changing landscape when it comes to accessing abortion. Preventing pregnancy through effective contraception is a paramount concern. It's against this backdrop that contraception methods, including the pill and apps, are being discussed online.

When used consistently, the oral contraceptive pill, a form of hormonal contraception, is highly effective. It prevents over 99% of pregnancies with perfect use and about 93% with typical use.[17] Hormonal experimentation on animals began in the 1940s, leading to drug trials for women's contraceptives in the 1950s. In 1957, the FDA approved their use for menstrual regulation and, by 1960, they were authorised for contraception by inhibiting ovulation.[18]

Some in the women's movement hailed this as a major medical breakthrough and embraced the pill as a symbol of liberation.[19] They suggested it revolutionised women's reproductive choices, granting them control over their health, and enabling greater freedom in education and careers. But safety concerns emerged a few years later, with reports of thromboembolisms.[20]

In 1961, without a drug pre-approval system, the UK's British Family Planning Association added the contraceptive pill to its Approved List of Contraceptives. It was a pivotal moment, given its role as the leading provider of family planning services. Official records show, however, there were deliberations that notably excluded women's perspectives.

On 4 December 1961, Tory MP Enoch Powell, now infamous for his 'rivers of blood' speech, who was minister for health at the time, announced that the pill would be available on the NHS. It was to be given to women whose health was put at risk by pregnancy and this was at a doctor's discretion.[21] In response to the announcement, Labour MP Marcus Lipton asked Powell if it would be 'left to the doctor to decide whether these pills shall be prescribed both for married and single women?' In a reflection of the paternalism at the time, Powell replied: 'It is always for the individual doctor to decide in each case what are the medical requirements.'

Since its inception, the birth control pill's core hormones haven't changed, though it is now available in various forms and dosages. Modern contraceptive options include pills, implants, injections, patches, vaginal rings and hormonal coils, each with distinct hormone combinations and effects. Understanding these effects requires identifying cause-and-effect relationships, but these are tricky to establish outside clinical trials and people's responses vary. For instance, weight gain after starting birth control might coincide with other life changes – such as starting college, entering a relationship or changing eating habits – that could be responsible.

Powell's comments about medical decision making are now outdated. Modern practice emphasises partnership between doctors and patients in making healthcare decisions. There is uncertainty about side effects of the pill: we do not always know who will experience them or how severely. Discussing these issues is crucial.[22]

## THE HASHTAG THAT SPARKED A BACKLASH

Research shows that women who feel involved in decisions about their birth control are generally more satisfied with their choices. However, contraceptive counselling often overlooks the potential side effects of the pill and alternatives to it.[23] In 2016, UK writer Holly Brockwell voiced her frustration on Twitter, declaring she was 'done with men telling me to take the pill'.[24]

Tech journalist Kate Bevan responded with a call to action. 'In support of @Holly, please share #MyPillStory. It's a great contraceptive – when it doesn't mess you up,' she wrote. Women took to Twitter and Instagram to share personal stories about the pill, highlighting side effects and health issues.[25] The campaign caught the attention of the media, inspiring articles and documentaries examining the impact of hormonal birth control. Unlike some trends that come and go, this movement has lasted almost a decade.

A 2024 study examined top TikTok videos about different kinds of birth control on a single day in May 2023.[26] Researchers found that while 57% of videos focused on side effects of the pill, only 20% mentioned any benefits. Nearly 50% of the videos featured creators who had quit hormonal contraception, citing issues ranging from headaches and mood swings to blood clots. The researchers stressed that while choosing non-hormonal options is a valid choice, TikTok videos tended to prioritise personal stories over scientific evidence. One of the authors, Emily Pfender, a researcher at the University of Delaware's Department of Communication, told me of a visual trope used in social media content to convey a sense of danger: creators would theatrically unfurl the long, densely written package inserts from birth control prescriptions like dramatic props.

But sociologist Dr Stephanie Alice Baker cautions against hastily labelling birth control discussions as 'misinformation'. A researcher at the City University of London, she studies wellness culture and social media, emphasising that in areas of medical uncertainty, where truth isn't always black and white, such accusations can be harmful. Dismissing personal experiences as misinformation risks alienating people from mainstream healthcare, she explains. In these grey areas of medicine, where personal stories overlap with scientific evidence, harsh criticism only deepens distrust. Baker likens this to a conversation with a close friend: if someone told you they had a bad experience with the pill, accusing them of spreading 'misinformation' would feel disproportionate, not to mention unkind.

Healthcare professionals who take to social media to 'debunk' claims about birth control side effects may find themselves in dangerous waters. While their aim may be to address misinformation, researchers suggest this myth-busting approach can seem dismissive.[27] When health professionals label patient experiences as myths, they risk perpetuating the same paternalism that led many women to turn to social media for support in the first place.

But our exposure to side effects on social media can shape how we experience them. Essentially, the power of the mind and belief, as we've seen, plays a role in how we perceive and respond to treatments. Dr Jenny Wu, an obstetrician and gynaecologist from Duke University in North Carolina, has studied how social media shapes expectations and influences physical experiences around contraception. 'When people read about nausea and fatigue on social media', she reflects, 'it might affect how they experience these side effects themselves.'

#MyPillStory allowed many women to feel affirmed in having adverse effects on the pill; that's valuable when their stories are so often overlooked. But there's an inherent bias with these stories. Women who take the pill and don't have anything bad to say about it are unlikely to be moved to post. The negative stories may then be further amplified by social media's algorithms. The more you engage with content emphasising the pill's side effects, the more of this content will be shown to you. Your feed doesn't reflect the average experience. And when it comes to making a decision about your own contraception, there's a risk of availability bias: leaning on the examples you see most and recall easily. The net effect is perhaps an overestimation of how likely bad side effects are.

Even if #MyPillStory took root organically, the ongoing renaissance of natural birth control methods can't be disentangled from the monetary incentives influencers have to tell *their* stories. Amelia, a British lifestyle influencer with 30,000 TikTok followers, says quitting the pill was transformative, enabling her to think clearly and feel less affected by emotions. While stressing she isn't offering medical advice, she promotes dietary changes for 'hormonal imbalance and gut health', alongside a discount code for a superfood brand – a partnership likely earning her commission.

UK influencer Ellie Mae-Grady, with 1.3 million TikTok followers, has built an image of authenticity: a relatable twenty-something navigating young adulthood. Her feed blends confessional storytelling and slice-of-life vlogs with sponsored content merging intimate moments with promotions for lifestyle and beauty brands. 'Five months since coming off the contraceptive pill, I feel so much better,' she shares. 'I don't know if it's partly a placebo effect, but I do feel happier, more in tune with myself and my emotions and my feelings, more motivated, my head's clearer.' She states she will '100% never go back on hormonal birth control'.

Jeana Reed, a TikTok creator from Kansas, recalls the pill being a teenage rite of passage in the 1990s. It was routinely prescribed for issues like acne and heavy periods. 'All my friends I did cheerleading with were on it; my mother and grandmother were like: "absolutely you're going on the pill,"' she tells me, explaining that both had been teen mums and wanted to spare her similar challenges. 'I thought, okay, I'll hop on this train too. I didn't question it,' she says.

Soon she started to experience side effects, however: intense headaches, occasional vomiting and drastic mood changes. 'I became really anxious, really depressed,' she recalls. She switched pills, but her symptoms persisted. She recalls doctors dismissing her struggles as typical for a sixteen-year-old girl. They would say: '"Of course you're anxious. Of course you're depressed. You're trying to figure out your place in the world,"' she recounts.

Years of frustration with unanswered questions about birth control eventually led to a breakthrough in her contraceptive choices. Today, she's turned that experience into a business, tapping into growing concerns about hormonal birth control side effects and the dependability of fertility tracking devices.

Oral contraceptive use in the UK and Europe had been declining since 2010, even before social media's influence became so widespread.[28] While it's difficult to quantify its exact impact, doctors report that patients increasingly bring social media discussions into consultations. Mawson has watched this 'hormone hesitancy' grow first-hand, driven by the surge of negative social media content about synthetic hormones. This trend, she explains, has instilled genuine fear in patients and changed contraceptive preferences. 'Lots of people want to get off hormones,' she says.

Brook's 2024 national survey supports what Mawson sees in her practice. Over 56% of respondents said that contraceptive experiences shared on social media – particularly stories about side effects – influenced their birth control choices. In the words of one participant, 'I use Google and the NHS website as well as different social medias to see other people's reactions to the contraceptive and side effects.'[29]

## DOING IT FOR THEMSELVES
The birth control pill isn't the sole contraceptive method under scrutiny on social media; the intrauterine device (IUD), or coil, has come in for scrutiny too. Highly reliable, the IUD is a small device placed in the uterus, available in two types: copper or hormone-releasing – both creating a hostile environment for sperm. These long-acting contraceptives last between five and ten years, depending on the type, and can be removed at any time.

Kate Sheridan, a researcher at Oxford University specialising in patient and public health monitoring tools, shared an account from a recent women's healthcare conference. Doctors reported encountering patients who had removed their own IUDs – a revelation that prompted audible gasps from the conference audience. 'People were like, "Oh my god, I don't know if that's a good idea." That was the reaction of some medical professionals too,' Sheridan tells me. 'Most of the people doing this are learning how on TikTok, and it's gone viral,' she adds.

One particular post received international attention. In a video (now taken down), TikToker Mikkie Gallagher is filmed performing a 'DIY IUD removal'.[30] It starts out with Gallagher showing off her hands in blue medical gloves, as a caption across the screen reads: 'Come along for a little IUD removal.' From there, she posts another caption 'Diving right in…', and she visibly winces as she 'goes fishing' for her inserted IUD. Within seconds, it's out: 'A lot easier than I thought, TBH,' and 'Catch of the Day: Mirena IUD 2 inches.' The accompanying hashtags #iudremoval and #diyiudremoval have had tens of millions of views.

The video itself clocked up millions of views and prompted a 'don't try this at home' response in the press with condemnation from some family planning organisations warning that 'It's just a ridiculous thing to do.'[31] Dr Semiya Aziz, GP and TV doctor, spoke to *The Mirror* about the complications that come with self-removal.[32] 'For doctors, removing an IUD can be a fairly quick and simple procedure.' Attempting to take it out by yourself, if unsuccessful, can cause a part of the IUD to break off or dislodge, causing intense pain and requiring urgent medical attention. Infection, sepsis, internal tears and significant bleeding, she says, are all risks.

Self-removal began as a response to America's healthcare costs, with US women sharing videos of removing them on TikTok and YouTube to avoid medical bills ranging from $50 to over $1,000.[33] But the practice spread far beyond its borders, as women reported healthcare providers sometimes resisting their requests for IUD removal.

Social media conversations about IUD self-removal have flourished even in the UK, despite free contraceptive care being available. During the Covid-19 pandemic, Mawson saw the consequences of restricted healthcare access first-hand in her Sheffield clinic. With sexual health services limited to remote consultations, women who wanted their IUDs or implants removed were unable to get it done. 'I heard of women desperate to try for pregnancy but unable to get coils removed due to the shutdown of services,' she says. This seems to have driven much of the discussion around self-removal.

Mawson says sexual health services can be fragmented and IUD removal has become increasingly difficult to access. Some clinics focus solely on insertion and don't have removal services. Many GPs aren't trained to do it, she says. 'I'm a coil fitter and remover, but I wouldn't take my own coil out. But I guess that if people have no other choice, they should be shown how to do it safely, but I wouldn't myself,' she says. 'It's a sad state of affairs when women aren't being listened to, and I suspect it's just a sign of chronic underfunding in services in the UK.'

Simply warning people about dangers often falls flat – especially when they already distrust the system or face barriers to accessing services. It's a pattern we've seen repeatedly, whether with drug use, excessive drinking or gambling. Telling people 'don't do this, it's harmful' rarely works as a stand-alone strategy.

One principle of public health is harm reduction. In a situation where you can't outright prevent someone from engaging in harmful behaviour, you do your best to reduce the harm caused to them and others. Harm reduction strategies rose in prominence in the 1970s and 1980s in response to infectious diseases such as hepatitis B and HIV.[34] This is why there is advocacy for syringe exchange programmes, safer injection facilities and opioid substitution treatments; these interventions help reduce infections in those engaging in high-risk behaviours. Some doctors are now trying to tackle contraception with a similar approach. If patients are going to look into removing implants themselves, some professionals argue they should show them how to do it safely.

Dr Jennifer Lincoln, a US obstetrician–gynaecologist, teaches self-removal on social media platforms. With millions of followers across TikTok, YouTube and Instagram, her content is – in her own words – the 'health class you wish you had in HS [high school]'. Her 2021 TikTok video on IUD self-removal became one of her most viral posts, nearing half a million views by June 2024. Dressed in her blue medical scrubs, she asks:

> Can you take out your own IUD? Honestly? Actually, probably you can. You do. Removals are actually really straightforward and really simple most of the time… If you're able to easily grasp the string and with a gentle tug, remove it. Cool. But if you can't get the string or it hurts, or you pull and it doesn't come out, you need to stop.

Lincoln says she has removed two of her own IUDs and suggests others may disagree with her. 'Going to the doctor to have an IUD removed can sometimes be a little difficult when it comes to childcare, costs… But by the same token, if you want to come in and have us do it, we're more than happy.'

Lincoln isn't the only health professional taking a different approach to social media. Influencer posts about health issues may sometimes lack medical rigour; they can also highlight critical gaps in patient care and unmet needs. The real challenge lies in distinguishing valid concerns from fleeting viral trends. 'We need to understand what patients are truly worried about, what values drive their decisions,' explains Wu. Social media is now a major source of health information, dismissing these concerns or practising paternalistic medicine is no longer viable, she adds.

Wu got on TikTok in the same way that most millennials did during Covid, as just a form of distraction, she tells me. 'I was just scrolling on TikTok and saw these videos of women recording themselves as they were getting the IUD placed,' she says. The first video she watched alternated between shots of the content creator's face and the health professionals conducting the procedure, capturing her expressions of pain during the insertion. In other graphic videos, young women described an 'explosion of cramps', a sensation of 'pulling, pushing and slicing' or being 'cut or ripped open inside'. Many of these patients said they were not warned of the potential for pain.[35]

There are other issues at stake too. In the UK, health professionals are growing concerned by patients who film their own medical treatment for TikTok and Instagram, saying it could distract staff or make them feel uncomfortable or anxious. They also say it risks publicising private medical data of other people who may be in the same part of the hospital. One described how the daughter of one of her patients filmed her putting in a cannula because it would be 'entertaining on social media' but she didn't ask permission. 'I spent the weekend afterwards worrying: did I do my job properly? I know I did, but no one's perfect all of the time,' the health professional said, adding, 'I don't think I slept for the whole weekend.'[36]

Hospital Trusts have had to put in policies around patients taking photos and filming procedures. NHS officials said it was vital that, if patients want to record any part of NHS care, they discuss it with staff first and it remains for their personal use only.[37]

'Watching someone's face contort in pain triggers something primal in us,' Wu explains. 'It's a visceral, emotional response that's fundamentally different from reading about pain in an article or Reddit post. When we see someone suffering in real time, our brains process that information in a way that makes us think, "I never want to experience that."'

Fear and anxiety can affect how we experience pain, a connection well documented in medical research, including with regard to IUD insertion.[38] The flood of TikTok videos showing painful IUD insertions may be inadvertently heightening patients' anxiety, making the actual procedure more painful when they undergo it, Wu adds. She suspects online content is affecting patients' choices, from her experiences at her clinic. Wu noticed her Gen Z patients were increasingly reluctant to choose IUDs, unlike their millennial predecessors. When she asked them why, many cited TikTok videos they'd watched – particularly ones showing painful experiences.

The lack of discussion around pain with IUD insertion was also cited in Brook's UK survey. 'I was also told the Mirena coil would be virtually painless. Big fat lie,' one respondent said, with another saying that she 'wasn't prepared for the immense pain during insertion'.[39] After noticing this trend, Wu and her colleagues analysed TikTok's 100 most-viewed IUD videos in a 2022 study.[40] They found negative content about IUDs (37.8%) outweighed positive messages (19.4%). In videos sharing patient experiences, every single one had either a negative or ambiguous tone, with nearly all emphasising pain and side effects.

Between them, the videos had amassed 471 million views, 32 million likes and 1 million shares. What troubled Wu was the deep mistrust of medical professionals evident in over a quarter of the videos. One comment in particular hit her: 'Your gynaecologist is worse than a politician.' Indeed, one Danish interview study of nineteen people between the ages of sixteen and twenty-four found that social media is reshaping relationships between young women and healthcare providers. Young women increasingly use social media for health information and view healthcare professionals mainly as prescription providers rather than partners in their contraceptive care, the researchers wrote.[41]

## FROM A VIRAL TREND TO A POLICY

The IUD videos caught the attention of both mainstream media and medical journals, appearing to influence federal health policy. 'After social media outcry, CDC tells doctors to better manage IUD pain,' the *Washington Post* declared in August 2024.[42] The Centers for Disease Control and Prevention (CDC) introduced new guidelines encouraging healthcare providers to discuss IUD insertion pain with patients. These conversations should cover all available pain management options, resulting in a 'person centred plan... based on patient preference.'[43] The new guidelines also expanded pain management options to include topical application of lidocaine as a cream or gel.

The earlier 2016 guidelines had suggested that lidocaine injections may be helpful in reducing pain but said there is only 'limited evidence'.[44] The evidence points in different directions. The updated 2024 recommendation was based on thirteen randomised control trials, of which six found a reduction in pain (at different points in the process), but seven did not find any. What's clear is that pain is now seen as a concern rather than just something people should put up with. 'What's striking is CDC guidelines typically focus on clinical evidence – medication indications and contraindications. Including patient experience like this isn't something you'd historically see in their recommendations,' Wu observes.

In post-*Roe* North Carolina, where abortion is illegal after twelve weeks, Wu says the issue of IUD pain needed to be resolved. Over seven years, she has watched abortion access shrink, while social media fuels the rise of 'natural' birth control methods, a trend she finds discomfiting given the limited options for unplanned pregnancies. 'It's scary to practice medicine in a state with restricted abortion access when patients reject the most effective contraception,' she says.

After *Roe v Wade* was overturned in 2022, TikTok saw a surge in DIY abortion content, from mugwort tea to high doses of vitamin C.[45] Users circumvented platform restrictions by rephrasing search terms. Hashtags related to herbal abortions had millions of views, while Facebook and Instagram posts shared lists of herbs alleged to induce miscarriage. Though some of the suggested remedies were relatively harmless, others, like pennyroyal, are toxic and can cause organ failure.

But social media, as ever, is a two-sided coin. Different platforms became lifelines for those seeking medical abortion, allowing health organisations to highlight how women could access medication kits to terminate pregnancies at home. Reproductive rights non-profits currently use 'shield laws' passed by liberal states to protect healthcare practitioners within their states from prosecution for providing abortions to patients in states where abortion is illegal or restricted.[46]

By 2023, seven states had also applied shield laws to telehealth, meaning their healthcare practitioners can post the pills required for medical abortion to patients in other states. While availability of these services is widely promoted on social media, it is unclear how well these shield laws will hold. Many states also require telehealth providers to be licensed in both their state and the patient's.[47]

There are also legal challenges to the medical abortion provision. Officials in both Texas and Louisiana are suing New York-based doctor Dr Margaret Daley Carpenter for violating state law by supplying pills by post. Depending on the outcome, this may be the first of many such lawsuits.[48]

Nonetheless, as it's the most accessible form of abortion for many America women, the information available about abortion pills online needs to be accurate. Wu's team analysed TikTok's top 100 videos on medical abortion in 2022.[49] To their surprise, most were accurate – 86% of scientific claims were correct. The videos had 12.1 million views and were largely educational, with 83% supporting abortion access and nearly half providing information about obtaining medical abortion.

However, even if social media is a vital tool for abortion providers to help women access their services, their reach can be hemmed in at the will of tech moguls. Shortly after President Trump's 2025 inauguration, reproductive health non-profits reported systematic suppression on Meta platforms. They said they had experienced post removals, image blurring and suspensions of their accounts.[50]

Some have accused Meta of 'shadow-banning' – the practice of blocking or partially blocking a user or their content from some areas of an online community without their knowledge. This has meant abortion service accounts have become harder to find through standard searches.[51] Meta claimed this was due to enforcement errors, but the Democrat senator Ruben Gallego accused Meta of 'pre-emptively bowing' to Trump's preferences following his election.

Against a backdrop of abortion restrictions and increased scepticism about conventional birth control methods, the Femtech industry has capitalised on the #offthepill movement. Some market their fertility trackers and period apps as 'hormone-free' alternatives, selling them as a form of 'empowerment' that gives back to women control over their reproductive health.

As one influencer put it: 'I will not accept synthetic hormones as my only option… We were sold a lie that the birth control pill was the magic pill for all our reproductive problems i.e. unwanted pregnancies, painful periods, acne, mood stabilising and much more.' Instead, she uses a digital fertility tracker: 'Less than sixty seconds per day is all it takes to be in control of my fertility.'

The 2023 TikTok analysis conducted by Pfender showed a difference in how contraceptives were portrayed. Non-hormonal methods were presented more positively and emphasised their benefits, such as fewer side effects.[52]

Meanwhile, a 2022 UK interview study of twelve women who used fertility apps felt they offered them a deeper insight into their bodies.[53] Some women initially viewed these apps as a 'magical solution', only to discover they demand significant personal commitment.

OVERSOLD AND UNDER-REGULATED
But, as Polis discovered, the fertility tracking market lacks adequate oversight. It's rife with questionable claims, especially on social media. Several studies have shown that many of these apps fail to deliver the accuracy they promise – a serious concern for technology women are using to prevent pregnancy. The algorithms often rely on a basic assumption: that ovulation occurs fourteen days after your period begins. But that's only true for about 10% of menstrual cycles, Polis explains. Ovulation timing varies considerably and can be affected by many factors. Tracking fertility can be challenging for people with unpredictable lifestyles or irregular cycles. For it to be effective, users need consistent daily routines, such as regular sleep patterns and reliable access to their thermometer. Life changes, travel, irregular schedules or disrupted sleep can all compromise the accuracy of these methods.[54]

Research has found inaccuracies in how fertility tracking devices predict ovulation and fertile windows.[55, 56] With hundreds of apps and trackers on the market but no independent evaluation system, fertility organisations warn that users face risks of unplanned pregnancy.[57] Indeed, UK data show that abortion rates have increased across all ethnicities, levels of deprivation and age groups over recent years.[58] At the same time, a study found that use of traditional birth control had decreased – hormonal methods nearly halved to 11%, while long-term options like IUDs fell to 0.6% in 2023 compared to 3% in 2018 in those seeking abortion. Though fertility awareness methods increased sixfold (from 0.4% to 2.5% of cases), the number of women using no contraception jumped from 56% to 70%.

The researchers warned that this move away from reliable contraception, combined with rising abortion rates, was putting pressure on healthcare services. They called for urgent investment in both contraceptive and abortion care.

Dr Rosie McNee, study author and public health specialist, reflects on her grandmother's legacy compared to today's trends. Dr Libby Wilson was a family planning doctor in 1970s Glasgow, secretly administering birth control injections to women whose husbands prohibited contraception. Facing fierce resistance, particularly from the Catholic Church, Wilson fought for reproductive autonomy.

McNee is circumspect. Her grandmother might feel disheartened by women turning away from the pill – a freedom she risked her career to secure – but McNee says her guiding principle was that a woman has a right to make her own healthcare decisions. She's supportive of expanding access to contraceptive options but argues that the priority should be providing women with complete information to make informed decisions. It's fine for people to opt for natural family planning, she says, but social media often fails to convey the full picture – particularly the higher typical failure rates compared to methods like the pill.

Some content creators portray natural family planning as foolproof when done correctly. It doesn't always engage in the detail of doing it correctly, nor does it raise the spectre of failure. Conversations about contraception take place detached from those about pregnancy and abortion.

However, Femtech apps are facing a backlash in light of the reversal of *Roe v Wade*, albeit not due to concerns about their accuracy. Digital privacy advocates urged women to delete period tracking apps from their phones lest their medical data become legal evidence in a hostile state. The call to action crystallised in a viral Twitter post from Gina Neff: 'Right now, and I mean this instant, delete every digital trace of any menstrual tracking. Please.' Her message resonated widely, gathering 177,000 likes and sparking a broader conversation about data privacy and reproductive rights. 'Let's get our bodies back,' she continued. 'There's work to be done and many more fights to fight for social and reproductive justice.'

Like other apps, period trackers collect and sometimes share user data. In states where abortion is criminalised, this digital trail of menstrual cycles and fertility information could potentially be subpoenaed by prosecutors building cases against women, criminal defence attorneys have argued.[59]

It seems that this isn't restricted to the US. In May 2025, UK police were given new guidance on searching women's homes for abortion drugs and checking their phones for menstrual tracking apps after pregnancy loss.[60] The National Police Chiefs' Council said officers may seize digital devices to examine internet searches, messages and health apps, including cycle trackers, to 'establish a woman's knowledge and intention in relation to the pregnancy'. The new guidance alarmed Dr Ranee Thakar, president of the Royal College of Obstetricians and Gynaecologists, who maintained it was 'not in the public best interest'.[61] 'Women in these circumstances have a right to compassionate care and to have their dignity and privacy respected, not to have their homes, phones, computers and health apps searched, or be arrested and interrogated,' she said. However, in England and Wales there are moves to decriminalise abortion, with MPs backing a change to legislation in June 2025.

In some countries, data have been handed over by providers themselves. In March 2024, Flo, a popular fertility tracking app, faced a Canadian class action lawsuit for allegedly sharing users' intimate health data with Facebook without consent.[62] The lead plaintiff, Jamie Kah Cate Lam, had used the app while trying to conceive, logging personal details about her menstrual cycle and sexual activity.

Though Lam deleted the app after her son's birth in 2018, she was shocked to later learn through a *Wall Street Journal* investigation that Flo had been sharing sensitive user data with Facebook and other companies. The lawsuit, which could affect millions of

Canadian users, seeks compensation for this privacy breach. Flo denies the allegations and maintains it protects user privacy.

After *Roe*'s reversal, Dr Ruba Abu-Salma, a computer scientist at King's College London, began investigating how fertility apps handle user data. Her study of the top twenty women's health apps in the US and UK showed several concerning practices.[63]

Some apps tricked users into sharing more personal information than they needed to. They made it hard to keep information private and pushed users to share sensitive details they didn't really need, including a person's medical history of miscarriage and abortion. Many apps also put basic features behind a paywall, meaning users had to pay and share identifying personal data just to use simple tracking functions. Women ultimately had to choose between protecting their privacy and using the app's core features.

Some apps did have anonymous modes, but these protections weren't widespread. Most companies, she found, treated user data more as a business asset than sensitive information requiring protection. As Neff and Nafus argue: 'In Silicon Valley, data is seen as a valuable general-purpose resource to stockpile – "the new oil" that might one day serve multiple, potential purposes.'[64]

According to Abu-Salma, this is especially troubling for pregnancy tracking apps, which collect highly intimate details yet may lack robust privacy safeguards. This means that deleting an app doesn't guarantee complete data erasure, as developers may retain past information. If you're concerned about keeping your medical information private, you should opt to use an app that stores your data on your device alone, instead of uploading it to its own servers (or 'cloud').

A 2025 report by Neff's team at Cambridge University backs this up. It suggested that these cycle tracking apps are 'a lucrative business because they provide the companies behind the apps with access to extremely valuable and fine-grained user data'. Data on who is pregnant, and who wants to be, was some of the 'most sought-after information in digital advertising' as it led to a shift in shopping patterns.[65]

'Menstrual cycle tracking apps are presented as empowering women and addressing the gender health gap,' Dr Stefanie Felsberger, lead author of the report, says. 'Yet the business model behind their services rests on commercial use, selling user data and insights to third parties for profit. There are real and frightening privacy and safety risks to women as a result of the commodification of the data collected by cycle tracking app companies.'

While the UK and EU have strong data protection laws (General Data Protection Regulation, GDPR) and a watchdog agency (Information Commissioner's Office, ICO), the sheer number of apps makes comprehensive oversight difficult. Just because an app's privacy policy follows GDPR rules on paper doesn't mean its actual handling of user data complies with the law. Compliance with the law is assumed rather than verified; the ICO will investigate after someone raises a complaint. But most of us lack the tools to work out if our data is being misused.

The task of monitoring how companies use data and market their products may default to independent researchers like Abu-Salma and Polis, rather than regulatory bodies. And these researchers, as Polis would find out, can face a backlash from manufacturers. In 2017, Valley Electronics, the maker of Daysy, claimed their device was over 99% effective as contraception, despite acknowledging that the FDA had 'blocked' them from calling it a contraceptive.

Polis questioned the evidence behind these claims. The distinctions between company claims, supporting evidence and presentation need careful attention. The words used make all the difference in regulatory terms. Marketing a product as contraception requires government approval from agencies like the UK's MHRA or the US's FDA. As medical devices, such products must undergo studies showing their effectiveness in preventing pregnancy, much like pills or IUDs.

However, there's a key regulatory difference between preventing pregnancy and aiding conception. Fertility tracking products are subject to lighter oversight than contraceptives. While struggling to conceive can take a big emotional toll, regulatory standards reflect different levels of risk. Unplanned pregnancies may bring more immediate and life-altering consequences. That's why fertility tracking products face less scrutiny than contraceptives from regulatory agencies.

This leaves a gap. Even when companies advertise their products solely for conception planning, users may still rely on them to avoid pregnancy. By displaying fertile windows, these tools inherently imply 'safe' periods for unprotected sex, though they lack formal approval as contraceptives. To date, two apps have been cleared by US regulators as digital contraception – Natural Cycles and Clue Birth Control. The studies that underpin their effectiveness for the average user (about 93% for Natural Cycles and about 92% for Clue), however, have been criticised as they are observational rather than the controlled trials required for other FDA-approved birth control methods.[66] In the UK, NICE prepared a briefing for Natural Cycles in 2021 as a contraception method, while stating in its summary 'Other more reliable forms of contraception are available.'[67]

Natural Cycles and Clue are exceptions in conducting studies about how well their technology works to prevent pregnancy. Some companies do not make it sufficiently clear to their users that fertility tracking is distinct from contraception – and that their product should not be used as contraception.

John Powell, professor of digital health at Oxford University, focuses on healthcare and digital technology. He is also an expert advisor to UK health agencies including NICE and the MHRA. Powell's concerns are not confined to fertility apps and he says it's often unclear which health apps you can actually trust. Many lack robust scientific evidence to support their effectiveness. Some companies exploit regulatory loopholes by obscuring the true purpose of their apps and how they are presented for approval: 'Maybe it is genuinely a health and wellness device, but people could use it as a medical device.' If you don't want to go through the lengthy and costly process of gathering evidence to register your app or wearable as a medical device, you can market it as a wellness product.

Even when evidence exists, it can be hard to track down, Powell explains. Companies might not share their research, or they may have tested the app under a different name. More troubling is that companies can simply rebrand unsuccessful apps rather than acknowledge negative results, he notes. If studies show an app doesn't work, they can just change its name and start afresh.

## THE DANGEROUS WORK OF DEBUNKING

It's easy to see why influencers might be confused as to how medically reliable an app is, and what purposes it's intended to be used for. But Valley Electronics should've known better. The company had been marketing Daysy for pregnancy prevention, but they had actually registered it with the FDA as a 'proceptive' device meant to help people conceive. Yet this was the opposite of how many users understood its purpose. Polis reported this discrepancy as potential regulatory misconduct to the FDA. The agency launched an investigation and ultimately forced the company to change how they marketed the device. They were not allowed to promote it for contraceptive use without proper approval.

Polis then investigated the company's 99% effectiveness assertion. She uncovered that the evidence was based on a flawed 1998 study of an earlier device, conducted sixteen years before Daysy even existed.[68] It was a retrospective study and she found issues in both the data collection and analysis methods. She contacted the company privately to raise her scientific concerns. Prospective clinical studies are needed to show how effective a given contraceptive method is and Polis told the company that they needed to conduct one. They dismissed her concerns, saying for them 'the costs and benefits are all out of proportion'. 'This statement shocked me, because it completely ignores the costs to their users or potential users of a potential unintended pregnancy,' Polis says.

In 2018, Valley Electronics published a study in the journal *Reproductive Health*, authored by company insiders, including their medical director Niels van de Roemer and Martin Koch (who would later join their scientific advisory board).[69] The research claimed Daysy was 99.4% effective at preventing pregnancy, suggesting it was a highly reliable form of contraception.

The company was promoting these figures across social media directly to consumers in a way that is illegal for drug companies in most of the world. The company used Facebook to promote their claims about Daysy, stating in one post that they were 'proud to be able prove' their system was 'highly trustworthy and reliable' for preventing pregnancy. They also responded to queries on the platform reiterating these data.[70]

Initially, Polis felt hopeful when she saw the company had published new research, thinking they might have addressed her previous concerns about evidence quality. But as she read the paper, her optimism faded. The study contained serious methodological problems, many of them similar to the flaws she had identified in the 1998 research paper and already brought to the company's attention. 'Unfortunately, this paper contains fatal flaws in the estimation of effectiveness of the Daysy device and DaysyView app for prevention of unintended pregnancy, which render the published effectiveness estimates unreliable,' she wrote in a peer-reviewed commentary.[71] She was worried that the research 'inappropriately inflated consumer confidence in the contraceptive effectiveness of Daysy'.

Instead of conducting a proper prospective study with regular pregnancy tests, the company had mailed surveys asking users to report unplanned pregnancies – an unreliable method for accurate data collection. There were other flaws. Only 13% of people responded to the survey, raising concerns about selection bias – a type of systematic error that occurs when the participants in a study are not representative of the broader population the study aims to understand. Most respondents (64%) were also using other forms of birth control, and researchers questionably excluded certain pregnancies from their calculations. The authors failed to address how these methodological problems might have skewed their results. The study had been designed to show the product in a favourable light rather than assess its effectiveness rigorously.

Agreeing with Polis, the journal editors retracted Daysy's paper in 2019. This led to media coverage. In interviews, Polis spoke bluntly about Valley Electronics, calling their practices 'unethical' and their research 'junk science'. This, she felt, was justified by their regulatory violations and the paper's retraction. The company did not take these criticisms lightly.

One Friday afternoon in May 2020, Dr Polis received a call at her home office in New York. It was John from the building's front desk. He was usually calm and composed, but he was now noticeably distressed about a delivery left in the lobby, where packages were put during the pandemic. To Polis' shock, it was a legal complaint. Valley Electronics claimed her statements were defamatory, and were suing her for $1 million for what she had said on social media, in the press and on blogs.

When a company faces federal reprimands and paper retractions, how should critics describe their practices? Some point out that scientific understanding is fluid. New research can up-end established beliefs, and experts often disagree about methodology and interpretation. But in digital health, where products reach consumers before studies are completed, some companies seem to treat robust science as an afterthought. Their priority is getting technology to market, regardless of uncertainty.[72]

In the case of Daysy, this created an environment where marketing outpaced the evidence, and those insisting on scientific rigour faced pushback for questioning claims. After nearly two years of costly and emotionally draining legal battles, the courts dismissed the case against Polis. But influencers continued to promote

Daysy as a contraceptive option, despite her work exposing its lack of evidence.

'The best natural non-hormonal form of birth control,' one influencer declared. 'Here's to menstrual cycle education and taking our power back! #womenempowerment.' Another posted: 'Did you know there is birth control that is hormone-free? Daysy is a cycle tracker and it can reliably help you know when you're fertile.' Although regulatory bodies, scientific journals and courts eventually addressed Daysy's questionable claims, misleading information remained widespread on social media.

A study by Dutch and Australian researchers examined how influencers with over 10,000 followers discussed Daysy on Instagram, focusing on posts made after Polis exposed flaws in the company's research.[73] Among the ninety-eight influencers studied (half European, 30% American), over 95% – including verified influencers with blue ticks – marketed Daysy as contraception despite FDA prohibitions. They emphasised its 'natural, hormone-free' benefits and shared personal stories of switching from traditional birth control. Only two posts acknowledged any uncertainty about Daysy's effectiveness claims.

The influencers relied heavily on personal storytelling. Many offered discount codes and giveaways, though few disclosed if they were being paid by the company. With no registry of influencer payments, it's impossible to know the full extent of these commercial relationships. In essence, companies can benefit from exaggerated claims made by content creators while maintaining plausible deniability. Health regulators seem powerless to control this dubious information. People at the regulatory authorities aren't sitting around scrolling on Instagram or X or TikTok, so violations and false marketing can continue on these platforms. They just can't keep up and the platforms themselves don't check, Polis tells me.

Even when scientists like Polis publish clear evidence in academic journals, their findings often fail to reach the public. These critical debates might be trapped behind paywalls or buried in academic publications that few people access. 'Folks are kind of on their own if they want to use these fertility awareness-based methods,' Polis says. But if patients feel dismissed by medical professionals they won't return for guidance. Instead, they'll seek information from potentially unreliable sources. We're in a bit of a bind.

Mawson also says she supports people using fertility awareness methods. 'But they need proper instruction,' she adds. Teaching these methods requires time – something that's in short supply in general practice and sexual health clinics. This gap has created an opportunity for others. Contraception and fertility coaches have stepping into the void. Some say they offer superior guidance on natural birth control compared to apps and devices alone.

## THE NEW JOB TITLE IN WOMEN'S HEALTH

Jeana Reed is a vocal critic of fertility apps on social media cautioning her followers that relying them is equivalent to 'winging it'. In 2015, while teaching yoga, a nurse and student introduced her to a different fertility awareness method. It involved tracking menstrual cycles without apps to pinpoint both fertile and infertile periods. 'She said it's not just a bunch of mumbo jumbo. We've known this since the 1940s and 50s, and it's really heavily researched,' Jeana tells me. 'And I was like, are you sure? And she's like, yeah, come over and I'll teach you it. So I went over to her house and she taught me FAM [fertility awareness methods] in an afternoon,' she says.

Fertility awareness methods come in various forms, but Jeana specialised in the 'symptothermal method'. It's a technique that combines monitoring body temperature, observing cervical fluid changes and noting menstrual cycle start dates. Seeking community, she joined a Facebook group of over 50,000 members, quickly realising her experience was part of a broader movement. A Canadian mentor refined her understanding, helping her to master the intricacies of this approach.

In autumn 2022, a conversation over a leisurely brunch changed the course of Jeana's life. A friend, musing about changing her birth control, turned to her and asked, 'What are you on?' 'I told her I wasn't on any,' Jeana recalls. 'She just stared at me. "What do you mean you're not on it?"'

If brunch etiquette dictated that certain topics – politics, money, the precise mechanics of cervical mucus – should be avoided, Jeana was unbothered. She launched into an explanation of her chosen method, a practice of tracking her body's biomarkers to monitor fertility naturally. The reaction from her friends was astonishment. 'They were shocked they hadn't heard of this,' she says. Seizing the moment, Jeana declared, 'So, my girl, welcome to the world of fertility awareness and understanding your body. It's controversial. It's taboo.'

Jeana had long thought that there were big gaps in reproductive health education and that women's knowledge of their own bodies was, at best, piecemeal. 'Google is not your friend when it comes to filling in those gaps,' she says to me. 'Social media is where you need to go.' Recognising her passion, her friends urged her to take her insights beyond the brunch table. 'Talk about this to everyone and anyone who will listen,' they told her.

And so she did. By the end of 2022, Jeane had set up TikTok and Instagram accounts under the handle @serialhealers using the titles menstrual cycle coach and fertility awareness educator. When it came to building an online audience and capturing momentum, Jeana nailed it. She is part informed confidante, part approachable friend. Her content strategy chimes with social media's fast-paced aesthetic – kinetic, provocative videos designed to grab scrolling attention. Bold, urgent headlines flash across the screen. The delivery is breathless and direct: 'Breaking up with your birth control is one of the hardest breakups you're ever going to have...'

But Jeana's approach to content creation isn't just intuitive – it's scientifically strategic. A 2023 study dissected the anatomy of viral reproductive health content. It found that such content used the same techniques she employs.[74] The research identified key elements that make health communication compelling:

authenticity trumps clinical detachment;

videos that succeed are intimate, casual and deeply personal;

women creators who speak from lived experience, dress casually and are filmed in home-like settings, generate more engagement than traditional medical communicators.

Relatability is the critical currency. Emotion, spontaneity and a sense of shared experience outperform sterile, professional presentations. Jeana doesn't just create content. She crafts a narrative that resonates with her audience's experiences and anxieties about reproductive health.

Within just three months, her follower count shot to 50,000 and kept climbing. People worldwide messaged her, telling her they had navigated years of formal schooling without receiving basic, critical information about their own reproductive biology she tells me. It was a gap Jeana was attempting to fill. Those who follow her say they're being 'medically gaslit' by their doctors. 'They're not being seen, not being heard,' she tells me. 'There's this overwhelming consensus with a lot of clients that they're tired of not understanding their cycles.'

When Jeana started her TikTok account, she was midway through her fertility awareness coach certification. Her training involved intensive Zoom instruction and months of client work before she was fully certified. Similar training programmes exist globally for various fertility tracking methods.

If you're teaching yourself these methods, the efficacy rate is around 76%, she tells me. This equates to roughly twenty-four pregnancies for every 100 women using the method a year. 'The method that I teach is 99.6% effective when learned with an instructor,' she says: you work with a coach one-to-one to understand your cycle over a number of months.

If hormonal birth control appears more suitable for a client, she readily refers them to her network of healthcare professionals, she tells me. Nearly all her clients find her through TikTok. She says this has been transformative allowing her to go from part-time work to a full-time career. The platform has also connected her with clients from Mexico, Canada, Europe, Abu Dhabi and Guam, turning her business into an international venture.

Dozens of other fertility awareness method educators have joined the space with names ranging from 'Menstrual Cycle Educator' to 'Cervical Mucus Queen'. They use viral hashtags such as #fertilityawarenessmethod and #hormonefree to amplify their coaching services.

But what about the evidence for Jeana's claims? Polis has researched and published on different fertility awareness methods in medical journals. One systematic review of the medical literature, a research strategy that looks for all the available evidence on a medical intervention, found that if the methods are used perfectly FABMs could be about as effective as condoms, sponges or diaphragms.[75]

And there are two FABMs (including the symptothermal method) that evidence suggests *might* be as effective as contraceptive pills, patches or rings. However, high-quality prospective trials have not been conducted on *any* of these methods, and so these findings need to be treated with caution. These methods may prove to be less effective if and when they are examined in more robust studies or in different populations. For example, the evidence for the technique Jeana Reed advocates is only medium quality.[76]

'I think many in the fertility awareness advocacy movement have honed in on this one study and used it as their banner to say: "Look, your doctors have been lying to you and this can be as effective as hormonal contraception,"' Polis tells me. 'But you never want to base what you know on a single study, especially not a single study that's of moderate quality. And a small number of moderate quality studies on the effectiveness of various FABMs is all we really have to go on right now,' she adds.[77]

Much of this comes down to money to do the necessary trials looking at their effectiveness. 'It's hard enough to find funding to do contraceptive research and development, let alone on a method that might be used by a very small percentage of the population,' Polis says. Moreover, while manufacturers of contraceptives have to do effectiveness studies to get them past a regulator and onto the market, fertility coaching is an unregulated space.

This applies to coaching more generally too. There are low barriers to entry, minimal professional oversight and no standardised certification process.[78] Coaches can command hundreds of dollars per session, often without formal credentials. Some influencers have even begun offering their own training programmes, providing certificates to attendees of basic webinars. This has created a self-perpetuating ecosystem of coaches with little external validation.

'I don't know if what they get in those courses is evidence-based or not. I know some fertility awareness educators who are extremely dedicated to being evidence-based. But I've seen enough of the kind of things that a variety of many other fertility coaches say on social media to know it ain't all evidence-based,' Polis adds.

Helping people to develop a deeper awareness of their bodies and better understand the fertile and infertile phases of the menstrual cycle is valuable. However, helping people to apply that knowledge as a form of contraception carries a far greater level of responsibility.

What's obvious by the popularity of fertility tracking apps, DIY IUD removal and #MyPillStory is that women have been let down by our healthcare services: many simply do not feel their reproductive health is taken seriously. A 2024 survey by the British Pregnancy Advisory Service of 1,300 women who terminated a pregnancy found that 36% cited the inability to access contraception they wanted as a factor.[79] Sexual health services, some of which are funded by local government grants, have come under significant financial pressure. This has, perhaps, made it harder for people to access consultations and certain types of contraception.

Social media steps into this vacuum. Content creators are effectively promoting a form of DIY reproductive health, where women don't have to rely on anyone but themselves. It's seductive. But when things go wrong, women might be left to pick up the pieces by themselves. We should perhaps listen to women when they express disillusionment with conventional healthcare.

# 9

# A HORMONAL QUICK FIX

Old politicians aren't usually known for being gym rats. So it's no surprise images of Robert F. Kennedy Jr working out went viral. The erstwhile Democrat, now a prominent figure in President Donald Trump's 'Make America Healthy Again' initiative, is an outspoken critic of the corporate capture of healthcare and the influence of 'big pharma'. When unveiling Kennedy as his choice to spearhead health programmes, Trump claimed that Americans had for too long suffered at the hands of food and drug companies, which he accused of trafficking in 'deception, misinformation, and disinformation'.[1]

The rhetoric dovetailed with Kennedy's own long-held convictions, particularly his view that these industries and government regulators share responsibility for the nation's health problems. Health problems he was not succumbing to. In a video that has already had more than 5 million views on X, he performs a gymnastic flip over an exercise machine to Survivor's 'Eye of the Tiger' dressed only tracksuit pants.[2] His caption quipped, 'Practicing moves for my confirmation hearing.' But he doesn't give all the credit to workouts when it comes to his physique.

'I'm on an anti-ageing protocol from my doctor that includes testosterone replacement. But I don't take any anabolic steroids or anything like that,' RFK Jr told Lex Fridman on his eponymous podcast, which boasts over 4 million mostly male subscribers, in 2023. There's an undeniable irony: in that offhand remark, the man who condemns the pharmaceutical industry inadvertently offered a compelling endorsement for hormonal treatments. These are a growing segment of the industry he criticises.[3]

In this admission, Kennedy joins the growing cohort of male celebrities and influencers who speak openly about their waning testosterone levels, a topic that was once only discussed in hushed tones. Supplementing them is now a badge of enlightened masculinity.

Joe Rogan admits to using these treatments and even challenges fitness personalities to do the same on his podcast, the *Joe Rogan Experience*. These frank discussions consistently attract millions of viewers, while selected clips shared across social platforms sometimes reach audiences in the billions. 'I started doing hormone replacement therapy at forty', he said on YouTube. It makes a big difference, makes your body work way better. You can avoid a host of ailments and conditions related to your body breaking down due to age, he added.[4]

There's a stigma attached to taking the hormone, Rogan complains. 'A lot of people are like, "Where do you get your testosterone from? I get mine from my balls."' But it doesn't matter where you get it from, he adds, the key thing is having it in your system. Without it, you won't feel as good. If you're okay with that, fine. 'TRT [testosterone replacement therapy] exists for a reason,' he says.

## THE SCIENCE BEHIND TRT

Alongside other hormones, testosterone is one of the body's chemical messengers, regulating essential processes including growth, metabolism and sexual function in both men and women. It is an anabolic-androgenic steroid hormone, its name referring to its role in building muscle tissue (the anabolic effect) and developing male sexual characteristics (the androgenic effect), from facial hair and deeper voices to the development of male sex organs. In men, testosterone levels reach their peak around age seventeen before beginning a gradual decline after forty, decreasing approximately 1% annually.

As well as being produced naturally, TRT is available in several forms, including patches, gels, injections, creams, nasal gels, capsules and tablets, all of which come with different side effects. These treatments help to raise testosterone levels in the blood.

Many of Rogan's followers embraced his stance on TRT, with one calling it 'a major lifesaver'. Others reported benefits ranging from improved mood, sex drive and energy to relief from joint pain. Rogan was widely praised for 'increasing awareness' of TRT, which some saw as the male counterpart to hormone replacement therapy (HRT) long used by women to manage menopause.

Testosterone is having a moment. It's now one of the most talked about men's health topics on both TikTok and Instagram, second only to semen retention, according to a 2024 study.[5]

Dr Brooke Nickel, a researcher at the University of Sydney's School of Public Health, has examined the online portrayal of testosterone, analysing two hundred posts on Instagram and TikTok. Online, medical normalcy was seen as insufficient – a kind of hormonal mediocrity to be avoided. She tells me:

> Normal wasn't good enough. Even if men were within the normal range, the message was that they should aim for 'optimal' or 'peak' levels, as high as possible, to feel better. There was a push toward testosterone supplementation, especially for those on the low end of the normal range, with companies and doctors linked to big pharma promoting these products.

Testosterone use has spiralled since Dr Luke Turnock first began researching it in 2010. Shortly after finishing his degree, he entered the world of powerlifting under the mentorship of his friend, a former national champion. In this community, testosterone use wasn't hidden but silently understood through subtle acknowledgements.

## MASCULINITY ONLINE

Over fifteen years later, Turnock says that any stigma has gone. Its use is now widely promoted on TikTok and Instagram. Younger men are subjected to the message that high doses of testosterone are essential for achieving the muscular physiques idolised by Hollywood or those on *Love Island*. Some fitness influencers and content creators outright assert that testosterone use is the secret to their success.

Take Kade, who began injecting testosterone at twenty-one. Despite looking healthy, he struggled with anxiety so severe he couldn't drive.[6] Now, four years later, he has built a following of over 74,000 TikTok users by documenting his transformation through bi-weekly injections. At twenty-five, Kade describes himself as a completely changed man. He is now muscular, bearded and sexually reinvigorated. 'If you wake up in the morning and your soldier is not standing at full salute or your tent is not fully pitched, you have low testosterone,' he declares in one video brandishing a syringe for emphasis.

Social media is intensifying the pursuit of the 'ideal male self'.[7] Men are told, much like women have been for decades, that if they feel ugly, unfit or plain worn out, it's their fault. But redemption is supposedly within grasp through a readily available hormone therapy that pledges total renewal.

Nickel found this messaging relies on a rather retro form of gender panic, implying that insufficient testosterone levels are a precipitous slide toward an emasculated existence. The messaging suggested that low testosterone levels made men 'too feminine' or delivered the crushing comparison of being 'like a girl'.

Much of the content on the posts she analysed centred on sex drive and muscle mass, featuring a parade of gleaming, muscular, shirtless men captured mid-flex. Testosterone was not so much a medical treatment but the missing ingredient in the recipe for masculine fulfilment, packaged and marketed to those made vulnerable by cultivated self-doubt.

On Reddit, forums about TRT are filled with users sharing their experiences. Many post 'before-and-after' photos, showing off their gains, with others asking how they achieved their sculpted physiques. Even the co-founder of the platform, Alexis Ohanian, shared his elevated testosterone results on X in 2024. He attributed these levels to weightlifting, reducing meat and alcohol consumption and taking testosterone-boosting supplements from Ro, a healthcare company he invests in.

In the UK, testosterone is being used for more than enhancing men's physiques. It has become a stopgap solution for those let down by social and economic systems. It's a way of gaining status, Dr Channa Jayasena, a consultant in reproductive endocrinology at Imperial College London, tells me. This trend is particularly noticeable in post-industrial areas such as South Wales and parts of the North, where low-paid work and social deprivation are common. For many, gym culture offers a source of prestige and is sometimes a coping mechanism.

Jayasena understands the appeal of testosterone as a 'fix-all' hormone. 'Getting a personal trainer or eating well selects for the socially advantaged, given the cost of one-to-one training and fresh food, high in nutrition. The most vulnerable in society have the least access to these,' he says.

While one group of users includes young men seeking to address insecurities about their status, the other comprises middle-aged men, inspired by figures like RFK Jr, who turn to testosterone supplementation to counter the effects of naturally declining hormone levels. These older users look nostalgically at their youth, viewing testosterone as a way to 'turn back the clock' to recapture the energy and vitality they experienced at twenty-one.[8] Older men at Turnock's gym suggested that symptoms like fatigue or depression might indicate low testosterone levels. It's a simple fix: take it, and you'll feel better, Turnock explains. This phenomenon has been popularised with terms like 'manopause' or 'andropause': the implication is that TRT is the fountain of youth.

This idea has filtered down to younger men. Turnock recounted the story of one man in his thirties – whom we'll call Andrew – who complained of persistent fatigue and low mood. Andrew had become convinced these symptoms stemmed from insufficient testosterone. When he consulted an NHS doctor, he was informed that his levels fell within the 'normal range'. Unsatisfied with this assessment, Andrew remained convinced his testosterone was inadequate. Determined to address his self-diagnosed hormone deficiency, he bypassed conventional medicine and turned to the illicit market, acquiring testosterone through connections at his gym.

In the UK, testosterone is a class C drug under the Misuse of Substances Act 1971, which means it can only be issued by pharmacists with a prescription. As for other anabolic steroids, it's legal to possess testosterone for personal use. However, it's illegal to possess, import or export anabolic steroids if there's suspicion of supplying or selling them, including giving them to friends.[9]

The once-cloaked networks for obtaining testosterone that were marked by discreet gym connections, knowing nods and locker-room referrals have evolved into a far more accessible system. Today's testosterone users need only scroll through their social media feeds to access an underground market where content creators use carefully coded language and strategic emoji placement to suggest they sell the hormone.[10] Despite Instagram's attempts at a crackdown, content creators direct users to encrypted platforms like WhatsApp to continue the conversation off-platform.

But you don't even have to buy it illegally anymore if you have the right reason. TRT is now increasingly mainstream. You don't have to be online for long before adverts for testosterone pop up, Turnock says. For people like Andrew, getting hold of TRT to treat symptoms that he associates with having low testosterone is now straightforward compared to when he was sourcing it in his gym and it's all above board.

## HORMONE EVANGELISM

Like TRT, HRT has enjoyed a similar surge in celebrity-led popularity. But there are similarities and differences in their respective stories. For women, HRT for the treatment of menopausal symptoms has long been a source of confusion and complexity, with evolving evidence, scare stories and changing recommendations. One major controversy was the Women's Health Initiative published in 2002, which indicated that long-term combined HRT was linked to increased risks of breast cancer and heart disease leading to a drop in use.[11] Critics have since questioned these findings, pointing out that study participants weren't representative of typical HRT users. Most were older, often ten or more years past menopause. The research also only tested one specific type of hormone therapy. This left open the question of whether alternative forms of HRT – using different hormones, combinations, dosing patterns or application methods like patches or creams – carry the same risks.[12] But thanks to increased awareness, its use has picked up since then.

Menopause is a natural biological event that occurs when a woman's ovaries stop releasing eggs. Women are born with a finite number of eggs, which declines over time. By menopause, so few remain that ovulation ceases. The follicles that once nurtured eggs also produce hormones – primarily oestrogen, which drops considerably during this stage. Since oestrogen receptors exist throughout the body, its decline can affect many systems.

Levels of progesterone, produced after ovulation to prepare the uterus for pregnancy, also fall. Testosterone – another hormone made by the ovaries – declines too. These changes can lead to symptoms, commonly hot flushes and night sweats, though mood changes and vaginal dryness also occur. Some women, however, experience no symptoms at all.

Today, the view of menopause has changed from seeing it as an unavoidable natural stage women just have to endure to understanding it as a condition that can be effectively treated. Gone are the days when women were expected to shut up and put up with their hot flushes – a time darkly referred to as 'the Change'. There are menopause cafes – spaces for women to come together and share experiences – in person and also online. In 2025, the UK health secretary announced that menopause checks are to be done in addition to the NHS Health Check at GP practices that look out for early signs of stroke, kidney disease, heart disease, type 2 diabetes or dementia. They have also called for more understanding in the workplace for issues and symptoms of menopause.[13]

This phenomenon, dubbed the 'Davina Effect', is named after Davina McCall, whose substantial influence comes in part from her personal podcast and over 2 million Instagram followers. She's become a prominent advocate for menopause awareness, hosting the documentary *Davina McCall: Sex, Myths and the Menopause* in 2021, where she shared her own experiences of the perimenopause, which started when she was forty-four.

'I used to think that menopause was an age thing and now I realise it's a woman thing. For far too long, there's been a shroud of embarrassment, shame and fear around this topic, and this is where it stops!' she says.[14] On Instagram she shares personal stories, hosts live Q&A sessions with experts and provides information to help women navigate this stage of life. 'When it happens, the menopause is tough (for some of us, that's a massive understatement) – it can have a really detrimental effect on our work, mental health, relationships and family,' she says in one 2023 video. She has accelerated the acceptability of talking more openly about the struggles women face as they age.

There's a fine line between addressing the challenges of menopause that produces very real symptoms and over-medicalising a natural stage of life. While it's long been under-discussed and under-treated, there's growing concern it may now be over-marketed. Rachel Weiss, who founded the Menopause Cafe in 2017, isn't convinced this has been an entirely positive development. 'The pendulum has swung from "put up and shut up, women have done this for generations, keep going with your career at breakneck speeds just like you kept going with your periods,"… to "It is awful, here are all the symptoms, everyone is going to have them big time and be disabled and have to give up jobs,"' she says.[15] 'People are frightened and it's getting commercialised and there are false facts out there,' she adds.

You can see glimpses of this on McCall's Instagram, where an occasional comment will accuse her of profiteering from medicalising the menopause. As we've seen with other health conditions, increased advocacy and awareness typically accompany a rise in treatment. This pattern holds true for menopause as well, with prescriptions for HRT more than doubling in England between 2017 and 2021.[16] Medical professionals specialising in women's health have described this uptick in HRT use as nothing short of explosive. But that of course does not mean its use is wrong. Women have described banging on the doors for help and effectively being ignored.

NICE recommends offering HRT as the first-line treatment for menopause symptoms. In the latest guidelines published in November 2024, NICE states that HRT can be used to treat hot flushes, sweats, poor sleep and depressive symptoms 'not meeting the criteria for a diagnosis of depression'.[17] The guidelines drew criticism for some quarters, including the British Menopause Society, which said it failed to discuss the impact of early menopause on long-term health and it contests some of their interpretation of evidence on harms.[18] The interpretation of evidence is often not straightforward – even when there are robust studies.

The MHRA advises that HRT should only be prescribed to relieve symptoms that are adversely affecting quality of life and say that 'treatment should be reviewed regularly to ensure the minimum effective dose is used for the shortest duration'.[19] These regulations are in place to prevent the risk of side effects. HRT is associated with a slightly increased risk of breast cancer.[20, 21] This risk increases the longer you take it and the older you are. The risk falls again after you stop taking it. There is little or no increase in the risk of breast cancer from oestrogen-only HRT, which can be taken after a hysterectomy. HRT tablets also increase the risk of blood clots, even if the risk is low.[22] HRT has also been shown to help maintain bone strength and lower the risk of osteoporosis. NICE recommends it for specific groups. But 'risk' can mean different things to different people. Deciding whether to take HRT during menopause often involves weighing up competing risks

A SOLUTION TO AGEING?

Social media has reshaped perceptions of HRT. It's now seen not just as a treatment option but as a solution to the challenges of ageing. Across platforms, doctors can be found enthusiastically promoting HRT, suggesting it offers protection against future heart disease, strokes – women are at increased risk of strokes following menopause – and dementia. But the latest guidance from NICE specifically advises against using HRT to prevent cardiovascular disease or dementia, stating that scientific evidence does not support these claims.[23] 'People are using HRT as a panacea and it's not a panacea,' says Professor Annice Mukherjee, an endocrinologist specialising in complex menopause, who works at Spire Hospital in Manchester.

For some, the public conversation about menopause was a business opportunity. A full-fledged menopause industry has burgeoned, offering an array of products that promise relief, from specialised facial masks and cooling pillows to elaborate vitamin blends.

Actress Naomi Watts, of *Mulholland Drive* fame, has launched her own menopause products line, Stripes, to 'address the skin and body changes of menopause'. Like her Reddit co-founding husband, tennis superstar Serena Williams has also invested in a supplement company. Called Wile, it produces plant-based supplements targeting pre-menopause and perimenopause. Williams has appeared in the company's promotional videos.

Some experts distinguish HRT, a valid medical treatment, from the wider commercialisation surrounding menopause. But in social media circles, these distinctions often become muddled. Influencers passionately advocate for the idea that stabilising hormone levels using HRT is the definitive solution to every difficulty a woman faces. Some even go so far as to claim that hormone therapy is the elixir of youth, effectively returning a woman to her younger self. It's portrayed as a relationship saver, a fountain of youth for skin and a revitaliser of sexual vitality.[24]

If this sounds dated and misogynistic, it's because it is. In 1966, the bestselling book *Feminine Forever*, by British-born Manhattan-based gynaecologist Dr Robert Wilson, declared that 'every woman alive today has the option of remaining feminine forever'. 'No longer need she fret about the cruel irony of women aging faster than men. It is simply no longer true that the sexuality of a woman past forty necessarily declines more rapidly than that of her husband,' he wrote.[25]

Twenty-four years before Wilson's book appeared, the FDA had approved oestrogen produced by pregnant mares to treat menopausal symptoms, specifically hot flushes. But Wilson proselytised that HRT could achieve much more than just relieving symptoms. He made the case that menopause was a serious disease – 'a mutilation of the whole body' – and that post-menopausal women were deficient. 'A woman's physical, social, and psychological fulfilment all depend on one critical test: her ability to attract a suitable mate and to hold his interest for many years.'

Wilson maintained that femininity, both physical and emotional, is determined by the amount of oestrogen in the body. Oestrogen therapy, therefore, could increase femininity in young women, preserve it in middle-aged women, and restore it in the aged. Though some feminists fought back, many health activists embraced the view that, like contraception, HRT was a key to women's liberation. But what wasn't common knowledge at the time was that Wilson was funded by the HRT industry.[26]

Wilson was a relatively early pioneer in a tactic we've seen repeatedly in the pharmaceutical industry. He classified a natural human condition as a disease and promoted the use of a drug as the remedy, which healthy women would take daily for the rest of their lives.[27] Wilson would have never imagined how the essential messages of *Feminine Forever* are now being championed by women themselves, in the language of feminist empowerment. Now, taking hormones is framed as an act of reclaiming control over your body, a means of harnessing inner strength and even a way to enhance your role as a partner and lover.[28] In today's enlightened era, it's not about fulfilling a man's expectations but prioritising your own sexual wellbeing.

A sceptic might argue that the some of the symptoms influencers label as 'menopause' could, in fact, arise from the various social challenges women encounter at this stage of life. Many women juggle roles as primary carers for both children and ageing parents, navigate workplace difficulties and face the financial repercussions of the gender pay gap.[29] This is especially evident as they near retirement, only to find their pension savings diminished by career interruptions or limited progression opportunities. Against this backdrop, disrupted sleep and increased stress could be seen as understandable reactions to these overwhelming demands.

Simple burnout seldom elicits sympathy from employers. Menopause, on the other hand, is recognised as a legitimate medical condition. In workplaces where employers show little willingness to assist employees with specific challenges, and face minimal legal obligations to do so, women often struggle to secure accommodations like flexible working hours or carer's leave to lighten their burden. What they can do, however, is turn to HRT. Yet when HRT doesn't resolve their symptoms, patients can end up on escalating doses, instead of exploring what else could be causing their symptoms. It's important to parse all these contributing factors out. Understanding and sympathy goes a long way – something that social media creators have mastered.

Additionally, anxiety, weight gain, fatigue and low mood are becoming more common throughout society, which leads to poorer health in middle age – precisely when menopause typically occurs, says Mukherjee. However, because of the HRT 'propaganda campaign', women attribute any of these symptoms to the menopause, she says. 'They go on HRT and this doesn't help.' 'It'll treat flushes, but they weren't a problem anyway,' she continues. 'And then they'll say that they have heavy bleeding or weight gain or bloating, or migraines are getting worse. Some doctors will then just escalate the doses up, and up, and up.' This leads to problems – problems that the health service has to pick up.

## THE MAKING OF LOW-T

This is also the case for testosterone. Testosterone treatment is genuinely medically necessary for a specific group of men, namely those with hypogonadism. It's a condition caused by identifiable medical issues that result in insufficient testosterone production.[30] For these men, low testosterone can result in reduced bone density, heightening their risk of fractures, as well as infertility. This condition is distinct from the so-called 'manopause'. But ageing men are a far bigger market than those diagnosed with hypogonadism.

For Steven Woloshin, co-director of the Center for Medicine and Media at the Dartmouth Institute, the current influencer and celebrity-led advocacy for testosterone as a panacea for 'ageing' is history repeating itself. Woloshin refers to himself as the 'Face of Low-T' due to his extensive research over the years into marketing of 'low testosterone'. It's a classic example of disease mongering, he says.

In 2013, Woloshin and his late wife Professor Lisa Schwartz documented the art of creating a disease.[31] First, hypogonadism needed a rebrand. It had no name recognition. But one drug company knew how to remedy this. Abbott's (now AbbVie) testosterone therapy, AndroGel, was approved by the FDA in 2000, for men with hypogonadism due to disorders of the testicles, pituitary gland, or brain, which cause low testosterone levels. Their blueprint was HRT, where a drop in oestrogen leads to a well-defined set of symptoms.

Their PR agencies decided to market their drug as a treatment for 'Low-T' – shorter, more memorable and much more relatable for middle-aged men. They coupled the name change with a disease-awareness campaign. Their messaging invited middle-aged men to ask their doctors if their expanding waistlines, unpredictable moods or post-meal drowsiness might be because of a treatable hormonal deficiency. The marketing team created the phrase 'Is it Low-T?', which functioned less as a genuine question and more as an implicit diagnosis that inevitably led to a prescription.

'A man on TV is selling me a miracle cure that will keep me young forever. It's called AndroGel … for treating something called Low T, a pharmaceutical company-recognized condition affecting millions of men with low testosterone, previously known as getting older,' *The Colbert Report*, quipped in December 2012.[32] But for those with low testosterone not caused by classic hypogonadism, there's a lack of good evidence that testosterone therapy really helps for many issues. Testosterone has been tested in hundreds of trials across different doses and groups. While some studies show benefit, others show no effect at all. That's why we rely on systematic reviews and meta-analyses – remember, those studies that sit at the top of the evidence pyramid.

A 2020 meta-analysis examined the benefits and harms of testosterone treatment in mostly older men without medical conditions causing low testosterone.[33] The findings showed that while testosterone therapy led to slight improvements in sexual function and quality of life for men with low testosterone, these gains were modest and supported by evidence of low to moderate certainty. However, the treatment showed minimal impact on physical abilities, depression, energy levels or cognitive function.

There was insufficient data on potential harms. Most research tracked participants for under a year and omitted people at higher risk of conditions such as heart disease, leaving long-term effects unknown. Limited information was available on younger men (eighteen to fifty years old), and definitions of 'low testosterone' varied across studies. Other trials showed testosterone therapy merely led to improvements in lean body mass of around 2 kg and reduction in body fat.[34]

These results are perhaps not a surprise. Various studies have shown that sexual symptoms are the only reliable sign of low testosterone. Even low testosterone levels in themselves don't indicate you will have any health problems.

The 2009 European Male Ageing Study examined 3,000 men over forty across Europe, looking at a wide range of symptoms. While 25% to 30% of these men had low testosterone on blood tests, most of them were otherwise healthy and did not report symptoms directly related to their hormone levels. Only 2% met the clinical criteria for testosterone deficiency, meaning they had both low testosterone and a specific set of sexual symptoms, such as reduced libido and erectile dysfunction.[35] In other words, the study suggests that most age-related symptoms in men are not due to low testosterone and that true testosterone deficiency is relatively rare.

This didn't concern the drug's marketers, who were starting to ramp up their campaign. AbbVie sponsored a website called IsItLowT.com, asking men about symptoms like decreased libido, energy, mood, sports performance and their erections. They even encouraged wives and partners to prompt the men in their lives to speak with doctors about these issues.[36]

The next issue the testosterone marketers faced was how to label as many people as possible with Low-T. Even today, there is no universal standard for diagnosing and treating low testosterone in men, with medical guidelines differing across professional societies. Testosterone levels in the blood vary greatly throughout the day and over time. Often, low testosterone is not the primary issue but rather a symptom of something else.

'At any time in life, your testosterone drops if you're ill for any reason,' explains Dr Richard Quinton, a consultant endocrinologist at the Royal Victoria Infirmary in Newcastle. 'And I mean for any reason. If you are up all night, the next day your testosterone will be very low. You have a big meal – that can affect your testosterone level. Any kind of underlying disease can lower your level.'[37]

Medical professionals assess your levels compared to a reference range based on the values found in a healthy population. This involves setting statistical boundaries, often two standard deviations beyond the mean, which classify 5% of the population as abnormal. Moving these boundaries closer to the mean increases the abnormal population. For testosterone, saying anyone who falls below a serum level of 230 ng/dL labels 7% of men over fifty as abnormal, but raising the threshold to 350 ng/dL bumps this proportion up to 26%.[38]

You can guess what happened here. In medical statements Abbott funded, it was claimed that those who fell below 350 ng/dL would be considered to have 'Low T'. It was an effective tactic. They created a $1.6 billion market for testosterone replacement treatment. Between 2003 and 2013, TRT use increased fourfold in men aged eighteen to forty-five, alongside a threefold increase in men between the ages of fifty-six and sixty-four in the US.[39] This trend was mirrored in the UK, where prescriptions almost doubled over a similar period.[40]

'Whether the campaign is motivated by a sincere desire to help men or simply by greed, we should recognize it for what it is: a mass, uncontrolled experiment that invites men to expose themselves to the harms of a treatment unlikely to fix problems that may be wholly unrelated to testosterone levels,' Woloshin wrote.[41] And not everyone was convinced that the benefits of taking TRT for low testosterone outweighed the risks, including the FDA.

As prescriptions surged, likely for its off-label use as a drug for ageing, the FDA issued multiple warnings. In 2015, the agency requested that manufacturers change their labelling to clarify that 'prescription testosterone products are approved only for men who have low testosterone levels caused by certain medical conditions'. The mandate extended to explicit warnings about heart attacks and strokes.[42] UK regulators had an equally circumscribed approach, approving testosterone only for hypogonadism (testosterone deficiency with clinical symptoms). It is not considered a treatment for low testosterone caused by ageing.

As we've seen in previous chapters, off-label marketing is illegal. But AbbVie and others were able to circumvent the regulations that prevent advertising off-label uses of the drug through framing 'Low-T' as a disease-awareness campaign. This strategy won them plaudits. While some in the medical profession were becoming increasingly concerned, the medical marketing press had a different view. AbbVie was being celebrated for the 'vim, vigour and sales drive' for its AndroGel campaign.

The company 'took a taboo topic and, via a cagey media-and-marketing strategy, rendered it less wince-inducing among its target audience', *Medical Marketing & Media* enthused.[43] Moreover, it 'did so at a time when a number of critics voiced their concerns that the marketing and use of testosterone-boosting products had gotten ahead of the science'.[44]

Some lawyers sniffed an opportunity. Testosterone manufacturers could be charged with failing to adequately warn patients of the risks of TRT, like the FDA had recommended. AbbVie itself settled 4,200 lawsuits related to AndroGel in September 2018.[45] But many years after testosterone hit the market for those without hypogonadism and lawsuits have been settled, there are still unresolved questions about the benefits versus the harms.

Some positive news came via the 2023 TRAVERSE trial studying 5,246 men aged forty-five to eighty with hypogonadism who were at high cardiovascular risk – so not men with normal levels just wanting a testosterone boost. Funded and overseen by manufacturers of testosterone replacement therapy, it was published in the *New England Journal of Medicine* comparing testosterone gel to placebo.[46] Both groups had similar cardiovascular event rates (about 7%) and overall adverse events, with slight increases in arrhythmias, kidney injury and lung blood clots in the testosterone group.

But some caution against saying that TRT provides a clean bill of health.[47] Over 60% of participants stopped taking the medication before the study concluded, possibly due to side effects or perceived lack of benefit. While short-term use appears safe, long-term safety is as yet unclear. Even this large trial found only very subtle effects from TRT. So subtle, in fact, that any individual benefit is likely to be more placebo than truly physiological, Jayasena says.

But the saga over harms and the ultra-conservativeness of the medical establishment might have created a knowledge gap, into which private clinics offering excessively high doses of testosterone have stepped, Jayasena adds. There's a 'U-shaped curve' for testosterone, meaning too little is bad for you and too much is bad for you, he says.

The TRAVERSE trial focused on carefully controlled doses. But the inappropriate doses being prescribed by some private providers – what Jayasena calls 'TRT plus plus plus' – fall outside this evidence base. These elevated doses come with potential harms, including increased blood pressure, worsened cholesterol and perhaps a higher risk of heart disease, he adds.

Jayasena has analysed health websites offering TRT across the globe, systematically categorising their claims against international medical guidelines. He tells me he's shocked by his findings, saying that most UK websites were peddling false claims about testosterone's benefits.

The UK and North America are the 'major epicentres' of this marketing, with roughly a fifth of the sites asserting that testosterone has rejuvenating, anti-ageing effects. One particularly egregious example came from a UK online pharmacy that overstated the risks of 'very low testosterone', warning visitors that it 'can be linked to a host of serious diseases in later life and older age'. Taking advantage of pandemic fears, the site cites a single study of thirty-one male patients in intensive care for Covid-19 in May 2020 to say there is research suggesting that very low testosterone 'can make men more vulnerable to the effects of Coronavirus'.

As we saw in previous chapters, companies have found ways to work around the ban on direct-to-consumer advertising of prescription drugs and it's no different for TRT. One UK website includes an article that discusses why celebrities like Joe Rogan, Jeff Bezos and Hugh Jackman use testosterone. Reasons include preserving their appearance, muscle mass and strength. The article also features embedded YouTube clips of these celebrities endorsing the advantages of testosterone therapy.

As I was investigating the evidence around the benefits and harms of testosterone, I asked various large language models to give me information in a general query. They used some of the information from these websites in their evaluation of the evidence. Thus the advice is far from impartial. The sources for the information these sites offer will be worth considering in the future.

A new generation of questionnaires has also sprung up, which Jayasena has tested. These surveys ask vague, leading questions like 'Do you feel tired? Do you want more energy?' – essentially questions that virtually any man over fifty could answer 'yes' to. 'I answered "no" to everything', he says, 'but it still ended with, "You may have low testosterone. Call us for a consultation." I've had patients from such clinics who were told they needed treatment when their levels were completely normal.'

Given that testosterone treatment is typically framed as a lifelong commitment, men's health clinics throughout the UK and US have developed lucrative subscription models. These typically cost several hundred pounds or dollars per month, offering comprehensive packages that include routine blood tests, hormone injections, and periodic doctor consultations. To boost retention and secure revenue streams, some offer discounts for patients willing to commit to extended six-month or annual contracts upfront.

## GATEWAY TESTING

Sometimes they use the need to get tested as a way to get people through the door. Nickel's analysis of 200 Instagram and TikTok posts showed that over two-thirds had financial motives tied to promoting testosterone testing. Naturally, testing sets the stage for pursuing TRT and may include the promotion of related supplements. As with other health issues, testing is increasingly a way to offer people a range of other services and treatments. But increasing medicalisation can lead to uncertain benefits and perhaps tilt the equation in the direction of harms.

A Facebook advert for the company 'Let's Get Tested' depicts a man and woman sitting side by side on the edge of a bed. Captioned with the words: 'Sex isn't everything said the guy with low testosterone.' The ad says that levels can be tested at home with a 'quick and easy testosterone test'.

In 2022, urologist Justin Dubin grew alarmed at patients being prescribed testosterone without valid medical reasons or warnings about side effects. To investigate what was going on, he went undercover as a secret shopper at seven men's online health clinics, publishing his findings in *JAMA Internal Medicine*.[48] Following a script, he posed as a happily married 34-year-old man experiencing low energy, decreased sex drive and erectile dysfunction. He told potential prescribers he read about low testosterone and was worried he might have it.

Dubin submitted his lab results showing healthy hormone levels. 'It was pretty clear that I did not need testosterone,' he said. Yet six of the seven clinics offered to prescribe injectable testosterone, defying medical society guidelines. They also suggested several other inappropriate testosterone-boosting drugs and supplements for his hypothetical case. 'As DTC [direct-to-consumer] testosterone therapy increases in popularity, patients and clinicians should be educated about the potential pitfalls of these platforms,' he wrote.

When Woloshin read the secret shopper paper he thought 'What the fuck?' he tells me. What Dubin found 'was just egregious,' he said. Despite Dubin's script clearly stating his desire to have a child soon, half of the online clinics offering testosterone didn't warn him about the hormone's potential to reduce fertility – among other harms. 'For this simulated patient, it could interfere with his goal to have children, and they were treating something he didn't have,' Woloshin said. 'It just seemed like terrible medical practice.'

A content analysis by sexual health specialists of TikTok videos posted between October 2022 and October 2023 examined information about TRT circulating on the platform. Not a single video mentioned the long-term impact that TRT has on sperm production.[49]

At his clinic at Beth Israel Deaconess Medical Center at Harvard Medical School, endocrinologist Dr Michael S. Irwig tells me he feels like he's swimming against the tide of demand for testosterone. Encouraging men to take an interest in their health is positive. Historically, men have not visited health services when necessary and have engaged in fewer health-promoting behaviours than women. But these clinics don't always promote genuine health improvement, he says.

Many of Irwig's patients arrive armed with prescriptions after obtaining diagnoses from online clinics. He finds himself devoting substantial time to dissuading men from purchasing testosterone off the internet and urging them to steer clear of what he terms 'predatory' men's health clinics.

Irwig believes it's irresponsible to prescribe testosterone to men with borderline low levels, even when these men are actively seeking treatment. He prefers recommending lifestyle modifications as the first approach for many symptoms. However, he acknowledges the difficulty of promoting this approach in a society that gravitates toward immediate quick-fix solutions like medication or surgery – options heavily promoted by clinics, social media personalities and online pharmacies.

He illustrates his point with a portrait of a typical fifty-year-old patient, who is overweight, has type 2 diabetes or pre-diabetes, hypertension, elevated cholesterol, sleep apnoea and a largely sedentary lifestyle. For this man, the most effective intervention would come from losing weight and exercising more. Even without weight loss, exercise would improve his cardiovascular health, and if he does shed some pounds, it would help address his diabetes, high blood pressure, high cholesterol and sleep apnoea. These are problems that testosterone therapy cannot fix. A meta-analysis of twenty-four studies suggests that weight loss is an effective way to boost testosterone levels in obese men, offering the best chance to alleviate symptoms and improve health.[50] In fact, testosterone levels can reflect a man's overall health status. Men with lower testosterone may have problems because they are less fit or have lower health status, he says.

Depression is another critical issue. In a study of 200 men with borderline total testosterone levels, 56% had depression and/or depressive symptoms.[51] However, depression is a diagnosis that many men find difficult to accept. Irwig says that while his patients are quick to embrace testosterone therapy, they often hesitate to seek professional treatment for depression. There's still a stigma attached. There's a notion that feeling depressed might suggest weakness. When people connect their moods to physical causes, they're often seeking a way to understand themselves without wrongly feeling like they're somehow to blame.

Irwig worries that his cautious approach to prescribing testosterone often drives men towards online men's health clinics, some of which are much less scrupulous. 'I wonder if my quest to dissuade men from jumping on the testosterone bandwagon is similar to

Don Quixote's battle with windmills,' he muses.[52] It might be that we're witnessing a change in what's wanted and expected.

Talking to men about testosterone can be challenging, Jayasena explains. Many patients arrive confidently armed with extensive information gathered from social media and internet forums. Some turn to the NHS having already obtained testosterone from elsewhere and some have suffered ill-effects from taking it. Recognising this growing phenomenon, Jayasena has begun to develop a specialised national service designed specifically for these patients.

In Glasgow, the NHS has introduced an Image and Performance Enhancing Drugs Clinic, providing injecting equipment, blood tests and information sessions to help clients manage their dosages. The clinic also advocates for reducing use and, in some instances, cessation. It is harm reduction as discussed in previous chapters.

John Campbell, who manages needle exchanges across over seventy sites, says that social media has heavily influenced expectations. 'TRT is a concern for us – it's a term that's crept in over the last five years,' Campbell says. 'Many clients' doses far exceed what we could expect to prescribe medically for TRT. That continuous use brings with it the increased likelihood of more side effects and complications in the long term.'[53] Some clients in the clinics have testosterone levels so high they're not measurable. Others have reduced sperm production or erectile dysfunction, which can last for many months or even years. 'It's a really difficult place for people to be. They often have no energy, feeling very down, bordering on depression,' Campbell says.

Moreover, stopping testosterone becomes increasingly difficult the higher your dosage has been. Once you begin taking testosterone, the body naturally responds by shutting down its own production of the hormone. This may cause the testosterone-producing cells to stop working and the testicles to soften and shrink, Dr Harry Fisch, former director of the Male Reproductive Center of New York Presbyterian Hospital, says.[54]

The impact of this on withdrawal is debated in medical circles. 'If a guy suddenly stops taking testosterone after using it for more than a month or so, he's very likely to feel terrible – he could have low energy, low sex drive, be irritable and even feel depressed. These withdrawal symptoms powerfully motivate guys to keep refilling their "T" prescriptions,' he adds. Recovery of testicular function may be prolonged.

It's only in Reddit forums that you hear what happens after men start testosterone therapy, such as the additional drugs they take to manage the side effects. These can include treatments to keep the testicles functioning to preserve fertility, and others to reduce excess oestrogen (testosterone naturally converts to oestrogen in the body to support bone health). These complexities rarely feature in podcasts or glossy TRT adverts, which tend to focus on the promises about what it can treat.

## CORRECTING THE BALANCE

The rosy picture of replacement hormones, while potential harms are glossed over, is also a problem in women's healthcare, despite HRT being an established treatment with clear evidence of benefit. I've talked with multiple consultant gynaecologists and women's health specialists who report spending considerable time correcting misconceptions about hormones, while simultaneously dealing with the consequences of private prescriptions that were never clinically indicated in their NHS practice. They stress that HRT and the different preparations often need tweaking, and decisions are very much down to individual choice.

However, to try to combat the hyperbole around HRT, Mukherjee created her own Instagram account. She explains that her challenge is presenting balanced information: 'HRT is good for this, not good for that. Some women do well, others don't.' This nuanced approach, she laments, doesn't align with social media algorithms that thrive on extreme perspectives such as 'I love HRT,' or 'I hate HRT,' or 'I'm having a terrible menopause.' 'We've got a situation where you've got social media algorithms where you see more of what you like and against this backdrop women are looking for information,' Mukherjee says.

The platforms heavily favour those with dedicated PR teams who understand how to manipulate algorithms to their advantage and consistently produce content that keeps followers engaged. Whole new markets flourish here that encompass menopause coaches, nutritionists, acupuncturists and self-styled healers, all competing for attention and clients. These job titles were completely non-existent just a decade ago, Professor Bassel Wattar, a consultant obstetrician and gynaecologist, tells me.

Of course, there are the predictable opportunists – those with large followings who monetise their online popularity by selling or endorsing countless supplements, tests and wellness products that have no scientific evidence supporting their effectiveness. But more concerningly, there are qualified and licensed doctors offering treatments that lack an evidence base, disregarding the risk of harm. Once a niche subspecialty, menopause has now become a thriving area for private healthcare. 'There was no demand. There was certainly no private practice in it,' Wattar says. Now there's been a rush to fill that void, with some making their living from referrals from Instagram.

'Online, private clinics can claim they have no conflicts of interest, while they may be selling huge amounts of products,' Mukherjee says. 'They'll tell you, "if you do this, you'll be amazing, and I care about you," while also vilifying traditional doctors as people who don't listen or care.' And there are plenty of people I've spoken to who feel dismissed by the NHS. They find the care and support they need on social media.

It's fair to say doctors don't always agree on interpretation of evidence, and Dr Louise Newson is a polarising figure in the field. Some specialists view her practice as problematic, yet many patients praise her for providing much-needed help. Referred to as the 'medic who ignited the menopause revolution', she began focusing on the topic in 2018 and has mastered Instagram, where she posts as @menopause_doctor. Through this platform, she also promotes her podcast, her 'Menopause Masterclass', and Newson Health, her network of private clinics.

Newson makes regular television appearances and is the go-to voice for many non-medical celebrity menopause influencers. However, in 2023, the British Menopause Society removed Newson from its register of menopause specialists because of concerns that 'aspects of her practice' did not fit with 'established guidance'.

In 2024, a BBC *Panorama* investigation raised serious concerns about her practice. They alleged she was prescribing high doses of oestrogen without increasing progesterone accordingly. This can lead to complications, including thickening of the womb lining, which can be a precursor to cancer. Some of her patients told the programme that they had been on higher than licensed doses and had developed such thickening.[55] Others said doctors treating them at Newson Health had continued to increase their doses of oestrogen, despite worsening symptoms, and they had not been informed that the safety of doing so had not been established. Some patients experienced heavy bleeding as a result.

Newson Health said it used a 'wealth of clinical experience and data' to treat patients on an individualised basis to 'provide the best possible menopause care'. Newson Health said on Instagram that: 'The BBC Panorama programme attempted to frame a biased narrative, which has ultimately restricted women's access to informed care.' They have submitted a formal legal complaint to Ofcom. At the time of writing, they were awaiting their response. The post was liked nearly 45,000 times.[56] Newsom has also pointed out that the British Menopause Society is a charity and not a regulatory authority saying she will continue to challenge 'misinformation'.[57] Newson said that there is no evidence connecting higher doses of oestrogen to an increased risk of long-term harm. She maintains that more damage is likely to result from not providing women with the doses they require. On Instagram she says that people are sensationalising the issue worrying women needlessly. She says that she's 'seen people have their dose reduced [by other doctors]' and 'seen them have very difficult consequences with horrendous symptoms that have returned.'[58] But as the old medical adage goes, absence of evidence is not evidence of absence. 'The bottom line is her practice is not founded or based on evidence. It's based on the lack of evidence, which is not a cautious and safe approach to help patients,' Wattar says.

Following the broadcast, the *Daily Mail* reported that a tearful Newson had described the distress the programme caused her. 'I don't care if they don't like me as a person. I don't even care if they don't like the way I prescribe because I'm an independent practitioner.' 'These clinics are like my fourth child,' she said. 'I don't actually know any more what these people want. Do they want to see me dead? Do they want to see me in an asylum? I don't understand.'[59]

Many of her followers were unhappy and rushed to sympathise. 'The press should be ashamed of themselves. Where was the story of the NHS depriving women of HRT?' one fumed. 'How dare they call out Louise for the amazing work she is doing in trying to redress the balance in this badly overlooked aspect of women's health' another commented. Another accused the press of doing 'a hatchet job' with 'persistent medical misogyny and gaslighting'.

Davina McCall took to Instagram to express her disappointment in a seven-minute video that the documentary will deter women from taking the 'lifeline' medicine. 'I felt like – once again – it was designed to kind of put us off trying to take hormone replacement therapy,' she said crediting Newson for giving her the courage to take HRT. Other celebrities joined her in this criticism.

Newson isn't the only doctor using Instagram to promote her menopause services. There are plenty of others. And, of course, they provide services that many women want, while they also have a right to choose treatment that goes outside medical guidelines. But this creates a challenge for the NHS.

When patients return to NHS care, still struggling with the symptoms that prompted them to seek HRT in the first place, some doctors have told me they face challenges correcting the idea that higher and higher doses lead to better and better results. Even when presented with the medical guidance, some patients still want to continue up the dosage escalator. 'Some people I've seen may then increase the dose themselves at home, despite the lack of supporting studies,' Wattar says.

At his NHS hospital, Wattar had to establish a policy that their clinic was not obliged to continue out-of-guidance prescriptions from private clinics. 'We inform patients: "We respect your previous prescriber, but we cannot continue this prescription. We only provide HRT according to national guidelines,"' he tells me.

Mukherjee also spends significant amounts of time explaining to patients why the information they've received from their previous prescriber is incorrect; she estimates that 70% of her patients have misconceptions about HRT. 'Can you imagine GPs in the NHS trying to do that in ten minutes? It's almost impossible for them. As a specialist, it's difficult for me because I have less time to focus on the empowering things I want to share with my patients, and instead, I spend more time myth-busting,' she says.

Mukherjee has encountered several women who were prescribed ten times the licensed dose of HRT from private clinics. They sought her help because they suspected something was wrong. They were being charged for every call and test while their doses kept increasing. Many experienced severe bleeding without getting any relief from their symptoms.

Women have told her they've tried every type of HRT without success. According to some of these clinics, testosterone is supposedly the crucial missing element needed to treat their anxiety, energy, stress and even their troubled marriages. Newson for one says it's 'barbaric and wrong that women aren't able to access their own hormone'.[60]

Again, not everyone agrees. 'The evidence for testosterone helping with those general symptoms is zero. Again, that's all propaganda,' Mukherjee says. Testosterone might be offered for sex drive after other interventions have been tried. To date, clinical trials of testosterone have not shown a beneficial effect on cognition, mood, energy and musculoskeletal health in women.[61] The safety profile is in some ways less well studied in women than in men. A large trial is currently under way based in Cardiff, investigating the non-libido effects of testosterone on general wellbeing, mood, bone density and muscle strength, with results expected in a couple of years.

In the short term, Mukherjee says women have come to her with their hair falling out, a deepening voice or new acne and hair growth on their bodies. When she measures their testosterone, it's sometimes equivalent to a man's level. But we know very little about the longer-term effects.

There's a reluctance by the pharmaceutical industry to 'finance further clinical studies' to allow female androgenic products, such as testosterone, to get a licence, the British Menopause Society says.[62] But perhaps there's little incentive either. Even in the NHS, testosterone prescriptions for women are increasing, despite access being more controlled there than in the private sector.[63]

In July 2024, in what is a damning statement from a medical organisation whose members could arguably benefit financially from prescribing drugs, the British Menopause Society said: 'Misinformation risks medicalising a normal life stage and render[s] women dependent upon clinicians, some of whom may also be overly promoting treatment with testosterone, which is associated with a high placebo response.'[64]

## BIOHACKING MENOPAUSE

Others outside more conventional medicine have made a career out of treating the menopause too. If the 'Davina Effect' has helped normalise HRT, the 'Davinia Effect' has led to a championing of an alternative, 'natural' approach to menopause.

Former *Hollyoaks* actress Davinia Taylor is a biohacker and wellness enthusiast who champions supplements and lifestyle modifications over conventional HRT. Her *Sunday Times* bestseller, *Hack Your Hormones* – reverentially referred to as the 'hormone bible' by some followers – advocates for a holistic approach to managing menopause symptoms. While few would argue against comprehensive wellness strategies and other ways to mitigate symptoms, it's the accompanying products that have raised eyebrows. With over a million Instagram followers, Taylor shares natural wellness tips while promoting her supplement brand, Willpowder. She's also on TikTok.

Former human resources manager Erica (not her real name) was captivated by Taylor's approach when she was struggling with menopausal symptoms. During a sabbatical from her draining job, she spent more time on social media. She spoke to me candidly about her experiences. 'Davinia is so down-to-earth,' she says. 'We all know what she's been through, and she just says it how it is.'

Erica opted not to take HRT because of a family history of cancer. Frustrated that her doctor only discussed HRT without offering alternative options, she turned to social media to explore what she could potentially do. 'Watching people go through their menopause journeys and learning from different creators has been eye-opening. TikTok helped me find the best supplements to support myself through menopause,' she says.

It wasn't long before Erica went from being a TikTok consumer – buying trending water bottles, make-up brushes and supplements – to becoming a creator and seller. She now sells supplements through her own TikTok Shop. We can see how this may be problematic for healthcare and wellbeing when we look at how it works. TikTok content creators use a feature called 'Product Marketplace', enabling them to browse products, integrate them into their videos and share them with their audience. The platform also allows creators to request free samples from brands and select which ones to endorse.

If a creator/seller selects a product to endorse, then they must create a video or do a live show within fourteen days. 'When I create the video I add the link to the product for customers to select on that video, which then ultimately pays me a commission,' Erica says. At first, she says, she was earning 'probably a pound or two a day', but a few months later 'things picked up super quickly'. Now Erica's making a living from her shop. 'TikTok has changed my life for the better in so many ways,' she says.

Erica selects products for her shop based on her personal use. She openly acknowledges that she avoids diving into the scientific details, as she finds them difficult to grasp. Instead, she relies on company websites to learn about the products and reviews to guide her choices. 'I trust the website is honest and go by how I feel,' she says.

Standing casually in her kitchen with cupboards visible behind her, she posts videos describing the supplements she takes. It's a dizzying list, including magnesium, lion's mane, turmeric, berberine, chondroitin and psyllium husk. One particular brand finds favour as it's been developed by someone with a PhD. 'I feel I've found my own happy balance now,' she says in one post accompanied by a series of hashtags: #menopause #supplements #health #wellbeing #tiktokmademedoit #tiktokmademebuyit.

'It's mind-blowing how many options there are, but it's about trial and error to find what works,' Erica insists. But Erica, like many others, has a financial incentive in saying something works: her income is linked to the content she puts out. No matter how genuine and well-meaning her recommendations are, the line between advice from a peer and a sales pitch from a promoter has become blurred.

Baroness Alexandra Freeman has reviewed the evidence on menopause treatments and collaborated in developing a decision aid for the NHS to explain the various options. This tool is designed to help GPs discuss treatments with patients so they can make informed choices based on the best available evidence. However, the issue is more complex than simply determining whether a treatment works or not, as the data for many interventions are often limited or of poor quality.

She explains that the scientific evidence for supplements and complementary medicines is frequently inadequate, including for menopause treatments. The research studies are typically small in scale, and there's often publication bias – research tends to be published only when it shows results. This means that all the studies showing a particular supplement had no effect typically stay unpublished. Many women, understandably, take both Davina and Davinia's advice to heart, combining HRT with various supplements, willing to try anything that might help them feel better.

This is not just a medical issue; it's shaped by culture, business interests and gender roles. Hormones are framed as fixes for existential discomfort, mid-life malaise and the feeling of being left behind. Behind the idea of empowerment is a system that at times medicalises normal human experiences and monetises them.

Why does this matter? As Newson argued in defence of her practice, if a woman chooses HRT, why shouldn't she have it? Surely how we manage our bodies' challenges should be our decision, especially when we're the ones paying for it?

Men and women may be making potentially life-altering decisions based on misleading information. Would so many men eagerly take testosterone if they fully understood the risk that their bodies might never produce it naturally again? That isn't to say that these treatments can't play an important role. It's just that perhaps they're not the quick fix we might hope they are.

# 10

# THE NEW PREVENTIVE MEDICINE

It was a dinner party for the ages. The Kardashians, Stanford University neuroscientist and podcast host, Professor Andrew Huberman, together with other influencers making a show of feasting on rather austere fare: broccoli, cauliflower, black lentils and nutty pudding – a concoction of walnuts, macadamia nuts, pomegranate juice, berries and cinnamon.[1] The occasion was one of US multi-millionaire biohacker Bryan Johnson's bi-weekly 'Don't Die' dinners, starting at 5 p.m. and ending at 7:30 p.m. Sleep, of course, had to be optimised. As one punter on Instagram quipped, this was 'the collab nobody asked for'.

Party host, Utah-born Johnson, a former Mormon missionary, has become the infamous tech entrepreneur poster child for a movement focused on achieving immortality. After serving as a missionary in Ecuador, he founded a web payments company that later acquired Venmo, the money transfer app. This was later sold to PayPal.[2]

Johnson uses multiple platforms – including Instagram – to promote his bespoke 'Blueprint Protocol' online. This offers a selection of health supplements, blood-testing kits and other products, conveniently available for purchase through his website – targeting those with enough disposable income seeking optimal health. 'By doing Blueprint, one of the key objectives is to achieve the lowest possible biological age,' he claimed. He added that his health regimen had 'reversed [sic]' his by 5.1 years.[3]

With a legion of dedicated followers, Johnson is not just one of the most famous and controversial faces in longevity: he's at the vanguard of self-experimentation. A cadre of scientists who obsessively read the scientific literature on ageing and longevity, use Johnson as a guinea pig for what they consider to be the most promising treatments.[4]

The regime he reportedly follows amounts to a lonely full-time occupation. It includes sleeping alone and taking dozens of supplements a day – as well as blasting his pelvic floor with electromagnetic pulses to improve muscle tone in hard-to-reach places. He operates on a strict caloric deficit: consuming 1,977 each day. In the past he has also used off-label prescription drugs, popular among Silicon Valley types in their bid to defy death.

When Greek philosophers created the maxim 'know thyself,' they could not have imagined someone as dedicated as Johnson. Through extreme self-quantification – blood glucose, heart rate variability, oxygen saturation and even his nocturnal erections – Johnson attempts to assess the effectiveness of his interventions.[5] All of this is shared on social media. It's unlikely that anyone's medical data has ever been so widely viewed on a daily basis. In the not too distant future, he suggests, human body management will all be outsourced (and his, likely open source) to AI.

Johnson's quest for longevity extends to extreme experimentation. In 2023, he involved his seventeen-year-old son, Talmage, and his seventy-year-old father, Richard in the 'the world's first multigenerational plasma exchange', a procedure approved by Johnson's team of over thirty doctors.[6]

The idea of rejuvenation through 'young blood' might evoke tales of 'Countess Dracula', Elizabeth Báthory, more than credible medical science. However, drawing on limited studies in mice – where plasma infusions appeared to enhance the memory of older mice[7] – Johnson speculated that receiving plasma from his son could help repair age-related cellular damage and lower his biological age. Talmage had a litre of blood drawn, which was separated into plasma, red blood cells, white blood cells and platelets. The plasma was then infused into Bryan, who later donated some of his own plasma for his father's benefit.

Plasma constitutes about 55% of blood. It acts as a transport system, carrying platelets, red blood cells and white blood cells throughout the body. It is rich in antibodies, proteins and other vital substances. Plasma is used in clinical practice, such as in transfusions to treat severe blood loss resulting from events like car accidents or complications during childbirth. The antibodies it contains, known as immunoglobulins, can be used to create medicines for people whose immune systems aren't working properly. But there aren't any trials that show that receiving plasma from a younger donor has any anti-ageing effect, although various biotech firms worked on the hypothesis that it could.

In 2019, the FDA issued a public warning in response to the now-defunct company Ambrosia, which had offered plasma infusions to the public for $8,000 as part of a 'trial'. The agency said that plasma infusions are not approved to treat conditions like normal ageing, memory loss, Alzheimer's or Parkinson's disease. Additionally, such treatments carry risk of harm, including allergic reactions, acute lung injuries and, in rare cases, infections from contaminated plasma.[8] But that didn't stop Johnson. Nor the clinic he visited.

After undergoing the infusion, Johnson conceded that it yielded no tangible benefits for him personally. However, he declared on Twitter that his 'super blood reduced my Dad's age by 25 years… my father is now aging at the rate of a 46 year old'. 'I am my dad's blood boy,' he wrote. Dr Oliver Zolman, the physician leading Johnson's team in in 2023, admitted, 'We have not achieved any remarkable results. In Bryan, we have achieved small, reasonable results, and it's to be expected.'[9]

Independent observers were more scathing. When Johnson showed up at the annual retreat for the Academy for Health &

Lifespan Research in 2023, a doctor in attendance told *Time*: 'He looked sick. He was pale. I don't know what he did with his face.'[10] Johnson, however, says he welcomes the 'haters'. 'They're engaging with me, they're offering me their perspectives, and I love it.'

His website proclaims that he is 'at war with death and its causes'. And it's one that commands all of his considerable resources. But he's not unique in this anxiety, only enabled by his wealth to take it to extremes.

## THE MANY DRIVERS OF AGEING

Ageing is a complex process, influenced by genetic and environmental factors. It starts with subtle biological changes, often unnoticed, which gradually build up from mid-life onward. This plays a role in causing common age-related diseases and multiple health conditions at once (known as multi-morbidity).[11] Recent studies of thousands of people's genetic and personal data in the UK suggest that for many of these illnesses someone's environment – their living conditions, physical activity and smoking – plays a bigger role than genetics.[12]

As you age, you are more likely to develop an age-related condition, like high blood pressure, which carries a lifetime risk of 90%.[13] Changes in the body's functions also increase the risk of illnesses like diabetes, cancer, heart disease and dementia.

Ironically, reaching this stage of life is considered a form of success. In 1900, life expectancy (how long you can expect to live, on average) in England and Wales was forty-four years for men and forty-eight years for women.[14] This was largely influenced by high infant mortality rates,[15] with one-third of all deaths occurring among children under the age of five.[16] But advances in sanitation, antibiotics and vaccines in the twentieth century played a big role in fighting infectious diseases, helping people live much longer lives. By 2011, a baby boy could be expected to live to the age of 79.0 and a baby girl 82.8.

This, however, varies depending on where you live. There's a north–south divide in England, with people in southern regions typically having longer life expectancies than those in northern regions.[17] Progress has slowed recently, and modern medicine has extended life mostly by saving older lives rather than younger ones, leading to longer periods of poor health. Data from the Centre for Ageing Better show that, on average, people in England spend a little over sixty years in good health. Men spend about 78% of their lives in good health, while women spend about 74.5%. But again this varies a lot depending on where you live.[18]

As we know, socioeconomic status shapes health outcomes. The poorer you are, the more likely you'll face chronic conditions including type 2 diabetes, cardiovascular disease, respiratory illnesses and mental health conditions.[19] The wealthy not only live longer but enjoy better health throughout those additional years.

These factors, known as social determinants of health, are among the most powerful drivers of ageing – and there's no single pill or medical intervention that can address them. Preventive healthcare, a long-standing branch of medicine dedicated to illness prevention through population and individual strategies such as vaccinations, healthy diet and exercise promotion, smoking cessation initiatives and cancer screenings, often calls for these determinants to be given greater attention.[20]

Meanwhile, vast sums are being invested in the pursuit of specialised treatments and tailored regimens, widening the divide between what wealthy individuals can access and what is available to the broader population – a disparity dubbed the 'Wellth Divide'.[21] Longevity clinics have sprung up with hefty annual fees promising the ultimate asset: extended years of healthy living. This asset has captivated Silicon Valley, which is perhaps unsurprising. Conquering death would be the ultimate holy grail in disruption: the most extreme act of self-exaltation.

Funding for the market has come from people who have built their fortunes in tech and perhaps believe ageing is a code that can be cracked. Such modern-day Gilgameshes include Peter Thiel, the founder of PayPal, who has poured millions into the

Methuselah Foundation, which aims to make '90 the new 50 by 2030'.[22] Jeff Bezos apparently invests in Altos Labs, based in Cambridgeshire, a firm which has reportedly raised no less than $3 billion in funds to cure ageing.[23] Bryan Johnson is on the extreme end, and it's easy to dismiss his routines and experiments as performative gimmicks. But there's a broad network of longevity influencers – mostly male podcasters, YouTubers and content creators – who promote their protocols, and champion 'science-supported' strategies to slow ageing or maintain healthier lifestyles into later years.

'A lot of the attraction of longevity for people who are already in good health is "Where do I go from here?" and they come to the conclusion that they don't want to die, like this is a priori a totally logical thing to want,' Dr Rohin Francis, a YouTuber, NHS consultant cardiologist and a researcher at University College London, says. Many begin with a solid foundation. They often overlook the role of luck in being forty-five, slim and affluent, overestimating how much their good health is the result of their actions. For Francis, this is symbolic of a hyper-individualistic culture. We're encouraged to believe we have total control over our own fate and these painstaking rituals can make you feel that you're in control of your health.

But this begs an ethical question. By some calculations $2 million – Johnson's annual spend on fighting ageing – would roughly cover the cost of vaccinating over 27,000 infants against eleven different diseases in developing countries.[24] It could cover the cost of 1 million malaria nets for families, helping to prevent a disease that takes over 600,000 lives a year, mostly of children.[25] In a token attempt to redress the balance, at least three public longevity clinics have launched in Singapore, Israel and the US in the last few years. Unlike private facilities, these clinics are connected to public hospitals and charge patients lower fees, in theory making longevity medicines more accessible to those with less money.[26] But on the whole, the ethical question is not one Silicon Valley and the longevity gurus are keen to answer.

Bryan Johnson repeatedly stresses the more egalitarian elements of his protocol in interviews; when speaking to the Indian *Economic Times*, he said that sleep, exercise and diet were the most powerful drugs on the market.[27] But he has no qualms about selling 440 g of 'blueberry nut mix' (dried blueberries, walnuts and macadamia nuts) for almost £40 a pop.

## DIY ANTI-AGEING

This expense and extremity is compelling for some. Platforms like Reddit have dedicated discussions on how to achieve a longer and seemingly healthier life. The spectrum of potential actions includes relatively simple interventions like ice baths but escalates to increasingly radical self-experimentation. Users share regimens involving supplement stacks, TRT and other off-label prescription drugs, hyperbaric oxygen chamber sessions and obsessive monitoring of their 'biological age' through various genetic and biological testing services. Enthusiasts publish their own modified protocols referencing scientific studies – or their interpretations of them – to support their methods.

It's overwhelmingly male-dominated. Interventions are sold in the language of tech and finance. Habits have become 'investments', routines are now 'protocols' and self-care is about 'biohacking' and 'optimisation'. Proponents offer a detailed menu of what to do and when – the kind of personalised advice that 'outdated' mainstream doctors are very unlikely to offer.

People like Daniel Lewis, however, have found solace in the longevity community. The thirty-something corporate lawyer from Austin, Texas tells me the idea of his 'body slowly breaking down over time has always been a bit disturbing'. His discomfort with ageing began during a childhood visit to a retirement home as a seven-year-old choirboy. 'Half of them [residents] were asleep, not even paying attention, and it was so hot and stuffy inside,' he says. 'That experience left a mark on me. I thought, "I don't want to end up like this, feeling this way. I want to stay strong all the way to the end."'

Daniel now assiduously follows 'the advancements in the longevity science community'. He shares his own 'protocols' for others to follow while measuring the biological impact of his anti-ageing routine. It's not Daniel's view, but a distrust of doctors and traditional preventive healthcare prevails. They're seen to be unhelpful and behind the times.

'Doctors – why bother?' asks one poster on Reddit. 'I use them for blood work to ensure I'm not actively dying, but they're always behind the latest research and give generic advice.' 'The standard of care is outdated, and most doctors have no incentive to tailor treatment to individual needs,' another bemoans.

Ryan Crownholme, as we might expect from his data-driven approach to life, is also part of an LA-based longevity group. 'I'm working with a wealth advisor who believes we're all going to live much longer – he's planning for 130 years, not just 80 or 100. He's gathered a group of people interested in longevity, and we've had a few lunches to share ideas.'

Ryan is drawn to experimental technologies, whether or not doctors recommend them. But he hasn't yet gone as far as those who've decamped to Próspera, an experimental town on the Honduran island of Roatán in the Caribbean.[28] Backed by a Delaware-based company, Próspera operates outside the usual regulations of the Honduran government. It's a private, for-profit city with its own governance system, designed to attract foreign investors through low taxes and minimal regulations.

It's an Ayn Rand-style free-market utopia that has attracted investments from Silicon Valley luminaries Peter Thiel, Sam Altman and Marc Andreessen in a bid to transform it into the world's most advanced start-up hub. This includes experimental medical facilities. One healthcare prospectus boasts that it 'injects market mechanisms into the regulatory system', offering flexibility and efficiency for health and biotech innovators.[29]

Businesses are free to adopt regulatory frameworks from other countries or design their own, with the promise of faster market entry and reduced costs, unencumbered by the more stringent standards of the US and Europe. Companies vie to attract medical tourists offering a range of services banned elsewhere. Bryan Johnson visited to have muscle-building gene therapy: 'Follistatin gene therapy ranks seventh among lifespan studies, extending mouse lifespan by over 30%,' he told his followers on Instagram.

Patri Friedman, grandson of free-market economist Milton Friedman, exemplifies the experimental spirit – implanting a Tesla-linked chip into his hand while on the island. During other visits, he used genetically modified bacteria to brush his teeth, reportedly to prevent cavities, and received protein booster injections designed to enhance strength and speed.[30]

For people wanting to try experimental treatments closer to home, Montana has become an officially sanctioned playground for those who want to push scientific boundaries. In May 2025, the state passed a bill to allow anyone to access drugs that have gone through just one phase 1 clinical trial – the first in human safety studies. This might not necessarily result in the promised outcomes, as we'll see later. The bill was passed after lobbying by a longevity group. It expanded on the state's existing Right to Try law, which allows seriously ill people to apply for access to experimental drugs.[31]

The law allows Montana to become a hub of medical tourism with a new licensing system for 'experimental treatment centers'. In exchange, companies have to give 2% of their profits towards helping low-income patients afford treatments.[32] But a clutch of science and health podcasters are steadily bringing what perhaps seem the outlandish obsessions of wealthy entrepreneurs into more mainstream conversations. Where traditional science is slow, methodical and cautious, these podcasters are fast, confident and hyper-capitalist. They bypass safeguards and offer seductive, personalised advice cloaked in sciencey language. With their new vocabulary, they subtly undermine evidence-based medicine, creating new norms.

## PODCASTING HEALTH GURUS

These podcasters reinforce one another's reach. Their views then find their way into the mainstream, feeding an appetite for content about living longer and shaping public discourse. These aren't fringe YouTubers. They're bestselling authors, supplement moguls and TED-style authorities.

In the world of longevity influencers, two in particular stand out: Dr Peter Attia, US-based physician and podcaster, and Professor Andrew Huberman, host of the *Huberman Lab*. With over 6 million subscribers on YouTube and millions more followers on Instagram, it's one of the world's most popular health podcasts. Both heavily emphasise their academic credentials, having collectively attended a number of prestigious universities across the United States.

Each has either dismissed the term 'biohacking' (Huberman – 'it implies people are taking shortcuts when they're just harnessing science')[33] or certain high-profile figures the longevity movement (Attia – 'just smells of snake oil… Most of what I see out there is what I think of as sci-fi longevity').[34]

In an era of waning trust in science, their profiles have taken on extra importance. A 2023 hagiographic feature in *Time* magazine praised Huberman for 'Getting America to care about science'.[35] It portrayed him as a scientific evangelist, achieving the extraordinary feat of drawing millions of Americans into lengthy, in-depth conversations about neuroscience and human biology. And that's no understatement. His podcasts are routinely two to three hours long covering a host of topics – from dopamine and sleep optimisation to exercise protocols, stress resilience frameworks, nutritional biochemistry, longevity pathways and mental health interventions. It's science as self-improvement.

He's been praised for offering 'a fabulous service for the world,' and 'opening the doors' to the often-exclusive world of science sparking excitement for learning among the masses.[36] At a packed New York City show in 2022, Huberman captivated a diverse audience for hours. Patagonia-clad finance bros sat alongside elderly couples and families out with their adult kids, listening to him talk about everything from his childhood to his views on brain science.

Unlike Huberman, Attia is a practising doctor. After dropping out of surgical training, he became a consultant for McKinsey and worked for an energy company before returning to medicine after growing concerns about his 'sausage-like' frame. He has coined his own terminology to describe the different eras of medicine. 'Medicine 1.0' is a pre-modern system to diagnosis and treatment, relying on observation, anecdote and superstition.[37] Think use of leeches, bloodletting and remedies based on humours or spirits.

Current medical practice – what Attia dismissively terms 'Medicine 2.0' – emerged during the seventeenth century's scientific revolution and has come to define modern healthcare. Rooted in the scientific method, germ theory and randomised controlled trials, it has given us major developments in diagnostics, such as MRI and CT scans, pioneering drugs like antibiotics and insulin, and life-saving surgical interventions.

In his view, however, conventional medicine excels at crisis intervention but fails at its more important mission: preventing the crisis entirely. For instance, it resorts to inserting stents to reopen narrowed or blocked coronary arteries, rather than proactively addressing the root causes of these blockages from the outset. He has relabelled this approach 'disease care', emphasising how it addresses pathology rather than cultivating optimal function.

Through his Austin-based telemedicine practice, he practises what he calls 'Medicine 3.0' – a model that emphasises proactive, personalised prevention aimed at improving both 'healthspan' (the period of life spent in good health) and lifespan. (Although some are sceptical that you get this long life where you're healthy and 'then you fall off a cliff'.)[38] His methods involve diagnostic and genetic testing, exercise plans and supplements, catering to an affluent and select clientele for an undisclosed fee.

Healthy ageing is like investing in retirement, he says, emphasising that the only real power we have lies in our individual choices.

He's aware that what he advocates encourages a widening divide – but, he told the *New Yorker*, 'it's absolutely not a problem I'm interested in addressing'.[39]

## SO HOW DO WE LIVE LONGER, HEALTHIER LIVES?

Much of what both Attia and Huberman advocate is obvious. Try to get good quality sleep, a nutritious diet and regular exercise. We know it's wise to avoid smoking and drinking to excess. But some defy the statistics.

Professor S. Jay Olshansky, a public health professor at the University of Illinois, explains that ageing is influenced by a stochastic, or random, component. Some people can lead perfectly healthy lifestyles yet still succumb to diseases like cancer at a young age. Even if something has less than a one in a million chance of happening, it will happen to someone. 'There are random things that go wrong – changes that occur to the DNA of cells, tissues, organs – that lead things to go wrong that are outside our control,' he tells me.

There are others who seem to benefit from unique good fortune. Smoking and obesity are well-known predictors of earlier death, but some people manage to live longer lives than average in spite of their vices. Olshansky points to Jeanne Calment, a French national treasure dubbed 'la doyenne de l'humanité', who still cycled at the age of 100 and recorded a rap album, *Mistress of Time*, when she was 121. She died in 1997, aged 122 – the longest validated human lifespan in history. But she smoked after dinner for most of her life, only giving up at 117.

'Those folks are really interesting to those of us who study ageing because there's something different about them – they are somehow protected. It's not just stochasticity that's influencing what's going on,' he explains. 'Centenarians die of the same things as the rest of us, but later,' he says, adding: 'You might live to a hundred if you could pick your genes. Oh, and don't be lonely.'

Sometimes, the most powerful interventions come from the simplest, most affordable lifestyle choices. Those that have been celebrated in songs and poems throughout history. It might not be Ryan Crownholme's tracked data or Daniel Lewis's structured routines that enhance their health, but the community they've developed around their pursuits. In trying to beat mortality with the latest tech, they've rediscovered one of humanity's oldest remedies: connection. It's something that both Attia and Huberman agree on too.

In 1938, during the hardships of the Great Depression, researchers at Harvard University launched a radical study to uncover the secrets to a healthy and happy life. The study initially focused on 724 boys, some from disadvantaged families in Boston and others Harvard undergraduates. It would become one of the world's longest studies of adult life.[40] Among the original recruits were president-to-be John F. Kennedy and long-time *Washington Post* editor Ben Bradlee. Over time, the study expanded to include the spouses of the men and, more recently, over 1,300 descendants of the original participants.

Over the years, as the study changed hands between different lead scientists, the research continued uninterrupted. Participants were regularly asked to complete questionnaires and monitored for their physical health and emotional wellbeing – including their careers, family lives and friendships. Poring over the data, including vast arrays of medical records and the hundreds of in-person interviews and questionnaires, the researchers came to 'a simple and profound conclusion'.[41]

Writing in the *Atlantic*, lead scientists Robert Waldinger and Marc Schulz said that good relationships are associated with health and happiness. 'The trick is that those relationships must be nurtured.'[42] More than wealth or fame, close relationships with family, friends and community are what keep people happy throughout their lives. Those ties seemed to protect against life's hardships, slow mental and physical decline, and are more associated with a long and happy life than social class, IQ, or even genes – and was true for both Harvard participants and their inner-city counterparts.

One obvious problem with this study is it's observational. It cannot definitively establish causality. For example, while strong relationships are associated with greater happiness and longevity, it's difficult to determine whether good relationships cause happiness or if happier people are more likely to form strong relationships. Another criticism is its lack of racial diversity (participants were mostly White), making it difficult to determine how the findings apply across different cultures.[43]

Findings such as these from observational studies carry extra weight when they're replicated by others. And this is the case here. Other studies seem to lend their support to Waldinger and Schulz's conclusions – but are also limited by their design. One meta-analysis published in *PLoS Medicine* looked at 148 studies that tracked whether people lived or died based on their social connections.[44] It found a strong association between social relationships and mortality risk, noting that people with weak social connections had a mortality risk as high as those who smoke, drink excessively or are physically inactive or overweight.

However, the researchers were conclusive in how their observations related to each other. Their evidence, they said, suggested that good relationships actually lead to longer life, rather than the other way around.

Proving that relationships directly cause longer life is tricky. You can't ethically force some people to be lonely and others to have great friendships, just as you can't randomly assign people to be smokers or non-smokers. But we accept that smoking causes disease because decades of research from multiple angles all point to the same conclusion. Lots of pieces of evidence stack up together to create a fuller picture. Likewise, other research has found that loneliness takes a physical toll on the body, being associated with an increased risk of cardiovascular, metabolic and neurological disorders.[45]

A 2023 systematic review and meta-analysis of prospective studies analysed data from ninety studies involving over 2.2 million adults. The research found that both social isolation and loneliness significantly increase the risks of all-cause mortality, cancer-related deaths and cardiovascular disease to differing degrees.[46] But alleviating it isn't always straightforward. Loneliness is a subjective experience stemming from the gap between the social connection you desire and the connection you actually experience.[47]

A person with a partner and countless friends can still feel lonely, while someone living alone with just a few close connections might feel deeply connected. Loneliness isn't simply explained by the circumstances of someone's life – it depends on how they perceive their social connections. We need to check in and reflect on our needs, Waldinger and Schulz wrote.[48]

Social media has a mixed impact on social connections and loneliness. Scientific evidence shows that social media use is associated with social isolation and loneliness, but the relationship is complex and depends on how, why and how much people use these platforms. Overall, there's also a lack of high-quality evidence from longitudinal studies and trials looking at the impact in different groups.[49]

Dr Amrit Purba Kaur, a researcher at the Digital Mental Health Programme at the Cognition and Brain Sciences Unit, University of Cambridge, agrees with this. She points to one experimental study of 143 undergraduates that found that limiting social media use to thirty minutes per day across multiple platforms for three weeks significantly reduced feelings of loneliness and depressive symptoms compared to a control group.[50] But this can't necessarily be generalised to other demographics and age groups. 'This requires further longitudinal and developmentally specific research,' she tells me.

Other studies have identified similar associations, though the direction of causality remains unclear, as their findings are based on surveys rather than experimental designs. They suggested that young adults who feel isolated might turn to social media for connection, yet excessive use could intensify isolation by replacing genuine social interactions or creating a sense of exclusion through idealised and curated content.[51] This is particularly the case for passive scrolling.

But it's not all negative. Some evidence suggests social media can help alleviate isolation for certain groups, including those with rare diseases, disabilities or people who are geographically or physically isolated. For these people, online communities and support networks offer a sense of connection and belonging that may be difficult to achieve in offline settings.[52] But again the evidence is limited, complicated and mixed.

But insisting on the basics of a good life – such as a good diet, exercise and developing connections – doesn't cut it for growing their audience or securing lucrative sponsorship deals. To stand out in the attention economy, they venture into speculative areas of research.

## THE CONTENT TREADMILL

The need for fresh insights is where scientific rigour fractures, leaving audiences overwhelmed by a flood of information. Episodes must still be produced, sponsors satisfied and audiences engaged. This content treadmill explains the genre's characteristic obsession with minutiae: Attia devoting entire segments to the biomechanical advantages of specific rucksack designs for running; Huberman enumerating the optimal minutes of sun exposure in the morning; Johnson meticulously documenting his supplement regimen down to the milligram. Huberman's team even created an AI tool to help users sift through the thousands of health tips in his content archive – a tech fix to a problem his own prolific output helped create.

People around the world have embraced Huberman and Attia's 'protocols'. They willingly buy supplements, adhere to fasting guidelines, purchase the fitness trackers they sponsor and undertake the medical tests they recommend. However, Ezekiel Emanuel, an oncologist and health policy professor at the University of Pennsylvania and former special advisor to the Obama administration, criticised figures like Attia in the *New Yorker*. They overcomplicate simple advice, he said: 'The idea that you're going to get another healthy decade of life just by doing the things he says is hocus-pocus... No one's got that evidence.'[53]

Instead of acknowledging it outright, they reshape how evidence is discussed, citing reams of studies. 'The general public may not always be aware of how science operates, and people who run these podcasts don't always convey the message of how science works,' Olshansky says.

Many longevity interventions involve supplements, ranging from basic vitamins to complex formulations with extensive ingredient lists. Since they aren't classified as medicines treating specific conditions, they fall under food safety regulations in the UK. While these rules ensure supplements are produced safely and accurately labelled, their availability on the market does not guarantee effectiveness.

Supplements tend to have the most evidence behind them when they are for specific deficiencies or issues. The NHS advises women who are planning to conceive to take folic acid daily, starting before pregnancy and continuing through the first twelve weeks. Folic acid, the synthetic form of folate (vitamin B9), helps to produce healthy red blood cells and is found in certain foods. This supplement helps lower the risk of developmental issues in the early stages of pregnancy. But the picture becomes much murkier when it comes to life extension

Inspired by Johnson, Lewis told one Reddit forum that he had gone from eating a Mediterranean diet with regular exercise, quality sleep and limiting sweets and alcohol to a complex supplement-laden protocol that you'd need a PhD in biochemistry to understand. He described his protocol in detail, which included six carefully measured supplements taken daily: vitamin C, liposomal green tea extract, spermidine, NMN, NAD+ and liposomal Ca-AKG. This all led to increased energy, better gym endurance, less need for sleep, reduced morning grogginess and even a significant decrease in eye puffiness, he said.

Lewis keeps an eye on the scientific studies and uses them to tweak what he is doing – although he admits that there's a lack of robust evidence to support many of his interventions. 'There's certainly no evidence for them on the level you'd find with a prescription drug, so it does require a bit of a leap of faith,' he says.

High price tags can trigger an exaggerated placebo effect. In effect, you cannot afford to not be satisfied. Research also suggests expensive placebos are more effective than cheap ones.[54] 'You consider: is it worth the money? Is it worth taking risks to potentially prevent something inevitable, like ageing and death?' Lewis asks. This is pretty much what Attia says. He owns there's 'great uncertainty'. 'Does the risk outweigh the reward? Everyone has a different tolerance for risk,' Attia says.

There's an obvious problem with this line of thinking. When the hypothetical reward is decades of additional healthy life almost any risk seems acceptable by comparison. The scales are tipped from the outset. That's why longevity advocates will promote extensive testing regimens while dismissing evidence that their interventions lack meaningful benefits. The theoretical prize is simply too seductive to relinquish, regardless of how speculative it is.

What presents itself as sophisticated risk analysis ultimately reduces to something far more elemental: how much are you willing to pay for hope? The answer, for many, is nearly everything – thousands of dollars, uncomfortable regimens and the organisation of daily life around theoretical benefits that may never materialise. If simply selling the promise is enough to attract buyers, there's little motivation to provide evidence that the product will deliver the intended results.

The scepticism around the length of time it takes to generate evidence seen on forums and in Central American enclaves is echoed, to a certain degree, by Attia. He's branded his approach as 'evidence-informed medicine', but is dismissive of using gold-standard randomised controlled trials to generate that evidence. For him, conventional medical guidelines are excessively cautious. For many longevity interventions, waiting for rigorous studies would not only consume decades but would be either unethical or practically impossible. (One example is how exactly would you design a study randomly assigning infants to ketogenic diets from birth through to adulthood?)[55]

Attia rejects the medical principle of doing no harm, calling it 'sanctimonious bullshit' that traps doctors in passivity and resignation to decline, yielding to disease rather than fighting it head-on. But this reasoning creates an elastic standard of evidence. It opens the door to extrapolation from animal studies, mechanistic reasoning and theoretical models. Almost any intervention can be justified as 'evidence-informed' despite lacking robust evidence of either efficacy or safety in humans.

In the absence of high-quality data, Attia suggests that people need to look at the mechanism of action, as well as the short-term and long-term risks both of taking a treatment and of not taking it.

Francis calls this 'mechanistic bias'. The body is more than a 'complex computer' – a machine that can be hacked if you just fiddle with the right processes. 'We've done a bad job of teaching uncertainty, stochastic processes and biological complexity. Their belief [i.e. that of some in the longevity and tech world] that they can micro-manage these things is due to a lack of understanding about reality,' he says.

A compound may have a particular effect in a lab – such as the chemicals in popular herb ashwagandha having anti-inflammatory properties – but that doesn't mean that when you buy it in pill form you will get that effect. The mechanism of action is only the beginning. It suggests there's an avenue worth pursuing in developing a treatment.

There are multiple hurdles in the journey from the lab to the bedside. Is the compound strong enough? Can it survive stomach acid and pass through the intestinal wall? Will it reach the right tissues in an active form and in therapeutic quantities?

There are differences in our metabolisms, gut bacteria, medications and genetics, affecting how something works in the body. Even when scientists feel confident about a compound's mechanism of action, nearly 90% of drug candidates fail clinical trials and never get to patients.[56] Many compounds fail to effectively treat the intended condition, cause unexpected side effects or fall short in how they are absorbed, distributed and processed by the body.

Supplement marketing, however, hinges on claims about mechanisms of action and broad statements. Manufacturers are prohibited from asserting that supplements can treat, prevent or cure diseases, including conditions linked to ageing. However, since ageing is not classified as a disease, supplements can be advertised as supporting ageing, preserving youth or promoting overall health, Dr Pieter Cohen tells me that the UK has a clearer regulatory framework than the US, but the principles are similar.

Described as 'the toxic supplement hunter' by *Men's Health*, Cohen has spent fifteen years uncovering dangerous dietary supplements and flaws in FDA oversight.[57] He began this work in 2006 after his patients started experiencing serious side effects from weight-loss supplements laced with amphetamines. 'You can say "In this petri dish, these cells lived an extra day or two," and boom, you have your anti-ageing data. It doesn't matter that it has nothing to do with humans or actual health,' he adds.

Cohen tells his patients that if a supplement has any effect on the body, it comes with potential harms – very little is risk free. Plus if you're taking multiple supplements, or taking them alongside medications, there's a chance of adverse interactions. 'There are serious researchers who believe there will eventually be mechanisms to slow ageing, and that might be true. But we're clearly not there yet, and selling dietary supplements before this is worked out is not going to be successful,' Cohen says.

When someone like Attia shares his own supplement protocols, he often qualifies his endorsements. But whatever caveats he gives, the fact that he uses a product at all serves as an endorsement to his fans. Francis is concerned about the weasel words that are used by some of the podcasters to describe what they're doing. 'While Dr Attia isn't directly telling others to do the same, he knows people trust him deeply. Many look up to him and think: "If he's doing this, maybe I should take these supplements every day too." That's the grey area where an influencer might say, "I didn't tell anyone to do this,"' he says.

Research by the Advertising Standards Authority (ASA) in 2024 has explored what they call a 'uniquely intimate and personal bond between podcast hosts and their listeners' that changes how advertising functions in this medium.[58] When hosts share personal stories and experiences a bond develops that mimics friendship. The relationship intensifies with well-known hosts, because listeners feel they're receiving privileged access to 'unfiltered' and 'authentic' perspectives. Premium subscription models cement this connection by creating a sense of exclusivity and deepening listener loyalty.[59]

The podcast space – just like social media – is awash with commercial conflicts of interest. On podcasts, hosts often discuss various recommendations for sleep, supplements, devices and wearables, only to swiftly segue into an advertisement. Sometimes, these hosts are not just promoters; they're also sponsors, investors, or even co-founders of the brands and products they're endorsing – a relationship they justify by claiming they only partner with products they use personally.

What concerns regulators is how listeners perceive these arrangements. Rather than recognising paid promotions, audiences may think that the host has carefully selected a brand based on genuine belief in their product's quality. This becomes particularly problematic when the host is seen as an expert in their field. It can be difficult for listeners to distinguish between evidence-based recommendations and commercial interests, the ASA report suggested. The study found this dynamic especially troubling in health and wellness podcasts, where unregulated advice could impact consumers' wellbeing. As one participant noted: 'If it is a health programme, you obviously care about your health...then you are more vulnerable if someone [the host] talks about "these vitamins being good"...that might be coercive.'

The audio-only format compounds these issues. Unlike visual media where disclosures like '#ad' signal sponsored content, podcasts don't offer these visual cues. Despite seeming like radio, podcasts fall under the UK's Non-broadcast Advertising Code, which lacks comparable regulatory frameworks.

Huberman, for example, shares his supplement protocol and is an advocate of Athletic Greens nutritional supplement – now AG1. He, along with Attia, is on AG1's Scientific and Medical Advisory Council to 'educate consumers on the science around nutrition and healthy habits'.[60] They're also a sponsor of his podcast on which he talks about how he uses the AG1 supplement to help cover his 'nutritional bases'. Like Attia, he uses complicated scientific terminology in his podcasts, covering neurons and circadian rhythms and endogenous opioids, and mechanistic descriptions about what he's doing.

This is 'scienceploitation': the use of scientific terminology to sell products, says Timothy Caulfield, a professor in the Faculty of Law and the School of Public Health at the University of Alberta, who has written about what he calls the 'manosphere' space. Caulfield says about Huberman's podcasts that 'you never leave one of his episodes thinking, "The science is pretty underwhelming here," or, "I probably shouldn't be doing this."' 'No, the takeaway is always, "You've got to do this,"' he says.

When potential doubts arise, strategic disclaimers like 'I'm not saying this' or 'this is just a possibility' provide plausible deniability

– though these caveats are sometimes followed by 'extremely interesting' results that effectively override the nominal caution. Huberman has his own terminology to explain his rationale. He uses terms like 'science-supported' and 'evidence-informed' to describe studies and evidence, and pairs this with podcast footnotes full of references to research papers.

Dr David Nunan, senior researcher and educator in evidence-based healthcare at Oxford University, suggests this is 'reference-based medicine': 'Somewhere the essence of what evidence-based medicine is has got a little bit lost and we think that it just means there's a study,' he tells me. Sharing research papers where an abstract seems to prove your perspective is 'scienceploitation' in action, especially given how many listeners might not be able to access the papers cited themselves. Citing research can lend an exaggerated sense of scientific legitimacy. References act more as symbols of authority than genuine engagement with the literature.

What is sometimes absent from these discussions is candid acknowledgement of research limitations – methodological flaws, contradictory findings or studies that fail to replicate initial promising results. Selective presentation creates an impression of overwhelming scientific support where often only preliminary or contested evidence exists. What's more, instead of presenting absolute risks – the actual statistical likelihood of a particular outcome – hosts talk about relative numbers that sound more dramatic. This also very common in mainstream media reporting. A treatment that reduces a 1% risk to 0.5% becomes 'cuts your risk by 50%' rather than 'reduces your risk by one-half of one percent'.

'Anyone can just share a study and cite the reference and say I have evidence to support my view,' Nunan says. It's harder to unpick and unpack what that study actually says. Podcasts lack the structure for critical reflection and active audience engagement, making them less open to scrutiny compared to platforms like Instagram or YouTube shorts, where inaccuracies can be easily flagged.[61]

The environment becomes even less conducive to critical thinking when the same longevity influencers appear on each other's shows, creating what Olshansky describes as 'a semi-scientific, pseudoscientific echo chamber'. Scientific findings undergo subtle distortions driven by 'vested monetary interests in the effort to modulate ageing', he says. Questionable claims gain credibility through repetition. When the same message – about a supplement, protocol or theoretical framework – comes from five different 'experts' a listener follows, it creates an illusion of scientific consensus.

Scott Carney, an investigative journalist and anthropologist studying wellness culture, sees a parallel to improvisational comedy. 'It's related to the "Yes, and" principle, where you always agree and build on what someone else says,' he explains. 'You could say, "Today, I met a talking cat," and the next person might add, "Yes, and it said it got an enema from Peter yesterday." The goal is to keep the story going. If anyone says "No", the fun stops.'

This dynamic governs interactions between podcast hosts, who maintain just enough agreement to preserve their place in the ecosystem. Rather than challenging questionable claims, they pivot with phrases like 'That's interesting' before adding their own perspective to keep the conversation flowing. Those who break this unspoken rule by offering substantive criticism tend to disappear from the circuit, Carney says. 'At the top of the social media hierarchy, there's a reciprocal gift exchange,' Carney says. 'It's about giving and receiving status. Attia works with influencers like Tim Ferriss and Esther Perel, creating a cycle of mutual support that feels off to me. There's money and influence involved, which I don't fully trust.'

## SCIENCE OR SHOWMANSHIP?

Some in the longevity space think of themselves as pioneers. But self-experimentation wasn't always the domain of shirtless billionaires livestreaming extreme routines. It has played a role in science. In the 1980s Australian scientists Dr Barry Marshall and Dr Robin

Warren identified a type of bacteria called *Helicobacter pylori* in the lining of the stomach of people with gastritis and peptic ulcers. Up until then the prevailing understanding was that these were caused by stress or spicy foods.

Marshall and Warren hypothesised the bacteria were the cause of these symptoms and undertook painstaking lab work. Unable to create a model by infecting an animal, Marshall experimented and consumed a broth containing *H. pylori*. Within three days, he developed acute gastritis symptoms, confirmed through endoscopy. *H. pylori* was cultured from a biopsy, and after fourteen days, he began antibiotic treatment, which resolved his symptoms.[62]

The self-experiment was impactful, but it didn't end there. The discovery was substantiated by larger studies, treatment trials and epidemiological evidence. These confirmed *H. pylori* was the cause of peptic ulcer disease and led to changes in medical practice.[63] The pair were awarded the 2005 Nobel Prize in Physiology or Medicine for their efforts.

Marshall's self-experiment is an example of what is called an 'N-of-1' study where he acted as his own control. His experiment featured a clear hypothesis (*H. pylori* causes gastritis and ulcers), a single intervention (drinking bacterial culture), observable outcomes within a defined timeframe (development of measurable symptoms and signs of gastritis) and importantly, reversibility (antibiotics clear it up).

But the complex regimens used by many in the longevity world 'N-of-1' studies aren't feasible. One key principle of determining causality – changing one variable while holding others constant – collapses entirely when you're doing lots of things at once and perhaps changing your behaviour, as we've seen.

Lewis acknowledges this limitation in his own protocol. 'It's still debatable and uncertain just how meaningful this will be long term,' he says. He finds value in feeling like he's making progress, but his cautious approach isn't universal. Unlike Lewis, who avoids prescription medications, some in the longevity community experiment with drugs like rapamycin and metformin for their purported anti-ageing properties.

Rapamycin, also known as sirolimus, was isolated in 1972 from a bacterium found on Easter Island (Rapa Nui), which is how it got its name. It was originally developed as an immunosuppressant for people with organ transplants. 'It seems like people notice a big reduction in inflammation, aches and pains of old age seem to disappear. People get more energy,' Lewis explains, though he personally draws the line at taking it: 'It's a lot less scary to buy supplements than to ask a doctor for a prescription drug that wasn't created with longevity in mind, particularly one developed for organ transplant patients to suppress their immune system.'

The effects of both rapamycin and metformin are genuine areas of scientific interest. Andrew Steele, who researches ageing, is particularly excited about rapamycin, despite 'frustratingly little human data'. The animal data are promising, however. 'There are loads of different ways that this drug can extend lifespan,' he says, adding that it's the first drug to extend lifespan in late life in a mammal.[64]

Rapamycin is hypothesised to extend life by mimicking the effects of eating less – caloric restriction – which has been shown to increase lifespan in non-human animals albeit inconsistently. 'Many studies have described how interventions such as dietary restriction can extend lifespans in experimental settings. However, the impact that some of these approaches have on lifespans has occasionally been inconsistent, or not observed, when repeated in different animal species or laboratories,' says Professor Neil Mabbott, personal chair of immunopathology, Roslin Institute & Royal (Dick) School of Veterinary Sciences, University of Edinburgh. A 2025 meta-analysis of animal studies showed that dietary restriction or treatment with rapamycin were equally effective in extending lifespans in the animal species used in those studies.[65]

Rapamycin does this by targeting a molecule called mTOR that helps cells sense nutrients. When food is scarce, mTOR is turned off, activating systems that help us survive starvation. One of these systems is autophagy, where cells clean out damaged components and use them for energy. It's a central mechanism by which ageing can be slowed down, Steele explains. This process reduces the build-up of cellular waste that clogs our tissues as we age and, as the theory goes, slows the ageing process. 'You can take all these old bits of cells and repair them, rejuvenate them and make new proteins from the component parts,' he says. But Mabbott cautions that while advances in healthcare are increasing lifespans worldwide, this also strains health systems. The 2025 meta-analysis assessed how well different interventions extend life, though it's unclear if they also improve healthspan – the years lived in good health. Living longer with illness isn't ideal; the real goal is more healthy years, which may also boost overall lifespan.

While Steele is cautiously optimistic; he doesn't take rapamycin himself, but certain podcasters do, including Attia, and talk about it publicly in the longevity space. Attia told *Men's Health* that he's taking rapamycin. 'On some level I've decided it's a smart option.'[66] And he goes on: 'But I haven't prescribed it to any patients, except one, who is himself a scientist studying rapamycin. And I think that speaks to my desire to better understand the risks, not only of taking too much but also of not taking enough.'

How he can assess these risks is unclear as he is taking a host of other supplements. But Cohen also says that, in order to test whether a longevity drug works, 'you'd have to randomise people for a lifetime and prove they live ten years longer, and that's nearly impossible.'

As a specialist in evidence-based healthhcare, Nunan has looked at the most up-to-date evidence on rapamycin. He stresses the importance of focusing on human studies. Benefits seen in animals don't always translate to humans.

One 2024 systematic review analysed the impact of rapamycin on ageing-related physiological changes and diseases in adults.[67] It suggested that the drug led to better health markers related to ageing in the immune, heart and skin systems of both healthy people and those with age-related diseases. Nunan says the systematic review is largely well done, but there are major limitations. The studies included are short – one lasted just a day, another two days, with the longest around seven hundred days. 'Even five years is relatively brief when studying longevity,' he says.

Nor is it clear if the reported effects are clinically meaningful. A reduced heart rate by a few beats per minute might be statistically significant but not provide health benefits. As we've already discussed, modifying a particular biomarker doesn't always translate into positive, long-term health outcomes.

For all its hoped for benefits, rapamycin is a strictly controlled drug carrying a black box warning in the US, the most serious alert possible, about using and prescribing it. It can be fatal for lung and liver transplant recipients and is immunosuppressive, increasing the risk of lymphoma, skin cancer and infections.[68] Those taking rapamycin for anti-ageing benefits may well be taking the drug at a lower dose than transplant recipients, but we don't know at what dosage the risk of adverse effects increases. If consistently taking low-dose rapamycin increases the risk of cancer, it may be a decade, if not more, before a link is established.

Some researchers who study rapamycin caution against prescribing it off-label for longevity, describing such practice as 'bordering on unethical' given our limited understanding of long-term effects.[69] Despite the concerns, it's not hard to find someone who will sell it. Expensive online clinics in the UK offer 'personalised longevity medicine', which includes off-label drugs like rapamycin – treatments the companies claim will improve lifespan, optimise healthspan and even reverse or slow down ageing.

Metformin is much easier to procure. As the world's most commonly prescribed oral medication for type 2 diabetes, it's both inexpensive and readily available. Recent research on its anti-ageing potential has transformed this decades-old diabetes treatment into a gateway drug for aspiring age-hackers everywhere.

Beyond Johnson's endorsement (who stopped taking rapamycin in 2024 because of the 'hefty' side effects), the drug has gained an anti-ageing profile thanks to its championing by medical influencers like Professor Tim Spector – founder of the ZOE dietary app – and Attia. These high-profile admissions of use have cascaded through online communities, with one Reddit member in the r/biohackers forum sharing: 'I am taking it daily for anti-aging/anti-cancer benefits… It's cheaper than peanuts and it's getting more and more interest in mainstream medicine.'

One particular study piqued interest in metformin for ageing. In 2014, a retrospective observational study of 180,000 UK patients compared the survival of people with type 2 diabetes taking metformin to those using sulphonylurea – another type 2 diabetes drug – and to non-diabetics, matched for various factors like age, sex and smoking status. Metformin users showed a small but statistically significant improvement in survival compared to non-diabetics. Those without diabetes had a 15% shorter survival time compared to metformin users, while sulphonylurea was associated with a 38% shorter survival time.

But there are lessons to be learned about relying on single observational studies to make treatment decisions. Another observational study, published eight years later, produced different findings. In 2022, a large Danish case-control study of 445,662 singletons and 151,091 individual twins found that metformin use among people with type 2 diabetes 'was not associated with survival equal or superior to that of the general population without diabetes'.[70] The fundamental problem with observational studies is their inability to eliminate bias and confounding variables – factors like lifestyle choices, socioeconomic status and medical history – that might influence outcomes. Additionally, metformin prescription criteria vary across countries, potentially explaining the contradictory results.

Professor Miles Witham, an academic geriatrician specialising in clinical trials for older adults at Newcastle University, has conducted more rigorous research on metformin's effects. Studies to date have been mixed with no consistent improvements across all measures. For example in one small randomised controlled trial, healthy adults over sixty-five either took metformin or a placebo for fourteen weeks. Both groups had resistance exercise training. Results showed that the placebo group achieved greater muscle growth and density than the metformin group, suggesting that metformin may hinder the usual benefits of exercise on strength and endurance.[71]

Other trials, however, have shown benefits of metformin in people starting to become frail, with slight improvements in walking speed and grip strength.[72] Witham devised a randomised controlled trial to evaluate if metformin improved the overall health of older people with frailty – a challenging group to research who rarely participate in clinical trials.[73]

They gave metformin or a placebo to frail older adults for four months but found there were no improvements in physical function or quality of life. Worse, the group taking metformin experienced significant side effects, with 40% stopping the treatment due to issues like nausea and diarrhoea. Frail older adults are more vulnerable to side effects, meaning that even minor ones can severely impact their health.

'Our findings suggest that metformin is not suitable for frail older people. It's not going to be a good answer for improving overall health in that group,' Witham says. He goes on:

> What we're seeing at the moment doesn't suggest that metformin is going to be some marvellous panacea. The longevity advocates tend to say, 'Ah, yes, well, you're giving it at the wrong time. You need to give it when you're fit and healthy, and you need to take it over decades.' And there's no easy way of saying they're wrong, because you've got to conduct clinical trials to prove it.

One of the challenges in ageing research is the need to explore interventions across different stages of life as each group requires tailored approaches. But the kind of trials required, with long-term follow-ups and consistency in protocol over several decades, are challenging to design and realise. While securing funding for thirty years is daunting enough, these studies also pose ethical dilemmas.

Johnson appears unbothered by such uncertainties. When Steele questioned why he invests his substantial wealth into marketing personal products rather than funding rigorous clinical trials on X, Johnson blocked him.

'I said, "Look, Bryan, your net worth is supposedly $800 million… Why don't you use it to fund a trial to actually test whether metformin works?"' Steele tells me.

Meanwhile, Attia has quietly discontinued his own metformin regimen. During a 2023 appearance on Huberman's podcast, he revealed he'd stopped taking the drug after discovering it elevated his resting lactate levels. Lactate is a substance that, while normally produced during energy metabolism, can cause adverse effects when at high levels.

As we've seen, these retractions and reversals rarely achieve the same penetration as the bold initial claims. None of this invalidates longevity as a growing field of medical research. And there's a huge value in public figures like Johnson promoting healthier habits, in a way that might be more effective and attractive than posters at your doctor's clinic.

Some praise these longevity podcasters for democratising science and helping to bring complex research to the masses. But scratch beneath the surface, and it's clear their world is built for the wealthy and the already healthy. The agency they promise over biological destiny is in fact reserved for those who have the time and resources to shell out for specialist supplements and drugs, and constant medical monitoring. Moreover their approach blurs boundaries between scientific rigour and personal branding. They elevate self-experimentation to the status of robust data and advocate an elastic concept of evidence that often supports what they've chosen to do at any given time.

The pursuit of ways to defy death has captivated people for centuries. What's different today is how this enduring ambition has been rebranded as clickable content, turned into a revenue stream through supplements and subscriptions, and packaged in marathon podcast episodes. Yet these elaborate, expensive protocols offer little evidence of additional gains. In their obsessive pursuit of optimised futures, these longevity influencers may mistake quantity of life for quality of life. Those scrambling to follow their lead might find themselves spending their time chasing costly illusions rather than living their life to the full.

# EPILOGUE

## THE COMMODIFIED SELF

When Anna, from chapter 1, got her anti-Müllerian hormone test results back, the clinic gave her a choice but, in many respects, it felt more like an ultimatum. Her levels were low and time, she was told, was not on her side. Her ovarian reserve would only decline further, along with her chances of conceiving. One solution they offered was egg freezing. It's a process that mimics the first stages of IVF, involving hormone stimulation, daily injections and eventual egg retrieval under sedation. The clinic would collect and cryogenically store her eggs, preserving them for possible later use.

The test that had been marketed on social media as a prediction tool had turned out to be a gateway to expensive invasive procedures and promises of a fertile future. None of this was made clear in the clinic's marketing materials. Women looking for answers about their fertility were being led to make emotionally fraught and expensive decisions though they hadn't perhaps expected to.

After some thought, Anna chose not to pursue it. It didn't feel right for her. But several of her friends were considering freezing their eggs, having been prompted by the same test. Even though she has gone on to have a baby, the persistence of the algorithm means her feed still throws up sponsored tests, miracle supplements and fertility coaches promising to decipher her body. For Anna, this might be a thing of the past. But for others it's a daily reminder of their struggles and just one more thing – or not – they feel they must try.

Anna told me she's much more cautious now. 'I'm going to ask a few more questions next time and not just click "buy now,"' she told me a year or so later. 'I'm always going to go for the latest beauty treatment though. I'm not *that* sceptical!'

Anna isn't alone in feeling that the health service wasn't taking her struggles to conceive seriously. Around the world, many people live with unexplained symptoms and feel their concerns are going unheard. Mainstream medicine, for all its strengths, cannot effectively address all concerns. People everywhere have expressed the same sentiment – they feel they've been failed.

For example, in the UK, our choices are shaped by what the NHS can offer. Care is constrained by tight budgets and, at times, strict thresholds for clinical evidence. Health systems in other countries face similar challenges. These safeguards are there for a reason. When a health service spends taxpayers' money, it needs solid evidence that treatments work to justify their cost. Yet, for patients with ongoing health problems, this cautious approach may feel frustrating, not to mention exceedingly slow. Some of those who want to take proactive control of their health equate robust evidence requirements with a bygone era.

When I started to research this book, I wasn't sure what I'd find. Aware of the heat around social media use and the paucity of robust data about its impact, I kept an open mind. But what I saw was health information being put onto and shaped by what are – for all intents and purposes – shopping and advertising platforms. TikTok, Instagram, YouTube and Facebook are built to grab and retain attention, gather our data and drive consumption. More and more of us are turning to these highly commercialised, barely regulated spaces in search of health advice and support. Yes – some of what's out there is genuinely helpful. But some is not only a waste of money but harmful too. The issue is it's hard to know which is which.

Of course, commercial interests have long played a role in how we understand health. For nearly two decades, I've reported on how powerful industries shape health, both directly and indirectly. Companies not only sell products or offer services that affect our wellbeing but also shape the systems, policies and public conversations that define what health means, what problems get attention and who receives care. In public health, this is known as the 'commercial determinants of health'.[1] It refers to how private companies market to consumers, lobby policymakers, fund research and influence how society understands illness, prevention and responsibility. For example, the tobacco industry has a long track record of deception, aggressively protecting profits at the expense of public health. Even when the evidence was clear, for decades it denied the link between smoking and lung cancer by hiding internal data, funding misleading research and casting doubt in courtrooms and the media.[2] Likewise, corporate influence plays a key role in deciding which conditions get attention, which treatments are developed and whose health needs are prioritised – or ignored completely.

In this book, we've seen how drug and diagnostics companies redefine what counts as a disease; run comparative trials only when they know they'll come out on top; use selective statistics to hype their product; and, in some cases, invent new conditions to create markets where none previously existed. They employ influential health professionals as key opinion leaders and shape the information we ultimately receive.

To be clear, such companies don't all impact health in the same way, and their influence is far from being always bad. It would be grossly unfair to assume that's the case. Some of them play a critical role in keeping us healthy and add huge value to our economies. Not only do they employ millions of people but the pharmaceutical, diagnostics and devices industries have developed crucial tests, treatments and vaccines. Many of the past century's major lifesaving medical innovations wouldn't have reached the public without the pharmaceutical industry's involvement and resources.

They've helped to eliminate diseases and improve life expectancy for millions. Alongside the legacy industries that have long shaped our health, new players have entered the scene. It's wise to stay sceptical, but we should also remain open to the possibility that there may be much to gain.

For better or worse, social media giants like Instagram, YouTube, TikTok, X and Facebook are influencing both individual and public health in ways we're only beginning to understand. These major platforms wield immense, increasingly well-documented power. Yet the way they operate is opaque and still poorly understood.

And it's not just the platforms themselves. Health tech developers, app makers, diagnostics companies, private clinics, pharmacies, influencers, podcasters and coaches are all finding ways to monetise our health, and they often do so with the help of platforms. Researchers recently started to call this the 'digital determinants of health' – essentially, any aspect of our online world that affects our health.[3] This emerging field recognises that our phones, apps, algorithms and online interactions may influence everything from our mental health to our medical decisions. In fact, scientists are beginning to understand how our digital environments affect both individual and population health outcomes, likely shaping them in ways we don't yet fully understand. And it may be that they never catch up, as platforms iterate faster than grant funders and ethics committees can wrap their heads around the research methods needed.

Of course, there are potential up-sides. These interventions may help people control their symptoms and prevent illness in later life. As we've seen, the various platforms have also created space for support, connection and community. People can share their stories and take more control over their care. In under-resourced areas and for stigmatised conditions, digital tools have brought medical services to people who might otherwise go without. Healthcare and health information, in effect, have become more accessible. Some I have spoken to have found out about conditions they didn't know they had and treatments they didn't know were available. For others, new opportunities have opened up – including new careers. The language of health is being rewritten and with it, perhaps, our expectations.

But the major downside, the *bad* influence, is the commodification of our health. Health and wellness have become increasingly profitable, clickable and highly visual commodities. Our symptoms, our traumas, our treatments, and even the blurry line between sickness and simply being human, are being monetised. Over-diagnosis, self-diagnosis and medicalisation are thereby fast-tracked.

Nason Maani, a senior lecturer in inequalities and global health policy at Edinburgh University, has studied both the commercial determinants of health and social media. He likens the digital world to a company town. Each street and signpost is designed to direct you towards a path for engagement and profit, not health. Each of us is offered a different version of this town, tailored by the data we offer, making the experience deeply personal but also isolating. 'You and I don't see the same town. Each of us gets a different version, shaped by what we've clicked on before. The main signposts don't direct you or give good advice. They're there to keep you inside and get you to spend time and money,' he says. 'Because your town is different to everyone else's, you don't see what others see. One person gets endless offers for tests and supplements. Someone else gets targeted with ads for cheaper or riskier options. You don't see the gap, but it shapes what you think is normal,' he adds. But the problem is we don't have the keys to the town and this is vital to understanding what is going on.

Researchers have told me about their efforts to get data from social media companies, which they say actively restrict or control access to their data, making independent research and scrutiny difficult or impossible. Marco Zenone is a global health policy researcher working to create safer online environments for vulnerable and underserved groups at the University of Ottawa in Canada. He tells me that it's unacceptable how 'untransparent' social media are and suggests that their business models and advertising should be more transparent. 'This should be an expectation with social media. We contribute to social media with our labour. We're essential because we help them to make money,' he tells me. He describes the kinds of information you have to disclose as researchers if you're going to get it. 'I have to submit the equivalent of [the information required to apply for] a grant. It's not a small grant. It's like a full literature review. You've got to say exactly what you're going to study,' he explains.

'You can imagine the problem', he says. 'My research could reflect badly on them, but I have to hand over my entire research question first. They can reject it outright or approve it, then change whatever I'm meant to study to avoid bad PR.' And even if they grant access, you usually have to agree to let them monitor how you use the tools at any time, Zenone adds. 'Then if I want to publish research using the data they have given me, I have to send them a manuscript… before it comes out. And that's just not how science works. It completely undermines the integrity of what we're doing,' he says.

Similarly, Cambridge University researcher, Amrit Purba Kaur told me that we need more objective social media usage data to better understand the impact of social media on health. Directly accessing such data from social media companies has hitherto been challenging because of privacy laws and commercial sensitivities. But UK data protection rules allow 'user-facilitated data donation', she says. People can request their personal digital activity records, called data download packages. These include posts, images, time-stamped video views, likes given and received and time spent on platforms. The packages can be shared with researchers, offering richer, more granular insights than traditional self-report methods, Kaur explains. The EU has also introduced legislation to require platforms to allow users to securely transfer their data to third parties, including researchers, either once or on an ongoing basis.

In the UK, TikTok has said it would enable automated data transfers so people's engagement with online content can be studied at scale. 'Such tools can help our understanding of the relationship between digital media consumption and health outcomes,' Kaur says. But the success of this approach, and its promise for public health research, ultimately rests on users being willing to donate their data. There are now calls for mandated data sharing.

Many of the health professionals I've spoken to say they regularly see patients who have either enquired about, or already undertaken, procedures and tests they discovered through social media or digital ads. In some cases, the treatments were costly, unnecessary or even harmful. This doesn't yet take into account the rise of large language models – AI systems like ChatGPT and others – which are only beginning to be used for health information and to make decisions about our care. These tools can generate instant answers to health questions, summarise medical research and even simulate clinical conversations. In theory, they offer convenience and accessibility. But in practice, we don't yet know how reliable the information is, how biases are embedded in the data they're trained on and what happens when people treat AI-generated advice as medical fact. As ever, oversight and evidence are lagging behind.

There's clearly a shared responsibility among regulators, platforms, companies, clinics and influencers themselves to make sure information is accurate. But, as we've seen, not all influencers and content creators fully understand or even want to understand the impact they have on people. There's an ethical and moral responsibility that comes with their influence, especially when it involves unsubstantiated claims or advertising banned products. But for some, it's simply about earning as much money as possible, without regard for the consequences.

At the same time, it's apparent that not all influencers are in it for the fame or the money. Many of those I've spoken to genuinely want to do the right thing: they're just not always sure what that looks like. Beyond the attention-grabbing headlines, it's not so different from journalism. Journalists have got things wrong too, often not out of bad intent but because we're working under immense pressure from editors and deadlines. I've been trying to report responsibly for decades, and I've made plenty of mistakes along the way.

In the UK, the Influencer Marketing Trade Body is an organisation 'dedicated to building a robust, sustainable future for the influencer marketing industry'. Members have a code of conduct, ensuring they act with honesty, transparency and integrity. Countries such as France and the Netherlands have launched government-backed influencer training and certificate programmes that focus on responsible and ethical advertising. For example, the Dutch 'Certified by influencerregels.com' programme provides e-learning and certification, with certified influencers listed in a public registry.[4] Other countries are set to follow suit. But, as one Dutch academic I talked to noted, it's not clear as yet how effective this will be.

One thing is clear – and I am not the first to say it – we need to be better informed as consumers. These platforms can't actually empower people to make better health choices without a parallel effort to improve health literacy and numeracy. This is no small task – it took decades for the evidence-based medicine movement to achieve this among medical professionals. And even now they don't all follow the best available evidence.

In previous chapters, I suggested questions to consider before undergoing a test or having a treatment. These are not meant to be prescriptive. Others recommend the acronym BRAN – weighing up the benefits, risks, alternatives to the treatment on offer or doing nothing but seeing what unfolds. But asking yourself why you should believe someone (and that may include me) is not usually a bad idea.

We also need a greater awareness of what shapes the content we see online and better tools to control it. Once you're pulled into a certain stream – whether it's specific conditions, extreme diets or questionable treatments – it can be difficult to shift gears. The algorithms are sticky, reinforcing patterns that may not serve health or wellbeing. Some experts have called for 'algorithm awareness' to be built into attempts to improve digital literacy. These should help people understand how these systems work, why certain content keeps resurfacing and how to push back. But awareness alone isn't enough.

Platforms need to offer clearer and more accessible ways to reset or customise your feed. These should be tools that go beyond vague settings or buried preferences. When algorithms can shape what we think about our health, transparency and control aren't just nice to have: they're essential.

One finance expert I interviewed, who had just written a book on statistics and bias, was quite dismissive. 'I don't understand why people don't just use reliable websites with factual information,' he said. But that's a bit like simply saying 'don't smoke'. We know that simply instructing people from a position of authority often isn't enough. It doesn't always change behaviour.

Digital platforms are where people go for health advice and information. That trend isn't likely to go away any time soon. Instead of dismissing these spaces or viewing them as too messy or unreliable, public health bodies need to rethink their approach. They have to meet people where they are – online – and communicate in ways that are engaging and accessible. That means adapting to the tone, pace and formats of digital culture without sacrificing accuracy or integrity. It's not enough to point out 'misinformation' and try to correct misconceptions. This seems to ignore the fact much of health is in a grey or uncertain zone. It's about earning attention and building trust in the places where people are already looking for answers.

As we've seen throughout this book, rather than dismiss people's choices, some health professionals have stepped onto the different platforms to help them navigate their decisions more safely, even when they don't align with traditional medical advice.

Equally, there perhaps need to be better ways to communicate what evidence says clearly and concisely. People need to know when something is effective, when it likely has no meaningful benefit, when the evidence is inconclusive (whether due to conflicting results or a lack of robust studies) and when there are potential safety concerns. This clearly needs to work with social media feeds where the first few seconds matter and personalities are becoming the go-to resource.

To understand health today requires an understanding of how it's shaped by new commercial interests and the design of the platforms we use every day. What we see on our screens is driven by industries that have a direct line to our day-to-day lives and they can couple that with our spending.

There's no doubt about the growing appetite for integrating health with digital platforms – whether through symptom checkers, wellness apps or AI-powered diagnostics. But enthusiasm alone isn't enough. We still need to ask the hard questions: will these tools – on balance – do more good than harm? We can't dismiss evidence as an inconvenience. In an ideal world, the interventions with the strongest evidence should rise to the top – not just those with the slickest marketing or most viral PR. To get there, we must explore new language and better frameworks to understand how these platforms are reshaping the way we think about health. They're not merely changing how we access care but also how we interpret symptoms, track wellbeing and even define what it means to be 'healthy' in the first place. We deserve *good* influence so we can take better care of ourselves and each other.

# ACKNOWLEDGEMENTS

This book began with a flurry of questions – many from friends feeling increasingly confused by the health advice flooding their feeds. I understood the confusion. The only real difference between us is that, as a journalist, I've had the good fortune of being able to call on some of the most knowledgeable people and critical minds to explore complex issues in healthcare. This cast of hundreds over the years has proved crucial in writing this book.

This is a list, in no particular order, of people without whom this book would not exist. I've been touched by the generosity people have shown me, and time they have been willing to spend with me, sharing their ideas and experiences.

The same summer I discussed my cousin's friend buying an AMH test, I attended a conference in Copenhagen exploring overdiagnosis to talk about how this issue is covered in mainstream media. I've spent much of my career covering topics like screening, diagnostic tests and the expanding definitions of disease, but I hadn't really considered how social media might impact these. That changed after I heard Raffael Heiss speak. His presentation explored the surge of medical and wellness interventions being promoted by influencers online. I'm grateful to Raffael for the inspiration and for generously taking the time to talk to me about his research.

A heartfelt thank you also to Steve Woloshin – who first invited me into this space – for his patient explanations of evidence and for his support over the years.

I must also thank Carl Heneghan, one of the conference conveners and someone I've been in the journalistic trenches with on several occasions. He introduced me to the concept of medicalisation. Over the years, I've learned a great deal from him – often through expletive-laden debate. We don't always see eye to eye but, as Carl himself has pointed out, the fact that a Scouser and a Manc have even agreed to work together is a miracle in itself.

Thanks, of course, go to my agent, Caroline Hardman, for spotting the potential in the idea immediately and helping me craft it into something that would work as a book. I'm also deeply grateful to my brilliant editors, Cecilia Stein and Rida Vaquas, for their thoughtful guidance, sharp editorial instincts and willingness to challenge me when necessary. Their insight and patience brought clarity to complexity.

My thanks extend too to the wider team at Oneworld Publications including Sophie Richmond, Paul Nash and Hannah Haseloff for their support behind the scenes.

In the course of writing this book, I've had the privilege of interviewing over 200 people from dozens of different countries around the world. They come from various walks of life.

None of this would have been possible without the generosity of the content creators, influencer agencies, tech insiders and others who spoke about their experiences with such candour both on and off the record. Some of their stories became full chapters; others stayed behind the scenes. But each one offered invaluable insight. Their perspectives made it possible to look at how social media platforms are used to market and sell health-related interventions and how people interact with this content.

And deep thanks to all those who have studied digital platforms and generously took the time to speak with me. I was incredibly fortunate to learn from health professionals from different specialties, researchers, scientists, regulators and journalists who have thought deeply about this space. I'm also grateful to the health professionals around the world who have told me about their experiences online, and to those who spoke openly about how they see social media shaping clinical practice.

Thanks to John Powell, who took time to explain how the regulatory systems worked, invited me to events and introduced me to PhD students looking at digital health. And to Rohin Francis, cardiologist and YouTuber, for spilling the beans about the kinds of approaches he got to promote all and sundry, and how he tries to maintain his independence.

Also I'm incredibly grateful to the health literacy team at Sydney University – Brooke Nickel, Tessa Copp and Kirsten McCaffery – who have been a constant source of help and have been willing to speak with me at the drop of a hat. Thanks also go to Thea Stein, Mark Dayan and Leonora Merry at the Nuffield Trust, for talking to me about issues affecting the NHS and always being willing to offer their insights.

I also want to extend my heartfelt thanks to my colleagues at LSE, Huseyin Naci and Elias Mossialos. Both recognised early on the potential impact of digital platforms on public health and have offered me not only their insight but also a platform from which to explore and develop many of the issues raised in this book.

A big thanks must also go to two brilliant colleagues who became cherished friends. Margaret McCartney's critical thinking and fierce integrity have taught me so much. It's been a privilege to learn alongside you. And Tracey Brown, thank you for your unwavering encouragement and clarity of thought. Both sense-checked me along the way. I'd also like to extend my gratitude to Karsten Juhl Jørgensen for reading several chapters to make sure I'd stayed faithful to the principles of screening and measuring biomarkers

To Rob Hughes, who has kept me both sane and sceptical. An independent thinker – sharp, principled and unafraid to challenge

# ACKNOWLEDGEMENTS

groupthink or question the status quo. The same applies to Sunil Bhopal and Georgia Ladbury, for equally being independent thinkers and willing to challenge their own preconceptions – and mine!

Thanks go to the Unicorns – a ragtag group of paediatricians, public health doctors, epidemiologists, mathematicians and an exiled surgeon – who found each other in the chaos of the pandemic. So named because we joked that chasing Zero Covid was like chasing a unicorn; but the bond we forged was anything but mythical. They're always available to share their thoughts and explain stuff that I'm not sure about.

Thanks also go to the hundreds of people I've worked with over the years who have been part of the dramas that come with being an investigative journalist in health. My former colleagues at the *BMJ*, the BBC and ITV.

And to all my wonderful friends – far too many to name individually, but each one deeply appreciated. A special shoutout to Faisal Islam and Verity Evans, who fed me, watered me and dragged me out dancing when I genuinely thought I was losing the plot. To Natasha Loder and Sandie Kanthal – thank you for your fierce intelligence, fierce loyalty and the kind of friendship where you can disagree on just about everything and still hug it out over a pint at the end of a muddy walk.

Zoe Gascoyne, named because she'd kill me if I didn't mention her (or at least go through my tax returns with a fine-toothed comb). Not many people make me laugh until I cry the way she does, except maybe Amy Britton and Gail Kniveton, who were equally essential for the dancing, and the general life-affirming chaos.

Danielle Dickinson, Georgie Carter, Rachael Newton, Rachel Collins and Sol Rosenwink, the group who bring me constant laughter and white wine. You've been the inspiration behind this book – thanks for the many thoughtful and unfiltered questions you ask.

Thanks also go to Helen Oliver, Laura Dewis, Rebecca Thomas, Ellie Carding and Helen Parker; you've taken me to festivals, down rivers, across seas, up mountains and into tents where someone earnestly tells you to breathe. You've provided so much kindness and escapism.

To Dawn Scott, Jody Friedman, and Gemma Blackburn, Chantal Gautier, Kathleen King – for your love and relentless encouragement. Thank you for the late-night messages full of wisdom.

Thanks goes to my best mate from medical school, Stuart Wallace, and his husband, Rob Kenyon, who sent me irreverent Instagram videos to stop the algorithm populating my feed with increasingly outlandish claims about conditions I thought I had and products that I'd be far too tempted to buy. I promise that next time I'll do something less serious and concentrate on unearthing those stories about skateboarding squirrels.

And last but not least to the family, who never let me forget I'm Scouse. They keep me endlessly entertained with head-in-hands moments and commentary that could only come from them. Loyal, gobby and caring, I'm glad you're mine. Not least because I'd be terrified if you weren't. And also thanks to my dad's ever-patient partner, Jane, my *soeur de coeur*, Rosie, Jon and the boys. I promise I won't be on a deadline next time I visit.

To my dear brother, Phil, and his wonderful partner, Maria – thank you for your constant support, and kindness. And to Theo and Elsa, whose lives are just beginning to unfold in ways we can only imagine. Aunty Ded hopes your world is one filled with curiosity and the courage to always ask questions.

And of course, to Mum and Dad – both wilfully unconventional to the core. You gave me a sense of adventure, the instinct to ask hard questions, and the gift of knowing when to give all the shits, and when to give none at all.

# NOTES

## 1 A CONFLUENCE OF CHANGE

1. Harris BS, Jukic AM, Truong T, Nagle CT, Erkanli A, Steiner AZ. Markers of ovarian reserve as predictors of future fertility. Fertil Steril. 2023 Jan; 119(1): 99–106.
2. Nickel B, Moynihan R, Gram EG, Copp T, Taba M, Shih P et al. Social media posts about medical tests with potential for overdiagnosis. *JAMA Netw Open*. 2025: 8(2): e2461940. doi: 10.1001/jamanetworkopen.2024.61940.
3. Whittaker R. Top expert reveals the type of coffee that's linked to cancer – and the one that's the healthiest for you. *MailOnline*. 2024 Nov 14. Available from: https://www.dailymail.co.uk/health/article-XXXXXXX/Top-expert-reveals-type-coffee-linked-cancer.html. Accessed 2025 May 14.
4. Allen V. Coffee may reduce your risk of type 2 diabetes, study reveals – but only if you don't add this one thing to your drink'. *Daily Mail*. 2025 Feb 6. Available from: https://www.dailymail.co.uk/health/article-XXXXXXX/coffee-type-2-diabetes-risk.html. Accessed 2025 May 14.
5. Lewis P. Falling vaccination rates: the case of the MMR jab. House of Lords Library briefing. 2020 Jan 28. Available from: https://lordslibrary.parliament.uk/research-briefings/lln-2020-0033/. Accessed 2025 May 14.
6. Deer B. How the case against the MMR vaccine was fixed. *BMJ*. 2011: 342: c5347. doi: 10.1136/bmj.c5347.
7. Bradshaw P. Has the Covid-19 pandemic changed the doctor–patient relationship forever? *BMJ Opinion*. 2020 Jun 8. Available from: https://blogs.bmj.com/bmj/2020/06/08/has-the-covid-19-pandemic-changed-the-doctor-patient-relationship-forever/. Accessed 2025 May 14.

8. Kozyreva A, Lewandowsky S, Hertwig R. Citizens versus the internet: confronting digital challenges with cognitive tools. *Psychol Sci Public Interest*. 2020: 21(3): 103–56. doi: 10.1177/1529100620946707.
9. Mintel. British Lifestyles: the NHS tops list of UK's most cherished institutions. 2018 Jun 7. Available from: https://www.mintel.com/press-centre/british-lifestyles-the-nhs-tops-list-of-uks-most-cherished-institutions/. Accessed 2025 May 15.
10. Taylor B, Lobont C, Dayan M, Merry L, Jefferies D, Wellings D. Public satisfaction with the NHS and social care in 2024: results from the British Social Attitudes survey. London: The King's Fund and Nuffield Trust; 2025 Apr. Available from: https://www.kingsfund.org.uk/insight-and-analysis/reports/public-satisfaction-nhs-social-care-in-2024-bsa. Accessed 2025 May 15.
11. Jefferies D, Wellings D, Morris J, Dayan M, Lobont C. Public satisfaction with the NHS and social care in 2023: results from the British Social Attitudes Survey. London: The King's Fund and Nuffield Trust; 2024 Mar. Available from: https://www.kingsfund.org.uk/insight-and-analysis/reports/public-satisfaction-nhs-social-care-2023. Accessed 2025 May 15.
12. Ren M, Zhang H, Meltzer D, Arora VM, Prochaska M. Changes in patient perceptions of the provider most involved in care during Covid-19 and corresponding effects on patient trust. *J Patient Exp*. 2023 Apr 3.
13. Georgieva D. What do demographic changes mean for labor supply? *World Bank Blogs*. 2024 Apr 9. Available from: https://blogs.worldbank.org/en/developmenttalk/what-do-demographic-changes-mean-for-labor-supply. Accessed 2025 May 15.
14. Mikulic M. Global pharmaceutical industry – statistics and facts. Statista. 2024 Nov 22. Available from: https://www.statista.com/topics/1764/global-pharmaceutical-industry/. Accessed 2025 May 16.
15. Kollewe J. Private healthcare boom fuelled by NHS waiting lists. *Guardian*. 2024 Oct 25. Available from: https://www.theguardian.com/society/2024/oct/25/private-healthcare-boom-fuelled-by-nhs-waiting-lists. Accessed 2025 May 16.
16. UK Government. *Fit for the Future: 10 Year Health Plan for England*. London: Department of Health and Social Care; July 2025. Available from: https://assets.publishing.service.gov.uk/media/6866387fe6557c544c74db7a/fit-for-the-future-10-year-health-plan-for-england.pdf

17 Ofcom. Adults' media use and attitudes report. 2025 May 7. Available from: https://www.ofcom.org.uk/research-and-data/media-literacy-research/adults/adults-media-use-and-attitudes. Accessed 2025 May 16.

18 Ayre J, Cvejic E, McCaffery KJ. Use of ChatGPT to obtain health information in Australia, 2024: insights from a nationally representative survey. *Med J Aust.* 2025: 222(4): 210–12. doi: 10.5694/mja2.52598.

19 Menz BD, Kuderer NM, Bacchi S, Modi ND, Chin-Yee B, Hu T *et al.* Current safeguards, risk mitigation, and transparency measures of large language models against the generation of health disinformation: repeated cross-sectional analysis. *BMJ.* 2024;384:e078538. doi: 10.1136/bmj-2023-078538.

20 Armbruster J, Bussmann F, Rothhaas C, Titze N, Grützner PA, Freischmidt H. 'Doctor ChatGPT, can you help me?' The patient's perspective: cross-sectional study. *J Med Internet Res* 2024: 26: e58831.

21 McQuater K. Report shows influence of social media for healthcare information. *Research Live.* 2023 Feb 15. Available from: https://www.research-live.com/article/news/report-shows-influence-of-social-media-for-healthcare-information/id/5100282. Accessed 2025 May 16.

22 Ofcom. Adults' media use and attitudes report. 2025 May 7. Available from: https://www.ofcom.org.uk/research-and-data/media-literacy-research/adults/adults-media-use-and-attitudes. Accessed 2025 May 16.

23 Ibid.

24 McQuater. Report shows influence of social media for healthcare information.

25 Sattora EA, Ganeles BC, Pierce ME, Wong R. Research on health topics communicated through TikTok: a systematic review of the literature. *J Media.* 2024: 5(3): 1395–412. doi: 10.3390/journalmedia5030088.

26 Kirkpatrick CE, Lawrie LL. TikTok as a source of health information and misinformation for young women in the United States: survey study. *JMIR Infodemiology.* 2024: 4: e54663. doi: 10.2196/54663.

27 Celletti C. Ogilvy launches global health influence offering. *Ogilvy.* 2024 Apr 24. Available from: https://www.ogilvy.com/ideas/ogilvy-launches-global-health-influence-offering. Accessed 2025 May 16.

28 Ibid.

29 Sattora EA, Ganeles BC, Pierce ME, Wong R. Research on health topics communicated through TikTok: a systematic review of the literature. *J Media.* 2024: 5(3):1395–1412. doi: 10.3390/journalmedia5030088.

30 Wang Y, Bao S, Chen Y. How does social media use influence the mental health of pancreatic cancer patients: a chain mediating effect of online social support and psychological resilience. *Front Public Health*. 2023: 11: 1166776. doi: 10.3389/fpubh.2023.1166776.

31 O'Riordan L. I wouldn't have made it through cancer without my 'community of care'. *Telegraph*. 2025 May 1. Available from: https://www.telegraph.co.uk/health-fitness/conditions/cancer/cancer-community/. Accessed 2025 May 16.

32 NHS. Content policy. 2025. Available from: https://www.nhs.uk/our-policies/content-policy/. Accessed 2025 May 16.

33 Binlot A. Roger Federer on why he ditched Nike for a $300 million Uniqlo deal. Forbes. 2018 Aug 28. Available from: https://www.forbes.com/sites/abinlot/2018/08/28/roger-federer-on-why-he-ditched-nike-for-a-300-million-uniqlo-deal/. Accessed 2025 May 16.

34 Reuters. Most influencers fail to admit to advertising, EU study shows. 2024 Feb 14. https://www.reuters.com/technology/most-influencers-fail-admit-advertising-eu-study-shows-2024-02-14/. Accessed 2025 May 16.

35 Reinikainen H, Munnukka J, Maity D, Luoma-aho V. 'You really are a great big sister' – parasocial relationships, credibility, and the moderating role of audience comments in influencer marketing. *J Mark Manag*. 2023: 39(7–8): 655–78. doi: 10.1080/0267257X.2023.2201234.

36 Advertising Standards Authority (ASA). Influencer Ad Disclosure on Social Media: Instagram and TikTok Report. May 2024. Available from: https://www.asa.org.uk/static/3f7df70c-ca5c-499c-8aaa56e8b3e9572e/ASA-influencer-ad-disclosure-report.pdf

37 Vellani V, Zheng S, Ercelik D, Sharot T. The illusory truth effect leads to the spread of misinformation. *Cognition*. 2023: 236:105421. doi: 10.1016/j.cognition.2023.105421.

38 Center for Countering Digital Hate. Deadly by design. 2022 Dec. Available from: https://counterhate.com/wp-content/uploads/2022/12/CCDH-Deadly-by-Design_120922.pdf. Accessed 2025 May 18.

39 TikTok. Community guidelines: safety and civility. 2024 Apr 17. Available from: https://www.tiktok.com/community-guidelines/en/safety-civility. Accessed 2025 May 18.

40 Dunn N. Top 23 TikTok statistics and facts you need to know in 2025! Charle Agency. 2025 Jan 4. Available from: https://www.charle.co.uk/articles/tiktok-statistics/. Accessed 2025 May 16.

41 Statista Research Department. Global influencer marketing value 2015–2025. Statista. 2025 Mar 21. Available from: https://www.statista.com/topics/2496/influence-marketing/. Accessed 2025 May 18.

42 Ibid.

43 Teleprompter Team. Podcast influencers: powering the digital marketing game. Teleprompter. 2024 Sept 30. Available from: https://www.teleprompter.com/blog/podcast-influencers. Accessed 2025 May 18.

44 Influencity. AI influencers: how virtual personalities are shaping the future of marketing. 2025 Jan 3. Available from: https://influencity.com/blog/en/how-to-humanize-ai-content. Accessed 2025 May 18.

45 Sellman M. Meet the TikTok vigilante trying to enforce advertising rules. *Sunday Times*. 2025 May 1. Available from: https://www.thetimes.co.uk/article/meet-the-tiktok-vigilante-enforcing-advertising-rules-2025. Accessed 2025 May 18.

46 Influencity. AI influencers: how virtual personalities are shaping the future of marketing.

47 Nanji N. Katie Price low-calorie diet advert for Skinny Food banned. *BBC News*. 2024 Apr 3. Available from: https://www.bbc.co.uk/news/entertainment-arts-68713464. Accessed 2025 Jun 6.

48 General Medical Council. Identifying and managing conflicts of interest. 2024 Jan 30. Available from: https://www.gmc-uk.org/professional-standards/the-professional-standards/identifying-and-managing-conflicts-of-interest/identifying-and-managing-conflicts-of-interest. Accessed 2025 May 18.

49 Sismondo S. How to make opinion leaders and influence people. *CMAJ*. 2015: 187(10): 759–60. doi: 10.1503/cmaj.150032.

50 Van Zee A. The promotion and marketing of OxyContin: commercial triumph, public health tragedy. *Am J Public Health*. 2009: 99(2): 221–27. doi: 10.2105/AJPH.2007.131714.

51 University of Alabama Center for the Study of Tobacco and Society. The 'More doctors smoke Camels' campaign: the unfiltered truth about smoking and health. Available from: https://csts.ua.edu/ama/more-doctors-smoke-camels/. Accessed 2025 May 18.

52 Everybody Agency. TikTok's health revolution: how the platform is shaping the future of health information. 2024. Available from: https://www.everybodyagency.com/en-us/insights/tiktok-healthcare-trends/. Accessed 2025 May 18.

## 2 ARE STORIES MAKING US SICK?

1. Ghorayshi A. How teens recovered from the 'TikTok tics'. *New York Times*. 2023 Feb 13. Available from: https://www.nytimes.com/2023/02/13/health/tiktok-tics-gender-tourettes.html. Accessed 2025 May 18.
2. Olvera C, Stebbins GT, Goetz CG, Kompoliti K. TikTok tics: a pandemic within a pandemic. *Mov Disord Clin Pract*. 2021 Jul 28. doi: 10.1002/mdc3.13316.
3. Müller-Vahl KR, Pisarenko A, Jakubovski E, Fremer C. Stop that! It's not Tourette's but a new type of mass sociogenic illness. *Brain*. 2022: 145(2): 476–80. doi: 10.1093/brain/awab316.
4. Stokel-Walker C. The complicated truth about Tourette's and TikTok. *WIRED*. 2021 Mar 27. Available from: https://www.wired.co.uk/article/tourette-tiktok. Accessed 2025 May 18.
5. Stanfield L. TikToker goes viral raising Tourette's awareness – as she shares life with condition. *The Express*. 2021 Feb 12. Available from: https://www.express.co.uk/life-style/health/1396530/tiktok-tourettes-syndrome-awareness-tics. Accessed 2025 May 18.
6. Olvera *et al*. TikTok tics: a pandemic within a pandemic.
7. Fremer C, Szejko N, Pisarenko A, Haas M, Laudenbach L, Wegener C *et al*. Mass social media-induced illness presenting with Tourette-like behavior. *Front Psychiatry*. 2022: 13: 963769. doi: 10.3389/fpsyt.2022.963769.
8. *Britannica*. Dancing plague of 1518. Available from: https://www.britannica.com/event/dancing-plague-of-1518. Accessed 2025 May 18.
9. Dominus S. What happened to the girls in Le Roy. *New York Times Magazine*. 2012 Mar 11. Available from: https://www.nytimes.com/2012/03/11/magazine/teenage-girls-twitching-le-roy.html. Accessed 2025 May 18.
10. McVige J, Rooney M, Shukri S, Munir A, Mechtler L, Mangold S. Le Roy: Diagnosing mass psychogenic illness. *Neurology*. 2021 Apr 13. Available from: https://n.neurology.org/content/96/15_Supplement/2400. Accessed 2025 May 18.
11. Dominus. What happened to the girls in Le Roy.
12. Olvera *et al*. TikTok tics: a pandemic within a pandemic.
13. Ibid.
14. Harvard Health Publishing. The power of the placebo effect. 2024 Jul 22. Available from: https://www.health.harvard.edu/mind-and-mood/the-power-of-the-placebo-effect. Accessed 2025 May 18.

15 Baliatsas C, Van Kamp I, Lebret E, Rubin GJ. Idiopathic environmental intolerance attributed to electromagnetic fields (IEI-EMF): a systematic review of identifying criteria. *BMC Public Health*. 2012: 12: 643. doi: 10.1186/1471-2458-12-643.

16 Howard JP, Wood FA, Finegold JA, Nowbar AN, Thompson DM, Arnold AD et al. Side effect patterns in a crossover trial of statin, placebo, and no treatment. *J Am Coll Cardiol*. 2021: 78(12): 1210–22. doi: 10.1016/j.jacc.2021.07.022.

17 Ibid.

18 Wolters F, Peerdeman KJ, Evers AWM. Placebo and nocebo effects across symptoms: from pain to fatigue, dyspnea, nausea, and itch. *Front Psychiatry*. 2019: 10: 470. doi: 10.3389/fpsyt.2019.00470.

19 Quinn V, Pearson S, Huynh A, Nicholls K, Barnes K, Faasse K. The influence of video-based social modelling on the nocebo effect. *J Psychosom Res*. 2023: 165: 111136. doi: 10.1016/j.jpsychores. 2022.111136.

20 Saunders C, Tan W, Faasse K, Colagiuri B, Sharpe L, Barnes K. The effect of social learning on the nocebo effect: a systematic review and meta-analysis with recommendations for the future. *Health Psychol Rev*. 2024: 18(4): 934-53. doi: 10.1080/17437199.2024.2394682.

21 Ibid.

22 Simas C, Muñoz N, Arregoces L, Larson HJ. HPV vaccine confidence and cases of mass psychogenic illness following immunization in Carmen de Bolivar, Colombia. *Hum Vaccin Immunother*. 2019: 15(1): 163–6. doi: 10.1080/21645515.2018.1511667.

23 O'Sullivan S. *The Sleeping Beauties: And Other Stories of Mystery Illness*. London: Picador, 2021.

24 Simas et al. HPV vaccine confidence and cases of mass psychogenic illness following immunization in Carmen de Bolivar, Colombia.

25 O'Sullivan. *The Sleeping Beauties*.

26 Colombian president: No link of vaccine to illness. *Medical Xpress*. 2014 Aug 31. Available from: https://medicalxpress.com/pdf328715969.pdf. Accessed 2025 May 18.

27 de Bruijn G-J, Vandebosch H, eds. *Health, Media, and Communication*. Berlin, Boston: De Gruyter Mouton, 2025.

28 Simas et al. HPV vaccine confidence and cases of mass psychogenic illness following immunization in Carmen de Bolivar, Colombia.

29 NHS. Breast enlargement (implants). NHS website. Available from: https://www.nhs.uk/tests-and-treatments/cosmetic-procedures/cosmetic-surgery/breast-enlargement/. Accessed 2025 May 18.

30. Newby JM, Tang S, Faasse K, Sharrock MJ, Adams WP Jr. Understanding breast implant illness. *Aesthet Surg J.* 2021: 41(12): 1367–79. doi: 10.1093/asj/sjaa329.
31. Special Report 2019: Breast implant illness and BIA-ALCL. Breastcancer.org. Available from: https://www.breastcancer.org/treatment/surgery/breast-reconstruction/types/implant-reconstruction/illness. Accessed 2025 May 18.
32. Cohen Tervaert JW, Mohazab N, Redmond D, van Eeden C, Osman M. Breast implant illness: scientific evidence of its existence. *Expert Rev Clin Immunol.* 2022: 18(1): 15–29. doi: 10.1080/1744666X.2022.2010546.
33. Yang S, Klietz M-L, Harren AK, Wei Q, Hirsch T, Aitzetmüller MM. Understanding breast implant illness: etiology is the key. *Aesthet Surg J.* 2022: 42(4): NP222–8. doi: 10.1093/asj/sjab394.
34. Ibid.
35. Bresnick SD, Morris S, Lagman C. Findings consistent with a breast implant-associated somatic system disorder (BIA-SSD) among patients self-reporting breast implant illness. *Plast Reconstr Surg Glob Open.* 2024: 12(11): e6322. doi: 10.1097/GOX.0000000000006322.
36. Yang *et al.* Understanding breast implant illness: etiology is the key.
37. Bird GR, Niessen FB. The effect of explantation on systemic disease symptoms and quality of life in patients with breast implant illness: a prospective cohort study. *Sci Rep.* 2022: 12: 21073. doi: 10.1038/s41598-022-25411-5.
38. U.S. Food and Drug Administration. Breast implants – certain labeling recommendations to improve patient communication: guidance for industry and Food and Drug Administration staff. Silver Spring, MD: FDA; 2020. Available from: https://www.fda.gov/regulatory-information/search-fda-guidance-documents/breast-implants-certain-labeling-recommendations-improve-patient-communication. Accessed 2025 May 18.
39. Medicines and Healthcare products Regulatory Agency (MHRA). Symptoms sometimes referred to as Breast Implant Illness: information for clinicians and patients. 2020 Jan 17 [updated 2023 Apr 28]. Available from: https://www.gov.uk/guidance/symptoms-sometimes-referred-to-as-breast-implant-illness-information-for-clinicians-and-patients. Accessed 2025 May 18.
40. Special Report 2019: Breast implant illness and BIA-ALCL.

41 U.S. Food and Drug Administration, Center for Devices and Radiological Health. FDA update on the safety of silicone gel-filled breast implants. June 2011. Available from: https://www.fda.gov/files/medical%20devices/published/Update-on-the-Safety-of-Silicone-Gel-Filled-Breast-Implants-(2011).pdf. Accessed 2025 May 18.

42 Institute of Medicine (US) Committee on the Safety of Silicone Breast Implants. *Safety of Silicone Breast Implants*. Bondurant S, Ernster V, Herdman R, eds. Washington, DC: National Academies Press, 1999. doi: 10.17226/9602.

43 NHS. PIP breast implants. NHS website. Available from: https://www.nhs.uk/conditions/pip-implants/. Accessed 2025 May 18.

44 U.S. Food and Drug Administration, Center for Devices and Radiological Health. FDA update on the safety of silicone gel-filled breast implants. June 2011.

45 NHS. PIP breast implants.

46 British Association of Plastic, Reconstructive and Aesthetic Surgeons (BAPRAS). ALCL risk from breast implants. Available from: https://www.bapras.org.uk/professionals/clinical-guidance/baprs-bia-alcl-statement-july-2021/alcl-risk-from-breast-implants. Accessed 2025 May 18.

47 Nelson JA, McCarthy C, Dabic S, Polanco T, Chilov M, Mehrara BJ *et al*. BIA-ALCL and textured breast implants: a systematic review of evidence supporting surgical risk management strategies. *Plast Reconstr Surg*. 2021: 147(5 Suppl): 7S–13S. doi: 10.1097/PRS.0000000000008040.

48 Longo B, Di Napoli A, Curigliano G, Veronesi P, Pileri S, Martelli M *et al*. Clinical recommendations for diagnosis and treatment according to current updated knowledge on BIA-ALCL. *Breast*. 2022: 66: 332–41. doi: 10.1016/j.breast.2022.11.009.

49 Allergan Ltd. Urgent Field Safety Notice: Allergan textured breast implants and tissue expanders. Marlow, UK: Allergan Ltd; 2018 Dec 19. Available from: https://associationofbreastsurgery.org.uk/media/h1pgcjqv/allergan-recall-finalpdf-received-from-mhra.pdf. Accessed 2025 May 18.

50 Ibid.

51 MHRA. Symptoms sometimes referred to as Breast Implant Illness: information for clinicians and patients. 2020 Jan 17.

52 Adidharma W, Latack KR, Colohan SM, Morrison SD, Cederna PS. Breast implant illness: are social media and the internet worrying patients

sick? *Plast Reconstr Surg.* 2020: 145(1): 225e–7e. doi: 10.1097/PRS.0000000000006361.
53 Tang S, Anderson NE, Faasse K, Adams WP Jr, Newby JM. A qualitative study on the experiences of women with breast implant illness. *Aesthet Surg J.* 2022: 42(4): 381–93. doi: 10.1093/asj/sjab204.
54 Ibid.
55 Kabir R, Stanton E, Sorenson TJ, Hemal K, Boyd CJ, Karp NS et al. Breast implant illness as a clinical entity: a systematic review of the literature. *Aesthet Surg J.* 2024: 44(9): NP629–36. doi: 10.1093/asj/sjae095.
56 Lieffering AS, Hommes JE, van der Hulst RRWJ, Rakhorst HA, Verheij RA, Mureau MAM, *et al.* Breast implant illness revisited: a cohort study of health symptoms in women with implant-based reconstruction. *J Plast Reconstr Aesthet Surg.* 2025: 102: 114–22. doi: 10.1016/j.bjps.2025.01.026.
57 Yang *et al.* Understanding breast implant illness: etiology is the key.
58 Bresnick SD. Self-reported breast implant illness: the contribution of systemic illnesses and other factors to patient symptoms. *Aesthet Surg J Open Forum.* 2023: 5: ojad030. doi: 10.1093/asjof/ojad030.
59 Keane G, Chi D, Ha AY, Myckatyn TM. En bloc capsulectomy for breast implant illness: a social media phenomenon? *Aesthet Surg J.* 2021: 41(4): 448–59. doi: 10.1093/asj/sjaa203.
60 Tang *et al.* A qualitative study on the experiences of women with breast implant illness.

## 3 THE WEIGHT-LOSS RACE, OR THE NEW DRUG MARKET

1 O'Brien SA. The name on everybody's lips at the Oscars: Ozempic. *Wall Street Journal.* 2023 Mar 13. Available from: https://www.wsj.com/articles/ozempic-oscars-weight-loss-11678630953. Accessed 2025 May 18.
2 Nnadi C. Kim Kardashian takes Marilyn Monroe's "Happy birthday, Mr President" dress out for a spin. *British Vogue.* 2022 May 3. Available from: https://www.vogue.co.uk/article/kim-kardashian-marilyn-monroe-dress. Accessed 2025 May 18.
3 Musk E. Fasting + Ozempic/Wegovy + no tasty food near me. *X* (formerly *Twitter*). 2022 Nov 16, 6:36 a.m. Available from: https://x.com/elonmusk/status/1592768518050574336. Accessed 2025 May 18.

4   *Good Morning Britain* [@goodmorningbritain]. *TikTok*. 2023 Nov 24. Available from: https://www.tiktok.com/@goodmorningbritain/video/7305035143440321825?_t=8p7A9Nau012. Accessed 2025 May 18.
5   NCD Risk Factor Collaboration (NCD-RisC). Worldwide trends in underweight and obesity from 1990 to 2022: a pooled analysis of 3663 population-representative studies with 222 million children, adolescents, and adults. *Lancet*. 2024: 403(10431): 1027–50. doi: 10.1016/S0140-6736(24)00490-2.
6   Celletti F, Branca F, Farrar J. Obesity and glucagon-like peptide-1 receptor agonists. *JAMA*. 2025: 333(7): 561–2. doi: 10.1001/jama.2024.25872.
7   NHS England. Health Survey for England 2019 [NS]. 2020 Dec 15. Available from: https://digital.nhs.uk/data-and-information/publications/statistical/health-survey-for-england/2019. Accessed 2025 May 18.
8   Celletti *et al*. Obesity and glucagon-like peptide-1 receptor agonists.
9   Department of Health and Social Care. *Fit for the Future: 10 Year Health Plan for England*. London: Department of Health and Social Care; 2025 Jul. Available from: https://assets.publishing.service.gov.uk/media/6866387fe6557c544c74db7a/fit-for-the-future-10-year-health-plan-for-england.pdf. Accessed 2025 Jul 6.
10  IQVIA data, April 2025, cited in Tony Blair Institute for Global Change. *Anti-obesity Medications: Faster, Broader Access Can Drive Health and Wealth in the UK*. London: Tony Blair Institute for Global Change; cited 2025 Jul 6. Available from: https://institute.global/insights/public-services/anti-obesity-medications-faster-broader-access-can-drive-health-and-wealth-in-the-uk. Accessed 2025 Jul 16.
11  Friedman JM. The discovery and development of GLP-1 based drugs that have revolutionized the treatment of obesity. *Proc Natl Acad Sci U S A*. 2024: 121(39): e2415550121. doi: 10.1073/pnas.2415550121.
12  Ibid.
13  Tait A. Weight-loss injections have taken over the internet. But what does this mean for people IRL? *MIT Technology Review*. 2023 Mar 20. Available from: https://www.technologyreview.com/2023/03/20/1069842/wegovy-mounjaro-ozempic-tiktok-weight-loss-injections/. Accessed 2025 May 18.
14  Healy E. Weight-loss drug maker Novo Nordisk becomes Europe's most valuable company. *Financial Times*. 2023 Sept 4. Available from: https://www.ft.com/content/19357584-62e0-452f-a06f-7cda1d8cd0e3. Accessed 2025 May 18.

15 Fick M, Gronholt-Pedersen J, Jacobsen S. Novo Nordisk ousts CEO after falling behind in weight loss market. Reuters. 2025 May 16. Available from: https://www.investing.com/news/stock-market-news/obesity-drug-maker-novo-nordisks-ceo-to-step-down-amid-market-struggle-4050383. Accessed 2025 May 18.

16 Diver T. Musk upgrades to 'King Kong' of weight-loss drugs. *Telegraph*. 2024 Dec 26. Available from: https://www.telegraph.co.uk/us/news/2024/12/26/musk-upgrades-to-king-kong-of-weight-loss-drugs/. Accessed 2025 May 18.

17 Basch CH, Narayanan S, Tang H, Fera J, Basch CE. Descriptive analysis of TikTok videos posted under the hashtag #Ozempic. *J Med Surg Public Health*. 2023: 1: 100013.

18 Smith R. Medical journals are an extension of the marketing arm of pharmaceutical companies. *PLoS Med*. 2005: 2(5): e138. doi: 10.1371/journal.pmed.0020138.

19 Handel AE, Patel SV, Pakpoor J, Ebers GC, Goldacre B, Ramagopalan SV. High reprint orders in medical journals and pharmaceutical industry funding: case-control study. *BMJ*. 2012: 344: e4212. doi: 10.1136/bmj.e4212.

20 *Nature Portfolio*. Reprints & Permissions. Springer Nature offers reprints and permissions services for authors, readers, and commercial entities, including author and commercial reprints, and permissions for reuse of published material. Available from: https://www.nature.com/nature-portfolio/reprints-and-permissions. Accessed 2025 May 22.

21 Wilding JPH, Batterham RL, Calanna S, Davies M, Van Gaal LF, Lingvay I *et al.*; STEP 1 Study Group. Once-weekly semaglutide in adults with overweight or obesity. *N Engl J Med*. 2021: 384: 989–1002. doi: 10.1056/NEJMoa2032183.

22 MHRA. Contribution of Yellow Cards to identifying safety issues. Updated January 2020, August 2020. Available from: https://assets.publishing.service.gov.uk/media/5f3fa4878fa8f53717418ef7/Contribution_of_Yellow_Cards_to_identifying_safety_issues.pdf. Accessed 2025 May 21.

23 MHRA. Women on 'skinny jabs' must use effective contraception, MHRA urges in latest guidance. 2025 Jun 5. Available from: https://www.gov.uk/government/news/women-on-skinny-jabs-must-use-effective-contraception-mhra-urges-in-latest-guidance. Accessed 2025 Jul 6.

24 Mahase E. Weight loss pill praised as 'holy grail' is withdrawn from US market over cancer link. *BMJ*. 2020: 368: m705. doi: 10.1136/bmj.m705.
25 European Medicines Agency. European Medicines Agency recommends suspension of marketing authorisation for sibutramine. 2010 Jan 22. Available from: https://www.ema.europa.eu/en/news/european-medicines-agency-recommends-suspension-marketing-authorisation-sibutramine. Accessed 2025 Jul 1; U.S. Food and Drug Administration. FDA Drug Safety Communication: FDA recommends against the continued use of Meridia (sibutramine). 2010 Oct 8. Available from: https://www.fda.gov/drugs/drug-safety-and-availability/fda-drug-safety-communication-fda-recommends-against-continued-use-meridia-sibutramine. Accessed 2025 Jul 1.
26 Onakpoya IJ, Heneghan CJ, Aronson JK. Post-marketing withdrawal of anti-obesity medicinal products because of adverse drug reactions: a systematic review. *BMC Med*. 2016: 14: 191. doi: 10.1186/s12916-016-0735-y
27 Sanyal AJ, Newsome PN, Kliers I, Østergaard LH, Long MT, Kjær MS *et al*.; ESSENCE Study Group. Phase 3 trial of semaglutide in metabolic dysfunction-associated steatohepatitis. *N Engl J Med*. 2025: 392: 2089–99. doi:10.1056/NEJMoa2403300.
28 Lincoff AM, Brown-Frandsen K, Colhoun HM, Deanfield J, Emerson SS, Esbjerg S *et al*.; SELECT Trial Investigators. Semaglutide and cardiovascular outcomes in obesity without diabetes. *N Engl J Med*. 2023: 389: 2221–32. doi: 10.1056/NEJMoa230756.
29 Novo Nordisk. Wegovy® approved in the US for cardiovascular risk reduction in people with overweight or obesity and established cardiovascular disease [company announcement]. 2024 Mar 8. Available from: https://www.novonordisk.com/news-and-media/news-and-ir-materials/news-details.html?id=167030. Accessed 2025 May 21.
30 Loftus P. Weight-loss drug Wegovy cuts stroke, heart-attack risk by 20% in new study. *Wall Street Journal*. 2023 Aug 8. Available from: https://www.wsj.com/health/pharma/wegovy-weight-loss-drug-heart-attack-stroke-570f435e. Accessed 2025 May 21.
31 Kessler D. Weight-loss drugs aren't really about weight: to figure out who will benefit most, doctors should consider a particularly toxic kind of fat. *The Atlantic*. 2025 May 12. Available from: https://www.theatlantic.com/health/archive/2025/05/weight-loss-drugs-visceral-fat/607123/. Accessed 2025 May 21.

32  Gasoyan H, Butsch WS, Schulte R, Casacchia NJ, Le P, Boyer CB et al. Changes in weight and glycemic control following obesity treatment with semaglutide or tirzepatide by discontinuation status. *Obesity*. 2025 Jun 10. doi: 10.1002/oby.24331.

33  Wilding JPH, Batterham RL, Davies M, Van Gaal LF, Kandler K, Konakli K et al.; STEP 1 Study Group. Weight regain and cardiometabolic effects after withdrawal of semaglutide: The STEP 1 trial extension. *Diabetes Obes Metab*. 2022: 24(8): 1553–64. doi: 10.1111/dom.14725.

34  Kessler. Weight-loss drugs aren't really about weight: to figure out who will benefit most, doctors should consider a particularly toxic kind of fat.

35  Blum D. The allure of 'microdosing' Ozempic. *New York Times*. 2024 Dec 5. Available from: https://www.nytimes.com/2024/12/05/well/ozempic-microdose-weight-loss.html. Accessed 2025 May 22.

36  Doheny K, Crist C. Some patients – and doctors – turn to microdosing GLP-1s. *Medscape Medical News*. 2025 Feb 6. Available from: https://www.medscape.com/viewarticle/some-patients-and-doctors-turn-microdosing-glp-1s-2025a10002y1. Accessed 2025 May 22.

37  Blum. The allure of 'microdosing' Ozempic.

38  Moore T. GLP-1s Done Right University. Docere Consulting Group LLC. Available from: https://www.drtyna.com/offers/VstUywXc/checkout. Accessed 2025 May 22.

39  Jastreboff AM, Aronne LJ, Ahmad NN, Wharton S, Connery L, Alves B et al.; SURMOUNT-1 Investigators. Tirzepatide once weekly for the treatment of obesity. *N Engl J Med*. 2022: 387: 205–16. doi: 10.1056/NEJMoa2206038.

40  National Voices. Addressing inequalities in clinical trials. 2024 May 16. Available from: https://www.nationalvoices.org.uk/publication/addressing-inequalities-in-clinical-trials/. Accessed 2025 May 22.

41  Aronne LJ, Bade Horn D, le Roux CW, Ho W, Falcon BL, Gomez Valderas E et al.; SURMOUNT-5 Trial Investigators. Tirzepatide as compared with semaglutide for the treatment of obesity. *N Engl J Med*. 2025: 393(1): 26–36. doi: 10.1056/NEJMoa241639

42  Eli Lilly and Company. Zepbound (tirzepatide) showed superior weight loss over Wegovy (semaglutide) in complete SURMOUNT-5 results published in The New England Journal of Medicine [news release]. 2025 May 11. Available from: https://investor.lilly.com/news-releases/

news-release-details/zepbound-tirzepatide-showed-superior-weight-loss-over-wegovy. Accessed 2025 May 22.

43 Stewart E. The bizarre Americanness of prescription drug commercials: before you'd heard of Ozempic, constant TV ads made sure you knew the Ozempic song. *Vox.* 2023 Feb 9. Available from: https://www.vox.com/23583280/prescription-drug-ads-commercials-ozempic-humira-fda. Accessed 2025 May 22.

44 Pharmaceutical Research and Manufacturers of America. PhRMA Guiding Principles: Direct to Consumer Advertisements About Prescription Medicines. Washington, DC: PhRMA; 2018. Available from: https://cdn.aglty.io/phrma/global/resources/PhRMA_Guiding_Principles_2018.pdf. Accessed 2025 Jul 2

45 The Human Medicines Regulations 2012, Part 14. 2012. Available from: https://www.legislation.gov.uk/uksi/2012/1916/part/14. Accessed 2025 May 22.

46 Menkes DB, Mintzes B, Lexchin J. Direct-to-consumer advertising: a modifiable driver of overdiagnosis and overtreatment. *BMJ Evid Based Med.* 2024: 29(6): 423–5. doi: 10.1136/bmjebm-2023-112622.

47 Ibid.

48 Mintzes B, Barer ML, Kravitz RL, Bassett K, Lexchin J, Kazanjian A *et al.* How does direct-to-consumer advertising (DTCA) affect prescribing? A survey in primary care environments with and without legal DTCA. *CMAJ.* 2003: 169(5): 405–12.

49 Kravitz RL, Epstein RM, Feldman MD, Franz CE, Azari R, Wilkes MS *et al.* Influence of patients' requests for direct-to-consumer advertised antidepressants: a randomized controlled trial. *JAMA.* 2005: 293(16): 1995–2002. doi: 10.1001/jama.293.16.1995

50 Ibid.

51 Franquiz MJ, McGuire AL. Direct-to-consumer drug advertisement and prescribing practices: evidence review and practical guidance for clinicians. *J Gen Intern Med.* 2021: 36(5): 1390–94. doi: 10.1056/NEJMoa241639

52 Ibid.

53 Chou R, Turner JA, Devine EB, Hansen RN, Sullivan SD, Blazina I *et al.* The effectiveness and risks of long-term opioid therapy for chronic pain: a systematic review for a National Institutes of Health Pathways to

Prevention Workshop. *Ann Intern Med.* 2015: 162: 276–86. [Epub 2015 Feb 17]. doi: 10.7326/M14-2559.

54 Sites BD, Harrison J, Herrick MD, Masaracchia MM, Beach ML, Davis MA, Prescription opioid use and satisfaction with care among adults with musculoskeletal conditions. *Ann Fam Med.* 2018: (1): 6–13. doi: 10.1370/afm.2148.

55 Martinez KA, Rood M, Jhangiani N, Kou L, Boissy A, Rothberg MB. Association between antibiotic prescribing for respiratory tract infections and patient satisfaction in direct-to-consumer telemedicine. *JAMA Intern Med.* 2018: 178(11): 1558–60. doi: 10.1001/jamainternmed.2018.4318.

56 Vestesson E, De Corte K, Chappell P, Crellin E, Clarke GM. Antibiotic prescribing in remote versus face-to-face consultations for acute respiratory infections in primary care in England: an observational study using target maximum likelihood estimation. *EClinicalMedicine.* 2023: 64: 102245. doi: 10.1016/j.eclinm.2023.102245.

57 Segarra E. 'RTT': Queen Latifah on destigmatizing obesity after 'being publicly scrutinized my whole career'. *USA Today.* Available from: https://www.usatoday.com/story/entertainment/celebrities/2025/05/22/queen-latifah-obesity-stigma-rtt/123456789/. Accessed 2025 May 22.

58 Missakian N. Novo Nordisk casts Queen Latifah in TV-themed awareness campaign for obesity. *Fierce Pharma.* 2021 Nov 1. Available from: https://www.fiercepharma.com/marketing/queen-latifah-tackles-obesity-tv-inspired-awareness-campaign-for-novo-nordisk. Accessed 2025 May 22.

59 https://www.facebook.com/QueenLatifah/videos/bigger-than-me/1227220604631724/

60 Kansteiner F. Novo Nordisk's semaglutide set to tackle obesity with hotly-anticipated FDA green light. *Fierce Pharma* 2021 Jun 4. Available from: https://www.fiercepharma.com/pharma/novo-nordisk-s-semaglutide-snags-hotly-anticipated-greenlight-obesity. Accessed 2025 May 22.

61 Pharma Forum. Advertising before approval – navigating pharma marketing. 2023 Apr 5. Available from: https://pharmaforum.com/news/advertising-before-approval-navigating-pharma-marketing. Accessed 2025 May 22.

62 Ibid.

63 Ibid.

64 Hayward E, Koronka P. 500,000 Britons buying weight-loss drugs online to beat 'slow' NHS rollout. *The Times.* 2024 Dec 20. Available from:

https://www.thetimes.co.uk/article/500000-britons-buying-weight-loss-drugs-online-to-beat-slow-nhs-rollout-2024. Accessed 2025 May 22.

65  Committee of Advertising Practice, MHRA. Enforcement Notice: Advertising of prescription-only weight-loss treatments. ASA; 2021. Available from: https://www.asa.org.uk/static/18371182-9943-4d43-b44ba781d88826af/Enforcement-Notice-Advertising-of-prescription-only-weight-loss-products.pdf. Accessed 2025 May 22.

66  Ibid.

67  Davis N. 'Wild west': experts concerned by illegal promotion of weight-loss jabs in UK. *Guardian*. 2024 Dec 26. Available from: https://www.theguardian.com/society/2024/dec/26/experts-concern-promotions-weight-loss-jabs-uk. Accessed 2025 May 22.

68  Chan W. 'I'm not a doctor just FYI': the influencers paid to hawk drugs on TikTok. *Guardian*. 2023 Mar 17. Available from: https://www.theguardian.com/us-news/2023/mar/17/patient-influencers-tiktok-instagram-medical-prescription-drugs. Accessed 2025 May 22.

69  Willis E, Friedel K, Heisten M, Pickett M, Bhowmick A. Communicating health literacy on prescription medications on social media: in-depth interviews with 'patient influencers'. *J Med Internet Res*. 2023: 25: e41867 doi: 10.2196/41867.

70  Chan. 'I'm not a doctor just FYI': the influencers paid to hawk drugs on TikTok.

71  Turner C, Cologne D, Carter R, Van Wymeersch V. Ever heard of health TikTok? Why health and wellness companies should explore TikTok. *Ogilvy Health*. 2024. Available from: https://www.ogilvyhealth.com/insights/why-health-and-wellness-companies-should-explore-tiktok. Accessed 2025 May 22.

72  Robinson J. More than half of pharmacists have been asked about medicines that patients had seen on social media, finds survey. *Pharm J*. 2022 Sept 21. Available from: https://pharmaceutical-journal.com/article/news/more-than-half-of-pharmacists-have-been-asked-about-medicines-that-patients-had-seen-on-social-media-finds-survey. Accessed 2025 May 22.

73  LiveWorld, Sermo. Social channels gain credibility with healthcare practitioners. February 2023. Available from: https://www.sermo.com/wp-content/uploads/2023/02/Social-Channels-Gain-Credibility-with-Healthcare-Practitioners.pdf. Accessed 2025 May 22.

74  Hayward, Koronka. 500,000 Britons buying weight-loss drugs online to beat 'slow' NHS rollout.

75  Ibid.
76  Pantony A. I had an eating disorder for most of my adult life. So why was I prescribed weight loss injections? *Glamour*. 2024 Jul 11. Available from: https://www.glamourmagazine.co.uk/article/weight-loss-injections-wegovy-eating-disorders. Accessed 2025 May 24.
77  Davis N. UK online pharmacies face stricter rules for sales of weight-loss jabs. *Guardian*. 2025 Feb 4. Available from: https://www.theguardian.com/science/2025/feb/04/uk-online-pharmacies-rules-wegovy-mounjaro-ozempic. Accessed 2025 May 24.
78  MHRA. GLP-1 receptor agonists: reminder of the potential side effects and to be aware of the potential for misuse. gov.uk. 2024 Oct 24. Available from: https://www.gov.uk/government/news/mhra-reminds-healthcare-professionals-to-advise-patients-of-the-side-effects-of-glp-1-agonists-and-to-report-misuse. Accessed 2025 May 24.
79  MHRA. Yellow Card: please help to reverse the decline in reporting of suspected adverse drug reactions. Drug Safety Update. 2019 May 17. Available from: https://www.gov.uk/drug-safety-update/yellow-card-please-help-to-reverse-the-decline-in-reporting-of-suspected-adverse-drug-reactions. Accessed 2025 May 24.
80  Diabetes UK. FAQs – GLP-1 RA shortages. 2025 Feb 4 [updated 2025 Feb 4]. Available from: https://www.diabetes.org.uk/about-us/news-and-views/our-response-serious-supply-issues-drugs-people-living-type-2-diabetes. Accessed 2025 May 24.
81  Ibid.
82  Fairclough S. Ozempic shortage hits diabetes patient after weight loss use. *BBC News*. 2023 Sep 6. Available from: https://www.bbc.com/news/uk-wales-66735012. Accessed 2025 May 24.
83  Walsh A, Rai P. Weight loss injection hype fuels online black market. *BBC News*. 2023 Nov 15. Available from: https://www.bbc.co.uk/news/health-67414203. Accessed 2025 May 24.
84  United Nations Interregional Crime and Justice Research Institute (UNICRI). Counterfeit medicines sold through the internet. 2019 Nov. Available from: https://unicri.org/sites/default/files/2019-11/Counterfeit%20medicines%20sold%20through%20the%20Internet.pdf. Accessed 2025 May 24.
85  Graham C. Ordering illicit weight loss drugs is 'dicing with death' – GP. *BBC News NI*. 2025 Apr 14. Available from: https://www.bbc.co.uk/news/articles/czd3n55enqyo. Accessed 2025 May 24.

86 Minsberg T. TikTok attempts to rein in weight loss posts. *New York Times*. 2024 May 17. Available from: https://www.nytimes.com/2024/05/17/well/tiktok-weight-loss-posts.html. Accessed 2025 May 24.

87 Ibid.

88 MHRA. UK medicines regulator warns against buying weight loss medicines without a prescription this New Year. 2024 Dec 30. Available from: https://www.gov.uk/government/news/uk-medicines-regulator-warns-against-buying-weight-loss-medicines-without-a-prescription-this-new-year. Accessed 2025 May 24.

## 4 A DIAGNOSTIC ODYSSEY

1 Endometriosis UK. Urgent government action needed to improve education for young people and healthcare practitioners: launch of Endometriosis Action Month March 2025. 2025 Mar 1. Available from: https://www.endometriosis-uk.org/news/urgent-government-action-needed-improve-education-young-people-and-healthcare-practitioners-launch. Accessed 2025 May 24.

2 Vogel L. Medicine slow to recognize social media as window into the patient experience. *CMAJ*. 2019: 191(3): E87–8. doi: 10.1503/cmaj.109-5701.

3 Moyer MW. Women are calling out 'medical gaslighting'. *New York Times*. 2022 Mar 28 [updated 2023 Jun 22]. Available from: https://www.nytimes.com/2022/03/28/well/live/gaslighting-doctors-patients-health.html#:~:text=Patients%20who%20have%20felt%20that,stories%20on%20sites%20like%20Instagram. Accessed 2025 May 24.

4 NHS. Medically unexplained symptoms. Available from: https://www.nhs.uk/conditions/medically-unexplained-symptoms/. Accessed 2025 May 24.

5 Cox C, Hatfield T, Fritz Z. How and why do doctors communicate diagnostic uncertainty: an experimental vignette study. *Health Expectations*. 2024: 27(1): e13957. doi: 10.1111/hex.13957.

6 Evans WRH, Rafi I. Rare diseases in general practice: recognising the zebras among the horses. *Br J Gen Pract*. 2016: 66(652): 550–1. doi: 10.3399/bjgp16X687625.

7 NICE. Recent-onset chest pain of suspected cardiac origin: assessment and diagnosis. Clinical guideline [CG95]. 2010 Mar 24 [updated 2016 Nov 30].

Available from: https://www.nice.org.uk/guidance/cg95. Accessed 2025 May 24.

8   NHS. Risks – Angiography. Available from: https://www.nhs.uk/conditions/angiography/risks/. Accessed 2025 May 24.

9   Cox *et al*. How and why do doctors communicate diagnostic uncertainty: an experimental vignette study.

10  Ibid.

11  MacGowan A. The TikTok Algorithm Knew My Sexuality Better Than I Did. *Repeller*. 2020 Jul 8. Smith B. How TikTok Reads Your Mind. *New York Times*. 2021 Dec 5. Available from: https://www.nytimes.com/2021/12/05/business/media/tiktok-algorithm.html. Accessed 2025 May 18.

12  Cotter K, DeCook JR, Kanthawala S, Foyle K. In FYP we trust: the divine force of algorithmic conspirituality. *Int J Commun*. 2022: 16: 2913–29. Available from: https://ijoc.org/index.php/ijoc/article/view/19289. Accessed 2025 May 24.

13  Simply Sensitivity Checks. Bioresonance checks. Available from: https://gb.simplysensitivitychecks.com/pages/bioresonance. Accessed 2025 May 27.

14  Memorial Sloan Kettering Cancer Center. BioResonance therapy: purported benefits, side effects and more. Available from: https://www.mskcc.org/cancer-care/integrative-medicine/herbs/bioresonance-therapy. Accessed 2025 May 27.

15  ITV. Are food intolerance home tests a waste of money? *This Morning*. 2024 Apr 16. Available from: https://www.itv.com/thismorning/articles/are-food-intolerance-home-tests-a-waste-of-money. Accessed 2025 May 27.

16  Jefferson-Brown N. YorkTest's turnover tops £6m as more turn to home health tests. 2022 Mar 30. Available from: https://www.yorkpress.co.uk/news/20028844.yorktests-turnover-tops-6m-turn-home-health-tests/. Accessed 2025 May 27.

17  Ibid.

18  Gram EG, Copp T, Ransohoff DF, Plüddemann A, Kramer BS, Woloshin S *et al*. Direct-to-consumer tests: emerging trends are cause for concern. *BMJ*. 2024: 387: e080460. doi: 10.1136/bmj-2024-080460.

19  Whiting P, Toerien M, de Salis I, Sterne JAC, Dieppe P, Egger M *et al*. A review identifies and classifies reasons for ordering diagnostic tests. *J Clin Epidemiol*. 2007: 60(9): 981–9.

20 Food Standards Agency. Patterns and prevalence of adult food allergy (PAFA): Final Report. FSA Contract Number: FS101174. University of Manchester, Manchester University NHS Foundation Trust, Amsterdam University Medical Centre, University of Southampton, Isle of Wight NHS Trust. 2025. Available from: https://doi.org/10.46756/sci.fsa.ehu454. Accessed 2025 May 27.

21 AllergyUK. Food allergy testing and diagnosing. Available from: https://www.allergyuk.org/resources/food-allergy-testing-and-diagnosing/. Accessed 2025 May 27.

22 AAAAI Adverse Reactions to Foods Committee. AAAAI support of the EAACI position paper on IgG4. May 2010. Available from: https://www.aaaai.org/Aaaai/media/Media-Library-PDFs/Tools%20for%20the%20Public/Conditions%20Library/Library%20-%20Allergies/eacci-igg4-2010.pdf. Accessed 2025 May 27.

23 Cleveland Clinic. Food intolerance. 2021 Aug 11. Available from: https://my.clevelandclinic.org/health/diseases/21688-food-intolerance. Accessed 2025 May 27.

24 Varney J. The science and pseudoscience of food allergy and intolerance testing. Monash University; 2021 Nov 8. Available from: https://lens.monash.edu/@medicine-health/2021/11/08/1383975/the-science-and-pseudoscience-of-food-allergy-and-intolerance-testing. Accessed 2025 May 27.

25 Kvehaugen AS, Tveiten D, Farup PG. Is perceived intolerance to milk and wheat associated with the corresponding IgG and IgA food antibodies? A cross sectional study in subjects with morbid obesity and gastrointestinal symptoms. *BMC Gastroenterol.* 2018: 18(1): 22. doi: 10.1186/s12876-018-0750-x.

26 Stapel SO, Asero R, Ballmer-Weber BK, Knol EF, Strobel S, Vieths S *et al.*; EAACI Task Force. Testing for IgG4 against foods is not recommended as a diagnostic tool: EAACI Task Force Report. *Allergy.* 2008: 63(7): 793–6. doi: 10.1111/j.1398-9995.2008.01705.x.

27 Shih P, Ding P, Carter SM, Stanaway F, Horvath AR, Langguth D *et al.* Direct-to-consumer tests advertised online in Australia and their implications for medical overuse: systematic online review and a typology of clinical utility. *BMJ Open.* 2021: 11(10): e049803. doi: 10.1136/bmjopen-2021-049803.

28 Young E, Stoneham MD, Petruckevitch A, Barton J, Rona R. A population study of food intolerance. *Lancet.* 1994: 343(8906): 1127–30.

29  Ibid.
30  Whiting P *et al*. A review identifies and classifies reasons for ordering diagnostic tests..
31  Association for Laboratory Medicine. Marketing of laboratory tests direct to the public. 2023 Sept 11. Available from: https://labmed.org.uk/our-resources/news/marketing-of-laboratory-tests-direct-to-the-public.html. Accessed 2025 May 27.

## 5 SICK UNTIL PROVEN HEALTHY

1  Mikhail A. I tried the $2,500 Prenuvo full-body MRI scan that Kim Kardashian endorsed. It may have benefits – but also some major downsides. *Fortune Well*. 2024 Feb 10 [updated 2024 Jun 24]. Available from: https://fortune.com/well/article/prenuvo-full-body-mri-scan-benefits-drawbacks/. Accessed 2025 May 27.
2  Davis D. The results of Kim Kardashian's butt X-ray are in. *Cosmopolitan*. 2011 Jun 24. Available from: https://www.cosmopolitan.com/entertainment/celebs/news/a3717/kim-kardashian-butt-x-ray/. Accessed 2025 May 27.
3  Kardashian K. Instagram post. 2023 Aug 8. Available from: https://www.instagram.com/p/CvszJqGyfqr/?hl=en. Accessed 2025 May 27.
4  Blum D, Holtermann C. The new status symbol is a full-body M.R.I. *New York Times*. 2023 Sept 19. Available from: https://www.nytimes.com/2023/09/19/well/live/full-body-mri-scan.html. Accessed 2025 May 27.
5  Warner B. Daniel Ek's next act: full-body scans for the people. *New York Times*. 2024 Apr 27 [updated 2024 May 23]. Available from: https://www.nytimes.com/2024/04/27/business/daniel-ek-neko-health-body-scans.html. Accessed 2025 May 27.
6  McCartney M, Cohen D. The truth about private health scans: there's a risk of over-diagnosis. *UnHerd*. 2025 Jan 20. Available from: https://unherd.com/2025/01/the-truth-about-private-health-scans/. Accessed 2025 May 27.
7  UK National Screening Committee. UK National Screening Committee: 25 years of recommendations. 2021 Sept 15. Available from: https://www.gov.uk/government/publications/uk-national-screening-committee-25-years-of-recommendations. Accessed 2025 May 27.

8  Tagami T. The truth about whole-body scans. *WebMD*. 2024 Oct 30. Available from: https://www.webmd.com/a-to-z-guides/features/truth-about-whole-body-scans. Accessed 2025 May 27.
9  Blum, Holtermann. The new status symbol is a full-body M.R.I.
10 Kwee RM, Kwee TC. Whole-body MRI for preventive health screening: a systematic review of the literature. *J Magn Reson Imaging*. 2019: 50(5): 1489–503. doi: 10.1002/jmri.26736.
11 Raz G. Full body preventive health care with Andrew Lacy of Prenuvo: how I built this podcast with Guy Raz. *Wondery*; 2023 Dec 7. Episode 577. Available from: https://wondery.com/shows/how-i-built-this/episode/10386-full-body-preventive-health-care-with-andrew-lacy-of-prenuvo/. Accessed 2025 May 27.
12 Elshaug AG, Rosenthal MB, Lavis JN, Brownlee S, Schmidt H, Nagpal S et al. Levers for addressing medical underuse and overuse: achieving high-value health care. *Lancet*. 2017: 390(10090): 191–202.
13 Anderson M, Molloy A, Maynou L, Kyriopoulos I, McGuire A, Mossialos E et al. Evaluation of the NHS England evidence-based interventions programme: a difference-in-difference analysis. *BMJ Qual Saf*. 2023: 32: 90–9. doi: 10.1136/bmjqs-2021-014478.
14 Ganguli I, Simpkin AL, Lupo C, Weissman A, Mainor AJ, Orav EJ et al. Cascades of care after incidental findings in a US national survey of physicians. *JAMA Netw Open*. 2019: 2(10): e1913325. doi: 10.1001/jamanetworkopen.2019.13325.
15 NHS. Abdominal aortic aneurysm (AAA) screening. 2024 Nov 11. Available from: https://www.nhs.uk/tests-and-treatments/abdominal-aortic-aneurysm-screening/. Accessed 2025 May 28.
16 Nickel B, Moynihan R, Gram EG, Copp T, Taba M, Shih P et al. Social media posts about medical tests with potential for overdiagnosis. *JAMA Netw Open*. 2025: 8(2): e2461940. doi: 10.1001/jamanetworkopen.2024.61940.
17 ten Hoor GA, Kok G, Peters GJY, Ruiter RAC. Fear appeals in health communication. In: de Bruijn GJ, Vandebosch H, eds. *Health, Media, and Communication*. Berlin, Boston: De Gruyter Mouton, 2025, ch. 5.
18 Jørgensen KJ, Gøtzsche PC. Content of invitations for publicly funded screening mammography. *BMJ*. 2006: 332: 538. doi: 10.1136/bmj.332.7540.538.

19  Petrow S. Cancer deaths are down, so why does cancer scare us so much? *Washington Post*. 2024 Jul 5. Available from: https://www.washingtonpost.com/wellness/2024/07/05/cancer-deaths-mortality-fear/. Accessed 2025 May 28.

20  Cancer Research UK. Cancer mortality statistics. Available from: https://www.cancerresearchuk.org/health-professional/cancer-statistics-for-the-uk. Accessed 2025 May 28.

21  Bae J, Fu J. Let's make social media a place for health education, not misinformation. *Harvard Public Health*. 2023 Jul 11. Available from: https://harvardpublichealth.org/tech-innovation/social-media-and-health-from-misinformation-to-education/. Accessed 2025 May 28.

22  Ropeik D. Cancer is a killer. So is the fear of it. *Stat News*. 2024 Apr 10. Available from: https://www.statnews.com/2024/04/10/cancer-can-kill-cancer-fear-delayed-presentation-make-it-worse/. Accessed 2025 May 28.

23  Smith J. How does cancer treatment in the UK measure up to other countries? Cancer Research UK. 2024 Feb 27. Available from: https://news.cancerresearchuk.org/2024/02/27/how-does-cancer-treatment-in-the-uk-measure-up-to-other-countries/. Accessed 2025 May 28.

24  NHS England. NHS cancer bus tours country as over two in five wouldn't visit GP about possible symptom. 2023 Nov 25. Available from: https://www.england.nhs.uk/2023/11/nhs-cancer-bus-tours-country/. Accessed 2025 May 28.

25  Khullar D. Will a full-body MRI scan help you or hurt you? *The New Yorker*. 2024 Jan 12. Available from: https://www.newyorker.com/science/annals-of-medicine/will-a-full-body-mri-scan-help-you-or-hurt-you. Accessed 2025 May 28.

26  Gray RE, Harris GT. Renal cell carcinoma: diagnosis and management. *Am Fam Physician*. 2019: 99(3): 179–84.

27  Kwee, Kwee. Whole-body MRI for preventive health screening: a systematic review of the literature.

28  Delaloge S, Khan SA, Wesseling J, Whelan T. Ductal carcinoma in situ of the breast: finding the balance between overtreatment and undertreatment. *Lancet*. 2024: 403(10445): 2734–46. Available from: https://www.thelancet.com/journals/lancet/article/PIIS0140-6736(24)00425-2/abstract. Accessed 2025 May 28.

29 Cancer Research UK. Ductal carcinoma in situ (DCIS). 2023 Jun 15. Available from: https://www.cancerresearchuk.org/. Accessed 2025 May 28.
30 Delaloge *et al.* Ductal carcinoma in situ of the breast: finding the balance between overtreatment and undertreatment.
31 Ahn HS, Kim HJ, Welch HG. Korea's thyroid-cancer 'epidemic' – screening and overdiagnosis. *N Engl J Med*. 2014: 371: 1765–7. doi: 10.1056/NEJMp1409841.
32 Ho J, Han M, Jung I, Jo YS, Lee J. Impact of thyroid hormone replacement on the risk of second cancer after thyroidectomy: a Korean National Cohort Study. *Sci Rep*. 2023: 13: 16280.
33 Storrs C. How much do CT scans increase the risk of cancer? *Scientific American*. 2013 Jul 1. Available from: https://www.scientificamerican.com/article/how-much-do-ct-scans-increase-cancer-risk/. Accessed 2025 May 28.
34 Royal College of General Practitioners. Screening position statement. London: RCGP. Oct 2019. Available from: https://www.rcgp.org.uk/representing-you/policy-areas/screening. Accessed 2025 September 30.

# 6 EXPANDING THE SYMPTOM POOL

1 Bartlett S. It turns out I have ADHD. LinkedIn. Available from: https://www.linkedin.com/posts/stevenbartlett-123_it-turns-out-i-have-adhd-a-few-weeks-activity-7125447379289268224-5TAr/. Accessed 2025 May 28.
2 McGrath N. Steven Bartlett: 'Not feeling like I was enough became a driving force in my life'. *Guardian*. 2023 Dec 16. Available from: https://www.theguardian.com/lifeandstyle/2023/dec/16/steven-bartlett-this-much-i-know. Accessed 2025 May 28.
3 McCabe DP, Castel AD. Seeing is believing: the effect of brain images on judgments of scientific reasoning. *Cognition*. 2008: 107(1): 343–52.
4 Farah MJ, Gillihan SJ. The puzzle of neuroimaging and psychiatric diagnosis: technology and nosology in an evolving discipline. *AJOB Neurosci*. 2012: 3(4): 31–41. doi: 10.1080/21507740.2012.713072.
5 Burns C. How many of us will end up being diagnosed with ADHD? *BBC News*. 2024 Sept 15. Available from: https://www.bbc.co.uk/news/articles/c3ejky0dy47o. Accessed 2025 May 28.

6   McKechnie DGJ, O'Nions E, Dunsmuir S, Petersen I. Attention-deficit hyperactivity disorder diagnoses and prescriptions in UK primary care, 2000–2018: population-based cohort study. *BJPsych Open*. 2023: 9(4): e121. doi: 10.1192/bjo.2023.512
7   O'Sullivan S. The number of people with chronic conditions is soaring. Are we less healthy than we used to be – or overdiagnosing illness? *Guardian*. 2025 Mar 1. Available from: https://www.theguardian.com/society/2025/mar/01/the-number-of-people-with-chronic-conditions-is-soaring-are-we-less-healthy-than-we-used-to-be-or-overdiagnosing-illness. Accessed 2025 May 28.
8   Burns C, Loader V, England R. Eight-year ADHD backlog at NHS clinics revealed. *BBC News*. 2024 Jul 25. Available from: https://www.bbc.co.uk/news/articles/c720r1pxrx5o. Accessed 2025 May 28.
9   Lange KW, Reichl S, Lange KM, Tucha L, Tucha O. The history of attention deficit hyperactivity disorder. *Atten Defic Hyperact Disord*. 2010: 2(4): 241–55. doi:10.1007/s12402-010-0045-8.
10  Ibid.
11  Ibid.
12  Ibid.
13  Kawa S, Giordano J. A brief historicity of the *Diagnostic and Statistical Manual of Mental Disorders*: issues and implications for the future of psychiatric canon and practice. *Philos Ethics Humanit Med*. 2012: 7: 2 (2012). doi: 10.1186/1747-5341-7-2.
14  First MB, Clarke DE, Yousif L, Eng AM, Gogtay N, Appelbaum PS. DSM-5-TR: rationale, process, and overview of changes. *Psychiatric Services*. 2023: 74(8): 869–75. doi: 10.1176/appi.ps.20220334.
15  Drescher J. Out of *DSM*: depathologizing homosexuality. *Behav Sci (Basel)*. 2015: 5(4): 565–75. doi: 10.3390/bs5040565.
16  Kawa, Giordano. A brief historicity of the *Diagnostic and Statistical Manual of Mental Disorders*.
17  American Psychiatric Association. The people behind *DSM-5*. 2013. Available from: https://www.psychiatry.org/File%20Library/Psychiatrists/Practice/DSM/APA_DSM_People-Behind-DSM-5.pdf. Accessed 2025 May 28.
18  Lange *et al*. The history of attention deficit hyperactivity disorder.
19  Boodman SG. Attention deficit disorder: do millions of Americans really have it? *Washington Post*. 1996 Mar 4. Available from: https://www.

washingtonpost.com/archive/lifestyle/wellness/1996/03/04/attention-deficit-disorder-do-millions-of-americans-really-have-it/. Accessed 2025 May 28.
20 Mayes R, Rafalovich A. Suffer the restless children: the evolution of ADHD and paediatric stimulant use, 1900–80. *History of Psychiatry.* 2007: 18(4): 435–57. doi: 10.1177/0957154X06075782.
21 Lange *et al*. The history of attention deficit hyperactivity disorder.
22 Moynihan R, Cassels A. *Selling Sickness: How Drug Companies Are Turning Us All into Patients.* Crows Nest, NSW: Allen & Unwin, 2005.
23 Eli Lilly and Co. First non-stimulant ADHD medication available in the United Kingdom. 2004 Jun 3. Available from: https://investor.lilly.com/news-releases/news-release-details/first-non-stimulant-adhd-medication-available-united-kingdom. Accessed 2025 May 28.
24 Moynihan, Cassels. *Selling Sickness: How Drug Companies Are Turning Us All into Patients.*
25 Ibid.
26 National Collaborating Centre for Mental Health (UK). Attention deficit hyperactivity disorder: diagnosis and management of ADHD in children, young people and adults. Leicester, UK: British Psychological Society and Royal College of Psychiatrists; 2009. (National Clinical Practice Guideline Number 72). Available from: https://www.nice.org.uk/guidance/ng87/evidence/full-guideline-pdf-4783651311. Accessed 2025 May 28.
27 Sanders S, Thomas R, Glasziou P, Doust J. A review of changes to the attention deficit/hyperactivity disorder age of onset criterion using the checklist for modifying disease definitions. *BMC Psychiatry.* 2019: 19: 357. doi: 10.1186/s12888-019-2337-7.
28 Ibid.
29 Epstein JN, Loren REA. Changes in the definition of ADHD in *DSM-5*: subtle but important. *Neuropsychiatry* (London). 2013: 3(5): 455–8. doi: 10.2217/NPY.13.59.
30 NICE. Attention deficit hyperactivity disorder: diagnosis and management. NICE guideline [NG87]. 2018 Mar 14 [updated 2019 Sep 13]. Available from: https://www.nice.org.uk/guidance/ng87. Accessed 2025 May 28.
31 Sanders *et al*. A review of changes to the attention deficit/hyperactivity disorder age of onset criterion using the checklist for modifying disease definitions.

32. Ibid.
33. Jønsson ABR. Negotiating normalcy: epistemic errors in self-diagnosing late-ADHD. *Cult Med Psychiatry*. 2025: 49: 369–91. doi: 10.1007/s11013-024-09888-y. Accessed 2025 May 28.
34. Mechanic M. Psychiatry's new diagnostic manual: 'Don't buy it. Don't use it. Don't teach it.' *Mother Jones*. 2013 May 14. Available from: https://www.motherjones.com/politics/2013/05/allen-frances-dsm-5-psychiatry-diagnostic-manual/. Accessed 2025 May 29.
35. Rubin L. Allen Frances on the *DSM-5*, mental illness and humane treatment. Psychotherapy.net. Available from: https://www.psychotherapy.net/interview/allen-frances-interview. Accessed 2025 May 29.
36. Ibid.
37. Karasavva V, Miller C, Groves N, Montiel A, Canu W, Mikami A. A double-edged hashtag: evaluation of #ADHD-related TikTok content and its associations with perceptions of ADHD. *PLoS One*. 2025: 20(3): e0319335. doi: 10.1371/journal.pone.0319335.
38. ADHD UK. Simone Biles. 2022 Aug 13. Available from: https://adhduk.co.uk/2022/08/13/simone-biles/. Accessed 2025 May 29.
39. PA Media. Singer Jessie J reveals she has been diagnosed with OCD and ADHD. *Guardian*. 2024 Jul 20. Available from: https://www.theguardian.com/music/2024/jul/20/singer-jessie-j-reveals-she-has-been-diagnosed-with-ocd-and-adhd. Accessed 2025 May 29.
40. Foulkes L, Andrews JL. Are mental health awareness efforts contributing to the rise in reported mental health problems? A call to test the prevalence inflation hypothesis. *New Ideas in Psychology*. 2023: 69: 101010. doi: 10.1016/j.newideapsych.2023.101010.
41. Young S, Moss D, Sedgwick O, Fridman MK, Hodgkins PS. A meta-analysis of the prevalence of attention deficit hyperactivity disorder in incarcerated populations. *Psychol Med*. 2015: 45(2): 247–58. doi: 10.1017/S0033291714000762.
42. Robins J. ADHD 'critically under diagnosed' in prisons, says report. *The Justice Gap*. 2022 Jun 21. Available from: https://www.thejusticegap.com/adhd-critically-under-diagnosed-in-prisons-says-report/. Accessed 2025 May 29.
43. Froehlich TE, Lanphear BP, Epstein JN, Barbaresi WJ, Katusic SK, Kahn RS. Prevalence, recognition, and treatment of attention-deficit/hyperactivity disorder in a national sample of US children. *Arch Pediatr*

*Adolesc Med.* 2007: 161(9): 857–64. doi: 10.1001/archpedi.161.9.857.

44 Shi Y, Hunter Guevara LR, Dykhoff HJ, Sangaralingham LR, Phelan S et al. Racial disparities in diagnosis of attention-deficit/hyperactivity disorder in a US national birth cohort. *JAMA Netw Open.* 2021: 4(3): e210321. doi: 10.1001/jamanetworkopen.2021.0321.

45 Boseley M. TikTok accidentally detected my ADHD. For 23 years everyone missed the warning signs. *Guardian.* 2021 Jun 3. Available from: https://www.theguardian.com/society/2021/jun/03/tiktok-accidentally-detected-my-adhd-for-23-years-everyone-missed-the-warning-signs. Accessed 2025 May 29.

46 Eagle T, Ringland KE. 'You can't possibly have ADHD': exploring validation and tensions around diagnosis within unbounded ADHD social media communities. In: Proceedings of the 25th International Conference on Computers and Accessibility (ASSETS '23); 2023 Oct 22–25; New York: ACM. doi: 10.1145/3597638.3608400.

47 Yeung A, Ng E, Abi-Jaoude E. TikTok and attention-deficit/hyperactivity disorder: a cross-sectional study of social media content quality. *Can J Psychiatry.* 2022: 67(12): 899–906. doi: 10.1177/07067437221082854.

48 American Psychiatric Association. *Diagnostic and Statistical Manual of Mental Disorders.* 5th edn, Text Revision. Washington, DC: American Psychiatric Association, 2022. p. 71.

49 Karasavva *et al.* A double-edged hashtag: evaluation of #ADHD-related TikTok content and its associations with perceptions of ADHD.

50 ADHD UK. Report: The ADHD medication crisis. 2023 Nov 28. Available from: https://adhduk.co.uk/adhd-medication-crisis-report/. Accessed 2025 May 29.

51 Duguid S. My ADHD medication ran out – then my life fell apart. *Sunday Times.* 2023 Nov 19. Available from: https://www.thetimes.co.uk/article/my-adhd-medication-ran-out-then-my-life-fell-apart-2023 Accessed 2025 May 29.

52 Das S. UK firms exploit ADHD medication shortage to promote unproven 'smart' supplements. *Observer.* 2023 Dec 17. Available from: https://www.theguardian.com/society/2023/dec/17/uk-firms-exploit-adhd-medication-shortage-to-push-unproven-smart-supplements. Accessed 2025 May 29.

53 Ibid.
54 The Decision Lab. Why do we believe our horoscopes? The Barnum effect, explained. Available from: https://thedecisionlab.com/biases/barnum-effect. Accessed 2025 May 29.
55 Karasavva *et al*. A double-edged hashtag: evaluation of #ADHD-related TikTok content and its associations with perceptions of ADHD.
56 Ibid.
57 Suffolk and North East Essex Integrated Care Board (ICB). Information for patients considering privately funding an ADHD assessment. NHS Suffolk and North East Essex. Available from: https://suffolkandnortheastessex.icb.nhs.uk/your-health-and-services/should-i-go-private/private-adhd-assessments/. Accessed 2025 May 29.
58 Chevalier O. 'It starts on TikTok': looping effects and the impact of social media on psychiatric terms. *Philos Psychiatry Psychol*. 2024: 31(2): 163–74. doi: 10.1353/ppp.2024.a930492.
59 Ibid.
60 Ginapp CM, Greenberg NR, MacDonald-Gagnon G, Angarita GA, Bold KW, Potenza MN. 'Dysregulated not deficit': a qualitative study on symptomatology of ADHD in young adults. *PLoS One*. 2023: 18(10): e0292721. doi:10.1371/journal.pone.0292721.
61 Ibid.

## 7 THE OPTIMISATION TRAP

1 Mazziotta J. Gwyneth Paltrow and Kim Kardashian are in a tense competition – over who gets more sleep! *People*. 2021 Aug 31. Available from: https://people.com/health/gwyneth-paltrow-and-kim-kardashian-are-in-a-tense-competition-over-who-gets-more-sleep/. Accessed 2025 May 29.
2 Evans M. Oura has made a gold-laced Gucci smart ring, and it's ludicrously expensive. *TechRadar*. 2022 May 30. Available from: https://www.techradar.com/news/oura-has-made-a-gold-laced-gucci-smart-ring-and-its-ludicrously-expensive. Accessed 2025 May 29.
3 Department of Health and Social Care. *Fit for the Future: 10 Year Health Plan for England*. London: UK Government, 2025. Available from: https://assets.publishing.service.gov.uk/media/6866387fe6557c544c74db7a/fit-for-the-future-10-year-health-plan-for-england.pdf. Accessed 2025 July 30.

4   Borgeaud A. Share of British owning a wearable device as of January 2025, by type of ownership. Statista. 2025 Mar 7. Available from: https://www.statista.com/statistics/1459686/wearable-ownership-by-type-uk/. Accessed 2025 May 30.

5   Laricchia F. Wearables in the U.S. – statistics and facts. Statista. 2025 Mar 6. Available from: https://www.statista.com/topics/12075/wearables-in-the-us/. Accessed 2025 May 30.

6   Brakenridge CL, Healy GN, Winkler EAH, Fjeldsoe BS, Eakin EG, Reeves MM. Effectiveness of wearable activity trackers to increase physical activity and improve health outcomes: a systematic review and meta-analysis. *Lancet Digit Health*. 2022: 4(8): e615–26.

7   Madigan CD, Daley AJ, Lewis AL, Aveyard P, Jolly K. Is self-weighing an effective tool for weight loss: a systematic literature review and meta-analysis. *Int J Behav Nutr Phys Act*. 2015: 12: 104.

8   World Health Organization. Social determinants of health. Available from: https://www.who.int/health-topics/social-determinants-of-health#tab=tab_1. Accessed 2025 May 30.

9   Bowden M. The measured man. *The Atlantic*. 2012 Jul/Aug. Available from: https://www.theatlantic.com/magazine/archive/2012/07/the-measured-man/309018/. Accessed 2025 May 30.

10  'WHOOP. Steven Bartlett's obsession? His health'. TikTok. 2023 Jul 14. Available from: https://www.tiktok.com/@whoop/video/7255738141791784234. Accessed 2025 Jul 11.

11  Inchauspé J. Commusings: My Origin Story as Glucose Goddess. *One Commune*. 2023 May 20. Available from: https://www.onecommune.com/blog/commusings-my-origin-story-as-glucose-goddess-by-jessie-inchauspe. Accessed 2025 Aug 22.

12  Silva C. Huberman husbands and the rise of self-optimization: stop trying to make yourself better. *Mashable*. 2023 Oct 13. Available from: https://mashable.com/article/huberman-husbands-rise-self-optimization. Accessed 2025 May 30.

13  Spartano NL, Sultana N, Lin H, Cheng H, Lu S, Fei D *et al*. Defining continuous glucose monitor time in range in a large, community-based cohort without diabetes. *J Clin Endocrinol Metab*. 2025: 110(4): 1128–34. doi: 10.1210/clinem/dgae626. Published online 2024 Sept 11.

14  Attia P. #54 – Kevin Sayer, CEO of Dexcom: Continuous glucose monitors – impact of food, sleep, and stress on glucose, the unmatched power

of CGM to drive behavioral change, and the exciting future of CGM. *The Peter Attia Drive* [podcast]. 2019 May 20. Available from: https://peterattiamd.com/kevinsayer/. Accessed 2025 May 30.

15 Donahue E, Birkenbach K. Continuous glucose monitoring to improve health in non-diabetics: individualizing blood glucose control and its benefits. *Peter Attia MD*. 2023 Nov 25. Available from: https://peterattiamd.com/cgm-in-non-diabetics/. Accessed 2025 May 30.

16 Attia P. #54 – Kevin Sayer, CEO of Dexcom: Continuous glucose monitors – impact of food, sleep, and stress on glucose…

17 Attia P. Are continuous glucose monitors a waste of time for people without diabetes? Some experts suggest CGMs are useless for nondiabetics. I disagree. *Peter Attia MD*. 2021 Jun 20. Available from: https://peterattiamd.com/are-continuous-glucose-monitors-a-waste-of-time-for-people-without-diabetes/. Accessed 2025 May 30.

18 Klein S, Gastaldelli A, Yki-Järvinen H, Scherer PE. Why does obesity cause diabetes? *Cell Metab*. 2022 Jan 4: 34(1): 11–20. doi: 10.1016/j.cmet.2021.12.012.

19 Veit M, van Asten R, Olie A, Prinz P. The role of dietary sugars, overweight, and obesity in type 2 diabetes mellitus: a narrative review. *Eur J Clin Nutr*. 2022: 76(11): 1497–501. doi: 10.1038/s41430-022-01114-5.

20 Oganesova Z, Pemberton J, Brown A. Innovative solution or cause for concern? The use of continuous glucose monitors in people not living with diabetes: a narrative review. *Diabet Med*. 2024: 41(9): e15369. doi: 10.1111/dme.15369.

21 Capoot A. As Covid-testing business drops, Abbott searches for new line of business with consumer wearables. *CNBC*. 2023 Oct 10 [updated 2023 Oct 10]. Available from: https://www.cnbc.com/2023/10/10/abbott-searches-for-new-line-of-business-with-consumer-wearables.html. Accessed 2025 May 30.

22 Fintech Finance News. Steven Bartlett's Flight Fund invests $2.5m in ZOE to improve the health of millions. *Fintech Finance News*. 2023 Mar 15. Available from: https://ffnews.com/newsarticle/funding/steven-bartletts-flight-fund-invests-2-5m-in-zoe-to-improve-the-health-of-millions/. Accessed 2025 May 30.

23 Cohen D, McCartney M. We need to talk about ZOE: how scientific is the must-have health app? *UnHerd*. 2023 Oct 12. Available from: https://unherd.com/2023/10/we-need-to-talk-about-zoe/. Accessed 2025 May 30.

24  Scrutiny Unit. Economics in practice: why is there public provision of healthcare? UK Parliament. Available from: https://www.parliament.uk/globalassets/documents/commons/Scrutiny/SU-Economics-in-practice-healthcare-1.pdf. Accessed 2025 May 30.
25  Blogs.cornell.edu. Asymmetric information in healthcare industry. 2016 Dec 1. Available from: https://blogs.cornell.edu/info2040/2016/12/01/asymmetric-information-in-healthcare-industry/. Accessed 2025 May 30.
26  Spector TD, Gardner CD. Challenges and opportunities for better nutrition science – an essay by Tim Spector and Christopher Gardner. *BMJ*. 2020 Jun 26: 369: m2470. doi: 10.1136/bmj.m2470
27  O'Neill R. Rethinking the 'wellness influencer': medical doctors, lifestyle expertise and the question of credentials. *Int J Cult Stud*. 2025: 28(3): 685–701. doi: 10.1177/13678779241307032.
28  Deliciously Ella. Our story. Available from: https://www.deliciouslyella.com/our-story/. Accessed 2025 May 30.
29  Wood Z. Deliciously Ella vegan food brand sold to Swiss group Hero. *Guardian*. 2024 Sept 17. Available from: https://www.theguardian.com/business/2024/sep/17/deliciously-ella-vegan-food-brand-sold-to-swiss-group-hero. Accessed 2025 May 30.
30  O'Neill R. Rethinking the 'wellness influencer': medical doctors, lifestyle expertise and the question of credentials.
31  General Medical Council. Continuing professional development: guidance for all doctors. Published June 2012. Available from: https://www.gmc-uk.org/-/media/documents/cpd-guidance-for-all-doctors-0316_pdf-56438625.pdf. Accessed 2025 May 30.
32  Brody H. Pharmaceutical industry financial support for medical education: benefit, or undue influence? *J Law Med Ethics*. 2009: 37(3): 451–60, 396. doi: 10.1111/j.1748-720X.2009.00406.x.
33  Fugh-Berman A. Industry-funded medical education is always promotion – an essay. *BMJ*. 2021: 373: n1273. doi: 10.1136/bmj.n1273.
34  Orlowski JP, Wateska L. The effects of pharmaceutical firm enticements on physician prescribing patterns: there's no such thing as a free lunch. *Chest*. 1992: 102(1): 270–3.
35  Van Zee A. The promotion and marketing of OxyContin: commercial triumph, public health tragedy. *Am J Public Health*. 2009: 99(2): 221–7. doi: 10.2105/AJPH.2007.131714.
36  Lopez G. The maker of OxyContin will finally stop marketing the addictive opioid to doctors. *Vox*. 2018 Feb 12. Available from: https://www.

vox.com/2018/2/12/17004258/oxycontin-purdue-pharma-marketing-stop. Accessed 2025 May 30.
37 Bermingham KM, Linenberg I, Polidori L, Asnicar F, Arrè A, Wolf J et al. Effects of a personalized nutrition program on cardiometabolic health: a randomized controlled trial. *Nat Med.* 2024: 30: 1888–97.
38 McCartney M, Cohen D. Does the METHOD study show that ZOE works? *BMJ.* 2024: 386: q1720. doi: 10.1136/bmj.q1720.
39 Ibid.
40 Halpert M. Trump administration to cut billions from biomedical research funding. *BBC News.* 2025 Feb 9. Available from: https://www.bbc.co.uk/news/articles/c15zypvgxz5o. Accessed 2025 May 30.
41 Callahan A. Leading nutrition scientist departs N.I.H., citing censorship. *New York Times.* 2025 Apr 16. Available from: https://www.nytimes.com/2025/04/16/health/nutrition-scientist-nih-censorship.html. Accessed 2025 May 30.
42 Howard R, Guo J, Hall KD. Imprecision nutrition? Different simultaneous continuous glucose monitors provide discordant meal rankings for incremental postprandial glucose in subjects without diabetes. *Am J Clin Nutr.* 2020: 112(4): 1114–19. doi: 10.1093/ajcn/nqaa198.
43 Stone JD, Rentz LE, Forsey J, Ramadan J, Markwald RR, Finomore VS Jr et al. Evaluations of commercial sleep technologies for objective monitoring during routine sleeping conditions. *Nat Sci Sleep.* 2020: 12: 821–42. doi: 10.2147/NSS.S270705.
44 Zeitzer JM. The utility of sleep wearables – well, that depends. *Sleep.* 2024: 47(4): zsae019. doi: 10.1093/sleep/zsae019. Published 2024 Jan 24.
45 Baron KG, Abbott S, Jao N, Manalo N, Mullen R. Orthosomnia: are some patients taking the quantified self too far? *J Clin Sleep Med.* 2017: 13(2): 351–7. doi: 10.5664/jcsm.6472. Published online 2017 Feb 15.
46 *Attia v. Oura Ring, Inc. et al*, No. 4:2023cv03433, Document 31 (N.D. Cal. 2024). Available from: https://law.justia.com/cases/federal/district-courts/california/candce/4:2023cv03433/415205/31/ Accessed 2025 May 30.

# 8 WHO'S REALLY EMPOWERED?
1 Kindelan K. Women turn to TikTok for health information and OBGYNs are there to meet them. *Good Morning America.* 2020 Feb 13. Available

from: https://www.goodmorningamerica.com/wellness/story/women-turn-tiktok-health-information-obgyns-meet-68824442. Accessed 2025 May 30.

2 Petrocchi S, Schulz PJ. Creating trust and understanding in doctor–patient relationships. In: de Bruijn GJ, Vandebosch H, eds. *Health, Media, and Communication*. Berlin, Boston: De Gruyter Mouton, 2025. doi: 10.1515/9783110775426.

3 Brook. Education, Access, Stigma and Young people (EASY): attitudes to contraception, condoms and sexual health. May 2024. Available from: https://www.brook.org.uk/wp-content/uploads/2024/05/EASY-REPORT-1.pdf. Accessed 2025 May 30.

4 Martinez MR, Thomas J, Carnevali A. Meet Ida Tin, the entrepreneur who coined the term 'femtech'. *Euronews*. 2024 May 2. Available from: https://www.euronews.com/next/2024/05/02/meet-ida-tin-the-entrepreneur-who-coined-the-term-femtech-europes-health-tech-pioneers. Accessed 2025 May 30.

5 Kaospilot Alumni. Meet Ida Tin: founder of Clue. Available from: https://www.kaospilot.dk/meet-ida-tin/. Accessed 2025 May 30.

6 Grand View Research. FemTech market size, share, and trends analysis report by type (devices, software, services), by application (pregnancy and nursing care), by end-use (direct to consumer), by region, and segment forecasts, 2025–2030. Report ID: GVR-4-68039-923-6. Available from: https://www.grandviewresearch.com/industry-analysis/femtech-market-report. Accessed 2025 May 30.

7 Ruaah L. High-growth femtech companies UK | 2024. *Beauhurst*. 2024 Aug 16. Available from: https://www.beauhurst.com/reports/high-growth-femtech-companies-uk-2024/. Accessed 2025 May 31.

8 Ibid.

9 Public Health England. What do women say? Reproductive health is a public health issue. Published June 2018. Available from: https://www.gov.uk/government/publications/reproductive-health-what-women-say. Accessed 2025 May 31.

10 Gorham B, Langham O. *Women's Health Economics: Investing in the 51 per cent*. NHS Confederation. 2024 Oct 2. Available from: https://www.nhsconfed.org/publications/womens-health-economics. Accessed 2025 May 31.

11 Gregory A. 'Concerning' lack of female-only medical trials in UK, say health experts. *Guardian*. 2025 May 7. Available from: https://www.

theguardian.com/society/2025/may/07/concerning-lack-of-female-only-medical-trials-in-uk-say-health-experts. Accessed 2025 May 31.

12  Liu KA, Dipietro Mager NA. Women's involvement in clinical trials: historical perspective and future implications. *Pharm Pract.* 2016: 14(1): 708. doi: 10.18549/PharmPract.2016.01.708.

13  Pinn VW. Sex and gender factors in medical studies: implications for health and clinical practice. *JAMA.* 2003: 289(4): 397–400. doi: 10.1001/jama.289.4.397.

14  National Institute on Drug Abuse Treatment Clinical Trials Network. Successfully including women in clinical trials: a guide for researchers. Available from: https://www.drugabuse.gov/sites/default/files/womens-brochure_1025-004_508.pdf. Accessed 2025 May 31.

15  Pinn VW. Sex and gender factors in medical studies: implications for health and clinical practice.

16  Center for Reproductive Rights. After Roe fell: abortion laws by state. 2025 Feb 28. Available from: https://reproductiverights.org/maps/abortion-laws-by-state/. Accessed 2025 May 31.

17  Drugs.com. Birth control failure rates – the Pearl Index explained. 2024 Dec 9.. Available from: https://www.drugs.com/medical-answers/birth-control-failure-rates-pearl-index-explained-3554953/. Accessed 2025 Jul 15.

18  Christin-Maitre S. History of oral contraceptive drugs and their use worldwide. *Best Pract Res Clin Endocrinol Metab.* 2013: 27(1): 3–12. doi: 10.1016/j.beem.2012.11.004.

19  Tyrer L. Introduction of the pill and its impact. *Contraception.* 1999: 59(1 Suppl.): 11S–16S. doi: 10.1016/S0010-7824(99)00011-8.

20  Ibid.

21  Iglikowski-Broad V. Just a pill: 60 years of the contraceptive pill on the NHS. The National Archives. 2021 Dec 4. Available from: https://blog.nationalarchives.gov.uk/just-a-pill-60-years-of-the-contraceptive-pill-on-the-nhs/. Accessed 2025 May 31.

22  Dehlendorf C, Grumbach K, Schmittdiel JA, Steinauer J. Shared decision making in contraceptive counseling. *Contraception.* 2017: 95(5): 452–5. doi: 10.1016/j.contraception.2016.12.010.

23  Littlejohn KE, Kimport K. Contesting and differentially constructing uncertainty: negotiations of contraceptive use in the clinical encounter. *J Health Soc Behav.* 2017: 58(4): 442–54. doi: 10.1177/0022146517736822.

24 Hall H. Women are sharing their experiences on the pill with #MyPillStory. *Stylist*. Available from: https://www.stylist.co.uk/health/my-pill-story-women-share-experiences/. Accessed 2025 May 31.

25 Schneider-Kamp A, Takhar J. Interrogating the pill: rising distrust and the reshaping of health risk perceptions in the social media age. *Soc Sci Med*. 2023: 331: 116081. doi: 10.1016/j.socscimed.2023.116081.

26 Pfender EJ, Tsiandoulas K, Morain SR, Fowler LR. Hormonal contraceptive side effects and nonhormonal alternatives on TikTok: a content analysis. *Health Promot Pract*. 2024: 26(3): 407–411. doi: 10.1177/15248399231221163.

27 Stevens LM. 'We have to be mythbusters': clinician attitudes about the legitimacy of patient concerns and dissatisfaction with contraception. *Soc Sci Med*. 2018: 212: 145–52. doi: 10.1016/j.socscimed.2018.07.024.

28 Johnson S, Pion C, Jennings V. Current methods and attitudes of women towards contraception in Europe and America. *Reprod Health*. 2013: 10: 7.

29 Brook. Education, Access, Stigma and Young people (EASY): attitudes to contraception, condoms and sexual health.

30 Cassidy C. Viral TikTok video of IUD removal at home prompts warning from health authorities. *Guardian*. 2021 Sept 24. Available from: https://www.theguardian.com/society/2021/sep/24/viral-tiktok-video-of-iud-removal-at-home-prompts-warning-from-health-authorities. Accessed 2025 May 31.

31 Ibid.

32 Wroe DK. Doctor warns never to try dangerous at-home IUD removal due to sepsis risk. *Mirror*. 2023 Sept 15. Available from: https://www.mirror.co.uk/news/health/doctor-warns-never-try-dangerous-30949944. Accessed 2025 May 31.

33 Becker A, Broussard K. Doctors are refusing to take out IUDs, so people are pulling them out at home – and posting how-to videos on TikTok and YouTube. *Business Insider*. 2021 Aug 30. Available from: https://www.businessinsider.com/people-pulling-out-their-iud-to-avoid-costs-doctor-refusal-2021-8. Accessed 2025 May 31.

34 Hawk M, Coulter RWS, Egan JE, Fisk S, Friedman MR, Tula M *et al*. Harm reduction principles for healthcare settings. *Harm Reduct J*. 2017: 14(1): 70.

35 Bever L. After social media outcry, CDC tells doctors to better manage IUD pain. *Washington Post*. 2024 Aug 8. Available from: https://www.

washingtonpost.com/wellness/2024/08/08/iud-pain-cdc/?utm_campaign=wp_main&utm_medium=social&utm_source=facebook. Accessed 2025 May 31.
36 Reed J. Warning over TikTok filming by hospital patients. *BBC News.* 2025 Jun 17. Available from: https://www.bbc.co.uk/news/articles/crk6mml5pemo. Accessed 2025 Jul 13.
37 Ibid.
38 Blair D, Peipert LJ, Zhao Q, Peipert JF. Anticipated pain as a predictor of discomfort with intrauterine device placement. *Am J Obstet Gynecol.* 2018: 218(2): 236.e1–9. doi: 10.1016/j.ajog.2017.10.017. Epub 2017 Nov 8.
39 Brook. Education, Access, Stigma and Young people (EASY): attitudes to contraception, condoms and sexual health.
40 Wu J, Trahair E, Happ M, Swartz J. TikTok, #IUD, and user experience with intrauterine devices reported on social media. *Obstet Gynecol.* 2023: 141(1): 215–17. doi: 10.1097/AOG.0000000000005027.
41 Schneider-Kamp, Takhar. Interrogating the pill: rising distrust and the reshaping of health risk perceptions in the social media age.
42 Bever. After social media outcry, CDC tells doctors to better manage IUD pain.
43 Curtis KM, Nguyen AT, Tepper NK, Zapata LB, Snyder EM, Hatfield-Timajchy K *et al.*; Centers for Disease Control and Prevention (CDC). U.S. selected practice recommendations for contraceptive use, 2024. *MMWR Recomm Rep.* 2024: 73(3): 1–77.
44 Curtis KM, Jatlaoui TC, Tepper NK, Zapata LB, Horton LG, Jamieson DJ, Whiteman MK. U.S. Selected Practice Recommendations for Contraceptive Use, 2016. *MMWR Recomm Rep.* 2016 Jul 29. 65(4): 1–66. Available from: https://www.cdc.gov/mmwr/volumes/65/rr/rr6504a1.htm
45 Brewster J, Arvanitis L, Pavilonis V, Wang M. Beware the 'new Google:' TikTok's search engine pumps toxic misinformation to its young users. *NewsGuard.* 2022 Sept 14. Available from: https://www.newsguardtech.com/misinformation-monitor/september-2022/. Accessed 2025 May 31.
46 Lee C. What are abortion shield laws? *Time.* 2025 Feb 24. Available from: https://time.com/7261130/what-are-abortion-shield-laws/. Accessed 2025 May 31.

47 Corbin B. Thinking of providing telehealth abortion services? Here are 3 legal frameworks you need to understand first. *MedCity News*. 2023 Apr 18. Available from: https://medcitynews.com/2023/04/thinking-of-providing-telehealth-abortion-services-here-are-3-legal-frameworks-you-need-to-understand-first/. Accessed 2025 May 31.

48 Lee. What are abortion shield laws?

49 Wu J, Greene M, Happ M, Trahair E, Montoya M, Swartz JJ. Medication abortion on TikTok: misinformation or reliable resource? *Am J Obstet Gynecol*. 2023: 228(6): 749–51. doi: 10.1016/j.ajog.2023.01.023.

50 Sherman C. Groups helping Americans find abortion pills report Instagram 'shadow-banning'. *Guardian*. 2025 Jan 29. Available from: https://www.theguardian.com/us-news/2025/jan/29/abortion-pills-instagram-shadow-banning. Accessed 2025 May 31.

51 Glenza J. Meta accused of 'bowing' to Trump by making abortion content harder to find. *Guardian*. 2025 Feb 3. Available from: https://www.theguardian.com/us-news/2025/feb/03/meta-abortion-content-trump. Accessed 2025 May 31.

52 Pfender *et al.* Hormonal contraceptive side effects and nonhormonal alternatives on TikTok: a content analysis.

53 Dudouet L. Digitised fertility: the use of fertility awareness apps as a form of contraception in the United Kingdom. *Soc Sci Humanit Open*. 2022: 5(1): 100261.

54 Phipps A. What lies behind the rise of the contraception app? *BBC News*. 2023 Apr 8. Available from: https://www.bbc.co.uk/news/uk-england-derbyshire-64405787. Accessed 2025 May 31.

55 Johnson S, Marriott L, Zinaman M. Can apps and calendar methods predict ovulation with accuracy? *Curr Med Res Opin*. 2018: 34(9): 1587–94. doi: 10.1080/03007995.2018.1475348.

56 Ali R, Gürtin ZB, Harper JC. Do fertility tracking applications offer women useful information about their fertile window? *Reprod Biomed Online*. 2020: 42(1): 273–81. doi: 10.1016/j.rbmo.2020.09.005.

57 Faculty of Sexual and Reproductive Healthcare, Family Planning Association, Pyper C. Sexual and reproductive health experts call for more independent research on fertility apps. Family Planning Association. 2018 Jul 31. Available from: https://www.fpa.org.uk/sexual-and-reproductive-health-experts-call-for-more-independent-research-on-fertility-apps/. Accessed 2025 May 31.

58 McNee R, McCulloch H, Lohr PA, Glasier A. Self-reported contraceptive method use at conception among patients presenting for abortion in England: a cross-sectional analysis comparing 2018 and 2023. *BMJ Sex Reprod Health*. 2025: 51(3): 186–90. doi:10.1136/bmjsrh-2024-202573.

59 Garamvolgyi F. Why US women are deleting their period tracking apps. *Guardian*. 2022 Jun 28. Available from: https://www.theguardian.com/us-news/2022/jun/28/why-us-women-are-deleting-their-period-tracking-apps. Accessed 2025 May 31.

60 Davis P. Police could search homes and phones after pregnancy loss. *Observer*. 2025 May 18. Available from: https://observer.co.uk/news/national/article/police-could-search-homes-and-seize-phones-after-sudden-pregnancy-loss. Accessed 2025 May 31.

61 Royal College of Obstetricians and Gynaecologists (RCOG). RCOG raises serious concerns around the National Police Chiefs' Council guidance on Child Death Investigation. 2025 May 21. Available from: https://www.rcog.org.uk/news/rcog-raises-serious-concerns-around-the-national-police-chiefs-council-guidance-on-child-death-investigation/. Accessed 2025 May 31.

62 Schmunk R. Lawsuit claiming Flo Health app shared intimate data with Facebook greenlit as Canadian class action. *CBC News*. 2024 Mar 8. Available from: https://www.cbc.ca/news/canada/british-columbia/flo-health-privacy-class-action-1.7137600. Accessed 2025 May 31.

63 Malki LM, Kaleva I, Patel D, Warner M, Abu-Salma R. Exploring privacy practices of female mHealth apps in a post-Roe world. In: *Proceedings of the CHI Conference on Human Factors in Computing Systems (CHI '24)*; 2024 May 11–16; doi: 10.1145/3613904.3642521.

64 Neff G, Nafus D. *Self-Tracking*. Cambridge, MA; London, UK: MIT Press, 2016.

65 Heywood H. Menstrual tracking app users cautioned about risks. *BBC News*. 2025 Jun 11. Available from: https://www.bbc.co.uk/news/articles/cgj8eq01vdxo.amp. Accessed 2025 Jul 13.

66 Glick M. People are replacing hormonal birth control with apps. *Discover Magazine*. 2022 Jan 12. Available from: https://www.discovermagazine.com/health/people-are-replacing-hormonal-birth-control-with-apps. Accessed 2025 May 31.

67 NICE. Natural Cycles for monitoring fertility. Medtech innovation briefing [MIB244]. 2021 Jan 19. Available from: https://www.nice.org.uk/advice/mib244/chapter/Summary. Accessed 2025 May 31.

68 Freundl G, Frank-Herrmann P, Godehardt E, Klemm R, Bachhofer M. Retrospective clinical trial of contraceptive effectiveness of the electronic fertility indicator Ladycomp/Babycomp. *Adv Contracept*. 1998: 14(2): 97–108. doi: 10.1023/a:1006534632583

69 Koch MC, Lermann J, van de Roemer N, Renner SK, Burghaus S, Hackl J et al. Improving usability and pregnancy rates of a fertility monitor by an additional mobile application: results of a retrospective efficacy study of Daysy and DaysyView app. *Reprod Health*. 2018: 15: 37. doi: 10.1186/s12978-018-0479-6. [Retracted]

70 Polis CB. Published analysis of contraceptive effectiveness of Daysy and DaysyView app is fatally flawed. *Reprod Health*. 2018: 15(1): 113. doi: 10.1186/s12978-018-0560-1.

71 Ibid.

72 Sheridan K, Ross C. In a defamation lawsuit, the hype around digital health clashes with scientific criticism. *STAT News*. 2022 Mar 2. Available from: https://www.statnews.com/2022/03/02/health-fertility-thermometer-valley-polis/. Accessed 2025 May 31.

73 Laestadius LI, Van Hoorn K, Wahl M, Witt A, Carlyle KE, Guidry JPD. Promotion of an algorithm-based tool for pregnancy prevention by Instagram influencers. *Journal of Women's Health*. 2024: 33(2): 141–51. doi: 10.1089/jwh.2023.0660.

74 Nair I, Patel SP, Bolen A, Roger S, Bucci K, Schwab-Reese L et al. Reproductive health experiences shared on TikTok by young people: content analysis. *JMIR Infodemiology*. 2023: 3: e42810. doi: 10.2196/42810.

75 Urrutia RP, Polis CB. Fertility awareness based methods for pregnancy prevention. *BMJ*. 2019: 366: l4245. doi: 10.1136/bmj.l4245.

76 Peragallo Urrutia R, Polis CB, Jensen ET, Greene ME, Kennedy E, Stanford JB. Effectiveness of fertility awareness-based methods for pregnancy prevention: a systematic review. *Obstet Gynecol*. 2018: 132(3): 591–604. doi: 10.1097/AOG.0000000000002784.

77 Ibid.

78 Gellman L. The girlbosses of fertility. *The Cut*. 2022 Jun 8. Available from: https://www.thecut.com/article/fertility-coaches.html. Accessed 2025 May 31.

79  British Pregnancy Advisory Service. The cost of living factor: The impact of the cost of living crisis on women's decisions to end their pregnancies. 2024 May. Available from: https://www.bpas.org/media/sbhh4w1o/the-cost-of-living-factor.pdf. Accessed 2025 Aug 28.

## 9 A HORMONAL QUICK FIX

1  McCausland P. What RFK Jr could do on US vaccines, fluoride and drugs. *BBC News*. 2024 Nov 15. Available from: https://www.bbc.co.uk/news/articles/c4gx3kkz8z3o. Accessed 2025 May 31.

2  Rissman K. RFK Jr shares bizarre shirtless workout video claiming he's 'practicing moves for my confirmation hearing'. *Independent*. 2024 Dec 2. Available from: https://www.independent.co.uk/news/world/americas/us-politics/rfk-jr-shirtless-workout-video-confirmation-hearing-b1771234.html. Accessed 2025 May 31.

3  Testosterone replacement therapy (TRT) global business research report 2024–2030. *GlobeNewswire*. 2024 Nov 6. Available from: https://www.globenewswire.com/news-release/2024/11/06/2975884/28124/en/Testosterone-Replacement-Therapy-TRT-Global-Business-Research-Report-2024-2030-Early-Detection-Growing-Awareness-Personalized-Medicine-Focus-on-Men-s-Health-Fueling-Market-Expansio.html. Accessed 2025 May 31.

4  Joe Rogan - TRT Makes a Big Difference! YouTube. 2018 Oct 28. Available from: https://www.youtube.com/watch?v=EEce1DRsRwQ. Accessed 15 February 2025.

5  Dubin JM, Aguiar JA, Lin JS, Greenberg DR, Keeter MK, Fantus R *et al*. The broad reach and inaccuracy of men's health information on social media: analysis of TikTok and Instagram. *Int J Impot Res*. 2024: 36(3): 256–60. doi: 10.1038/s41443-022-00645-6.

6  Becker A. Young men are getting testosterone boosts to feel stronger, sharper, and anxiety-free. *Business Insider*. 2024 Oct 26. Available from: https://www.businessinsider.com/young-men-testosterone-supplements-masculinity-2024-10. Accessed 2025 May 31.

7  Hirst M, Turnock L. Semaglutide, testosterone and sildenafil advertising on social media: the normalisation of lifestyle enhancement drugs. *Performance Enhancement & Health*. 2024: 12(1): 100303. doi:10.1016/j.peh.2024.100303.

8  Ibid.

9   NHS. Anabolic steroid misuse. Available from: https://www.nhs.uk/conditions/anabolic-steroid-misuse/. Accessed 2025 May 31.
10  Cox L, Gibbs N, Turnock LA. Emerging anabolic androgenic steroid markets; the prominence of social media. *Drugs: Education, Prevention and Policy*. 2023: 31(2): 257–70. doi: 10.1080/09687637.2023.2176286.
11  Writing Group for the Women's Health Initiative Investigators. Risks and benefits of estrogen plus progestin in healthy postmenopausal women: principal results from the Women's Health Initiative randomized controlled trial. *JAMA*. 2002: 288(3): 321–33. doi: 10.1001/jama.288.3.321.
12  Cagnacci A, Venier M. The controversial history of hormone replacement therapy. *Medicina*. 2019: 55(9): 602. doi: 10.3390/medicina55090602.
13  Parr E. Government looking to include menopause in QOF and NHS health checks. *Pulse*. 2023 Nov 1. Available from: https://www.pulsetoday.co.uk/news/clinical-areas/womens-health/government-looking-to-include-menopause-in-qof-and-nhs-health-checks/. Accessed 2025 May 31.
14  Channel 4. Channel 4 and Davina McCall to break the menopause taboo [news release]. 2021 Mar 8. Available from: https://www.channel4.com/press/news/channel-4-and-davina-mccall-break-menopause-taboo. Accessed 2025 May 31.
15  McElhone N. Perth's Rachel Weiss on how she broke the age-old taboo around the menopause. *The Courier*. 2024 Oct 11. Available from: https://www.thecourier.co.uk/fp/lifestyle/5094338/getting-to-know-menopause-cafe-founder-rachel-weiss/. Accessed 2025 May 31.
16  Quinn H. HRT prescriptions double in five years, despite supply shortages. *The Pharmaceutical Journal*. 2022 Mar 17. Available from: https://pharmaceutical-journal.com/author/helen-quinn. Accessed 2025 May 31.
17  NICE. Menopause: identification and management. NICE guideline NG23. Published: 12 November 2015. Last updated: 7 November 2024. Available from: https://www.nice.org.uk/guidance/ng23. Accessed 2025 May 31.
18  British Menopause Society. BMS statement in response to the publication of the updated NICE Menopause guideline (NG23). 2024 Nov 7. Available from: https://thebms.org.uk/2024/11/bms-statement-in-response-to-the-publication-of-the-updated-nice-menopause-guideline-ng23/. Accessed 2025 May 31.

19. MHRA. Hormone replacement therapy (HRT): further information on the known increased risk of breast cancer with HRT and its persistence after stopping. 2019 Aug 30. Available from: https://www.gov.uk/drug-safety-update/hormone-replacement-therapy-hrt-further-information-on-the-known-increased-risk-of-breast-cancer-with-hrt-and-its-persistence-after-stopping. Accessed 2025 May 31.
20. NICE. Menopause: identification and management. NICE guideline NG23.
21. MHRA. Hormone replacement therapy (HRT): further information on the known increased risk of breast cancer with HRT and its persistence after stopping.
22. NICE. HRT and the likelihood of some medical conditions: a discussion aid for healthcare professionals and patients. Menopause: identification and management (NICE guideline NG23). 2024 Nov 7. Available from: https://www.nice.org.uk/guidance/ng23/resources/communicating-the-benefits-and-risks-of-hrt-13553196013. Accessed 2025 May 31.
23. NICE. Menopause: identification and management. NICE guideline NG23.
24. Gunter J. The rise of misinformation about menopause hormone therapy on Instagram. *The Vajenda*. 2024 Aug 19. Available from: https://vajenda.substack.com/p/the-rise-of-misinformation-about. Accessed 2025 May 31.
25. Bazell R. The cruel irony of trying to be 'feminine forever'. *NBC News*. 2007 Jan 2. Available from: https://www.nbcnews.com/id/wbna16397237. Accessed 2025 May 31.
26. McCartney M, Cohen D. Has HRT propaganda misled women? Menopause is not a disease. *UnHerd*. 2024 Mar 7. Available from: https://unherd.com/2024/03/has-hrt-propaganda-misled-women/. Accessed 2025 May 31.
27. Bazell. The cruel irony of trying to be 'feminine forever'.
28. Orgad S, Rottenberg C. The menopause moment: The rising visibility of 'the change' in UK news coverage. *European Journal of Cultural Studies*. 2023: 27(4): 1–21. doi: 10.1177/13675494231159562.
29. McCartney, Cohen. Has HRT propaganda misled women? Menopause is not a disease.
30. Bhasin S, Brito JP, Cunningham GR, Hayes FJ, Hodis HN, Matsumoto AM *et al*. Testosterone therapy in men with hypogonadism: an Endocrine

Society clinical practice guideline. *J Clin Endocrinol Metab*. 2018: 103(5): 1715–44. doi: 10.1210/jc.2018-00229.

31  Schwartz LM, Woloshin S. Low 'T' as in 'template': how to sell disease. *JAMA Intern Med*. 2013: 173(15): 1460–2. doi: 10.1001/jamainternmed.2013.7579.

32  Ibid.

33  Diem SJ, Greer NL, Olson CM, MacDonald R, McDonagh MS, Rutks IR, Wilt TJ. Efficacy and Safety of Testosterone Treatment in Men. *Ann Intern Med*. 2020: 172(2): 133–140. doi: 10.7326/M19-0830.

34  da Silva A, Rodrigues da Silva F, de Oliveira J et al. Effectiveness of testosterone replacement in men with obesity having low testosterone levels: a systematic review and meta-analysis. *Arch Endocrinol Metab*. 2021: 65(6): 759–67. doi: 10.20945/2359-3997000000412.

35  Corona G, Lee DM, Forti G, O'Connor DB, Maggi M, O'Neill TW *et al*. Age-related changes in general and sexual health in middle-aged and older men: results from the European Male Ageing Study (EMAS). *J Sex Med*. 2010: 7(4 Pt 1): 1362–80. doi: 10.1111/j.1743-6109.2009.01601.x.

36  Schwartz, Woloshin. Low 'T' as in 'template': how to sell disease.

37  Kremer W. How many middle-aged men need HRT? *BBC News*. 2014 Apr 28. Available from: https://www.bbc.com/news/health-27183264. Accessed 2025 May 31.

38  Schwartz, Woloshin. Low 'T' as in 'template': how to sell disease.

39  Rao PK, Boulet SL, Mehta A, Hotaling J, Eisenberg ML, Honig SC *et al*. Trends in testosterone replacement therapy use from 2003 to 2013 among reproductive-age men in the United States. *J Urol*. 2017: 197(4): 1121–26. doi: 10.1016/j.juro.2016.10.063.

40  Gan E, Pattman SJ, Pearce S, Quinton R. A UK epidemic of testosterone prescribing, 2001–2010. *Clin Endocrinol (Oxf)*. 2013: 79(4): 564–70. doi: 10.1111/cen.12178.

41  Schwartz, Woloshin. Low 'T' as in 'template': how to sell disease.

42  U.S. Food and Drug Administration. FDA Drug Safety Communication: FDA cautions about using testosterone products for low testosterone due to aging; requires labeling change to inform of possible increased risk of heart attack and stroke with use. 2015 Mar 3. Available from: https://www.fda.gov/media/91048/download. Accessed 2025 May 31.

43  Dobrow L. 2013 All-Star Large Pharma Marketing Team of the Year: AndroGel. *Medical Marketing & Media*. 2013 Jan 2. Available from:

https://www.mmm-online.com/home/channel/features/2013-all-star-large-pharma-marketing-team-of-the-year-androgel/. Accessed 2025 May 31.

44 Gorski D. 'Low T': the triumph of marketing over science. *Science-Based Medicine*. 2013 Nov 25. Available from: https://sciencebasedmedicine.org/low-t-the-triumph-of-marketing-over-science/. Accessed 2025 May 31.

45 Gala D. Androgel lawsuit update: after Bellwether loss, AndroGel MDL down to last 9 cases. *TheLawFirm.com*. 2021 Dec 13. Available from: https://thelawfirm.com/androgel-lawsuit-updates-and-settlements/. Accessed 2025 May 31.

46 Lincoff AM, Bhasin S, Flevaris P, Mitchell LM, Basaria S, Boden WE et al., for the TRAVERSE Study Investigators. Cardiovascular safety of testosterone-replacement therapy. *N Engl J Med*. 2023: 389(2): 107–17. doi: 10.1056/NEJMoa2215025.

47 Labos C. Testosterone study results are reassuring, but come with caveats. *McGill Office for Science and Society*. 2023 Jun 30. Available from: https://www.mcgill.ca/oss/. Accessed 2025 May 31.

48 Dubin JM, Jesse E, Fantus RJ, et al. Guideline-discordant care among direct-to-consumer testosterone therapy platforms. *JAMA Intern Med*. 2022: 182(12): 1321–1323. doi: 10.1001/jamainternmed.2022.4928.

49 Clarke H. TikTok content on low testosterone lacks information on future risks, study finds. *Urology Times Journal*. 2024 Oct 22; 52(12). Available from: https://www.urologytimes.com/view/tiktok-content-on-low-testosterone-lacks-information-on-future-risks-study-finds. Accessed 2025 May 31.

50 Corona G, Rastrelli G, Monami M, Saad F, Luconi M, Lucchese M et al. Body weight loss reverts obesity-associated hypogonadotropic hypogonadism: a systematic review and meta-analysis. *Eur J Endocrinol*. 2013: 168(6): 829–43. doi: 10.1530/EJE-12-0955.

51 Westley CJ, Amdur RL, Irwig MS. High rates of depression and depressive symptoms among men referred for borderline testosterone levels. *J Sex Med*. 2015: 12(8): 1753–60. doi: 10.1111/jsm.12937.

52 Irwig MS. Battling the testosterone clinics and websites. *J Gen Intern Med*. 2022: 37: 3477–8. doi: 10.1007/s11606-022-07718-8.

53 O'Neill C, Dickinson O. The dark side of fitness: social media 'fuelling steroid use' among men. *STV News*. 2023 Dec 4. Available from: https://news.

stv.tv/scotland/anabolic-steroids-social-media-fuelling-rise-in-scots-taking-image-and-performance-enhancing-drugs. Accessed 2025 May 31.

54  Watson RA. Testosterone dependence: How real is the risk? *Urology Times*. 2014 Jul 23. Available from: https://www.urologytimes.com/view/testosterone-dependence-how-real-risk. Accessed 2025 Aug 30.

55  McEvinney K, Clegg R, Casserly J. TV menopause doctor concerns probed by watchdog. *Panorama*. 2024 Sep 30. Available from: https://www.bbc.co.uk/news/articles/cp8e5y4e83lo. Accessed 2025 May 31.

56  Newson L. [Instagram post]. menopause_doctor. 2025 Jun 17. Available from: https://www.instagram.com/p/DLARx-gIlKc/?img_index=2. Accessed 2025 Jul 13.

57  Newson L. A message from Dr Louise Newson [Internet]. 2025 Jun 17. Available from: https://www.drlouisenewson.co.uk/knowledge/a-message-from-dr-louise-newson. Accessed 2025 Aug 30.

58  Newson L. [Instagram reel]. menopause_doctor. 2025 Jul 7. Available from: https://www.instagram.com/reel/DLzXf_kK9AJ/?igsh=amxkaGJndTZ3M2Jl. Accessed 2025 Jul 13.

59  Howe M, Wolfisz F. More of Dr Louise Newson's patients criticise their care at clinic being probed by watchdog as TV celebrity menopause expert gives tearful interview defending her record. *Daily Mail*. 2024 Oct 5 [updated 2024 Oct 6]; Available from: https://www.dailymail.co.uk/news/article-13921085/HRT-TV-celebrity-menopause-doctors-Newson-Health.html. Accessed: 2025 Jul 13.

60  Geddes L. Prescribing of testosterone for middle-aged women 'out of control'. *Guardian*. 2024 Jul 5. Available from: https://www.theguardian.com/society/2024/jul/05/prescribing-of-testosterone-for-middle-aged-women-out-of-control. Accessed 2025 May 31.

61  Ibid.

62  British Menopause Society. Testosterone replacement in menopause: information for GPs and other health professionals. 2022 Dec. Available from: https://thebms.org.uk/wp-content/uploads/2022/12/08-BMS-TfC-Testosterone-replacement-in-menopause-DEC2022-A.pdf. Accessed 2025 May 31.

63  Connelly D. NHS testosterone prescribing in women rises ten-fold in seven years. *Pharm J*. 2023 Feb 17. Available from: https://pharmaceutical-journal.com/article/news/nhs-testosterone-prescribing-in-women-rises-ten-fold-in-seven-years. Accessed 2025 May 31.

64  British Menopause Society. BMS statement on testosterone. 26 July 2024. Available from: https://thebms.org.uk/2024/07/bms-statement-on-testosterone-2/. Accessed 2025 May 31.

## 10 THE NEW PREVENTIVE MEDICINE

1  Mikhail A. Longevity investor Bryan Johnson hosted Kim Kardashian and neuroscientist Andrew Huberman at a 'Don't Die Dinner,' where they discussed their own mortality. *Fortune*. 2024 Jun 14. Available from:https://fortune.com/well/article/bryan-johnson-kim-kardashian-andrew-huberman-dont-die-dinner-longevity/. Accessed 2025 May 31.
2  Braintree. Company profile. *Vault*. Available from: https://vault.com/company-profiles/financial-technology/braintree. Accessed 2025 May 31.
3  Wigle R. Biohacker Bryan Johnson, 47, boasts that he only ages 8 months every year – here's how. *New York Post*. 2025 Jan 16. Available from: https://nypost.com/2025/01/16/lifestyle/biohacker-bryan-johnson-47-boasts-that-he-only-ages-8-months-every-year-heres-how/. Accessed 2025 May 31.
4  Alter C. The man who thinks he can live forever. *TIME*. 2023 Sept 20. Available from: https://time.com/6315607/bryan-johnsons-quest-for-immortality/. Accessed 2025 May 31.
5  Ibid.
6  Prater E. Tech CEO defends using his 17-year-old son's blood plasma in pursuit of youth, despite it not working. *Fortune*. 2023 Jul 13. Available from: https://fortune.com/well/2023/07/13/blueprint-ceo-bryan-johnson-defends-plasma-donation-son-youth-aging-longevity-brainstorm-tech-fortune-utah/. Accessed 2025 May 31.
7  Hamzelou J. Blood from human teens rejuvenates body and brains of old mice. *New Scientist*. 2016 Nov 15. Available from: https://www.newscientist.com/article/mg23331184-300-old-blood-can-be-made-young-again-and-it-might-fight-ageing/. Accessed 2025 May 31.
8  U.S. Food and Drug Administration. Important Information about Young Donor Plasma Infusions for Profit. 2019 Feb 19 [updated 2024 Dec 6]. Available from: https://www.fda.gov/vaccines-blood-biologics/safety-availability-biologics/update-important-information-about-young-donor-plasma-infusions-offered-profit. Accessed 2025 May 31.
9  Vance A. How to be 18 years old again for only $2 million a year. *Bloomberg*. 2023 Jan 25. Available from: https://www.bloomberg.com/

news/features/2023-01-25/anti-aging-techniques-taken-to-extreme-by-bryan-johnson. Accessed 2025 May 31.
10. Alter. The man who thinks he can live forever.
11. Argentieri MA, Amin N, Nevado-Holgado AJ, Sproviero W, Collister JA, Keestra SM et al. Integrating the environmental and genetic architectures of aging and mortality. *Nat Med.* 2025;31(3):1016–1025. doi:10.1038/s41591-024-03483-9.
12. Ibid.
13. National High Blood Pressure Education Program. The seventh report of the Joint National Committee on prevention, detection, evaluation, and treatment of high blood pressure. Bethesda (MD): National Heart, Lung, and Blood Institute (US); 2004 Aug. Report No.: 04-5230.
14. Office for National Statistics. Mortality in England and Wales: average life span, 2010. 2012 Dec 17. Available from: https://www.ons.gov.uk/peoplepopulationandcommunity/birthsdeathsandmarriages/deaths/articles/mortalityinenglandandwales/2012-12-17. Accessed 2025 May 31.
15. Office for National Statistics. How has life expectancy changed over time? 2015 Sep 9. Available from: https://www.ons.gov.uk/peoplepopulationandcommunity/birthsdeathsandmarriages/lifeexpectancies/articles/howhaslifeexpectancychangedovertime/2015-09-09. Accessed 2025 May 31.
16. Office for National Statistics. Mortality in England and Wales: average life span, 2010.
17. Raleigh V. What is happening to life expectancy in England? The King's Fund. 2024 Apr 10. Available from: https://www.kingsfund.org.uk/insight-and-analysis/long-reads/whats-happening-life-expectancy-england. Accessed 2025 May 31.
18. Centre for Ageing Better. Health and wellbeing | The State of Ageing 2025. 2024 Feb 22. Available from: https://ageing-better.org.uk/health-and-wellbeing-state-ageing-2025. Accessed 2025 May 31.
19. Ibid.
20. Holmes J. What is a population health approach? Population health. Integrated care. London: The King's Fund; 2022 Jul 21. Available from: https://www.kingsfund.org.uk/insight-and-analysis/long-reads/population-health-approach. Accessed 2025 Jun 1
21. Global Wellness Summit. Trend: The Wellth Divide is widening: super-expensive wellness is on the rise. 2023. Available from: https://www.

globalwellnesssummit.com/blog/trend-the-wellth-divide-is-widening-super-expensive-wellness-is-on-the-rise/. Accessed 2025 Jun 1.
22 PayPal co-founder pledges $3.5 million to Methuselah Foundation. *Philanthropy News Digest.* 2006 Sept 30. Available from: https://philanthropynewsdigest.org/news/paypal-co-founder-pledges-3.5-million-to-methuselah-foundation. Accessed 2025 Jun 1.
23 Buntz B. Biotech Altos Labs emerges with $3B in funding to focus on 'cellular rejuvenation programming'. *Drug Discovery and Development.* 2022 Jan 20. Available from: https://www.drugdiscoverytrends.com/biotech-altos-labs-emerges-with-3b-in-funding-to-focus-on-cellular-rejuvenation-programming/. Accessed 2025 Jun 1.
24 UNICEF. Costs of fully vaccinating a child: countries eligible for Gavi vaccine prices. August 2024. Available from: https://www.unicef.org/documents/costs-fully-vaccinating-child. Accessed 2025 Jun 1.
25 Pulkki-Brännström AM, Wolff C, Brännström N, Skordis-Worrall J. Cost and cost effectiveness of long-lasting insecticide-treated bed nets – a model-based analysis. *Cost Eff Resour Alloc.* 2012: 10: 5. doi: 10.1186/1478-7547-10-5.
26 Hamzelou J. The quest to legitimize longevity medicine. *MIT Technology Review.* 2024 Mar 18. Available from: https://www.technologyreview.com/2024/03/18/1089888/the-quest-to-legitimize-longevity-medicine/. Accessed 2025 Jun 1.
27 ET Team. The hitchhiker's guide to immortality: tech entrepreneur Bryan Johnson on 'don't die' philosophy and mortality. *The Economic Times.* 2024 Dec 6. Available from: https://economictimes.com/industry/healthcare/biotech/the-hitchhikers-guide-to-immortality-tech-entrepreneur-bryan-johnson-on-dont-die-philosophy-and-mortality/articleshow/116048707.cms. Accessed 2025 Jun 1.
28 Corbett R. The for-profit city that might come crashing down. *New York Times Magazine.* 2024 Aug 28 [updated 2024 Sept 19]. Available from: https://www.nytimes.com/2024/08/28/magazine/prospera-honduras-crypto.html Accessed 2025 Jun 1.
29 The world's most flexible jurisdiction for health & biotech. Próspera; 2025. Available from: https://www.prospera.co/en/solutions/health. Accessed 2025 Jun 1.
30 Corbett. The for-profit city that might come crashing down.

31 Hamzelou J. Access to experimental medical treatments is expanding across the US. *MIT Technology Review*; 2025 May 16. Available from: https://www.technologyreview.com/2025/05/16/1116526/access-to-experimental-medical-treatments-expanding-us/. Accessed 2025 Jun 1.

32 Prada L. Experimental drugs without FDA approval are now legal in Montana. *VICE*; 2025 May 18. Available from: https://www.vice.com/en/tag/drugs/. Accessed 2025 Jun 1.

33 Ducharme J. How podcaster Andrew Huberman got America to care about science. *TIME*. 2023 Jun 28 [updated 2023 Jun 28]. Available from: https://time.com/6290594/andrew-hubman-lab-podcast-interview/. Accessed 2025 Jun 1.

34 Khullar D. How to die in good health. *The New Yorker*. Available from: https://www.newyorker.com/magazine/2023/04/03/how-to-die-in-good-health-peter-attia. Accessed 2025 Jun 1.

35 Ducharme. How podcaster Andrew Huberman got America to care about science.

36 Ibid.

37 Attia P. AMA #41: Medicine 3.0, developments in the field of aging, healthy habits in times of stress, and more. 2022 Nov 14. Available from: https://peterattiamd.com/ama41/. Accessed 2025 Jun 1.

38 Khullar. How to die in good health.

39 Ibid.

40 Mineo L. Good genes are nice, but joy is better. *Harvard Gazette*; 2017 Apr 11. Available from: https://news.harvard.edu/gazette/story/2017/04/over-nearly-80-years-harvard-study-has-been-showing-how-to-live-a-healthy-and-happy-life/. Accessed 2025 Jun 1.

41 Waldinger R, Schulz M. What the longest study on human happiness found is the key to a good life. *The Atlantic*; 2023 Jan 19. Available from: https://www.theatlantic.com/ideas/archive/2023/01/harvard-happiness-study-relationships/672753/. Accessed 2025 Jun 1.

42 Ibid.

43 Itkowitz C. For 79 years, this groundbreaking Harvard study has searched for the key to happiness. Should it keep going? *Washington Post*; 2017 Apr 17. Available from: https://www.washingtonpost.com/news/inspired-life/wp/2017/04/17/for-79-years-this-groundbreaking-harvard-study-has-searched-for-the-key-to-happiness-should-it-keep-going/. Accessed 2025 Jun 1.

44 Holt-Lunstad J, Smith TB, Layton JB. Social relationships and mortality risk: a meta-analytic review. *PLoS Med.* 2010: 7(7): e1000316. doi: 10.1371/journal.pmed.1000316. Accessed 2025 Jun 1.

45 Hawkley LC. Loneliness and health. *Nat Rev Dis Primers.* 2022: 8: 22. Available from: https://doi.org/10.1038/s41572-022-00355-9. Accessed 2025 Jun 1.

46 Wang F, Gao Y, Han Z, Yu Y, Long Z, Jiang X et al. A systematic review and meta-analysis of 90 cohort studies of social isolation, loneliness and mortality. *Nat Hum Behav.* 2023: 7(8): 1307–19. Available from: https://doi.org/10.1038/s41562-023-01617-6. Accessed 2025 Jun 1.

47 Hawkley. Loneliness and health.

48 Waldinger R, Schulz M. What the longest study on human happiness found is the key to a good life. *The Atlantic.* 2023 Jan 19. Available from: https://www.theatlantic.com/ideas/archive/2023/01/harvard-happiness-study-relationships/672753/. Accessed 2025 Jun 1.

49 Lei X, Matovic D, Leung WY, Viju A, Wuthrich VM. The relationship between social media use and psychosocial outcomes in older adults: a systematic review. *Int Psychogeriatr.* 2024: 36(9): 714–46. doi: 10.1017/S1041610223004519. Accessed 2025 Jun 1.

50 Hunt MG, Marx R, Lipson C, Young J. No more FOMO: limiting social media decreases loneliness and depression. *J Soc Clin Psychol.* 2018: 37(10): 751–68. doi: 10.1521/jscp.2018.37.10.751. Accessed 2025 Jun 1.

51 Primack BA, Shensa A, Sidani JE, Whaite EO, Lin LY, Rosen D et al. Social media use and perceived social isolation among young adults in the U.S. *Am J Prev Med.* 2017: 53(1): 1–8. doi: 10.1016/j.amepre.2017.01.010. Accessed 2025 Jun 1.

52 National Academies of Sciences, Engineering, and Medicine; Health and Medicine Division; Board on Population Health and Public Health Practice; Committee on the Impact of Social Media on Adolescent Health; Wojtowicz A, Buckley GJ, Galea S, eds. *Social Media and Adolescent Health.* Washington, DC: National Academies Press; 2024 Mar 25. 3, Potential Benefits of Social Media series. Available from: https://pubmed.ncbi.nlm.nih.gov/38713784/. Accessed 2025 Jun 1.

53 Khullar. How to die in good health.

54 Lowe D. Expensive placebos work better. *Science;* 2015 Jan 29. Available from: https://www.science.org/content/blog-post/expensive-placebos-work-better. Accessed 2025 Jun 1.

55 Khullar. How to die in good health.
56 Mullard A. Parsing clinical success rates. *Nat Rev Drug Discov.* 2016: 15: 447. doi: 10.1038/nrd.2016.136.
57 Clifford S. The toxic supplement hunter. *Men's Health.* 2021 Jul 9. Available from: https://www.menshealth.com/health/a36981623/toxic-supplement-hunter/. Accessed 2025 Jun 1.
58 Advertising Standards Authority (ASA). Ad labelling in podcasts: qualitative research report. May 2024. Available from: https://www.asa.org.uk/static/49b21053-2165-44df-b03f1d0d3896baa6/ASA-Ad-Labelling-in-Podcasts-Research-Report-Final-090424.pdf. Accessed 2025 Jun 1.
59 Clifford S. The toxic supplement hunter. *Men's Health.* 2021 Jul 9. Available from: https://www.menshealth.com/health/a36981623/toxic-supplement-hunter/. Accessed 2025 Jun 1.
60 Athletic Greens announces Dr. Andrew Huberman as scientific advisor. *Business Wire.* 2022 Mar 21. Available from: https://www.businesswire.com/news/home/20220318005080/en/Athletic-Greens-Announces-Dr.-Andrew-Huberman-as-Scientific-Advisor. Accessed 2025 Jun 1.
61 Wirtschafter V. The challenge of detecting misinformation in podcasting. *Brookings.* 2021 Aug 25. Available from: https://www.brookings.edu/articles/the-challenge-of-detecting-misinformation-in-podcasting/. Accessed 2025 Jun 1.
62 Aronson J. When I use a word… self-experimentation. *BMJ.* 2021 Mar 29. Available from: https://blogs.bmj.com/bmj/2021/03/29/jeffrey-aronson-when-i-use-a-word-self-experimentation/. Accessed 2025 Jun 1.
63 Mégraud F. A humble bacterium sweeps this year's Nobel Prize. *Cell.* 2005: 123(6): 975–6. Accessed 2025 Jun 1.
64 Selvarani R, Mohammed S, Richardson A. Effect of rapamycin on aging and age-related diseases – past and future. *Geroscience.* 2021: 43(3): 1135–58. doi: 10.1007/s11357-020-00274-1.
65 Ivimey-Cook ER, Sultanova Z and Maklakov AA. Rapamycin, not Metformin, mirrors dietary restriction-driven lifespan extension in vertebrates: a meta-analysis. *Aging Cell.* 2025. e70131. https://doi.org/10.1111/acel.70131
66 Easter M. This obscure, potentially dangerous drug could stop aging. *Men's Health.* 2019 Jul 19. Available from: https://www.menshealth.com/health/a28405352/rapamycin-anti-aging-drug/. Accessed 2025 Jun 1.

67 Lee DJW, Hodzic Kuerec A, Maier AB. Targeting ageing with rapamycin and its derivatives in humans: a systematic review. *Lancet Healthy Longev.* 2024: 5(2): e152–62. doi: 10.1016/S2666-7568(23)00258-1.
68 FDA Full Prescribing Information, Rapamune (Sirolimus), 2022. https://www.accessdata.fda.gov/drugsatfda_docs/label/2022/021083s069s070,021110s087s088lbl.pdf. Accessed 2025 March 15.
69 Easter. This obscure, potentially dangerous drug could stop aging.
70 Keys MT, Thinggaard M, Larsen LA, Pedersen DA, Hallas J, Christensen K. Reassessing the evidence of a survival advantage in Type 2 diabetes treated with metformin compared with controls without diabetes: a retrospective cohort study. *Int J Epidemiol.* 2022: 51(6): 1886–98. doi: 10.1093/ije/dyac200.
71 Walton RG, Dungan CM, Long DE, Tuggle SC, Kosmac K, Peck BD et al. Metformin blunts muscle hypertrophy in response to progressive resistance exercise training in older adults: a randomized, double-blind, placebo-controlled, multicenter trial: The MASTERS trial. *Aging Cell.* 2019: 18(6): e13039. doi: 10.1111/acel.13039. Epub 2019 Sept 26.
72 Laksmi PW, Setiati S, Tamin TZ, Soewondo P, Rochmah W, Nafrialdi N et al. Effect of metformin on handgrip strength, gait speed, myostatin serum level, and health-related quality of life: a double blind randomized controlled trial among non-diabetic pre-frail elderly patients. *Acta Med Indones.* 2017: 49(2): 118–27.
73 Witham MD, McDonald C, Wilson N, Rennie KJ, Bardgett M, Bradley P et al. Metformin and physical performance in older people with probable sarcopenia and physical prefrailty or frailty in England (MET-PREVENT): a double-blind, randomised, placebo-controlled trial. *Lancet Healthy Longev.* 2025: 6(3): 100695.

## EPILOGUE: THE COMMODIFIED SELF

1 World Health Organization. Commercial determinants of health. Geneva: World Health Organization; 2023 Mar 21. Available from: https://www.who.int/news-room/fact-sheets/detail/commercial-determinants-of-health. Accessed 2025 Jun 23.
2 Bero LA. Tobacco industry manipulation of research. In: *Late Lessons from Early Warnings: Science, Precaution, Innovation.* Luxembourg: European Environment Agency; 2013. pp. 151–68. (EEA Report No. 1/2013).

Available from: https://www.eea.europa.eu/publications/late-lessons-2/late-lessons-chapters/late-lessons-ii-chapter-7. Accessed 2025 Jun 27.

3  World Health Organization. *Addressing Health Determinants in a Digital Age: Project Report*. Copenhagen: WHO Regional Office for Europe; 2024. (Document number: WHO/EURO:2024-10917-50689-76724). Available from: https://www.who.int/europe/publications/i/item/WHO-EURO-2024-10917-50689-76724. Accessed 2025 Jun 23.

4  Julia V. The Netherlands launches a Responsible Influence certificate for content creators. Value Your Network. 2024 May 7. Available from: https://www.valueyournetwork.com/en/the-netherlands-launch-a-responsible-influence-certificate-for-content-creators/. Accessed 2025 Jun 28.